Rise of the Far Right

Rise of the Far Right

Technologies of Recruitment and Mobilization

Edited by Melody Devries,
Judith Bessant and Rob Watts

ROWMAN & LITTLEFIELD
Lanham • Boulder • New York • London

Published by Rowman & Littlefield

An imprint of The Rowman & Littlefield Publishing Group, Inc.
4501 Forbes Boulevard, Suite 200, Lanham, Maryland 20706
www.rowman.com

86-90 Paul Street, London EC2A 4NE, United Kingdom

Copyright © 2021 by The Rowman & Littlefield Publishing Group, Inc.

All rights reserved. No part of this book may be reproduced in any form or by any electronic or mechanical means, including information storage and retrieval systems, without written permission from the publisher, except by a reviewer who may quote passages in a review.

British Library Cataloguing in Publication Information Available

Library of Congress Cataloging-in-Publication Data Is Available

ISBN: 978-1-78661-492-6 (cloth: alk. paper)
ISBN: 978-1-5381-5890-6 (pbk: alk. paper)
ISBN: 978-1-78661-493-3 (electronic)

Contents

Contributors

JP Armstrong is a PhD candidate at York University. His research brings together social movement scholarship and critical sexuality studies to examine various forms of and resistances to LGBTQ activism.

Dr. Judith Bessant is a member of the Order of Australia, a professor at RMIT University and an adjunct professor at the School of Justice, QUT University, Australia. She publishes in the areas of sociology, politics, youth studies, media studies and history.

Dr. Simon Bradford was a reader in social science in the Department of Clinical Sciences at Brunel University London. His main research interests are in social policy initiatives that affect young people and communities, and the history and organisation of professional work in the public services, particularly education services.

Noel Brett is a PhD candidate in the Computing and Software Department at McMaster University, interested in the areas of mathematics and computer science, critical algorithm studies, social systems design and queer game studies. Brett studies the intersection of computer science and social sciences and uses these theories to explore gaming culture, design and how these reproduce exclusionary practices within gameplay.

Simon Copland is a PhD candidate in sociology at the Australian National University studying the online men's communities called the 'manosphere'. He has expertise in men's rights, male violence, misogyny and extremism online and the digital economy. He is also a freelance writer whose work has been published in *The Guardian*, *BBC Online* and *The Conversation*.

Luc S. Cousineau is a PhD candidate at the University of Waterloo who studies masculinity, men's rights and leisure online. Luc's research centres on gender and power relations in work and leisure spaces, with a particular focus on how masculinities are understood and interact with lives online. Using qualitative and digital ethnographic methods, Luc has written on the ethics of platform-based quarantines, leisure and digitality and geo-social networking applications.

Dr. Fin Cullen is a senior lecturer at St Mary's University, Twickenham, United Kingdom. Her teaching encompasses citizenship education, children and young people's rights and social policy. Her main research interests explore sex and gender equalities, young people's cultures and (inter)professional identities in education and youth services.

Melody Devries is a PhD candidate in the Communication & Culture Department at Ryerson University. Building from a masters in anthropology from the University of Toronto, her doctoral work uses ethnographic methods and theories of relationality and performativity to examine how contemporary far-right online communities exist in tandem with mainstream politics.

Sal Hagen is a PhD candidate in the Department of Media Studies at the University of Amsterdam. As part of the Digital Methods Initiative and co-founder of OILab, his research focuses on anonymous and pseudonymous online subcultures and their political engagements. Methodologically, his work combines media theory with computational methods.

Greta Jasser is a PhD student at Leuphana University Lüneburg, and a research associate at the University of Hildesheim, Germany. She researches far-right and misogynist online networks, and focuses her work on technology, platforms, affordances and ideologies.

Dr. Yowei Kang is an assistant professor at the Bachelor Degree Program in Oceanic Cultural Creative Design Industries at the National Taiwan Ocean University, in Taiwan. His research interests focus on new media design, digital game research, visual communication and experiential rhetoric. He has received government funding to support his research in location-based advertising and consumer privacy management strategies.

Andrey Kasimov is a PhD candidate in the Department of Sociology at McMaster University in Hamilton, Ontario, Canada. His research focuses on how the internet is used to promote and sustain far-right politics and movements. His most recent project looks at how decentralization impacts user experiences on sites like 4chan and Stormfront.

Jordan McSwiney is a PhD candidate in the Department of Government and International Relations at the University of Sydney. His research focuses on political parties and the far right, with an interest in their ideology, organising practices and use of technology. His research has been published in *Information, Communication & Society* and the *Australian Journal of Political Economy*.

Dr. Tanner Mirrlees is an associate professor of communications and digital media studies at Ontario Tech University and the president of the Canadian Communication Association. Mirrlees is the co-editor of *Media Imperialism: Continuity and Change* and *The Television Reader*, is the author of *Hearts and Mines: The US Empire's Culture Industry* and *Global Entertainment Media* and is the co-author of *EdTech Inc.: Selling, Automating and Globalizing Higher Education in the Digital Age*.

Dr. Marc Tuters is an assistant professor in the University of Amsterdam's Media Studies faculty. Previously a media artist, his PhD research focused on the relationship between the concept of location and new media. As a researcher affiliated with the Digital Methods Initiative (DMI) and as the director of the Open Intelligence Lab (OILab), his current work examines how online subcultures constitute themselves as political movements.

Dr. Rob Watts is a professor of social policy at RMIT University, Australia. He teaches criminology, politics, policy studies, the history of ideas and applied human rights. Recent books include *The Precarious Generation: A Political Economy of Young People* (with J. Bessant and R. Farthing; 2018) and *Criminalizing Dissent: The Liberal State and the Problem of Legitimacy* (Routledge 2020).

Dr. Kenneth C. C. Yang is a professor in the Department of Communication at the University of Texas at El Paso, United States. His research focuses on new media, consumer behaviour and advertising. He has edited or co-edited three books, *Asia.com: Asia Encounters the Internet* (Routledge, 2003), *Multi-Platform Advertising Strategies in the Global Marketplace* (IGI Global, 2018) and *Cases on Immersive Virtual Reality Techniques* (IGI Global, 2019).

Acknowledgements

Melody thanks her co-editors Dr. Judith Bessant and Dr. Rob Watts, her dissertation supervisor Dr. Chris Powell, Noel and Daniel for the help and support during the process of chapter writing and volume editing.

Judith and Rob would like to thank Royal Melbourne Institute of Technology University and their good colleagues and students.

Last and importantly, we thank Rowman & Littlefield for having faith in this project and seeing the promise in the initial proposal we sent some time back. In particular, we thank Dhara Snowden and Rebecca Anastasi for their ongoing professional and always helpful support, especially amidst the full effects of the Covid-19 pandemic.

Chapter 1

The Uncanny Political Involvement of Technologies

Melody Devries, Judith Bessant and Rob Watts

No doubt it has happened to you. Scrolling through Facebook or Twitter on phones or laptops, you spot a post that seems *off*. This 'offness' can be subtle or explicit. Perhaps it's an image of a Greek statue paired with some obscure quote about the grandeur of Western civilization (Zuckerberg 2018). Maybe you've been caught off guard by an image making fun of young climate activist Greta Thunberg (Neville & Langois 2019), or dismissing American *Black Lives Matter* activists, calling them 'irrational', 'naïve', or 'angry' and 'violent'. Maybe while browsing Reddit, a post links to an 'hilarious' YouTube video showing a character in a video game feeding a feminist to an alligator (Brett, this volume). Perhaps someone sends you a video from a popular YouTuber, which explains how political correctness and women's rights have gone too far and are leading us towards 'white genocide' (Lewis 2018; Tuters & Burton 2021). Or, you've noticed Instagram posts where users complain about government control via Covid-19 lockdowns, captioned with *#resistance*. Within each of these posts, there is no explicit reference to any 'far', 'extreme' or otherwise aberrant political ideology or orientation. Yet, a sense of offness remains (figure 1.1).

Similar 'off' scenes have filled non-digital streets and parks, for example, through the vague picket signs and green face paint reminiscent of the Alt-Right meme *Pepe* during a 'Straight Pride' parade in Boston (figure 1.2). Elsewhere around the world, we may pass by messages about the importance of the nuclear family and the detriment caused by gay marriage rights (Yang & Kang, this volume), or of nationalist pronatalism (Bradford & Cullen, this volume) on billboards and bus ads.

With no sign of slurs or outright hate in sight (as we might remember from other settings, such as during the infamous Westboro Baptist Church demonstrations in the United States; Barret-Fox 2011), these social media posts,

Figure 1.1. An 'off' or non-explicit image from far-right Facebook group.
Source: Collected by author, *American Sanity Magazine Facebook Page* (now defunct).

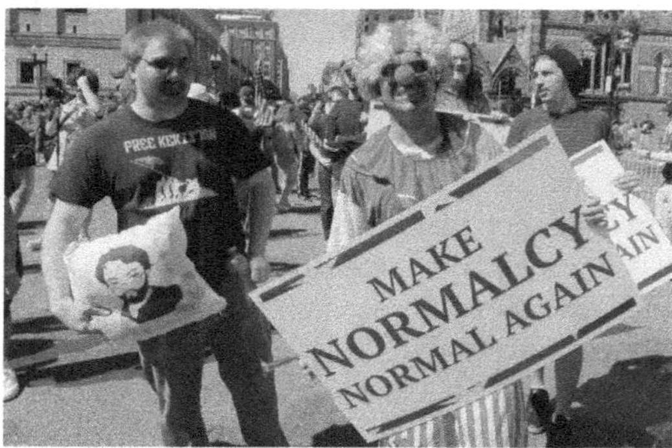

Figure 1.2. Straight Pride Parade, Boston, MA.
Source: Brian Snyder / Reuters. Appearing in the article "'Straight Pride Parade' in Boston draws counterprotesters and heavy police presence", Nicole Acevedo, NBC News. https://www.nbcnews.com/news/us-news/straight-pride-parade-boston-draws-counterprotesters-heavy-police-presence-n1048626.

printed posters and verbal slogans do not explicitly communicate what many might typically recognize as 'far-right ideology' or 'hate'. Still, these scenes pulse with an uncanniness that implicates a politics just below their surface.

The 'uncanniness' of what robotics designers refer to as the 'uncanny valley' results from a degree of incompleteness that prevents a viewer's full comfort or assuredness when attempting to find affinity with a robot that resembles, but doesn't quite achieve, the familiarity of humanness (Caballar 2019). A similar effect is happening here. While these images don't explicitly professes hatred, far-right scholars, journalists and digital activists have shown that such content nevertheless is derived from and dependent upon oppressive political traditions and current far-right movements that forward ethno-nationalism, misogyny, xenophobia and antipathy toward individuals and groups deemed as cultural 'others'. When we notice this discrepancy, even if we can't quite name it, an uncanniness is produced.

Yet when technologically mediated and distributed, these digital texts attain a shrewd subtlety which enables or encourages engagement from folks that might recognize and be sympathetic to their surface message: hilarity, national pride, Christianity, normalcy, peace or freedom. To extend the metaphor, the robot has passed as human. Recognition of the familiar can often negate, hide or welcome underlying implications and narrative ties to more harmful and undeniably hateful movements (Devries 2021). It is thus from this discrepancy between what is said and what is unsaid that a potential for reader recruitment or mobilized participation with uncanny content emerges.

Reflective of this distinction between the spoken and the unspoken, it is often the case that 'hate' or 'hateful' is not how folks that encounter and spread this content view themselves. To be hateful is not always the intention of passive or even more vocal participants. In our contemporary digital communications landscape, many of those (but certainly not all) who spread such uncanny media often vehemently deny their hatred towards minorities, feminists, liberals, globalists (Jewish folks) or 'Marxists', while in the same breath denouncing the evil that is supposedly associated with *those* folks.

Sara Ahmed pointed this out in her work on *Affective Economies*, when she stressed that the strong feelings and emotions which mobilize hate or white supremacy do not stem from within individual, emotive subjects. Rather, Ahmed (2004) shows that political affect forms as it passes between folks, and we would add, between media and digital platforms, when familiarity is recognized. Describing the rhetoric of the white nationalist group *Aryan Nations*, Ahmed (2004) says that this relational co-production and circulation of affect undergirds the logics of white supremacy and the motivation to pursue its ends.

Like how the circulation of labour and commodity produces value (for some), the circulation and exchange of love, trust and a sense of 'likeness' or deep affiliation between folks and certain political or national entities – between white people, the concept of 'the white race', the nuclear family, God, nationhood and promised land – produces a profound desire to affiliate, protect and defend. Yet, this same flow of love between similar entities necessarily produces distrust of difference. Circulating love of the same marks 'like-kinds' as that which is desired for preservation, and simultaneously marks those whom have historically been construed as a threat as 'other' as the very downfall of 'us' (Chun 2018). It is a toxic love indeed, as the very presence of these others is imagined as the threat to the object of love: that which is the same (Ahmed 2004).

Over the years, this affective economy of fervent love for the same and rejection of difference has helped shape many institutions, policies and technologies that compose a vastly unequal mainstream society (Chun 2018). Alongside this, it has helped maintain the camaraderie of fringe white nationalist groups, sticking folks together and against outsiders instead of affording a culture of comfort amidst difference (Chun 2018; Ahmed 2004). This 'stickiness' and the affective economy from which it emerges (Ahmed 2004) is just one example of an active social *process* which leads to recruitment into anti-egalitarian worldviews, and mobilization of action towards related goals. In this case, the circulation of affect is a process that reifies conviction of what or who must be protected, and that which must be destroyed. This reified, deeply felt conviction is exemplified in a video shared by a Facebook user to the Pro-President Trump Facebook group titled 'Rudy Giuliani [Common Sense]'. In the video, avid President Trump backer Mike Lindell declares in response to the then upcoming inauguration of President Joe Biden that: 'This isn't something we can ever get complacent on. This is a fight for everything we have grown up with. Everything we live for, and everything that this country stands for'.

In this sense, far-right populist politics are often a tangle of love that equates hate, which performs intolerance even under the presumption of acting in righteous anger to pursue justice (figure 1.3). The point here is not to defend those who are part of harmful and oppressive racist, anti-Semitic, homophobic or misogynist movements as misunderstood lovers. Rather, it is to point out the importance of frequent, ongoing relationships and *connectivity* within processes of far-right recruitment and mobilization. Connectivity is one of the most profound affordances of contemporary technologies; while certain online media may seem uncanny to some, it may affectively *stick* to others.

On 6 January 2021, members of so-called III% militias, Proud Boys, and other avowed white nationalists stormed the United States Capitol building (Somas 2021), intent on stopping the Senate's confirmation of President Biden's electoral defeat over Donald Trump. These organized groups were joined by what appeared to be thousands of individuals from across the nation – right-wing Trump supporters broadly, evangelical Christians, free-speech enthusiasts, gun hobbyists and conspiracy theorists – all engaged in an immense love for things that they felt assured their continued existence

YOU ARE NOT ALONE
ALL ACROSS AMERICA A QUIET RAGE
IS BUILDING AGAINST THE ASSAULT
UPON AMERICAN VALUES.
MORE SO THAN EVER IN THE HISTORY
OF AMERICA, THE CONCERNS AND
PATIENCE OF IT'S PEOPLE ARE BEING
TESTED, TRIED, AND ATTACKED
BY A GROUP OF ELITISTS THAT ARE
HELL-BENT ON THE DESTRUCTION
OF THIS COUNTRY.
REFUSE TO REMAIN SILENT

Figure 1.3. 'You Are Not Alone'. Image Circulated on Far-Right Facebook Page Sticks Users Together. Posted in 2021.

Source: Collected by author, *Rudy Giuliani [Common Sense] Facebook Page* (now defunct). Original creator unknown.

and an anger towards the constructed threat to these familiar things: The deep state, Biden's Democratic Party, a globalist elite (a dog whistle for anti-Semitic conspiracy). As one participant in the Capitol Siege told a reporter: 'Absolutely people are angry. And you can feel it, you can feel the rage, the madness' (Vice media 2021). Affect here is public, growing stronger as it passes between attendees.

While not all individual participants were drawn into this affective economy by traditional means like local proximity to like-minded folks and organized group affiliation, digital networks and infrastructures made up for this by connecting users with more media and folks *like them*, resulting in violent mobilization in defence of the familiar, the traditional and 'everything we have grown up with'. In effect, digital technologies rapidly multiplied and extended the effects of collective organizing across the United States, resulting in the coming together of folks with varying degrees of far-right conviction and strategy, but with a shared love of the same and hatred for the threat to such love posed by 'anti-Trump' law-makers inside the Capitol (Avevado 2021). In this sense, new media technologies and online platforms like Facebook, Twitter, YouTube, Parler and Gab enable the affective mediation and circulation of historic, racialized and gendered notions of nation, normalcy, belonging, 'us', 'them' and threat. As Jennifer Peterson (2011) writes on the mediation of political drive, our imagined relationships with strangers – whether those for or against us – are always 'highly mass mediated, informed by texts, images, and narratives emanating from the many mass-produced pages and screens that surround us. As such, these relationships and feelings are public issues, not private ones'.

Connective technologies and cryptic, uncanny posts (as well as less cryptic ones) have been changing the game of far-right recruitment and mobilization. They are part of the material infrastructure wherein these emotional and ideological processes operate to mobilize political participation. Whether we approach the uncanniness of far-right media as curious citizens or critical researchers, as concerned friends or relatives, or as members of a socially vulnerable or minority group, it can be difficult to understand exactly how those around us are convicted by its messages. This difficulty to parse points towards the complex entanglement between far-right rhetoric, policy, habits of everyday life, various user histories, media, platform features and institutional and economic power relations. Technologies are themselves shaped by reigning economic and socio-political systems, and the ways humans manufacture, use and understand them. This is a messy entanglement, but in order to make sense of what recruits and mobilizes so many people towards anti-egalitarian, far-right ends, we must begin to dissect these assemblages. This is what the chapters in this volume have set out to do.

Notably, the technologically mediated mobilization of the far-right is nothing new, nor is it unique to the United States. From the age of print to the digital present, media and communication systems have been used by fringe white nationalist groups (i.e. Don Black's *Stormfront*), far-right political parties, and reactionary movements. Over the past decade, far-right and/or authoritarian populist politicians including France's Marine Le Pen (National Front), Hungary's Viktor Orbán (Fidesz), Britain's Nigel Farrage (UK Independence Party), the Netherlands' Geert Wilders (Freedom Party), India's Narendra Modi (Bharatiya Janata Party) and Brazil's Jair Bolsonaro have seen parliamentary success amid both heavy-handed and subtly mediated political messaging through newspapers, billboards, TV and radio broadcasting and through social media platforms. Also, ethno-nationalist parties like Finland's The Finns, Greece's Golden Dawn and Austria's Freedom Party of Austria have successfully mobilized significant popular support.

While these current events show us the ongoing interplay of technologies in far-right politics, this book does not hold any technology solely responsible for this resurgent electoral and cultural popularity of far-right parties, movements and pundits. Instead, this volume highlights the connectivity involved in contemporary global processes of far-right recruitment and mobilization by exploring how communication technologies alter or contribute to these processes. In this sense, we have also avoided producing another volume that analyzes far-right rhetoric, ideologies and history as part of a distinct fringe group or movement. This work has been well done by a variety of scholars (Belew 2019; Hawley 2017, 2019; Miller-Idriss 2020; Renton 2019). Consequently, this volume features a variety of subjects and phenomena. It discusses material concepts, such as technological affordances, platform infrastructures and networked communities, as well as more abstract factors such as ideologies of pronatalism, belonging, micro-celebrity, playfulness and othering.

As this project developed, it became clear that these chapters scratched the surface of complex theoretical and methodological issues. These relate to how we classify the 'far'-right as such, given the fact that the inequities and oppressions which are often attributed to far-right politics or parties are also presided over and propagated by centrist and mainstream liberal governments. As well, these contributions left us thinking about how to constitute and thereby study mobilization and/or recruitment as processes. We think that this volume proves valuable for raising questions that future research in this area will need to address. These questions include: What constitutes far-right mobilization, effective recruitment or resistance? What qualifies a far-right online space? How do we mark moment(s) of 'recruitment' or political conversion? Where and when is it helpful to consider recruitment and mobilization as separate processes?

Having raised these questions, for the remainder of this introduction we attempt to achieve three goals. We provide a rationale for prioritizing the inclusion of chapters that refuse technological determinism, and that frame far-right recruitment and mobilization as processes shaped but not ordained by technology. We then briefly contextualize our chapters in the field by marking how the contemporary far-right has been addressed as a social movement and political entity. Lastly, we offer a preview of the contribution made by each chapter.

SWAPPING DETERMINISM FOR INVOLVEMENT

Contemporary professional and public discourses concerning technologies, especially digital technologies, commonly include a variety of clichés and buzzwords from Silicon Valley industries and publicists, government technology innovators and incubators, NGOs and techno-utopian media coverage. Such discourses suggest that we are collectively passing through a 'Fourth Industrial Revolution', or that 'data is the new oil', or even that new Silicon Valley tech will drive 'disruptive' 'revolution' (Bessant 2018; Mirrlees 2019). It is certainly the case that the current scale of digital activity – Facebook has 2.32 billion monthly users and 40,000 Google searches happen every second, for example – reveals an important social transformation in terms of how we interact with others, where we get our news and how we move about the world (Mirrlees 2019). Yet within these discourses is the suggestion that we must 'surf' only the 'technological waves' into a preordained future. This hastily implies that powerful technologies have escaped human, socio-political design and thus ordain our futures (Bessant 2018), or as Elon Musk might claim, ordain our AI overlords (Chandler 2020).

A similar technologically deterministic disposition appears in much scholarly work that has associated 'the digital' with a radical, even epochal, societal and political transformation (Kaufmann & Jeandesboz 2016). With the advent of micro-electronics in the 1970s, many scholars initially suggested that there was empirical evidence that an 'information society' was in the making (Fuchs 2013; Webster 2014). Other technologically deterministic ways of defining society from various disciplines continued to develop over time; discussion of the 'information society' in the 1970s and 1980s moved to talk of a 'network society' in the 1990s (Castells 1996, van Dijk, 2006, 2013). In the 2010s, we encountered debates about the revolutionary and harmful potential of 'big data' (Mayer-Schonberger & Cukier, 2013; cf. Bessant 2018, pp. 20–35). Generally, scholarship in this area invites us to imagine that the twenty-first-century world is 'being turned into digital data and is thus transformable via digital manipulation' (Packer 2013, p. 297). Moral panics about the overuse of smartphones, disgust or weird fascination with non-mainstream online forums or youth-centric technologies and the circulation of popular metaphors such as 'digital addiction' have accompanied these frameworks.

What connects these narratives together is the underlying logic that technology somehow asserts unbridled and unidirectional agency over its social and political uptake. But as Kaufmann and Jeandesboz (2016) argue, there are good reasons for avoiding this framing of social reality (Bessant 2014). A determinist framework inherently denies our ability to understand, let alone assess, the material and historic flows of social power that shape the development, production, circulation, uses and impacts of digital technologies (as Marx says is the case with the construction of any social history).[1] This is not only because the determinist framework is overly techno-utopian or techno-dystopian in how much unidirectional agency it grants technology. More pressingly, the determinist framework leaves intact an epistemological dualism between subject and object by implying that human subjects are dominated by out-of-control objects. In this sense, to move beyond techno-determinism means not just restoring our faith in human agency to make our own techno-destiny, but moving past the debate of whether technology controls us or whether we control technology altogether. In other words, a more thorough resistance to the pitfalls of techno-determinism might be to forward a relational view (see Bourdieu & Wacquant 1992; McFarlane 2013; Powell 2013; Stokers 2013), which understands human capacity to use, manipulate or politicize technology as co-constituted with the agencies of those technologies, as well as the conditions of their production. An anti-determinism thus considers the mediating features, affordances and political powers of any technology as inseparable from the historically classed, racialized, gendered and economic conditions that build and commoditize them.

Notably, inherently relational, non-determinist work concerning technologies is not new, and has been taken up by critical race and technology scholars including Safiya Noble (2018), Latanya McSweeny (2013), Wendy Chun (2016, 2018) and others. Also, other scholars have provided a historical political economy of the tech tradition, pointing out how capitalism and nation states intersect to shape new technological developments (H. Schiller 1991, 1992, 1998; D. Schiller 2000, 2014). As all this important work argues, the work of digital or other technologies cannot be divorced from the social, political and economic conditions that instantiate, use and shape the means by which we connect with each other and with politics.

In light of this, this volume includes both chapters that discuss how far-right social actors use or exert agency upon technologies in order to recruit or mobilize, as well as chapters that consider the active role that technologies play in social and political processes like recruitment and mobilization. This has functioned as a commitment to the fact that technologies also do work within in contemporary politics, while maintaining that the work they do is shaped by the conditions of their production and surrounding social histories and narratives (Kaufmann & Jeandesboz 2017, p. 315). These chapters ask not only how far-right actors use technologies for varied ends, but also how technologies are *involved* in such harmful politics, sometimes even in the absence of explicitly far-right adherents.

Following this direction away from technological determinism and towards technological involvement also means avoiding essentialist notions which might qualify certain objects or technologies as carrying a far-right or other un-alterable political essence or quality. Rather than carrying always-already political traits, technologies enter relationships that get them involved in politics. In this sense, platforms like Facebook or Twitter *become* ‘far-right’ technologies in the moments when they are used by and entangled with other far-right actors, circumstances or outcomes. Other technologies like Alt-Tech (Jasser, Brett) may encounter more consistent, frequent and more intentional entanglements with these harmful politics than other platforms like Facebook (McSwiney), open-world video games (Brett), virtual worlds (Devries), or forum communities (Cousineau). Thus, while certain Alt-Tech can more consistently be recognized as 'far-right', it is also important to consider what seemingly benign or apolitical technologies afford for the emergence of far-right figurations. As the chapters in this volume attest, digital objects operate as technologies of political mobilization or recruitment not because of any innate capacity to win over users or to serve oppressive powers, but because of the work they do in their relationships with users, their designers, other objects and historical precedents. This has enabled social movement scenes and other settings for mobilization (see also Kasimov, Brett, Hagen & Tuters, Devries, Copland, Cousineau, Armstrong, Jasser, this volume). Yet, as a relational view attests, technologies are neither innocent and apolitical objects, nor solely responsible for political movements (O'Neil 2016; Chun 2018; Noble 2018). Following this form, we assume technological redeemability, and conclude with a chapter that considers the potential of turning the affordances of these technologies, along with other institutional means towards progressive, even liberating directions (Mirrlees, this volume).

In sum, we bring a technological focus to far-right studies not because technologies determine our political movements and futures, but because they are – and always have been – critically *involved*. Subsequently, this book has many subjects. It addresses the socio-political, the technological, the collective and the interpersonal, and spans continents. What marries the chapters is a shared focus not on one categorizable political group, but on processual, relational, socio-political phenomena. Amidst ongoing folk panic about the harmful or manipulative effects of social media, or of the return of far-right politics in various cultural and institutional contexts, this volume's goal is to ask: What, exactly are technologies doing here? And to what extent are they involved in recruiting ideological adherents and mobilizing far-right action, enabling organization or garnering support?

CONFIGURING THE 'FAR' RIGHT

While we don't claim to have reached any definitive answers to these questions, this volume suggests what future studies of far-right recruitment or mobilization might entail. Comparing these to past work, we have found there are some common tendencies in social movement and far-right studies that produce valuable insights while also reaching limitations. We briefly discuss these tendencies in what follows.

Social movement studies have given much attention to how progressive movements have adopted participatory technologies to promote a revived public sphere, enhance deliberative democracy and mobilize support for liberal, anti-capitalist and anti-globalization movements. This work has also usefully examined how these same technologies are used by state and corporate actors to surveil and manage political action by citizens. However, less attention has been given to far-right or contemporary 'Alt-Right' groups, parties and movements in social movement studies. In his critical literature review, Manuel Caiani (2017) reinforces Donatella della Porta's (2013) earlier assessment that social movement research that emphasizes actors' strategic choices and the contextual opportunities for mobilization has focused mostly on left-wing radical activism.

Further, studies that do examine far-right social movements tend to feature a narrow framing of 'the far-right' in terms of 'extremism' or terrorism. This disposition is commonly expressed in 'breakdown theories' or models of relative deprivation that characterize far-right interventions as political pathologies (Caiani 2017). However, this approach relies on using certain features or traits as signs of 'far right' affiliation, which distinguish it from a supposed centrist, democratic and non-oppressive 'norm'. This becomes problematic because studies that define 'far'-right politics as social breakdowns tend to take for granted that these traits said to characterize far-right insurrection – such as resurgent ideological traditionalism, ethno-nationalism, protectionist economic policies, disdain for immigrants and asylum seekers, opposition to egalitarian tax policies, anti-Semitism, Islamophobia, misogyny or transphobia – do not hold mainstream sway within neoliberal democracies. In other words, an epistemological strategy that qualifies the far-right as having only 'anti-mainstream', 'terroristic' or extremist qualities can limit our ability to spot and critique these features in more mainstream liberal arenas. Further to this point on the limitations of 'extremist' framings, in the wake of increasing unrest in the United States after the electoral defeat of President Donald Trump, many activists have pointed out that a reliance on the concept of 'terrorism' in policy meant to address 'home-grown' white supremacist violence (i.e. 'far-right *terrorism*') pushes law-makers to contribute weapons, funding and other technology to state apparatuses of 'counter-terrorism' (Panjwani & Kayali 2021). This is problematic because these institutions continue to disproportionately surveil, police, and abuse Muslim, Arab, South Asian, Black and other People of Colour (Kundnani 2015; Maynard 2017). All considered, there are serious theoretical and practical limitations to the 'social breakdown' classification of far-right movements.

Relatedly, scholarly and journalistic texts within cultural studies, media studies and social movement studies tend to operate with a substantialist definition of the 'far-right'. Over the past few years especially, scholars have defined and described 'far-right online culture', highlighting the often carnivalesque, ironic or stoic discursive function of its memes and forum spaces. These have pointed out 'obscene', abnormal or violent political qualities of Internet communities that assumedly locate them within the political category of 'far-right' or adjacent (Beran 2019). These accounts do well at describing the features of these subcultures which entangled themselves with dangerous contemporary entities like the Alt-Right (Hawley 2019). Notably, this approach relies on identifying a given phenomena as far-right by assessing its features as meeting a definitional standard or checklist. In effect, we can consider this an essentialist or substantialist epistemological approach; in order for an entity, user, technology or party to qualify as far-right, it must possess a certain 'substance' or set of features that allow us to typify it as far-right, that is, outside the mainstream realm of conservative politics. This approach is useful for identifying and calling out the harmful work of organized far-right or white supremacist groups or parties, as is done effectively in the chapters here on Alt-Tech (Jasser), on parliamentary far-right movements (Bradford & Cullen; McSwiney) and manosphere communities (Cousineau).

Expanding from these foundations, alternative epistemological approaches may now be useful for discerning equally harmful or oppressive effects of socio-political phenomena that might not meet the colloquial definitional standard of a far-right group, organization or platform. Where and how sharply we draw these definitional borders of the 'far-right' is often dependent upon national histories and narratives, the capacity of contemporary activism to expose propagandic narratives, or the policy and leanings of a given parliamentary government. It is likely that more theoretical and methodological models will develop to account for all the factors that come together to configure more nebulous anti-egalitarian, nationalist or racist phenomena.

For us, this has meant an inclusion of chapters which analyse the recruitment and mobilization processes of less-than-explicitly far-right entities, such as the traditionalist movement against same-sex marriage laws in Taiwan (Yang & Kang), the Straight Pride movement (Armstrong) and the harassment campaign against sex workers, #thotaudit (Copland). As these chapters show, often these 'less extreme' phenomena are closely linked through digital and economic networks with more recognizably far-right entities. Also, we have included chapters that evaluate (Kasimov; Cousineau) or question (Devries; Brett; Hagen & Tuters) our capacity to categorize an entire online space as far-right, or as composed strictly of ideologically aligned far-right subjects with explicitly political motives.

In sum, we find this volume importantly brings together studies of the recruitment or mobilization processes of explicitly far-right groups, as well as study of the less expected, at times uncanny settings or circumstances where far-right politics may emerge, evolve or create harmful effects. In what follows, we give a brief preview of these chapters and the directions they initiate.

A LOOK AHEAD

Electoral and Institutional Resurgence: Campaigns and Wins

Many of these chapters include discussion of the technological affordances available for far-right mobilization. Chapters by Jordan McSwiney, Simon Bradford and Fin Cullen, and Kenneth C. C. Yang and Yowei Kang locate the effects and affects of these affordances in electoral wins and movements adjacent to the democratic process. Starting the volume with a swift and specific study, Jordan McSwiney addresses how three affordances – direct communication, connectivity and visibility – provided Pauline Hanson and the Australian 'far-right' with the capacity to build bonds with their followers, connect with like-minded organizations and reduce the threshold of participation. McSwiney argues that this resulted in the successful election of senators like Pauline Hanson and Malcom Roberts, who have made calls to halt Muslim immigration and the construction of mosques across Australia.

Simon Bradford and Fin Cullen's address of Hungary's far-right party *Fidesz* and its leader Viktor Orban discusses the mediation of cultural narratives and maintenance of popular support via various digital and analogue media technologies throughout the leader's decade in power. Orban's assertion is that nation, government and *Fidesz* itself are indivisible. This discourse of collective strength, especially in comparison to the denigrated 'other', is not only common to far-right populist movements, but also points to the mobilizing effects of 'collectivity' elsewhere online (Hagan & Tuters, Copland, Kasimov, Devries).

Distant from these explicit far-right and 'anti-gender ideology' politics in Hungary, Taiwan became the first Asian nation to legalize same-sex marriage in 2017. This win breaks past conservative notions of traditionalism and heterosexual norms, the origins of which emerge from a complicated imperial past. Yang and Kang employ a social movement studies lens to address this historical moment of gay-marriage legalization, and examine the push-back it has incited from Taiwanese Right-wing Christian groups, who unsurprisingly receive support from ultra-conservative and anti-LGBT Christian institutions and lobbies in the United States. In this sense, Yang and Kang provide an important discussion about how the maintenance of ultra-conservatism and the manufacture of a Taiwanese 'heritage of Biblical marriage' are dependent upon a global economic network of influence (Stewart 2020), as well as upon digital networks. The products of these varied networks appear on Taiwanese Facebook groups and the communication application Line, which Yang and Kang identify as an important tool in the Christian right's spread of homophobic content. These reactionary campaigns have since led to a landslide majority for far-right city and county representatives in 2018 local elections.

Social Network, Social Movement and the Gendered Far Right

Alongside Yang and Kang, JP Armstrong applies social movement studies to reactionary anti-LBGTQ movements. Armstrong investigates the brief emergence of a 'straight pride' hashtag that, while unable to accumulate mass popular support, successfully gained prominence on Twitter networks as a global trend. This mobilization on behalf of a supposedly silent, 'oppressed majority' (of straight people) shows how certain technological affordances like the Twitter hashtag can work against or despite more popular progressive trends. As Armstrong points out, the Twitter hashtag is a magnifying device, unilaterally amplifying any engagement. In the case of straight pride, this meant that engagement with reactionary hashtags by progressive actors meaning to refute their intent instead bolstered the hashtag's spread. These findings raise important questions about how to engage or defuse reactionary forms of hashtag activism like straight pride.

Simon Copland's chapter also follows a small yet harmful anti-women and anti–sex worker harassment campaign mobilized largely via Twitter: #thotaudit. Like straight pride, this campaign did not get much mainstream attention nor gather wide support outside of its ideological networks. Yet, Copland argues that it is important to consider the way participatory networks between different platforms like Twitter and YouTube (and the influential microcelebrities located therein) mobilize reactionary, far-right and anti-feminist violence against vulnerable communities like sex workers.

Luc Cousineau rounds off this discussion about the relationship between digital platform features and anti-feminist communities. Cousineau provides an important reminder of the links between contemporary male supremacist subreddits and a historical dissatisfaction with gender norms that, in some contradiction, still reject the egalitarian projects of feminist movements. Cousineau shows how the digitization of these aging movements provides new means of recruitment, and thus the evolution of new anti-feminist communities like /r/MensRights, and /r/TheRedPill. As these three chapters investigate the connections between technological affordances and anti-LGBT, anti–sex worker and anti-women movements, we are reminded not only of the varied ways that ultra-conservative anti-feminism petitions for validity amidst contemporary progressive discourses, but also of the extent to which they mobilize harm against a common 'other'.

Platforms and Alt-Tech Collectivity

Like Armstrong and Yang and Kang, Andrey Kasimov brings these concepts of social movement theory into uncommon applications. Emphasizing the lack in social movement studies as applied to the explicit 'far-right', Kasimov evaluates whether we can consider 4chan's /pol/ forum as a social movement scene that functions to recruit and mobilize far-right adherence. Kasimov finds that /pol/ indeed hosts activity that qualifies as persistent attempts at far-right ideological recruitment, along with calls to mobilize 4chan's userbase. However, Kasimov implies that recruitment and mobilization via the now notorious 4chan is more an appropriation of the medium by far-right actors, as opposed to solely the work of 4chan's technological features and cultural history of transgression.

Sal Hagen and Marc Tuters also address the compelling question of how anonymous 'dark-web' Internet forums contribute to forms of far-right recruitment and mobilization. In answering, however, these authors move past assumptions that recruitment arises through person-to-person contact, showing that this concept of recruitment fails to capture the nuanced group-making dynamics of 4chan's anonymous collectives. Instead, they introduce and demonstrate the concept of *group entitativity* on 4chan, arguing that researchers need to consider the collective construction of an in-group (as well as a typical hatred towards out-groups like the 'mainstream media') in order to more accurately understand how 4chan might function as a complex site of far-right ideological recruitment.

In contrast to these discussions of 4chan, Reddit and Twitter – all various forms of semi-accessible sites developed with no far-right intention – Greta Jasser addresses Alt-Tech: a series of online platforms developed for the specific, right-libertarian purpose of enabling 'anti-mainstream' (i.e. racist, offensive or violent) digital interaction typically censored by mainstream social media. Jasser presents a case study of *Gab*, a platform meant to counter the anti-hate-speech regulations imposed by Twitter in their monitoring of anti-Semitism and other harassment or abuse. Jasser finds that the use of pointedly anti-mainstream technology is commonly paired with a user attitude which conceives of themselves as a persecuted group. While typical Gab users don't qualify as a counter-public by nature of their location within dominant social groups, Jasser uses the analytical concept of an imitated counter-public to effectively dissect what mobilizes far-right appeal in Alt-Tech.

Assemblages and Assembled Tools: From Theory to Resistance

This qualification of Alt-Tech as imitated counter-publics juxtaposes Noel Brett's analysis of the intentionally far-right videogame, *Angry Goy 2*. Like other Alt-tech, *Angry Goy 2* was developed with politics at its forefront; every move the player makes constitutes an action which carries political weight. Compellingly, Brett uses qualitative analysis to compare *Angry Goy 2* to the very different game, *Red Dead Redemption 2* (*RDR2*). While *RDR2* is not encoded with an explicit politics, its open-world mechanics allow players to perform a wide set of mundane, non-campaign-related actions. These affordances for players to do almost any action resulted in players performing explicitly racist, sexist and violent acts against feminist and Black non-player characters. Whether reflective of the player's 'true' authoritarian politics or not, this gameplay highlights questions about from where and when far-right politics emerge. Providing an important turn towards analysing far-right outputs, Brett presents the theoretical concept of 'moments of political gameplay' to mark how game features combine with the latent political affordances to produce what in the end constitutes digitized far-right action.

Like Brett, Devries also presents a theoretical model that pushes past analysis of far-right intent and content towards the consequences of intentional *or* passive political action. Here, Devries develops 'the collective avatar', a conceptual tool paired with ethnographic methods that uses theories of performativity and relationality to account for how participants within online spaces not only reproduce far-right ends, but often do so unintentionally. Tying together two distinct case studies – the racist Ugandan Knuckles meme and 4chan's reaction to the New Zealand massacre – the collective avatar works as a means to understand how otherwise mainstream users are mobilized to perform far-right or racializing practice before they are fully recruited within far-right causes or groups. Devries argues that while a user does not have to be a fully formed or 'recruited' white supremacist to mobilize far-right ends, mobilized participation can produce affiliation with far-right politics. Further, Devries argues that developing concepts to map this process – wherein mobilized practices precede far-right ideological recruitment – is critical to forging new directions in contemporary qualitative studies of online far-right subcultures, and to conceptualizing modes of resistance.

Post these varied and vivid discussions of how technologies have been involved in recruiting far-right adherents or mobilizing far-right political practice, Tanner Mirrlees' chapter reminds us of our potential avenues for resistance. This chapter ends the volume with a detailed overview of the multi-faceted sources from where there exists potential to oppose the far-right. It focuses on what State actors, Big Tech corporations, entertainment and news industries, non-profit research communities and anti-fascist initiatives and media-makers do to counter the far-right. Importantly, Mirrlees is reflexive in assessing the limits of such resistance, with an eye to the racial capitalism and right-wing neoliberal blocs – progressive and reactionary – that perpetuate white class power and privilege. In this, we are left with implications for what avenues (and what technologies) might provide us with brighter, more egalitarian futures amidst the social settings that have afforded the global, contemporary far-right in the first place.

We hope that together, the chapters in this volume provide inspiration for further critical studies concerning the myriad evolving forms of mediated, contemporary far-right recruitment and mobilization.

NOTE

1. 'Men make their own history, but they do not make it just as they please; they do not make it under circumstances chosen by themselves, but under circumstances directly encountered, given and transmitted from the past' (Marx 2009, p. 15).

REFERENCES

Acevedo, N. 2019. '"Straight Pride Parade" in Boston Draws Counterprotesters and Heavy Police Presence'. *NBC News*. 3 September. https://www.nbcnews.com/news/us-news/straight-pride-parade-boston-draws-counterprotesters-heavy-police-presence-n1048626.

Acevedo, N. 2021. 'Woman Who Said She Wanted to Shoot Pelosi during Capitol Riot Arrested: At least 160 People Have Been Charged Federally with Crimes Related to the Riot that Left Five People Dead'. *NBC News*. https://www.nbcnews.com/politics/congress/woman-saying-she-wanted-shoot-pelosi-friggin-brain-during-capitol-n1256275.

Ahmed, Sara. 2004. 'Affective Economies'. *Social Text* 22 (2): 117–39.

Barret-Fox, R. 2011. 'Anger and Compassion on the Picket Line: Ethnography and Emotion in the Study of Westboro Baptist Church'. *Journal of Hate Studies*: Special Issue: Proceedings from the Second International Conference on Hate Studies 9 (1).

Belew, K. 2019. *Bring the War Home: The White Power Movement and Paramilitary America*. Cambridge, MA: Harvard University Press.

Beran, D. 2019. *It Came from Something Awful: How a Toxic Troll Army Accidentally Memed Donald Trump into Office*. St. Martin's Publishing Group.

Bessant, Judith. 2014. *Democracy Bytes: New Media and New Politics and Generational Change*. Basingstoke, Hampshire, UK: Macmillan Palgrave.

Bessant, Judith, 2018. *The Great Transformation, History for a Techno-Human Future*. New York, NY: Routledge.

Blanchette, J. F. 2011. 'A Material History of Bits'. *Journal of the American Society for Information Science and Technology* 62 (2): 1042–57.

Bourdieu, P., and L. Wacquant. 1992. *An Invitation to Reflexive Sociology*. Cambridge: Polity Press.

Caiani, M. 2017. 'Radical Right-Wing Movements: Who, When, How and Why?' *Sociopedia ISA*, DOI: 10.1177/205684601761.

Caiani, M., D. Della Porta, and C. Wagemann. 2012. *Mobilizing on the Radical Right: Germany, Italy and the United States*. Oxford: Oxford University Press.

Caballar, Rina Diane. 2019. 'What Is the Uncanny Valley?: Creepy Robots and the Strange Phenomenon of the Uncanny Valley: Definition, History, Examples, and How to Avoid It'. *IEEE Spectrum Magazine*.

Chun, Wendy Hui Kyong. 2016. *Updating to Remain the Same: Habitual New Media*. Cambridge, MA: MIT Press.

Chun, Wendy Hui Kyong. 2018. 'Queerying Homophily'. In *Pattern Discrimination*, edited by Apprich, Chun, Cramer, and Steyerl, 59–98. Minneapolis: University of Minnesota Press.

Chadler, Simon. 2020. 'Elon Musk Is "Distracting Us" From Real Tech Issues, AI Figures Warn'. *Forbes*, 18 May. https://www.forbes.com/sites/simonchandler/2020/05/18/elon-musk-is-damaging-tech-and-the-tech-industry/?sh=4db96aa519b8.

Devries, M. 2021. 'Archetypes vs. Homophilic Avatars: Re-defining Far/Right Facebook Practice'. Manuscript submitted for publication.

Fuchs. C. 2013. Capitalism or Information Society? The Fundamental Question of the Present Structure of Society. *European Journal of Social Theory*, 16 (4): 413–34.

Hawley, G. 2017. *Making Sense of the Alt-Right*. Chichester, NY: Columbia University Press.

Hawley, G. 2019. *The Alt-Right: What Everyone Needs to Know*. New York, NY: Oxford University Press.

Kaufmann, M., and J. Jeandesboz. 2017. 'Politics and "the Digital": From Singularity to Specificity'. *European Journal of Social Theory* 20 (3): 309–28.

Kayali, Lea, and Panjwani. 2021. 'The White Supremacist Agenda of the War on Terror'. https://medium.com/qalam/the-white-supremacist-agenda-of-the-war-on-terror-545f14799e91.

Kundnani, Arun. 2015. *The Muslims Are Coming! Islamophobia, Extremism, and the Domestic War on Terror*. Brooklyn: Verso Books.

Lewis, Rebecca. 2018. 'Broadcasting the Reactionary Right on YouTube'. Media and Manipulation Research Initiative. *Data & Society*. https://datasociety.net/library/alternative-influence/.

Marx, K. 2009 [1869]. *The 18th Brumaire of Louis Bonaparte*. 2nd ed. La Vergne, TN: Wildside Press.

Mayer-Schonberger, V., and K. Cukier. 2013. *Big Data: A Revolution That Will Transform How We Live, Work, and Think*. London: John Murray.

Maynard, Robyn. 2017. *Policing Black Lives: State Violence in Canada from Slavery to the Present*. Winnipeg: Fernwood Publishing.

McFarlane, Craig. 2013. 'Relational Sociology, Theoretical Inhumanism, and the Problem of the Nonhuman'. In *Conceptualizing Relational Sociology: Ontological and Theoretical Issues*, edited by Christopher Powell and François Dépelteau. New York: Palgrave Macmillan.

Miller-Idriss, C. 2020. *Hate in the Homeland: The New Global Far Right*. Princeton, NJ: Princeton University Press.

Mirrlees, T. 2019. 'Power, Privilege and Resistance in the Digital Age'. Canadian Centre for Policy Alternatives. 1 May. https://www.policyalternatives.ca/publications/monitor/power-privilege-and-resistance-digital-age.

Neville, S. J., and G. Langlois. 2021. 'Enemy Imaginaries: A Case Study of the Far-right in Canada'. *Canadian Journal of Communication* (accepted, pending revisions).

Noble, Safyia. 2018. *Algorithms of Oppression*. New York: NYU Press.

O'Neil, C. 2016. *Weapons of Math Destruction: How Big Data Increases Inequality and Threatens Democracy*. New York, NY: Broadway Books.

Packer, A., 2013. 'Epistemology Not Ideology or Why We Need New Germans. *Communication and Critical/Cultural Studies* 10 (2–3): 295–300.

Panjwani, Aly, and Lea Kayali. 2021. 'The White Supremacist Agenda of the War on Terror'. *Qalam: Medium*. https://medium.com/qalam/the-white-supremacist-agenda-of-the-war-on-terror-545f14799e91.

Peterson, Jennifer. 2011. *Murder, the Media, and the Politics of Public Feelings: Remembering Matthew Shepard and James Byrd Jr*. Bloomington, IN: Indiana University Press.

Powell, C. 2013. 'Radical Relationalism: A Proposal'. In *Conceptualizing Relational Sociology: Ontological and Theoretical Issues*, edited by Christopher Powell and François Dépelteau. New York: Palgrave Macmillan.

Renton, D. 2019. *The New Authoritarians: Convergence on the Right*. London: Pluto Press.

Schiller, D. 2000. *Digital Capitalism: Networking the Global Market System*. Cambridge, MA: MIT Press.

Schiller, D. 2014. *Digital Depression: Information Technology and Economic Crisis*. Chicago, IL: University of Illinois Press.

Schiller, H. I. 1991. 'Not Yet the Post-Imperialist Era'. *Critical Studies in Mass Communication* 8 (1): 13–28.

Schiller, H. I. 1992. *Mass Communication and American Empire*. New York: August M. Kelley.

Schiller, H. I. 1998. 'Striving for Electronic Mastery'. In *Electronic Empires: Global media and Local Resistance*, edited by Daya Kishan Thussu. New York: Bloomsbury Academic.

Somos, Christy. 2021. 'These Are Some of the Extremist Groups Responsible for the Violence on Capitol Hill'. CTV News. https://www.ctvnews.ca/world/these-are-some-of-the-extremist-groups-responsible-for-the-violence-on-capitol-hill-1.5259142.

Stewart, Katherine. 2020. *The Power Worshippers: Inside the Dangerous Rise of Religious Nationalism*. New York, NY: Bloomsbury Publishing.

Sweeney, L. 2013. 'Google Ads, Black Names and White Names, Racial Discrimination, and Click Advertising'. *ACM QUEUE* 11 (3). https://queue.acm.org/detail.cfm?id=2460278.

Tsekeris, Charalambos. 2013. 'Norbert Elias on Relations: Insights and Perspectives'. In *Conceptualizing Relational Sociology: Ontological and Theoretical Issues*, edited by Christopher Powell and François Dépelteau. New York: Palgrave Macmillan.

Tuters, Marc, and Anthony G. Burton. 2021. 'The Rebel Yell: Alt-Right Audiences & Burlesque Traditionalism on YouTube'. *Canadian Journalism of Communications*. Forthcoming.

van Dijk J., 2006. *The Network Society*. 2nd ed. London: SAGE.

van Dijk, J. 2013. 'Inequalities in the Network Society'. In *Digital Sociology: Critical Perspectives*, edited by K. Orton-Johnson and N. Prior, 105–24. London: Palgrave Macmillan.

Vice News Video. 2021. 'Inside the Capitol Hill Riots'. *Vice Media*. 9 January. https://www.youtube.com/watch?v=lfP_5L8epow.

Webster, F. 2014. *Theories of the Information Society*. 4th ed. London: Routledge.

Part I

ELECTORAL AND INSTITUTIONAL RESURGENCE: CAMPAIGNS AND WINS

Chapter 2

Far-Right Recruitment and Mobilization on Facebook: The Case of Australia

Jordan McSwiney

The Internet is a powerful tool for the far right.[1] By facilitating communication and participation across spatial boundaries, connecting like-minded organizations and spreading their messages (Caiani and Parenti 2016), the Internet, and in particular social networking platforms, have become vital to recruitment and mobilization for the far right today. This is especially the case in contexts where the far right faces institutional or social marginalization. This chapter explores how the far right utilizes the popular social networking platform Facebook through a case study of the Australian far-right Facebook fan page network in 2018. Though significant research has been conducted on the use of social media by the far right (e.g. Engesser et al. 2016; Ernst et al. 2016; Froio and Ganesh 2019; Klein and Muis 2019), these have tended to focus on the discursive or communicative utility of such platforms.

This chapter builds on this, first by focusing on mobilization and recruitment, and second, by contributing a case outside the 'usual suspects' (Mudde 2016) of the largely 'Eurocentric' (Castelli-Gattinara 2020) research on the far right. I argue that there are three central technological affordances which make the platform useful to the Australian far right: direct communications, connectivity and visibility. These provide the far right with the capacity to build bonds with their followers, connect with like-minded organizations and reduce the threshold of participation, the effect of which is to create new opportunities for both recruitment and mobilization.

Given the lack of historically strong and stable offline organizations, the Australian far right has had to rely on the Internet to build a movement (Fleming and Mondon 2018). Following nation-wide protest mobilizations to 'reclaim Australia' in 2015, the Australian far right underwent an organizational rejuvenation culminating in the electoral breakthrough of Australia's most successful far-right political party Pauline Hanson's One

Nation (thereafter One Nation) at the 2016 federal election. Though the size and capacities of the Australian far right remain marginal compared to its European or North American counterparts, policy makers, as well as law enforcement and intelligence agencies, are paying increasing attention to the potential threat the far right poses to public safety and social cohesion (Peucker and Smith 2019). However, limited research has been conducted into the role that social media networks play in the organization of the Australian far right (cf. McSwiney 2020).

The aims of this chapter are twofold. Using social network analysis, I first map the network of Australian far-right pages present on Facebook in 2018. The configuration of this network helps to identify key actors, as well as indicating offline opportunities available to the far right in so far as institutionalization and mobilization (Klein and Muis 2019). Second, I analyse the affordances of such a network in terms of its cooperative and communicative linkages and how it facilitates far-right mobilization and recruitment in the Australian context. I identify several distinct communities present in the network, corresponding to particular ideological, organizational and geographical configurations. These communities are structured around a selection of key Facebook pages, which serve as communicative and organizational hubs in the online network. Non-party actors (i.e. protest campaigns) are both the most numerous and the most structurally significant network actors, pointing to the limited space for institutionalized (i.e. parliamentary) far-right actors in Australian politics (Klein and Muis 2019). Nevertheless, One Nation occupies an important network position as the most electorally successful Australian far-right party. In addition, the party's founder and leader Pauline Hanson is even more popular on the platform than the One Nation party organization. This suggests that it is Hanson's significant public profile, as distinct from the party itself, which has created electoral opportunities for One Nation, taking full advantage of the communicative affordances of Facebook to build strong bonds with the party's supporters.

Owing to the limited political opportunities for the far right in Australia in terms of electoral politics, social movements campaigning against mosques and halal certification occupy key positions in this Facebook network, indicating they serve an important function as mobilizing outlets and spaces for recruitment. Connectivity helps foster a sense of community, while the lowered engagement threshold of 'liking' and 'sharing' lends itself to a 'commitment curve' of gradually increasing participation, with the aim of recruitment into the movement and participation in offline mobilization (Chen 2015, 136). Though a large number of violent street-based groups are present on the platform, they are relatively marginalized in the Australian far-right network on Facebook. So too are the explicitly fascist and white supremacist Australian organizations operating on Facebook. This suggests that such groups are unable to build broad alliances with other far-right actors in Australia, limiting their ability to mobilize effectively.

THE FAR RIGHT AND THE AFFORDANCES OF FACEBOOK

The Internet has long been a key tool for the far right, providing space for this notoriously internecine political family to connect and coalesce (Copsey 2003; Winter 2019; Caiani, Della Porta, and Wagemann 2012). Long before the uptake of social networking platforms, email lists, digital bulletin boards and dedicated web servers were used to develop a sense of shared community among the far right (Copsey 2003). Thanks to their accessibility and the ways in which they facilitate the 'sharing of experience, knowledge and information' by users and their 'potential collective mobilizing powers', social networking platforms have been seized upon by the far right as an organizational technology (Nixon, Mercea, and Rawal 2013, 2). The networks of the far right now span multiple mainstream platforms like Facebook, Twitter and YouTube (Ernst et al. 2017; O'Callaghan et al. 2013). However, access to these platforms has become increasingly difficult for the far right, particularly in the wake of the 2019 Christchurch Massacre in New Zealand. Following this attack, platforms including Facebook and Twitter introduced much stricter rules around hateful speech and white supremacist content (Cook 2019). While this has not resulted in the total removal of the far right from these platforms, it has noticeably limited the presence of high-profile far-right actors. Many have since turned the far-right's parallel Internet infrastructure in the so-called Alt-Tech (Jasser 2020, this volume). Nevertheless, social networking platforms like Facebook remain valuable tools for the far right due to their technological affordances of use for the intersecting processes of recruitment and mobilization. By mobilization, I refer to the motivation to act, either online or offline, such as engaging in collective action (i.e. protest). By recruitment, I refer to both the process of becoming an informal supporter of a group by adhering to a certain politics, as well as the formal act of joining an organization. In the following I outline three key technological affordances of Facebook and their utility to the Australian far right.

Firstly, Facebook allows pages to communicate directly with their followers. These networks provide a free and readily available means for disseminating the goal, mission and ideology of a political group to a large potential audience (Caiani and Kluknavská 2017). Pages are able to bypass the traditional gatekeeping function of media and bring their message directly to their supporters (Chadwick 2013; Pedersen and Saglie 2015; Stier et al. 2017). For those on the far right who adopt a populist communication style like

Pauline Hanson and One Nation (Moffitt 2016; Sengul 2020), the medium of Facebook is especially useful. Bypassing traditional media allows Hanson to appeal directly to 'the people', helping facilitate stronger and closer connections between populist actors and their supporters (Stier et al. 2017). Social media also affords a greater degree of immediacy, allowing users to quickly respond to events or livestream collective action such as protests through the 'Facebook live' feature.

Secondly, the connective architecture of a social networking platform like Facebook hinges the interaction between users. Users are encouraged to seek out and connect with those (be they organizations or individuals) with similar interests (Stier 2017). Low thresholds for engagement, such as a 'like' on Facebook, allow users to easily connect and remain up to date with an organization's activities. This facilitates interaction and participation across spatial barriers, enabling supporters to participate virtually even if an organization has no local presence offline (Burris et al. 2000; Ward and Gibson 2010). Users can support an organization by 'liking' and 'sharing' its content, becoming important links in chains of communication by disseminating an organization's message within their own personal networks (Gonzalez-Bailón 2014). These linkages may also serve as pathways of political recruitment and mobilization across different organizations. By facilitating communication between large numbers of individuals at low cost, Facebook affords significant mobilization potential. Users can easily receive and share a call to action or information regarding a demonstration. The platform also provides specific tools for organizing events (e.g. Facebook's 'event' feature), which help facilitate opportunities for developing connections offline, and hence recruitment, as well.

Thirdly, visibility, which relates to the amount of effort required to locate information (Treem and Leonardi 2013), facilitates accessibility making the far right's content easier to access and interact with. Facebook's connectivity, boosted by its indexing in search engines, internal search function and recommender algorithm showing similar pages, helps users build a like-minded community and more easily identify information, organizations or events. This has important implications for modes of far-right recruitment by making far-right ideas and communities accessible to those who may support some or all of the positions but are not yet engaged with the far right as a movement. The content shared in far-right networks is moreover aimed at creating a collective identity among supporters (Caiani and Kluknavská 2017). This socialization process helps to facilitate mobilizations by influencing 'individual behaviour and readiness to take part in collective action' (Bowman-Grieve 2009, 1003). Often, this takes the form of 'interpretive frames': content which gives clues to readers that they should mobilize around a certain issue in a certain way (Caiani et al. 2012). For the contemporary far right, key interpretive frames have generally centred on Islam and Islamophobia (Froio and Ganesh 2019; Minkenberg 2018; Miller 2017).

THE FAR RIGHT IN AUSTRALIA

The importance of a social networking platform like Facebook to the Australian far right is difficult to understate. The effective collapse of Pauline Hanson's One Nation in the early 2000s due to infighting and charges of electoral fraud left the Australian far right with few meaningful electoral players (Fleming and Mondon 2018). During this time, the Internet became the 'chief domain' of the Australian far right (Fleming and Mondon 2018, 662), with a multitude of blogs and social media pages coalescing around key issues including anti-immigrant and anti-refugee sentiments, and Islamophobia.

Lacking meaningful electoral opportunities, protest campaigns and small, localized social movement organizations became the central players in the Australian far-right scene. In particular, the emergence of a number of Islamophobic campaigns targeting the construction of mosques and halal food certification in Australia throughout the late-2000s and 2010s had an important effect on the far right's cultural milieu that can still be seen today. These campaigns served as key points for the coalescing of various far-right groups and individuals. The most notable of these was the *Stop the Mosque Bendigo* campaign in regional Victoria, a local campaign against an application to build a mosque and Islamic community centre, which evolved into a national flashpoint for the far right (Rudner 2019). One Nation would later recruit election candidates from this (and other) anti-mosque campaigns for both the 2016 and 2019 federal elections. Importantly, these relationships were not one-directional, with groups like Stop the Mosque Bendigo relying on their social media connections to the broader far-right networks for 'advice, propaganda material for distribution, funding and encouragement' (Markus 2018, ii).

In 2015, numerous anti-Islam, anti-immigrant and anti-refugee projects coalesced in the emergence of *Reclaim Australia* in 2015. Between 2015 and 2017, Reclaim Australia held dozens of rallies in capital cities and regional centres around the country. Collectively attracting several thousand people, these rallies were 'the most significant mobilization of the far right since the Hanson years [of the 1990s]' (Fleming and Mondon 2018, 662). Reclaim Australia opened the political space for a number of far-right activists and organizations to coalesce and organize, leading to the formation of several other groups. The most notable of these was the *United Patriots Front*, a more militant breakaway group that embraced confrontational tactics and violence in dealing with anti-racist and anti-fascist counter-demonstrators (Richards 2019). Other similar organizations to emerge from these protests include the *True Blue Crew* and the establishment of the Australian chapter of the *Soldiers of Odin* (Nilan 2019).

Reclaim Australia also provided the momentum for the return of One Nation as a viable electoral contender. The party's founder and leader Pauline Hanson participated three times as a headline speaker at Reclaim Australia rallies in the state of Queensland, the party's traditional heartland (Goot and Watson 2001). Her third appearance was part of her official 'Fed Up' tour, a key pillar of the party's political comeback ahead of the 2016 federal election, where the party achieved an electoral breakthrough with 4.3% of the first preference Senate vote. Though One Nation was the only far-right party to achieve electoral representation in 2016 with the election of four senators, a number of other far-right parties contested the federal election. Among them, the *Australian Liberty Alliance* was the most significant new party due to its extensive connections to the international counter-jihad movement (Hope Not Hate 2018). Founded in 2015 with the endorsement of Dutch far-right politician Geert Wilders, the Australian Liberty Alliance is the political party project of the secretive *Q Society of Australia*, which describes itself as Australia's leading 'Islam-critical movement' (Q Society 2011). While hesitant about participation in some anti-Islam protests in 2015 (Baxendale 2015), the Australian Liberty Alliance successfully incorporated leading anti-halal certification campaign organization *Halal Choices* into its party network.

Another important fixture is the neo-Nazi Australia First Party. Though electorally insignificant, the party is the longest-running neo-Nazi party in Australia. It played an important role in anti-mosque protests in Penrith in Sydney's west throughout the early to mid-2010s and has links to the Greek neo-Nazi party Golden Dawn. Founded by disgraced Australian Labor Party MP Graeme Campbell in 1996, the Australia First Party was taken over by Jim Saleam following Campbell's exit in 2001 (coincidentally, Campbell left to stand as a Senate candidate for One Nation; Fleming and Mondon, 2018). Saleam, who still leads the party today, is a veteran activist in Australia's white supremacist and neo-Nazi circles (e.g. Greason 1994).

Paramount to these developments within the Australian far right was the Internet, and more specifically, Web 2.0, with its ease of use, social and participatory focus and provision of platforms emphasizing user-generated content (Lovink 2011). Social media platforms like Facebook were central to this rejuvenation and the uptick in support that materialized with the Reclaim Australia rallies. These protests marked the first nationally co-ordinated mobilizations of a movement that until then primarily existed online (Fleming and Mondon 2018). Facebook's utility as a tool for recruitment and mobilization was crucial here. As one of the founders of Reclaim Australia, Catherine Brennan, told CNN: 'without social media we wouldn't exist, it's that simple' (cited in Fenton 2017).

DATA AND METHODOLOGY

This chapter uses social network analysis to map the relations among and between the Australian far right on Facebook. Social network analysis is distinguished by its focus on the network as its central theoretical and methodological focus. A network is a set of objects or actors ('nodes') and the relationships ('ties') that connect them (Borgatti, Everett, and Johnson 2018; Kadushin 2012; Scott 2017). The pattern of ties produces a network structure in which nodes occupy particular positions, and these positions influence 'the opportunities and constraints' a node is presented with (Kane et al. 2014, 3). Adapting the method developed by Burris et al. (2000), this chapter operationalizes Facebook fan pages as the relevant nodes, and the 'likes' between them as ties. The pattern of connections among and between various Australian far-right pages is read as a networked structure. The page-to-page likes, though not necessarily indicative of formal ties between organizations or persons, nevertheless points to 'ties of affinity, paths of communication, tokens of mutual aid in achieving public recognition and/or potential avenues of coordination' (Burris et al. 2000, 215). The analysis of these likes therefore maps the contours of the far-right (sub)cultural milieu, highlighting 'coalition building, overlapping membership, processes of collective action and counter mobilization' (Caiani 2014, 373), while also identifying different subgroups and potential channels of recruitment.

Though the entirety of this network spans multiple digital spaces, Facebook provides the most important window into the Australian far right. Facebook is the most popular social networking platform in Australia (Yellow 2018), providing the greatest opportunity for the far right to engage with its supporters as well as the general public. While a significant portion of the Australian far-right ecosystem was removed from Facebook in the wake of the 2019 Christchurch Massacre, many of the key players were still active on the platform in 2018 when data was collected for this chapter.

Lacking an exhaustive directory of Facebook, it is impossible to determine the complete dimensions of the network and hence, an entirely representative sample (Caiani 2014). Instead, a purposively selected sample of key actors in the Australian far right is used as a starting point for this analysis, with additional nodes added using the snowball method (Scott 2017). The thirty-five actors included in this starting list, which can be found in Figure 2.1, were selected based on their predominance in the literature concerning the contemporary far right in Australia (Dean, Bell, and Vakhtova 2016, Fleming and Mondon 2018; Peucker, Smith, and Iqbal 2019). The sample also aims to provide a cross-section of the different organizational forms and ideologies that make up the Australian far right. Of the thirty-five far-right actors included in the starting sample, only twenty had active Facebook pages at the time of

Present on Facebook	Not present on Facebook
Australia First Party	Adelaide Institute
Australian Defence League	Antipodean Resistance
Australian Liberty Alliance	Australian League of Rights
Australian Protectionist Party	Blood and Honour
Blair Cottrell	Full Blooded Skips
Citizens Electoral Council	Hellenic Nationalists of Australia
Cooks Convicts	National Action
Lads Society	National Democratic Party of Australia
Love Australia or Leave Party	Party for Freedom (Australia)
Nationalist Alternative	Patriotic Youth League
Nationalist Uprising	Right Wing Resistance
Pauline Hanson's One Nation	Southern Cross Hammerskins
Patriots Defence League	Squadron 88
Q Society of Australia	United Nationalists Australia
Reclaim Australia	United Patriots Front
Rise Up Australia Party	
Soldiers of Odin	
TheDingoes.xyz	
True Blue Crew	
XYZ	

Figure 2.1. Seed List of Australian Far-Right Organizations Present on Facebook, April 2018.
Source: Author.

data collection. The far-right groups absent from the platform were generally the more explicitly fascistic and violent actors included in the sample, such as neo-Nazi *Squadron 88* or the *Southern Cross Hammerskins*. These groups are likely not present on Facebook due to Facebook's community guidelines, which disallows explicit neo-Nazi content. However, these same guidelines nevertheless allow less explicitly white supremacist far-right actors to slip through the cracks, avoiding moderation or potential removal from the platform. A number of far-right groups in the sample had multiple pages, reflecting different branches or chapters within an organization. In such cases, all of these pages were used for the purposes of collecting network data.

Data was collected using Netvizz (v1.45; Rieder 2013), which collects only publicly available data using Facebook's application programming interface,

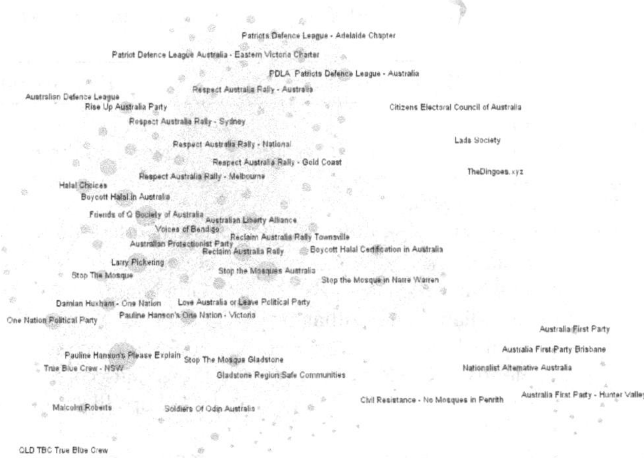

Figure 2.2. Network of Pages Belonging to the Australian Far Right on Facebook, April 2018.
Source: Author.

helping to ensure that the platform's legal requirements regarding data collection and use by third-party actors are met. Acknowledging ethical consideration regarding privacy, this chapter focuses only on public Facebook pages (Klein and Muis 2019). Only the names of public figures (i.e. spokespersons who have represented the groups in the press) are included in publication. Network visualizations were created using Gephi (version 0.9.2; Bastian, Heymann, and Jacomy 2009).

FINDINGS

In total, 198 pages (nodes) were identified, with 967 likes (ties) between them (figure 2.2). These 198 fan pages represent 65 different organizations when accounting for groups with multiple pages. The resulting directed network is fairly decentralized, though there are a number of key pages that structure the network. That is, pages which have a significantly higher number of in-bound likes, or sit on the shortest path between two otherwise unconnected pages. Three pages included in the starting sample are not connected to the network. Six sub-communities are identifiable. These communities are based on a higher level of local density among the pages within their cluster compared to the network as a whole. These are detailed in table 2.1. The names given to the communities are not deterministic, but rather reflect the general character of the most prominent pages within that community.

Centrality measures indicate the extent to which a network is organized around one or more key nodes, or in this case, Facebook fan pages. This helps to identify the most important pages in structuring a network (Caiani

Table 2.1. Table of Australian Far-Right Communities, Facebook Page-Like Network, April 2018

Community	*Key Nodes*	*Description*
Australia First Party	• Australia First Party • Australia First Party Brisbane • Australia First Party – Hunter Valley	Comprised largely of pages belonging to the neo-Nazi Australia First Party.
Pauline Hanson's One Nation	• Pauline Hanson's Please Explain • One Nation Political Party	Consists primarily of pages associated with Pauline Hanson's One Nation Political Party.
Q Society	• Australian Liberty Alliance • Halal Choices • Friends of Q Society of Australia • Stop the Mosques Australia	Comprised of various anti-halal and anti-mosque campaigns. Present also are local branches of groups like the Patriots Defence League.
Reclaim Australia	• Reclaim Australia Rally • Reclaim Australia Rally Townsville • Rise Up Australia Party	Comprised mostly of Reclaim Australia pages.
Respect Australia	• Respect Australia Rally – National • Respect Australia Rally – Gold Coast • Rise Up Australia Party	Structured around two Respect Australia Rally pages. However, the community itself is largely populated by Patriots Defence League pages.
Safe Communities Australia	• Gladstone Region Safe Communities • Love Australia or Leave Party • Stop the Mosque Gladstone	Comprised largely of pages belonging to Safe Communities Australia. Also present are the fan pages for the Soldiers of Odin and True Blue Crew.
Stop the Mosques – Victoria	• Stop the Mosque in Narre Warren • Boycott Halal Certification in Australia	Consists mostly of Victorian anti-mosque campaigns and the national Boycott Halal Certification in Australia page.

Source: Author.

and Parenti 2016). Based on betweenness centrality – the measure of how often a node appears on the shortest path between other nodes in the network – a number of campaign organizations emerge as vital to the overall network. This includes Respect Australia Rally – National, Stop the Mosque Gladstone, Stop the Mosque Australia and Respect Australia Rally – Gold Coast. These nodes have the greatest potential influence over internal network flows due to their structurally significant positioning 'between' other nodes (Scott 2017). It also highlights the importance of protest organizations and anti-mosque campaigns as spaces of both recruitment and mobilization as they bridge the gap between other pages, potentially introducing more diverse content onto their pages while also helping direct users towards other similar pages. The page of One Nation Party leader Pauline Hanson (*Pauline Hanson's Please Explain*) has a similarly high centrality measurement – one which is notably higher than the One Nation Party itself – suggesting Hanson is at the core of One Nation's appeal to the far right. Given their high centrality measures, these pages also unsurprisingly occupy central positions in a number of the identified sub-communities.

Degree measures the connectedness of a node, that is, how many likes a Facebook page receives. Those with a higher degree are considered to be 'in the thick of things' in that they are especially well connected, with a greater number of contacts (Scott 2017, 96). In-degree measures the number of in-bound likes a Facebook page receives. High in-degree often reflects a position of leadership and prestige within the network. Hanson's personal page, Pauline Hanson's Please Explain, is the most popular, with an in-degree measure of twenty-eight, meaning twenty-eight other pages in the network are directly connect to it. This reflects the symbiotic relation between Hanson, One Nation and the broader Australian far right. Hanson and One Nation's popularity within the Australian far-right points to their position of leadership and influence over the scene, as well as the far right's importance to One Nation's electoral competitiveness. Both the pages Friends of Q Society of Australia and Australian Liberty Alliance have significant in-degree measures (twenty and eighteen, respectively). While evidently not as popular as Hanson, it nevertheless indicates the potential challenge this party posed to One Nation in 2018 as an electoral alternative for the Australian far right. Other pages with high in-degree include Stop the Mosques Australia, Boycott Halal in Australia and Reclaim Australia Rally. Once again, their popularity demonstrates the importance of these protest organizations and campaigns in functioning as key spaces for both recruitment and mobilization, reflecting their vital role in the rejuvenation of the Australian far right.

Out-degree, the number of outbound links from a Facebook page, is generally interpreted as indicating a willingness to collaborate and organize while also trying to position themselves as communication and mobilization bridges between different pages (Kadushin 2012). Even if their connections are not reciprocated, fan pages with high out-degree have the potential to provide their audiences with a greater diversity of content from the pages they connect with and may introduce their followers to organizations within the milieu which they were previously unfamiliar. In this respect, they play an important role in the communicative chain, disseminating content throughout the broader network (Gonzalez-Bailón 2014). To this end, the various Respect Australia Rally fan pages are the most important, as their national, Gold Coast and Sydney pages are the top three in terms of out-degree measures. Moreover, these pages often provide the shortest path between other important communities or actors, like those structured around One Nation and the Q Society. In this sense, their large numbers of connections suggest that these organizations are attempting to position themselves as communication hubs within the broader Facebook network structure, functioning as bridges between different organizations.

DISCUSSION

Taking advantage of the connective architecture of Facebook's social networking features, the Australian far right has built a network of collaboration opportunities and communication multipliers. Facebook's technological affordances make the site a valuable tool for the far right to interact and coalesce with the aims of attracting new supporters and building a cohesive movement.

However, the Australian far-right network on Facebook is largely decentralized, with no single actor around which the network is unambiguously structured. A more centralized network would suggest hierarchical organization within the milieu able to more easily co-ordinate across different actors in a top-down manner. Instead, this decentralized network indicates that the Australian far right remains extremely heterogeneous, and not especially well suited to vertical coordination. These findings are consistent with existing scholarship on the make-up of the Australian far right (Dean et al. 2016; Peucker et al. 2019).

Three types of organizations make up most of the fan pages identified in the Facebook network: social movement organizations like Reclaim Australia or the various Stop the Mosque pages, militant street-level groups like the True Blue Crew or Soldiers of Odin and political parties such as One Nation. One Nation's leader Pauline Hanson is one of the most prominent actors and has clearly served as a focal point for this political Facebook network. Notably, her personal page is significantly better connected than the One Nation national party page, suggesting her personal brand – more than One Nation as an organization – is vital to the Australian far right. This is consistent with the direct communication affordances of Facebook, and the ways in which they especially benefit those with a populist communication style like Hanson (Stier et al. 2017). Overall, One Nation is well connected to the Australian far-right network on Facebook, with relations to all communities except the Australian First Party group – though these are predominantly unreciprocated, inbound links. Two important conclusions can be drawn from this. Firstly, the generally high in-degree and betweenness centrality of the One Nation pages and in particular the page Pauline Hanson's Please Explain reflect Hanson and the party's position of leadership within the milieu. However, One Nation's apparent unwillingness to reciprocate these ties on Facebook may suggest the party's wishes to keep such relationships at arm's length. While One Nation may use the network for both mobilization and recruitment, it can distance itself from the sometimes 'counterproductive' actions of some of its supporters (Hanson, cited in Anderson and Kozaki 2016).

There are a variety of communities structured around specific pages reflecting ideological, geographical or other organizational configurations. While some of these communities are structured around party groups, like the One Nation and Australia First Party communities, others have a more diverse range of actors and organizational forms. For one, the Q Society community combined multiple anti-halal and anti-mosque groups with the Australian Liberty Alliance and local chapters of groups like the Patriots Defence League. Likewise, the Safe Communities Australia cluster is made up of various branches of the anti-Islam community group, along with Queensland-based anti-mosque campaigns and various states' True Blue Crew chapters. By building more diverse connections, these communities are taking greater advantage of Facebook's connective affordances to build a wider network of relations. Expanding organizational networks in this way create greater opportunities for the dissemination of information (Gonzalez-Bailón 2014), as well as connecting with more potential supporters to try and grow their organizations. More generally, the sharing of content among and between different pages in the network has potential socialization effects for its audience, helping integrate them into the far-right milieu by creating a sense of shared identity (Caiani and Kluknavská 2017). This is further facilitated by the visibility afforded by the platform, both in terms of potential audience size and searchability. This socialization has mobilization impacts by increasing the readiness of individual supporters to take part in collective action (Bowman-Grieve 2009, 1003).

Anti-mosque campaigns emerged as the key spaces for the mobilization of existing supporters as well as the recruitment of new ones. Of these, there are three which stand out: the Bendigo and Narre Warren campaigns in the state of Victoria, and the Gladstone campaign in Queensland. These three campaigns have produced important offline flashpoints, including an arson attack in Narre Warren and violent clashes between anti-mosque demonstrators and counter-protestors in Bendigo. Most importantly, all three campaigns have seen other far-right fixtures heavily involved. In particular, Kim Vuga of the Love Australia or Leave Party in Gladstone and violent street-level movements like the United Patriots Front, True Blue Crew and Soldiers of Odin (among others) in Narre Warren and Bendigo. Bendigo in particular has been important to the recruitment of new far-right activists and efforts to build a local base of support (Markus 2018; Rudner 2019). It has also been an important site for the preselection of electoral candidates for parties like One Nation. In 2016 the party preselected Bendigo City councillor and one of the key organizers behind Stop the Mosque Bendigo, Elise Chapman, to lead the One Nation senate ticket in Victoria at the federal election (though the candidacy was later withdrawn). Similarly, at the 2019 federal election, a prominent New South Wales (NSW) anti-mosque activist Kate McCulloch was preselected to lead One Nation's NSW senate ticket. This highlights the importance of the networked relationships among various far-right organizations in Australia, both online and offline.

The overwhelming presence of pages belonging to protest campaigns and street-level organizations rather than political party pages – both in terms of quantity on Facebook and structural significance in terms of network measures – indicates that despite One Nation's successes, the broader far right has yet to fully institutionalize and organize primarily around electoral politics. In a party system open to far-right institutionalization, party organisations are expected to be predominant in the far right's digital networks (Klein and Muis 2019). Conversely, in a more closed party system, where the far right lacks elite allies or ownership of a salient issue, or perhaps faces state repression, non-institutionalized forms of mobilization like protest movements are expected to be predominant (Klein and Muis 2019). Therefore, the sizeable presence of non-party organizations in the Facebook network suggests a lack of political opportunity for the far right in Australia in 2018. A potential explanation for this can be found in the willingness of Australian centre-right parties such as the Liberal Party of Australia to adopt far-right talking points and incorporate them into government policy, therefore limiting the political space available to the far right (Mondon 2012, 2013).

On the other hand, the more violence-prone street-level organizations like the True Blue Crew are structurally insignificant, with generally limited connections to other actors in the network. This suggests that while such groups may have played a significant role in the protest phase of 2015–2017, their prominence has declined with the institutionalization of One Nation as a serious electoral contender with parliamentary representation. It may also be an indicator of some limited successes with regard to Facebook's attempts to crack down on hateful speech. This has made the platform (in theory at least) a less hospitable place for such groups, who may instead turn to alternative social networking sites like Gab.com (Hermansson et al. 2020; Jasser 2020, this volume). In addition, there is little in the way of network cleavages outside of the marginalization of the neo-Nazi Australia First Party and the community of pages built up around it. While this marginalization makes sense from the perspective of more 'moderate' electoral actors like One Nation, the Australia First Party still connects to the broader network via a front organization it established as part of the Penrith anti-mosque campaign Civil

Resistance, again emphasizing the importance of these protests as spaces of ideological crosspollination and recruitment opportunities. In addition, three nodes – the Citizens Electoral Council, The Dingoes.XYZ and the *Lads Society*, all of which were included in the starting sample – are completely isolated from the network. Given the extreme politics of the three, their isolation reflects the marginalization of more fascistic and explicitly white supremacist positions within the Australian far right on Facebook, even if an organization like the Citizens Electoral Council has the support of international backers (Gardner 1996).

CONCLUSION

The affordances provided by Facebook in terms of both recruitment and mobilization have been vital to the rejuvenation of the contemporary Australian far right. Direct communication has allowed the far right to bypass traditional media gatekeeping structures. Those adopting a populist communication style like Pauline Hanson stand to benefit the most from these affordances, as this allows them to develop stronger emotional bonds with their followers. By building a shared sense of collective identity, far-right actors like Hanson and One Nation can recruit followers to their cause, as either party members or informal supporters. At the same time, the connective logic of Facebook has aided in connecting this organizationally and ideologically diverse political family. While this has not produced a clearly structured network that can be coordinated by a single actor, these linkages afforded by Facebook nevertheless provide important communication multipliers and may introduce their supporters to other similar organizations, again aiding with recruitment, while also furthering the reach of individual calls to action to bolster mobilization. Additionally, the ease at which users can access Australian far-right content and organizations on Facebook allows these groups to reach a larger audience than ever before. By reducing the threshold for participation to a curve beginning with just 'like' and 'share', Facebook makes it easy for new followers to engage in collective action online.

While this research presents only one perspective into the re-emergence of the Australian far right, this Facebook network analysis points to a decentralized and heterogeneous movement, which is not amenable to vertical coordination by a single actor. Nevertheless, aided by the affordances provided by a platform such as Facebook, the Australian far right had enjoyed significant growth, resulting in a large – if decentralized – far-right movement across Australia. Rather than organizing through a number of larger entities, various smaller groups proliferate within the Australian far right. This decentralization helps to account for the predominance of non-party organizations in the

Facebook network, which also suggests that opportunities for parliamentary mobilization remain limited in the Australian context, even if One Nation has achieved state and national parliamentary representation. In addition, the structural insignificance of avowedly white supremacist and fascist organizations such as the Australia First Party, as well as violent street organizations like the True Blue Crew, to this more broad far-right Facebook network indicates that such actors are somewhat marginalized by contemporary Australian far-right groups. Instead, it is Islamophobic protest organizations, and particularly anti-mosque campaigns, which emerge as key sites of mobilization and recruitment. These campaigns inevitably play a key role in advancing far-right politics by providing opportunities to recruit new members and build local strongholds of support, effectively acting as 'gateways' to the broader far right.

Further research might extend the analysis, not only for cross-national comparison but also for cross-platform, looking not only at mainstream social media like Instagram, Twitter or Youtube, but also alternative platforms favoured by the far right like Gab, VK or Telegram. Cross-platform analysis would be of further value as practices of mobilization and recruitment likely vary across them too (Klein and Muis 2019). Further exploration of the representativeness of the online networks vis-à-vis the offline milieu would also no doubt be useful in understanding the 'real-world' practices of the Australian far right.

NOTE

1. I follow Mudde's (2007, 2019) classification of the far right as a heterogeneous family of political actors distinguished by a shared ideological core of nativism combined with authoritarianism.

REFERENCES

Anderson, Stephanie, and Danuta Kozaki. 2016. 'Pauline Hanson says anti-Islam group's Gosford Anglican Church stunt "counterproductive"'. *ABC*, 16 August. http://www.abc.net.au/news/2016-08-15/pauline-hanson-says-one-nation-not-linked-to-church-protesters/7735538.

Bastian, Mathieu, Sebastien Heymann, and Mathieu Jacomy. 2009. 'Gephi: An Open Source Software for Exploring and Manipulating Networks'. *Third International AAAI Conference on Weblogs and Social Media*, San Jose, California, 17–20 May. DOI: 10.13140/2.1.1341.1520.

Baxendale, Rachel. 2015. 'Beware "Bullies and Activists": Anti-Islam Group Shuns Planned Rallies'. *The Australian*, 9 October.

Borgatti, Stephen, Martin Everett, and Jeffery Johnson. 2018. *Analyzing Social Networks*. London: Sage.

Bowman-Grieve, Lorraine. 2009. 'Exploring "Stormfront": A Virtual Community of the Radical Right'. *Studies in Conflict and Terrorism* 32 (11): 989–1007.

Burris, Val, Emery Smith, and Ann Strahm. 2000. 'White Supremacist Networks on the Internet'. *Sociological Focus* 33 (2): 215–35.

Caiani, Manuela. 2014. 'Social Network Analysis'. In *Methodological Practices in Social Movement Research*, edited by D. Della Porta, 368–96. Oxford: Oxford University Press.

Caiani, Manuela, Donatella Della Porta, and Claudius Wagemann. 2012. *Mobilizing on the Extreme Right: Germany, Italy, and the United States*. Oxford: Oxford University Press.

Caiani, Manuela, and Alena Kluknavská. 2017. 'Extreme Right, the Internet and European Politics in CEE Countries: The Cases of Slovakia and the Czech Republic'. In *Social Media and European Politics: Rethinking Power and Legitimacy in the Digital Era*, edited by M. Barisione and A. Michailidou, 167–92. London: Palgrave Macmillan.

Caiani, Manuela, and Linda Parenti. 2016. *European and American Extreme Right Groups and the Internet*. New York: Routledge.

Castelli-Gattinara, Pietro. 2020. 'The Study of the Far Right and Its Three E's: Why Scholarship Must Go beyond Eurocentrism, Electoralism and Externalism'. *French Politics* 18: 1–20.

Chadwick, Andrew. 2013. *The Hybrid Media System: Politics and Power*. Oxford: Oxford University Press.

Chen, Peter. 2015. 'The Virtual Party on the Ground'. In *Contemporary Australian Political Party Organisations*, edited by N. Miragliotta, A. Gauja, and R. Smith, 127–40. Melbourne: Monash University Publishing.

Cook, James. 2019. 'Far-right Turn to Niche Social Network Amid Facebook Crackdown'. *The Telegraph*, 27 March. https://www.telegraph.co.uk/technology/2019/03/27/far-right-turn-extremist-social-network-amid-crackdown-facebook/.

Copsey, Nigel. 2003. 'Extremisim on the Internet: The Far Right and, the Value of the Internet'. In *Political Parties and the Internet: Net Gain?*, edited by R.Gibson, P. Nixon, and S. Ward, 218–33. London: Routledge.

Dean, Geoff, Peter Bell, and Zarina Vakhitova. 2016. 'Right-wing Extremism in Australia: The Rise of the New Radical Right'. *Journal of Policing, Intelligence and Counter Terrorism* 11 (2): 121–42.

Engesser, Sven, Nicole Ernst, Frank Esser, and Florin Büchel. 2017. 'Populism and Social Media: How Politicians Spread a Fragmented Ideology'. *Information, Communication & Society* 20 (8): 1109–26.

Ernst, Nicole, Sven Engesser, Florin Büchel, Sina Blassnig, and Frank Esser. 2017. 'Extreme Parties and Populism: An Analysis of Facebook and Twitter across Six Countries'. *Information, Communication and Society* 20 (9): 1347–64.

Fenton, Andrew. 2017. 'Australia's Far Right Fighting for Attention'. *CNN*, 22 September. https://edition.cnn.com/2017/09/22/asia/australia-far-right/index.html.

Fleming, Andy, and Aurelien Mondon. 2018. 'The Radical Right in Australia'. In *The Oxford Handbook of the Radical Right*, edited by J. Rydgren, 651–66. Oxford: Oxford University Press.

Froio, Caterina, and Bharath Ganesh. 2019. 'The Transnationalisation of Far Right Discourse on Twitter'. *European Societies* 21 (4): 513–39.

Gardner, Paul. 1996. 'Paranoid Anti-Semitic Con-men: The CEC and the Larouche Movement'. B'nai B'rith Anti-Defamation Commission Australia, 16 February. http://www.wej.com.au/adc/profiles/paranoid.html.

Gonzalez-Bailón, Sandra. 2014. 'Online Social Networks and Bottom-Up Politics'. In *Society and the Internet: How Networks of Information and Communication Are Changing Our Lives*, edited by M. Graham and W. Dutton, 209–22. Oxford: Oxford University Press.

Goot, Murray, and Ian Watson. 2001. 'One Nation's Electoral Support: Where Does It Come from, What Makes It Different and How Does It Fit?'. *Australian Journal of Politics and History* 47 (2): 159–91.

Scott, John. 2017. *Social Network Analysis*. London: Sage.

Sengul, Kurt. 2020. ' "Swamped": The Populist Construction of Fear, Crisis and Dangerous Others in Pauline Hanson's Senate Speeches'. *Communication Research and Practice* 6 (1): 20–37.

Stier, Sebastian, Lisa Posch, Arnim Bleier, and Markus Strohmaier. 2017. 'When Populists Become Popular: Comparing Facebook Use by the Right-Wing Movement Pegida and German Political Parties'. *Information, Communication & Society* 20 (9): 1365–88.

Ward, Stephen, and Rachel K. Gibson. 2010. 'European Political Organizations and the Internet: Mobilization, Participation, and Change'. In *Routledge Handbook of Internet Politics*, edited by A. Chadwick and P. Howard, 25–40. London: Routledge.

Winter, Aaron. 2019. 'Online Hate: From the Far-Right to the "Alt-Right" and from the Margins to the Mainstream'. In *Online Othering: Exploring Digital Violence and Discrimination on the Web*, edited by K. Lumsden and E. Harmer, 39–62. Cham: Palgrave Macmillan.

Yellow. 2018. 'Yellow Social Media Report 2018: Part 1 – Consumers'. Retrieved from https://www.yellow.com.au/wp-content/uploads/2018/06/Yellow-Social-Media-Report-2018-Consumer.pdf.

Chapter 3

Populist Myths and Ethno-Nationalist Fears in Hungary

Simon Bradford and Fin Cullen

The ruling Hungarian Civic Alliance (*Fidesz*) and its coalition partner, the Christian Democratic People's Party (*KDNP*), have been in power in Hungary since 2010. Victor Orbán has been prime minister throughout this period. In this chapter we ask how Fidesz and Orbán have mobilized political support and gained a two-thirds parliamentary majority in Hungary. What specific factors have contributed to Fidesz's capacity to secure such popular consent? We explore some of the ideological and discursive work undertaken in support of Fidesz's project. The run-up to the European Parliamentary (EP) election of 2019 offers examples of how Fidesz discourse was used in various media forms to rally support. In particular, Fidesz has constructed a narrative of Hungarian history that provides an authority based on tradition and reverence for a sacred and shared national past. The narrative is intercut with discourses of Hungarian *exceptionalism*, the *victimization* of Hungary and the conviction that *treachery* (internal and foreign) threatens Hungary's present circumstances. These form a composite discourse from which Fidesz claims to embody the interests of the Hungarian nation. The assertion, typical of populist right parties, is that nation, government and Fidesz itself are indivisible. Its description of its own regime as the so-called System of National Cooperation (NER: Nemzeti Együttműködés Rendszere) is one manifestation of an ideological compact that permeates Hungarian political and cultural life (Batory 2016). Traditional and contemporary media technologies – billboards and social media – have been widely deployed to propagate the Fidesz message.

We recognize that precisely what counts as populism or 'the right' implies diverse positions with shifting political, ideological and conceptual boundaries. Populism claims to speak for 'the people' (itself a discursive construction) against the power of established elites. Essentially, 'populism' denotes *forms* of political practice rather than content. However, precise definition of the right or far right is problematic (Krekó 2017). These ideas, practices and groups are constituted in shifting and locally specific combinations, neither static nor inert. To appear relevant, the substantive content of right or far-right politics must speak to local audiences. In Hungary, these ideas can be understood as responses to the consequences of post-communist social change and a global neo-liberal order and expressed in anxieties about the role of the nation-state in late modernity.

However, despite definitional problems, there is a shared substantive base that underlies any plausible definition of populist-right/far-right ideology. This includes xenophobia, an ethno-nationalism which privileges both the nation-state and 'the people' and an authoritarianism entailing the centralization of political power under strong leadership. The basic ideas which compose Fidesz discourse are historically rooted in Hungarian culture and, for some, suggest the risk of a slide into fascism or post-fascism (Tamás 2013, 24).

Emerging from student activism in the 1990s and governing Hungary between 1998 and 2002, Fidesz's subsequent failures in the national elections of 2002 and 2006 (though still achieving 41% and 42% of the vote, respectively) signalled that a change of political focus was necessary. Scandal in the then-governing socialist party and the impact of the 2008 global financial crisis facilitated this shift to a populist-right position. Fidesz's ethno-nationalism (embodied in anti-migrant and anti-Roma discourse) seems calculated to bolster its support from voters who might find popular racism and anti-migrant sentiments persuasive. The European migration crisis of 2015 heralded the most radical (and opportunistic) change for Fidesz's policies and diverted attention from government corruption, poor levels of health and education, public services and so on.

This chapter is structured in the following way. First, we contextualize the present political situation in Hungary and Fidesz's place within it. We go on to outline the broad media environment in Hungary. We then offer an analysis and discussion of Fidesz's discursive work in recruiting political support, drawing on data from the run-up to the 2019 European Parliamentary election. Our focus is on the juxtaposition of and interplay between older and newer technologies and how these have been harnessed to key political messages in Fidesz's successful mobilization of support. In doing this, we examine two technologies used during the run-up to that election: the campaign billboard and campaign Facebook posts. Finally, we offer some brief conclusions.

HUNGARY AND FIDESZ

Hungary lies in Central Europe, a region shaped by feudalism, 'semi-peripheral gentry capitalist and autocratic traditions' (Krausz 2019). In Hungary these have fostered a historically rooted conservative worldview especially marked in rural and small-city areas of the country. Until 1918 Hungary was part of the Austro-Hungarian Empire. The 1920 Trianon Peace Treaty, signed at Versailles, led to the loss of two-thirds of Hungary's population and territory to neighbouring states. Trianon remains a symbolically powerful and justified grievance in Hungarian collective memory. During the inter-war years, a period of authoritarian 'Christian nationalism' flourished, and a symbiotic relationship formed between fascist groups and the regime of the Regent Miklos Horthy.[1] An openly fascist government collaborated with the Nazis prior to and during their occupation of Hungary in 1944. This culminated in the deportation of some 600,000 Jewish Hungarians to Nazi extermination camps. There is evidence of resilient anti-Semitism and anti-Roma prejudice in Hungary (EVZ 2018; Hann and Róna 2019). Between 1945 and 1989, Hungary was situated in the Soviet communist sphere of influence. The country acceded to the European Union (EU) in 2004 and is a member of the 'Visegrad 4', a political alliance with Poland, Czech Republic and Slovakia.

Fidesz has shifted from an original 1990s conservatism to a populist-right position. It has colonized political territory hitherto the terrain of Jobbik (Movement for a Better Hungary), currently the largest opposition party in the Hungarian Parliament. Jobbik has a history of neo-Nazi, anti-Semitic and anti-Roma activity, but has recently moved towards the political centre. Its principal significance, and that of its extremist offshoot Mi Hazánk Mozgalom (Our Homeland Movement), has been a broad dissemination of rightist political discourse in Hungary.[2] Jobbik and Mi Hazánk Mozgalom continue to be influential locally and in relation to distinct local events. Their propagation of discourses of 'gypsy crime' and 'gypsy terror', for example, and their use of these powerful anti-Roma discourses and signifiers as framing devices in recent cases of street violence have achieved high-profile press coverage. Fidesz similarly reflected negative representations of Roma people.[3] However, Fidesz uses surrogates in the distribution of rightist discourse. Arguably, it is in Fidesz's interests for 'extremist' politicians or right-wing journalists to perpetuate racist or anti-migrant discourse throughout a hybridized media landscape. Those agents undertake the discursive dirty-work that might discredit Fidesz politicians, but from which the latter can draw political capital.

Fidesz has been significantly more influential than Jobbik in far-right discourse becoming normative in Hungary. Such discourse is increasingly *respectable* rather than extremist, the latter depiction being readily attached to Jobbik. Respect entails judgements of moral legitimacy. Fidesz's widely disseminated version of Hungarian ethno-nationalism implies an authentic, singular and patriotic national identity central to Fidesz's politics and policy around which Fidesz seeks to solidify its support. One significant example of this is the strong anti-migrant sentiments expressed by Hungarians (European Commission 2018).

According to former Fidesz member of EP György Schöpflin (regarded by some as a Fidesz intellectual), Fidesz has sought to develop a Hungarian state systematically cleansed of Budapest's left-liberal 'comprador elite' and organized around a communitarianism eschewing individual rights in favour of duty 'conservatism and Christian Democracy, solidarity, family, nationhood and statehood . . . in tune with historically inherited traditions, social aspirations and democracy' and proclaiming 'the importance of the state as an instrument of solidarity, redistribution and security' (Schöpflin 2013, 13). This signals resistance to Western liberalism, especially policies associated with inward migration, multiculturalism and what Fidesz refers to as 'gender ideology'. Despite recurrent denunciation of 'globalism', Fidesz has promoted neo-liberal economic liberalization, flexible labour markets, workfare and diminished welfare and social protections. Hungary is characterised by austerity, inequality and a precarious labour market (Scheiring 2020).

Christianity and 'the nation' are central to Fidesz politics, 'Christian culture . . . is anti-immigration . . . (and) . . . rests on the foundations of the Christian family model' (Orbán 2018b), constituting the principal elements of Orbán's so-called illiberal democracy in which Fidesz has positioned itself as the protector of Christian Europe. Ironically, a minority of Hungarians regard themselves as religious (Pew Research Centre 2019), but Christianity is formally acknowledged in the 2011 Constitution (the 'Fundamental Law of Hungary'). Christianity is deployed as a legitimating marker, affirming that Hungary represents authentic European values in contrast to a multi-cultural and, implicitly, 'lost' West. A 'paganized' (Ádám and Bozóki 2019, 102) and nominal Christianity, rehearsing the inter-war Horthy regime's 'Christian nationalism', assumes a high profile in Fidesz discourse.

Fidesz's neo-liberal economics has supported the development of a 'national bourgeoisie' – an 'oligarchy' – benefiting extensively from state contracts. Following Weber, Szelényi (2015, 50) analyses Fidesz's prebendalist system (a form of political patronage) which distributes opportunities for capital accumulation to Fidesz associates. They, in turn, serve Fidesz's political interests. This is especially important in relation to media ownership in Hungary. Allies occupy key roles in elements of the Hungarian state apparatus which, in classical democracies, are intended to counter-balance the powers of the political executive. These include the constitutional court, the state audit office, the office of the ombudsman and the competition authority (Kornai 2015, 281), as well as the National Bank, media, sports, arts and cultural institutions. Some analysts suggest Fidesz has achieved state capture (Fazekas and Tóth 2016), even describing contemporary Hungary as a 'post-communist Mafia state' where public interests are subordinated to private interests, the state becoming a 'privatised form of parasite state' (Magyar 2016). In 2018 Hungary was identified as the twenty-sixth most corrupt of the twenty-eight EU member states (Transparency International 2019).

Hungary has attracted international censure for its erosion of civil liberties, academic freedom, the rule of law and judicial independence, corruption and, particularly, its recent response to refugees and asylum seekers. Freedom House has described Hungary as 'partly free', the only country in the EU to attract such a classification (Freedom House 2019). An increasingly centralizing and autocratic Hungarian polity lies somewhere between dictatorship and democracy (Kornai 2015).

Fidesz gained a two-thirds parliamentary 'super majority' in Hungary's 2018 national election, with 133 seats from 199 achieved from about 49% of votes cast on a turnout of 70%. In the 2019 EP election Fidesz achieved about 52% of the vote, thirteen seats from twenty-one, on a turnout of 44%. Both results demonstrate Fidesz's political power and its ability to mobilize consistent support although consistent allegations of wide-ranging electoral irregularities have been made.[4] In achieving a near-political hegemony, Fidesz has successfully articulated its own interests with those of the rural and urban working class, parts of the middle-class, the Hungarian business class as well as transnational capital. Fidesz's electoral support emerges as a complex amalgam of generally older, nominally Christian, small- and medium-size town dwellers, moderate conservatives and some middle-class voters, many of whom felt abandoned in the social disintegration following the 2008 financial crisis in Hungary (Republikon 2015). In another study (Juhász, 2017), Fidesz voters reflected Hungary's gender profile (56% of Fidesz voters women, 44% men) and blue/white-collar employment status (64% and 36% of Fidesz voters, respectively). Fidesz voters are concentrated in sections of population with vocational certificates/high school diplomas (33% and 34% of Fidesz voters, respectively). Broadly, this reflects Hungary's population profile, suggesting the party's extensive support.

HUNGARIAN MEDIA AND POLITICAL MOBILIZATION

For Anderson (1991), the nation is produced as an *imagined* political community through common language and the printed word. These form the unifying bonds of nation. Constructing such an imagined community in Hungary entwines ideological integration and identification with the nation-state, Christianity, populism and representations of the 'good Hungarian' (Fekete 2016), in the attempt to create a national hegemony. Hungarian media and propaganda mechanisms (broadcast, digital and print news media, national consultations, billboards, advertisements, social media, etc.)

create a hybrid media landscape, juxtaposing older and newer technologies (Chadwick 2017).

Chadwick's work is helpful here in explaining how formations, reconfigurations and interplay of old and new media are used in political communication and mobilisation. He argues that old and new media practices are coexistent and interdependent. The diversification of political communication strategies could be seen to erode public trust in political elites and democratic institutions. Citizen activists, loyal party members and casual users can now become knowledge producers *and* consumers. However, Chadwick argues that political elites have begun to adapt to these shifts, attempting to push their agendas both on and offline. The resulting mixed media logics include a renewal of old media systems such as broadcast and print, alongside attempts to utilize influential platforms such as Facebook.

A diversity of media forms underlies Fidesz's mobilization of political support. The party's media practices extend through regional newspapers, television and radio to billboards, online news sites and social media platforms. While audiences inevitably engage differently with these formats and messages, a unity of campaign message and powerful evocation of nation, identity and *the Other* runs across these media forms. We explore two ends of this 'hybrid media' spectrum: Fidesz's use of billboards and social media sites in mobilizing key political messages.

Although the Hungarian media environment appears diverse, one estimate puts Fidesz-friendly ownership at 78% (Mérték Media Monitor, 2018). This is consolidated under the rubric of the Central European Press and Media Foundation (KESMA), some 400 media outlets. KESMA is subject neither to competition rules nor to independent scrutiny. As Bátorfy and Urbán note, Hungary shows governments 'can generate pseudo-diversity as the state uses its unlimited access to state resources to disburse funds among private owners who are loyal to the government in exchange for propaganda' (2019, 47). Despite some diversity, state and some non-state television channels and daily newspapers remain loyal to Fidesz.

Television remains the most important source of political information in Hungary (Eurostat 2017; Mérték Media Monitor 2018) other than for young people who increasingly rely on social media (NDI, 2018). According to Eurostat, 74% of Hungarians use social network platforms, 96% of sixteen to twenty-four year-olds (Eurostat, 2018). The Fidesz 'media juggernaut' (Krekó and Enyedi 2018, 46) overshadows state, national, regional and online media and is a key site for securing ideological dominance. Traditional media forms such as billboards, many owned by Fidesz associates and covering the country at election times, are also well-funded propaganda tools.[5]

As a platform for political mobilization, social media is vital. It enables new patterns of engagement, increased visibility of key campaigning messages and the development of a stronger forum for smaller political parties (Lilleker et al. 2017; Wilkin et al. 2015; Bene 2017, 2018). However, as traditional media remain influential in determining voter intentions, social media sources like Facebook, YouTube and Instagram occupy supplementary positions within a broader hybrid strategy (Klinger and Russman 2017).

The influence of Facebook in shaping elections and spreading 'fake' viral news has received much research attention (Chadwick 2017; Goździak and Márton 2018; Bennett and Livingston 2018). Bene notes that peer engagement and sharing of political posts reinforce existing political affiliations rather than reaching out to new potential supporters (Bene 2017, 2018). Bíró-Nagy et al. (2016) argue that the links and networks between 'likes' on Hungarian Facebook posts demonstrate tightly segregated and insular patterns of use, with little cross-engagement between political posts and party supporters. This suggests that the 'traditional' tools of political mobilization remain influential and are interwoven with online forms in attracting support (Klinger and Russman 2017; Lilleker et al. 2017).

In Hungary, party political engagement is mobilized through a broad web of campaign material spreading a common message across TV and radio advertisements, newspapers, mass mailings, citizen consultations and billboards. This inter-textual media coverage promotes an agenda that amplifies Fidesz's core messages when reaching out to the electorate (Krekó and Enyedi 2018). Key campaign messages and slogans remain remarkably consistent with little apparent attempt at segmenting the audience or reaching out to potential Fidesz voters. Indeed, the ' "tilted electoral playing field" for Fidesz is also founded on "genuine support from the people" ' (Krekó and Enyedi 2018, 41) and a large existing voter base. Fidesz remains dominant, its position consolidated through state media support and an expansive pro-government oligarchic media network.

FIDESZ: USING THE MIGRATION CRISIS

We now consider Fidesz's resurgence in the past five years, drawing on analysis of political messaging from billboard campaigns and social media during that period. During the run-up to the 2019 EP election, we monitored the official Fidesz Facebook and Twitter feeds, identifying key campaign messages and attempts to distribute and engage with an ethno-nationalist agenda.

Here, billboards and Facebook are platforms for discourse, important media texts that seek to mobilize political approval. They contain visual and textual symbols that create representations of key political actors, attract identification and form relations between audiences and politicians (Fairclough 1995, 5). Following Laclau (1977, 2005), we understand the political mobilization process as a form of national populist 'mythmaking' that operates in Fidesz's hegemonic interests. Laclau's post-Gramscian account clearly shows how populism works as a discursive process in shaping political identification. Laclau identifies the significance of a strong and popular leader able to rescue the nation, and notes that in order to mobilize support it is important to develop an 'us' (the people) and a 'them'. In Hungary, the populist 'us' is constructed as a fictive, ethnically 'pure' kin-nation: truly *Magyar* and Christian. The 'others' (non-Magyar, Roma, Muslims, refugees, globalists, the UN, the EU or George Soros)[6] are represented as a corrosive threat to the enduring culture of the Hungarian nation.

We share methodological aspects of Balzacq's (2005) discursive view of *securitization*, a process that articulates audiences, contexts and power. Existential threats to key audiences are defined by powerful actors, who argue that they are amenable to political intervention. Fidesz has comprehensively securitized migration discourse in Hungary, categorizing migration as a fundamental threat to Hungarian life and identity, deploying a range of xenophobic discursive practices, border closures and other deterrents that have reinforced resistance to migration and secured popular consent for increasing authoritarianism. Threats from migration resonate with historic anxieties about national annihilation 'by alien, rootless state powers' (Bibo 1946, 149). Such anxiety has a history of fomenting an 'anti-democratic nationalism' across East and Central Europe, in which 'oppressive powers . . . search for the "hirelings" of the enemy, the "traitors"' (Bibó 1946, 149–152). The 2015 European migration crisis provided rich material on which Fidesz's then weakening political position was reversed.[7] In 2015, billboards positioning Fidesz as the protector of the nation quickly covered the country. Ironically, though ostensibly targeting migrants, their texts were in Hungarian, clearly aimed at domestic audiences and citing key threats to the security of the nation and its members. 'If you come to Hungary you should respect our culture' and 'If you come to Hungary don't take Hungarians' jobs'.

Billboard and social media campaigns subsequently constructed a composite Fidesz discourse about threats from migration, constituting a 'common sense' that has pervaded Hungarian culture. Three elements of this discourse are evident. First, a Hungarian exceptionalism, second, the imputed victimization of Hungary and its people and, third, accusations of treachery. We consider these in turn.

HUNGARIAN EXCEPTIONALISM

Nationalism invariably claims the nation's exceptional status or identity. National belonging is evoked through a series of historical 'us' and 'them' binaries (Goździak and Márton 2018): Christian/Muslim, native/migrant, civilized/barbarian, and so on. In this context exceptionalism entails an almost metaphysical claim that the spirit of the Hungarian people is somehow beyond the norm, incomparable and, implicitly, superior to *unexceptional others*. Orbán recurrently invokes Hungarian uniqueness, citing its linguistic and cultural isolation and marking some predestined duty: 'The Hungarian people's most valuable asset is that which sets it apart from all others. If we were the same as others, what purpose would we serve in the world and on what grounds could we seek God's assistance in the face of our opponents?' (Orbán 2015).

Hungary's unique status is consistently evoked in relation to a series of others, construed as 'our opponents', part of boundary setting and distancing 'us' 'from all others'. This was materialized in 2015 when a 500-kilometre fence, patrolled by some 12,000 soldiers, police and guards, was constructed on Hungary's southern border. The steel and barbed wire fence, designed to prevent refugees crossing Hungary's borders, denotes inside and outside, the 'us' and the 'them' and symbolizes Hungary's Christian presence on European terrain. 'When we draw the boundaries of our identity, we mark out Christian culture as the source of our pride' (Orbán 2017). The text in the following 2016 poster, part of a series focusing on government reforms, states, 'We don't want illegal immigrants!' (figure 3.1).

The young woman in the poster, white, casually dressed and seemingly representing contemporary Hungary, maintains eye contact and connection with the viewer. Ironically, she attempts to symbolically reference a youthful constituency, and not typical Fidesz voters. The conjugation of the verb in the text signifies the young woman is speaking on behalf of 'we', an emotional appeal for identification with her (as representative) and the wider 'raced'

Figure 3.1. Hungarian Government billboard, 2016, (photo source: Budapest Beacon).
Source: Photo: Budapest Beacon.

kin-nation. Projecting 'we' she symbolizes a 'good' Hungarian, white, Christian woman whose duty is the reproduction of the ethnically pure and *exceptional* kin-nation, central to Fidesz discourse. As Orbán put it, 'We don't want to become a mixed country; we don't want migration; we want to preserve our security; and even without migrants we will be able to sustain Hungary's biological future through our family policy' (Orbán 2019b).

Fidesz's narrative forgets or ignores Europe's non-Christian heritage in classical culture. Hungary's multi-ethnic history and segments of its present and non-Christian populations are erased by this historical amnesia that privileges an exclusionary identity defined in historico-ethno-biological and Christian terms, reliant on an illusory sense of ethno-national purity (Goździak and Márton 2018).

In the run-up to the 2019 EP election, social media threads framed concerns about the declining Hungarian population[8] due to a low birth rate (1.55 births per woman in 2018; Eurostat 2020), an ageing population and youth emigration. Fidesz's counter-immigration pronatalist policy stance promotes an ethno-nationalist, 'family-friendly' agenda which includes tax breaks and credit deals for the upper middle-classes who already benefit from a 'flat-tax' regime. Campaign messages emphasize the true 'Magyar' (non-Roma)[9] woman as wife, mother and producer of future citizens, suggesting the gendered and ethnicized nature of the Fidesz project. Pronatalism draws its power from the idea 'that the members of a nation are part of an extended family, ultimately united by ties of blood' (Muller 2008, 20). It emphasizes the imagined community of the kin-nation in order to preserve and affirm an exceptional and authentic national identity (Yuval-Davis 1997; King 2002; Brown and Ferree 2005). Pronatalist programmes are not new in Eastern Europe. From the mid-twentieth century, communist states followed such policy in response to declining fertility, and Hungary has engaged with pronatalism since then (McIntyre 1975). Recently, nationalist anxieties have framed pronatalism in terms of women's duty to the exceptional Hungarian nation and its biological and cultural reproduction. Fidesz ideology has configured Hungarian responses to declining population as integral to its anti-immigration family policy. This resonates with earlier twentieth-century authoritarian regimes using women's fertility as a driver of ethno-national success.

A series of posts on Fidesz's official Facebook account during the 2019 EP election reflects this:

> God bless Hungarian mothers! (14 May 2019)
>
> We stand by Hungarian families, and we will protect and support them with every possible means. (15 May 2019)
>
> Instead of immigration, the future of Europe should be based on good family policy. (17 May 2019)

Throughout the election, Fidesz's ethnicized pronatalist agenda was contrasted with unwanted immigration and presented in social media as a means of revitalizing the exceptional nation.

VICTIMHOOD

Victimization signifies 'harm perpetrated against a person or group, and victimhood as a form of collective identity based on that harm' (Jacoby 2015, 513). Fidesz's mythmaking casts Hungary as the victim of global forces and supranational powers. It outlines defensive action necessary to preserve national and cultural integrity. External threats menace autonomy and sovereignty and are discursively framed to imply a threat to 'the Hungarian people' whose linguistic, cultural and ethnic integrity are jeopardized by liberalism, sexual politics or feminism. Victimhood permeates a Hungarian culture currently represented as under siege from hostile forces: globalization, transnational institutions like the UN and EU, multi-culturalism and, especially, migration.

Hungarian victimhood is invariably framed in terms of loss and harm, especially with reference to the Trianon Treaty of 1920 or the virtually continuous successive occupation of Hungary since the sixteenth century by the Turks, Austrians, Nazis and Soviets. For Fidesz, an authoritarian EU similarly seeks to undermine an independent and sovereign Hungary. EU accession was accompanied by sometimes disparaging representations of 'eastern Europeans' in Western media and public opinion, encouraging a perception of a second-class European citizenship. Some analysts argue this is a consequence of failed attempts by Central and East European states to imitate Western liberal democracies, leading to humiliation and fuelling a victimhood narrative (Krastev and Holmes 2018, 118). Cultural texts, including those of the billboards identified in this chapter, institutionalize and reproduce the narrative.

Referring to inward migration as a question of national security, in which Hungary becomes the victim of terrorism, Orbán warned: 'Migration has become the trojan horse of terrorism, and the discourse of liberal political correctness is unable to understand the real dangers of migration' (Origo 2017). The following image of an election poster widely displayed on billboards across the country in 2018 signals Hungary as the potential victim of mass migration. This is symbolized by the apparently unending line of threatening, mainly male and seemingly dystopian figures, and contrasts with the innocence and hopefulness of the young woman in figure 3.1. The image appears cynically intended to alarm a population with little recent experience of inward migration.[10] It establishes a clear 'us' and 'them' and adds the 'red-for-danger' injunction to 'stop' them.[11]

During the 2019 EP election campaign, a triple threat emerged in social media posts. The threat linked EU, global and transnational political actors and migrant groups, portraying them as overwhelming Hungarian culture and evoking the alleged threat of terrorism from which Hungarians and Hungary would be potential victims. A Fidesz Facebook post from April 2019 highlights how these concerns are discursively linked: Victor Orbán's 7-point program is especially current now. . . . Brussels only increases migration and the terror threat to Europe (25 April 2019).

The 7-point programme forms a securitized approach to migration including exclusion of migrants without valid identity papers from EU territory, no compulsory relocation of migrants in any EU state and compulsory return of migrants to countries of origin. This post was followed with: 'After the European Parliament elections, we must return to the protection of external borders, the Europe of nation states' (26 April 2019).

The post interlaces the EU, the migrant crisis, and an underlying fear of 'terror' in familiar form, inseparable from the logic of nationalized Hungarian victimhood. The terror threat emerges from religious, social and cultural *Others*; from illegal and economic migrants, like those in figure 3.2, represented as jeopardizing Hungarian (and European) security and society. Ironically, this sense of dread is palpable in media and public discourse despite the

Figure 3.2. Hungarian Government billboard, 2018 (photo source: authors).
Source: Photo: Authors.

almost complete absence of migrant communities in Hungary. State media, a crucial relay in the dissemination of Fidesz propaganda, sustains this in regular news stories of migrants massing in Turkey or Greece, on the border with Serbia, and digging tunnels under or breaking through the Hungarian border fence.

TREACHERY

Resentment over others' treachery is the third central feature of Fidesz discourse. The treaty of Trianon stands as the seminal treacherous act against Hungary. Collective memory of Trianon has been carefully managed as a 'clear symbolic system, which communicated a whole universe of national resentment' (Kovács 2016, 528).[12] Resentment is a highly mobile force that can be easily manipulated and whose focus can be rapidly shifted. Fidesz has constructed George Soros as a contemporary and high-profile target of resentment, the necessary (Jewish) counter to the sanctified figure of Orbán. Soros is vilified as traitor to Hungary for his so-called Soros plan,[13] and his Soros network (more recently the Soros orchestra), which allegedly manipulates EU politicians, EU policy and NGOs in an effort to promote migration. Underlying Soros's vilification is a strong notion of conspiracy invoking the allegedly covert entry of Soros agents into institutions like the UN, the EU and a range of Europe- and Hungary-based NGOs. This narrative relies on familiar, coded anti-Semitic tropes, vigorously protested by Hungarian Jewish organizations, which incorporate the idea that Soros seeks to undermine the government and aspirations of the Hungarian people. Soros is regularly portrayed by Fidesz-sympathetic media as a globalist traitor to his homeland.

The following, grinning, Soros image from 2017 cautions Hungarians not to let Soros 'have the last laugh' and that '99% reject illegal immigration'. Soros is represented here as the artful trickster, sneering at those about to be fooled by his deception. Figures 3.3 and 3.4 represent Soros as cultural enemy and as a Jewish *other*. Existing extensive anti-Semitism in Hungary both contribute to and inform such propaganda. The text implicitly warns 'us', the readers, of the danger of Soros. 'We' are his potential victims. Viewed in conjunction with figure 3.2 (representing impending migration), the impact of figure 3.3 is especially powerful.

For Fidesz, Soros's goal is '*transforming Europe and moving it towards a post-Christian and post-national era*' (Orbán 2018b). Described as 'open society' ideologue and predatory capitalist (Schmidt 2017), Soros's alleged collusion with 'Brussels' is a potent recurring symbol in Hungary. Figure 3.4 from a 2019 EP election poster insinuates that the then European Commission president Juncker was either collaborating with Soros or that Soros was behind Juncker (*literally* so in this image) and the EU's plans. It states,

Figure 3.3. Hungarian Government billboard, 2017 (photo source: Attila Károly NAGY/ Index.hu).

Source: Photo: Attila Károly NAGY/Index.hu.

Figure 3.4. Hungarian Government billboard, 2019 (photo source: authors).

Source: Photo: Author.

'You too have a right to know what Brussels is doing'. The Brussels-Soros conspiracy to replace Christian culture with Western multiculturalism, the essence of the so-called Soros plan, is constantly rehearsed in Fidesz propaganda. In a population with little experience of inward migration, this has demonstrated considerable potential to create fear and suspicion of 'global' conspiracy. Controversy around this image eventually led to Fidesz's membership suspension and departure from the European People's Party, a centre-right grouping within the EP.

In a 2018 national election campaign speech, Orbán suggested the existence of an unseen and sinister enemy, evoking 'rootless cosmopolitans' (Gelbin and Gilman 2017, 192), whose particular target is symbolized by the colours of the Hungarian national flag:

> We must fight against an opponent which is different from us. Their faces are not visible, but are hidden from view; they do not fight directly, but by stealth; they are not honourable, but unprincipled; they are not national, but international; they do not believe in work, but speculate with money; they have no homeland, feel that the whole world is theirs. They are not generous, but vengeful, and always attack the heart – especially if it is red, white and green (Orbán 2018a).

These meticulously crafted representations of external and concealed enemies appeal to 'our' identity symbolized by the red, white and green. They contain typically emotive injunctions to stand firm against the unified nation's enemies. The notion of a 'hidden power' or (invariably foreign) conspiracy underlying Hungary's troubles has considerable traction in the Hungarian popular and tabloid media. Fidesz-associated television, print and online sources have carried stories based on ideas of veiled powers acting on behalf of external agents. NGOs are discredited and invariably represented as political activists paid by shadowy foreign or Soros-inspired interest groups (Szombati 2018, 13). For example, invoking an enduring Judeo-Bolshevik conspiracy myth (Ablovatski 2010, 475), environmentalists are portrayed as international 'climate communists' and 'green commandos' (Farkas 2019; Megadja 2019). Seemingly, there is always another 'Other' to confirm the existence of anti-Hungarian powers.

We noted earlier that Laclau identifies the importance of populist leaders in rescuing the nation from treacherous others. The figure of Victor Orbán is central to Fidesz's success. Orbán is effectively the face of Fidesz, and his public identity has been carefully constructed. He is positioned as the embodiment of rural Hungary's resilient Christian agrarian populism (Hann 2016, 608) that reflects a historical antipathy towards urban, left, liberal (and Jewish) elites. This endears Orbán to significant sections of the population, cementing the relation that has formed between him and his followers. Orbán's Instagram account, for example, constructs a carefully curated complex of ordinariness, political gravitas, Christian iconography, self-conscious parochialism, sentimentality and a grounded vision of traditional Magyar masculinity, seemingly calculated to appeal to those sympathetic to such imagery and symbolism. His deceptive proximity appears to permit the cultivation of a personal relationship with supporters. Yet, extraordinary powers are vital and Orbán has skilfully managed public emotion by representing himself and Fidesz as safeguarding the nation at a time of looming chaos symbolized in supposedly uncontrolled migration. Orbán has become a charismatic presence in Hungarian politics. However, as Weber argued (Gerth and Wright Mills 1948, 248), charisma is impermanent, volatile and, when no longer able to enchant, can quickly recede.

CONCLUSIONS

We began this chapter by asking how Fidesz has been successful and what factors have contributed to its mobilization of support. Insofar as Fidesz's achievement of parliamentary dominance and an almost total hold over state institutions is construed as 'success', there seems little ambiguity. Fidesz has achieved a national hegemony in which consent is cemented both by the increasing and authoritarian centralization of powers, and discursively through its (populist) appropriation of national history, memory and nativism in the context of a crisis of migration. Of course, the *relative* stability of the Hungarian economy (post-2010) is also a vital factor. It remains to be seen what impact the Covid-19 pandemic will have.

A familiar worldview has been (re)normalized in Hungary, harnessing diverse media forms to propel Fidesz to a position of power. Fidesz discourse coalesces across media forms and is deployed to send a unified message to Hungarian society. This manipulates long-held popular fears and resentments and uses representations of an imagined 'traditional' national community and symbolic others. The chapter has presented an exploration of how various media forms (in this case billboards and social media platforms) have been used to solidify Fidesz's electoral and broad political support. We have argued that key messages are consistently presented *across* media, a kind of inter-textuality which creates clear meanings (e.g. around migration and Soros) that resonate between media forms. In that sense, a hybridized media landscape in Hungary has facilitated Fidesz's political practices.

Fidesz has skilfully constructed a dominant and emotive vision of Hungary. Almost fundamentalist, seemingly terrified by the ambiguity and contingency implied by the *Other's* presence, a desire for purity is echoed in relentless centralization and control of the state apparatus. This vision articulates ethno-nationalism, Christianity and a volatile underlying national resentment focusing on injurious historical events. It manifestly appeals to substantial sections of the population. Yet, it relies on an exclusionary and restrictive representation of Hungary and Hungarians, in which a multi-ethnic Hungarian history and the contemporary presence of minorities is forgotten. This is further manifested in a tension between a constrictive Fidesz notion of 'tradition' (often set in a discourse about the virtues of rural life) and a modernity that appears on a broader European register, and represented by opposition politicians and parties. Interestingly, in municipal elections in late 2019, opposition parties took control of Hungarian cities, including Budapest, illuminating a historic rural–urban tension in Hungary that may yet have implications for Fidesz hegemony.

Our exploration suggests how the realm of the imaginary (powerfully linked to emotion and sensibility) and a continuously confected collective memory shape national identity in a discourse of Hungarian 'illiberal democracy' embodying the repudiation of liberal constitutionalism. Fidesz has re-cast older myths in new forms in order to speak to contemporary anxieties about nation and identity. Mythmaking and a politics of memory have become vital components in contemporary Hungarian statecraft. Memory marks out what is to be remembered but necessitates historical forgetting. It is therefore partial. Fidesz's EP campaign, following from national elections in 2018, emphasized formations of (an implicitly authentic) national and cultural identity in a combative *Magyarság*: 'Hungarian-ness'.

Fidesz's move rightwards provides insights into how populist discourse functions, as well as how populist, far-right nationalist rhetoric can become normalized to reshape mainstream political discourse in a modern European nation. Indeed, in Hungary, Fidesz has been more significant in shifting Hungarian politics to the right than other more obviously 'extreme' Hungarian political groups.

NOTES

1. Hungary introduced the first anti-Jewish law in Europe in 1920 (*Numerus Clausus*) followed by further laws in 1938, 1939 and 1941. Fidesz celebrates the Horthy regime as the high point of modern Hungarian history and that regime's interests and those of the Christian churches were shared, especially in terms of a deeply held anti-Semitism. The current relationship between the churches and the state is complex, but some have been supportive of and supported by Fidesz. Indeed, there is an argument that some Christian churches have been co-opted by the current regime.

2. There is a range of right/far-right websites and social media accounts in Hungary. Kuruc.info and Elég are well known. There are also high-profile Fidesz-supporting publicists (Zsolt Bajer or Tamás Pilhál are examples) who relentlessly push a far-right position.

3. In a recent court case, Roma children in the village of Gyöngyöspata were awarded 99 million HUF (about €280,000) in compensation because their school had segregated them on the basis of ethnicity. Orbán's response to this was considered by many to embody anti-Roma sentiments (Szurovecz 2020).

4. This includes manipulation of electoral rules, gerrymandering, initiating forms of clientelism and 'vote-buying' (Kreko and Enyedi 2018, 40; Mares and Young 2019, 451; Scheppele 2019, 317).

5. One source indicated that Government spent about €28,000,000 on 'communication and consultation . . . propaganda' in the 2018 national election period, including billboard posters (Oroszi, 2020).

6. Hungarian-born Soros is a liberal Jewish financier-philanthropist who funds a range of broadly 'progressive' causes and organizations. His 'Open Society Foundation' draws on the work of the philosopher Karl Popper.

7. Hungary refused to accept 1,294 refugees under the EU's 2015 plans to relocate 120,000 refugees, mainly from Syria. The Fidesz government initiated a referendum in 2016 on the acceptance of the EU's compulsory migrant quota. Although the result was constitutionally invalid (a 44% turnout gave a 98% rejection), the referendum mechanism placed migration firmly on the political agenda and marked the EU as attempting to undermine Hungarian sovereignty.

8. Hungary is identified by the UN as one of a number of European countries set to see their population decline by more than 15% by 2050. Over the past thirty years, the population has declined by 1 million to 9.8 million.

9. Currently the Hungarian Roma community is estimated to be between 3% and 9% of the population.

10. Hungary is an 'emigration' country with significant numbers migrating to the west in recent years creating justifiable demographic anxiety (Gödri, Soltész, B., and Bodacz-Nagy 2014).

11. This image, showing refugees on the Slovenian border, was also used by Nigel Farage in the 2016 UK Brexit referendum campaign. Critics then noted similarities to Nazi propaganda, and Farage claimed that it 'won' the referendum.

12. Initiated by Fidesz, since 2010 an annual Trianon commemoration day articulating national grievance has been held annually. A Trianon memorial was recently erected in Budapest amidst significant controversy. One Fidesz-associated historian claimed a thousand years to be insufficient to process the trauma and tragedy of Trianon (Schmidt 2018).

13. The 'Soros plan' refers to a corpus of ideas presented by Soros about migration, the preservation of the EU and support of developing countries. In fact, Soros has argued for a managed system of migration into Europe accompanied by strong borders.

REFERENCES

Ablovatski, Eliza. 2010. 'The 1919 Central European Revolutions and the Judeo-Bolshevik Myth'. *The European Review of History* 17 (3): 473–89. DOI: 10.1080/13507486.2010.481947.

Ádám, Zoltan, and András Bozóki. 2019. 'Radical Right-Wing Populism and Nationalized Religion in Hungary'. In *Resisting Exclusion: Global Theological Responses to Populism*, edited by S. Sinn and E. Harasta. Geneva: The Lutheran World Federation.

Anderson, Benedict. 1991. *Imagined Communities: Reflections on the Origin and Spread of Nationalism* (revised edition). London: Verso.

Balzacq, Thierry. 2005. 'The Three Faces of Securitization: Political Agency, Audience and Context'. *European Journal of International Relations* 11 (2): 171–201.

Batorfy, Agnes. 2016. 'Populists in Government? Hungary's "System of National Cooperation"'. *Democratization* 23 (2): 283–303, DOI: 10.1080/13510347.2015.107621.

Bátorfy, Agnes, and Agnes Urbán. 2019. 'State Advertising as an Instrument of Transformation of the Media Market in Hungary'. *East European Politics* 36 (1): 44–65.

Bene, Marton. 2017. 'Influenced by Peers: Facebook as an Information Source for Young People'. *Social Media+ Society*, 3 (2): 1–14, DOI: 10.1177/2056305117716273.

Bene, Marton. 2018. 'Post Shared, Vote Shared: Investigating the Link between Facebook Performance and Electoral Success during the Hungarian General Election Campaign of 2014'. *Journalism & Mass Communication Quarterly* 95 (2): 363–80.

Bennett, W. Lance, and Steven Livingston. 2018. 'The Disinformation Order: Disruptive Communication and the Decline of Democratic Institutions'. *European Journal of Communication* 33 (2): 122–39.

Bibó, I. 1946. 'Miseries of East European Small States', in I.Z. Dénes, *The Art of Peacemaking. Political Essays by István Bibó*, Newhaven: Yale University Press.

Bíró-Nagy, Andras, and Tamas Boros, 2016. 'Jobbik Going Mainstream: Strategy Shift of the Far Right in Hungary'. In *L'extreme droite en Europe*, edited by Jérome Jamin, 243–63. Brussels: Bruylant.

Brown, John, and Myra Ferree. 2005. 'Close Your Eyes and Think of England: Pronatalism in the British Print Media'. *Gender & Society* 19 (1): 5–24.

Chadwick, Andrew. 2017. *The Hybrid Media System: Politics and Power*. Oxford: Oxford University Press.

European Commission. 2018. *Integration of Immigrants in the European Union*. Special Eurobarometer 469. Report. Brussels: European Commission.

Eurostat. 2017. 'Are You Using Social Networks?' https://ec.europa.eu/eurostat/web/producteurostat-news/-/DDN-20170713-1, accessed 18 December 2019.

Eurostat 2018. 'Digital Economy and Society in the EU'. https://ec.europa.eu/eurostat/cache/infographs/ict/index.html, accessed 1 July 2020.

Eurostat 2020. 'Total Fertility Dataset'. https://ec.europa.eu/eurostat/databrowser/view/tps00199/default/table?lang=en, accessed 20 February 2020.

EVZ, 2018. *Antigypsyism and Antisemitism in Hungary: Summary of the Final Report*. Budapest: EVZ Foundation.

Fairclough, Norman. 1995. *Media Discourse*. London: Arnold.

Farkas, Örs. 2019. 'Jogi blabla helyett zöldkommandó'. *Magyar Nemzet*, 13 December. https://magyarnemzet.hu/velemeny/jogi-blabla-helyett-zoldkommando-7565282/, accessed 29 January 2020.

Fazekas, Mihaly, and Istvan Tóth. 2016. 'From Corruption to State Capture: A New Analytical Framework with Empirical Applications from Hungary'. *Political Research Quarterly* 69 (2): 320–34. DOI: 10.1177/1065912916639137.

Fekete, Liz. 2016. 'Hungary: Power, Punishment and the "Christian-National Idea"'. *Race & Class* 57 (4): 39–53.

Fidesz, 2020. 'Gender Ideology Is Incompatible with Conservative and Christian Democratic Values'. https://fidesz.hu/int/news/gender-ideology-is-incompatible-with-conservative-and-christian-democratic-values, accessed 8 July 2020.

Freedom House, 2019. 'Freedom in the World 2019: Hungary Country Report'. https://freedomhouse.org/report/freedom-world/2019/hungary, accessed 20 January 2020.

Gelbin, Cathy, and Sander Gilman. 2017. *Cosmopolitanisms and the Jews*. Ann Arbor: University of Michigan Press.

Gerth, Hans, and C. Wright Mills. 1948. *From Max Weber: Essays in Sociology*. London: Routledge and Kegan Paul.

Gödri, Iren, Bela Soltész, and Roroka Bodacz-Nagy. 2014. 'Immigration or Emigration Country? Migration Trends and Their Socio-economic Background in Hungary: A Longer-Term Historical Perspective'. Working Papers on Population, Family and Welfare, 19, Hungarian Demographic Research Institute, Budapest.

Goździak, Elzbieta, and Peter Márton. 2018. 'Where the Wild Things Are: Fear of Islam and the Anti-Refugee Rhetoric in Hungary and in Poland'. *Central and Eastern European Migration Review* 7 (2): 125–51.

Hann, Chris. 2016. 'Overheated Underdogs: Civilizational Analysis and Migration on the Danube-Tisza Interfluve'. *History and Anthropology* 27 (5): 602–16.

Hann, Chris, and Elzbieta Róna. 2019. *Anti-Semitic Prejudice in Today's Hungarian Society*. Budapest: Action and Protection Foundation.

Jacoby, Tami. 2015. 'A Theory of Victimhood: Politics, Conflict and the Construction of Victim-Based Identity'. *Millennium* 43 (2): 511–30.

Juhász, Attila (ed.). 2017. *The Year of Rearrangement: The Populist Right and the Far-Right in Contemporary Hungary*. Budapest: Political Capital Kft. and Social Development Institute Kft.

King, Leskie. 2002. 'Demographic Trends, Pronatalism, and Nationalist Ideologies in the Late Twentieth Century'. *Ethnic and Racial Studies* 25 (3): 367–89.

Klinger, Ulrike, and Uta Russmann. 2017. 'Beer Is More Efficient than Social Media – Political Parties and Strategic Communication in Austrian and Swiss National Elections'. *Journal of Information Technology & Politics* 14 (4): 299–313.

Kornai, Janos. 2015. 'Hungary's U-Turn'. *Society and Economy* 37 (3): 279–329. DOI: 10.1556/204.2015.37.3.1.

Kovács, Eva. 2016. 'Overcoming History through Trauma: The Hungarian Historikerstreit'. *European Review* 24 (4): 523–34, DOI: 10.1017/S1062798716000065.

Krastev, Ivan, and Stephen Holmes. 2018. 'Explaining Eastern Europe: Imitation and Its Discontents.' *Journal of Democracy* 29 (3): 117–28.

Krausz, Tamas. 2019. 'Searching for Alternatives in Eastern Europe'. *Monthly Review*. https://monthlyreview.org/2019/04/01/searching-for-alternatives-in-eastern-europe/, accessed 28 January 2020.

Krekó, Peter, and Zsolt Enyedi. 2018. 'Explaining Eastern Europe: Orbán's Laboratory of Illiberalism'.' *Journal of Democracy* 29 (3): 39–51.

Krekó, Peter, and Attila Juhász. 2017. *The Hungarian Far Right: Social Demand, Political Supply and International Context*. Stuttgart: Ibidem-Verlag.

Laclau, Ernesto. 1977. *Politics and Ideology in Marxist Theory*. London: NLB.

Laclau, Ernesto. 2005. *On Populist Reason*. London: Verso.

Lilleker, Darren, Karolina Koc-Michalska, Ralph Negrine, Rachel Gibson, Thierry Vedel, and Sylvie Strudel. 2017. 'Social Media Campaigning in Europe: Mapping the Terrain'. *Journal of Information Technology & Politics* 14 (4): 293–98, DOI: 10.1080/19331681.2017.1397239.

Magyar, Balint. 2016. *Post-Communist Mafia State: The Case of Hungary*. Budapest: Central European University Press.

Mares, Isabela, and Lauren Young. 2019. 'Varieties of Clientelism in Hungarian Elections'. *Comparative Politics* 51 (3): 449–80.

McIntyre, Ronald. 1975. 'Pronatalist Programmes in Eastern Europe'. *Soviet Studies* 27 (3): 366–80.

Megadja, Gabor. 2019. 'A klímakommunizmus kísértete'. *Magyar Nemzet*, 1 October. https://magyarnemzet.hu/velemeny/a-klimakommunizmus-kisertete-7351562/, accessed 28 January 2020.

Mérték Media Monitor. 2018. *Sources of Political Information in Hungary, Trends 2015–2018*. Budapest: Médiaelemző műhely.

Muller, Jerry. 2008. 'Us and Them: The Enduring Power of Ethnic Nationalism'. *Foreign Affairs* (March/April): 18–35.

NDI. 2018. *Youth, Democracy and Politics: Hungary*, available at https://www.ndi.org/sites/default/files/NDI%20Hungary%20Youth%20Polling%202018_0.pdf, accessed 8 July 2020.

Orbán, Viktor. 2015. 'Viktor Orbán's Speech on the Anniversary of the Hungarian Revolution of 1848'. *Website of the Hungarian Government*, 15 March, available at https://www.kormany.hu/en/the-prime-minister/the-prime-minister-s-speeches/viktor-orban-s-speech-on-the-anniversary-of-the-hungarian-revolution-of-1848, accessed 28 January 2020.

Orbán, Viktor. 2017. 'We Must Defend Christian Culture'. *Website of the Hungarian Government*, 27 December, available at https://www.kormany.hu/en/the-prime-minister/news/we-must-defend-christian-culture, accessed 29 January 2020.

Orbán, Viktor. 2018a. 'Orbán Viktor's Ceremonial Speech on the 170th Anniversary of the Hungarian Revolution of 1848'. *Website of the Hungarian Government*, available at https://www.kormany.hu/en/the-prime-minister/the-prime-minister-s-speeches/orban-viktor-s-ceremonial-speech-on-the-170th-anniversary-of-the-hungarian-revolution-of-1848, accessed 29 January 2020.

Orbán, Viktor. 2018b. 'Prime Minister Viktor Orbán's Speech at the 29th Bálványos Summer Open University and Student Camp'. *Website of the Hungarian Government*, available at https://www.kormany.hu/en/the-prime-minister/the-prime-minister-s-speeches/prime-minister-viktor-orban-s-speech-at-the-29th-balvanyos-summer-open-university-and-student-camp, accessed 29 January 2020.

Orbán, Viktor. 2019a. 'Address by Prime Minister Viktor Orbán at the 2nd International Conference on the Persecution of Christians'. *Website of the Hungarian Government*, available at https://www.kormany.hu/en/the-prime-minister/the-prime-minister-s-speeches/address-by-prime-minister-viktor-orban-at-the-2nd-international-conference-on-the-persecution-of-christians, accessed 4 February 2020.

Orbán, Viktor. 2019b. 'There Can Be No Compromise on Defending Christian Culture'. *Website of the Hungarian Government*, available at https://www.kormany.hu/en/the-prime-minister/news/there-can-be-no-compromise-on-defending-christian-culture, accessed 29 January 2020.

Origo, 2017. 'Orbán Viktor: A migráció a terrorizmus trójai falova'. *Origo*, 30 March, available at https://www.origo.hu/itthon/20170330-orban-a-migracio-a-terrorizmus-trojai-falova.html, accessed 28 January 2020.

Oroszi, Babet. 2020. 'Csak 100 milliárdot költhetett Rogán Antal tárcája kormánypropagandára'. *HVG*, 20 January, available at https://hvg.hu/gazdasag/20200120_miniszterelnoki_kabinetiroda_zarszamadas_kormanyzati_kommunikacio?s=hk, accessed 2 February 2020.

Republikon, 2015. *A Fidesz Szavazói*. Budapest: Republikon Intézet.

Scheiring, Gabor. 2020. *Orbanomics: A Polarising Answer to the Crisis of Liberal Dependent Capitalism*. Budapest: Friedrich-Ebert-Stiftung.

Scheppele, Kim. 2019. 'The Opportunism of Populists and the Defense of Constitutional Liberalism'. *German Law Journal* 20: 314–31. DOI:10.1017/glj.2019.25.

Schmidt, Maria. 2017. 'The Gravedigger of the Left'. *About Hungary*, 25 April. http://abouthungary.hu/blog/the-gravedigger-of-the-left/, accessed 28 January 2020.

Schmidt, Maria. 2018. 'Trianon feldolgozására ezer év sem elegendő', *Mandiner*, 10 December. https://mandiner.hu/cikk/20181210_schmidt_maria_trianon_feldolgozasara_ezer_ev_sem_elegendo, accessed 29 January 2020.

Schöpflin, Gyorgi. 2013. 'Hungary: The Fidesz Project'. *Aspen Review* 1: 11–16.

Szelényi, Ivan. 2015. 'Capitalisms after Communism'. *New Left Review* 96: 39–51.

Szombati, Kristof. 2018. 'Viktor Orbán's Authoritarian Regime'. In *The Far Right in Government: Six Cases from Across Europe*, edited by Stefanie Ehmsen and Albert Scharenberg. New York: Rosa Luxembourg Stiftung.

Szurovecz, Illes. 2020. 'Orbán szerint igazságtalan, hogy kártérítést kaphatnak a roma gyerekek, akiket éveken át elkülönítettek az iskolában'. *444*, 9 January. https://444.hu/2020/01/09/orban-szerint-igazsagtalan-hogy-karteritest-kaptak-a-roma-gyerekek-akiket-eveken-at-elkulonitettek-az-iskolaban, accessed 7 July 2020.

Tamás, Gaspar. 2013. 'Words from Budapest'. *New Left Review* 80: 5–26.

Transparency International. 2019. *Corruption, Economic Performance and the Rule of Law in Hungary*. Budapest: Transparency International Hungary Foundation.

Wilkin, Peter, Lina Dencik, and Eva Bognár. 2015. 'Digital Activism and Hungarian Media Reform: The Case of Milla'. *European Journal of Communication* 30 (6): 682–97.

Yuval-Davis, Nira. 1997. *Gender and Nation*. London: Sage Publications.

Chapter 4

Multi-Platform Social Capital Mobilization Strategies among Anti-LGBTQIA+ Groups in Taiwan

Kenneth C. C. Yang and Yowei Kang

On May 24, 2017, Taiwan's Constitutional Court (equivalent to the Supreme Court in the United States) made a landmark ruling that the existing legal definition of marriage in the Civic Code was not constitutional, and that marriage should not be a legal status limited to a relationship between a man and a woman (Horton 2017a, b; Tcheng 2017). Following this, Taiwan's Parliament was given two years to develop legislation to include gay marriage (ibid.). On 17 May 2019, Taiwan became the first country in Asia to legalize gay marriage after the passage of the *Enforcement Act of Judicial Yuan Interpretation No. 748* (Hollingsworth 2019; Rich and Eliassen 2019; Zhang 2019). Since then, over 3,000 couples have been married (*Today* 2020). The law has offered marriage equality to same-sex couples so that they may 'manage a life together, conclude a permanent union that is intimate and exclusive' (Article 2) and have the rights to 'matrimonial property regimes' (Article 15), and 'inheritance' (Article 23) (cited in Zhang 2019, n.p.). However, unlike in heterosexual marriage, these same-sex couples are still not allowed to adopt children from their biological parents (Article 20; cited in Zhang 2019, n.p.). In addition, international same-sex marriages are presently not recognized to receive immigration benefits in Taiwan (*Today* 2020).

In East Asia, attitudes toward homosexuality have traditionally been less tolerant than in Western countries (Adamczyk and Cheng 2015). Similarly, homosexuality has long been a taboo topic in Taiwan, an ethnic Chinese majority country, because of its strong ideological roots in traditional Chinese cultural and religious traditions that strongly emphasize heterosexual family values (Kong 2016) and Confucianism (Cheng, Wu, and Adamczyk 2016). Cultural stigma and social discrimination commonly lead to an overall unfriendly environment for LGBTQIA+ minorities in Taiwan (Tcheng 2017). Homosexuality is often criticized by religious groups for being 'unnatural and . . . against the normal biological and psychological human development' (Liu 1988, cited in Kong 2016, 495). In addition to the discrimination and stigmatization experienced by LGBTQIA+ individuals in Taiwan, their rights to property ownership or to be involved in medical decisions about their same-sex partner are often breached because of a lack of legal recognition of their relationship (Smith 2016). The tragic death of a French professor, Jacques Picoux, at National Taiwan University, after his Taiwanese partner of thirty-five years died of cancer, is one example of the unintended consequences of the legal invisibility of LGBTQIA+ minorities, and has become 'a pivotal moment' in Taiwan's gay rights movement (Smith 2016, n.p.).

However, when compared with social and legal practices common in other Asian countries (such as Indonesia's public caning and Singapore's colonial sodomy law; Chan 2008), feelings towards LGBTQIA+ minorities in Taiwan are relatively accepting (Tcheng 2017). Taiwan has seen the gradual transformation of its society into a more gay-tolerant one (Kingston 2016). Longitudinal survey data from 1995, 2006 and 2016 have reported the growing tolerance of LGBTQIA+ minorities in Taiwan as a result of its economic development, democratization and evolving social values (Cheng, Wu, and Adamczyk 2016). The changes in attitudes towards homosexuality have been attributed to 'cohort succession and partly intra-cohort changes in attitudes' (Cheng et al. 2016, 317).

While Taiwan can be considered a comparatively LGBTQIA+-tolerant country, the legalization of gay marriage unexpectedly polarized its society (Kingston 2016). Public polls have shown the contestation between modern and traditional attitudes toward homosexuality. In 2016, the public poll showed that 46.3% of the population supported the legalization of gay marriage, while 45.4% opposed the change (Kingston 2016). Factors like age, education, residence and political orientation act as significant predictors of Taiwanese attitudes toward homosexuality and gay marriage (Ho 2018; Kingston 2016). Social intolerance against homosexuality and gay marriage has significantly increased in 2012 among the Christian community, which has traditionally made up the major ideological support for anti-gay marriage groups like those in the United States (Cole 2017; Wilson 2014).

As the legalization of gay marriage became a contentious issue in Taiwan, far-right anti-gay political and religious groups (such as Taiwan Marriage League and New Party) became more prominent. The collaboration between foreign anti-gay marriage right and far-right groups as well as local conservative and religious groups has given some momentum to what is now a widespread social movement (Cole 2017). Many of these anti-LGBTQIA+ groups have been aided by a Massachusetts-based hate group, *MassResistance*, which lobbies anti-gay influencers among U.S. local religious groups, Taiwanese Americans and conservative political figures in the United States (ibid). Some of these Taiwanese right and far-right groups include Hope Family League, Taiwan Marriage League, Stability of Power, Protection of Family Value Students Organization, The Nationalist Party, For Public Good Party, People First Party, Non-Partisan Solidarity Union and New Party. The close ties between local and foreign right and far-right anti-gay religious groups – such as International House of Prayer, Bread of Life Christian Church and Agape Christian Church – have been well documented, highlighting their leadership role in shaping this rhetoric across international waters (Cole 2013).

These anti-gay marriage groups in Taiwan share many ideological similarities, including a strong emphasis on traditional family values, the notion that marriage is a sacred institution only between men and women, and stereotypical gender roles. In ways similar to those of far-right groups in the United States after the Supreme Court ruling in 2015, some of these anti-gay groups create messaging that warns Taiwanese citizens that they face 'imminent divine judgment and civil war' and the destruction of 'our nation's heritage of Biblical marriage' (Tashman 2015, n.p.). Other more absurd statements claim that Taiwan's legalization of gay marriage will promote 'sex with animals and . . . lure children into homosexuality and sadomasochism' and 'bestiality, promiscuity, incest, rape, chaos, [and] the destruction of the traditional family' (Cole 2017, n.p.). Alarmingly, these domestic and foreign anti-gay marriage groups have aptly employed new technological platforms such as Facebook or Twitter to spread 'hate, or attack or call for the exclusion of others on the basis of who they are' (Hern 2019, n.p.). This phenomenon bears alarming resemblance to the rise of technology-empowered alt-right groups in Europe and North America (*TRT World* 2019).

Justifications and Objectives of This Study

The rise of right and far-right anti-gay marriage groups in Taiwan provides an excellent case study to examine how otherwise unpopular, traditionalist ideas can become mainstream by amassing and contributing a large amount of financial, technological, human and networking resources to promote their anti-LGBTQIA+ agendas. This chapter examines how anti-gay marriage groups have benefited from mobilizing social capital through multi-platform technologies for their anti-LGBTQIA+ referendums before and during the 24 November 2018 elections. We focus on multi-platform resource mobilization because, in addition to Facebook and Line, traditional media such as bus advertising and leaflets were also used to advocate these right and far-right agendas. This topic is of critical importance to studies of far-right and right-wing political and economic influence, yet, there is little existing research that explores this phenomenon in the context of new East Asian marriage equality laws. In sum, the objectives of this chapter are to examine the mobilization of social capital resources among anti-LGBTQIA+ groups in Taiwan that seek to influence public opinion in harmful, traditionalist directions which oppress minority groups. We also provide a detailed analysis of social capital mobilization strategies by these anti-LGBTQIA+ groups.

LITERATURE REVIEW AND THEORETICAL FOUNDATION

Mobilizing Social Capital Resources for Anti-Gay Marriage Groups

Resource Mobilization Theory has been used to examine 'the dynamics and tactics of social movement growth, decline, and change' (McCarthy and Zald 1977, 1213) by focusing on the role of resource mobilization to explain the success of social movements (Hara and Estrada 2005). The utilization of critical resources such as money, facilities, labor, land, legitimacy and technical expertise has been tied to the success of civil society groups in achieving their agendas (Hara and Estrada 2005). Other scholars have argued that the mobilization of authority, financial contribution, connective public goods and trust are important resources in achieving organizational goals (Corte 2013; McCarthy and Zald 1977).

Successful resource mobilization through multi-platform technologies is a topic that has generated substantive interest among scholars who studied resource mobilization strategies among non-profit organizations (Büscher 2014; Butler 2012; Choi and Shin 2017; Yang and Kang 2020). These scholars have examined how cultural, human, material, moral, social organizational and technological proficiency resources could help these organizations (Edwards and McCarthy 2004, cited in Corte 2013, 29). In recent years, a growing body of literature has explored social capital mobilization through multi-platform technologies (Choi and Shin 2017; Mou and Lin 2017; Zúñiga, Barnidge, and Scherman 2017). The emergence of social media has rekindled scholarly interests in social capital accumulation (Zúñiga et al. 2017). Social media platforms have been extensively examined because of their capabilities to create and maintain social interactions and interpersonal relationships, from which social capital can be subsequently mobilized (Hara and Estrada 2005; Mou and Lin 2017). The mobilization of social capital through multi-platform technologies is particularly relevant to the present study since many right and far-right groups have been found to depend on these new media technologies to foster and maintain social interactions among their members, which may ultimately contribute to the mobilization of social capital (*TRT World* 2019).

According to Bourdieu (1986), social capital refers to 'the aggregate of the actual or potential resources which are linked to possession of a durable network of varying, institutionalized relationships of mutual acquaintance or recognition' (248–9). Bourdieu's conceptualization of social capital is derived from his sociological perspective that links social capital with 'social reproduction' and 'symbolic power' (Claridge 2015). The accrual of social capital can be influenced by class, gender and race because of the structural constraint placed on equal access to these social capital resources (Claridge 2015). In spite of the richness of Bourdieu's (1986) approach to study social capital, we surmise that access to emerging technologies to mobilize social capital resources may be less influenced by these pre-existing constraints. Both anti- and pro-gay marriage groups have the same technological capabilities to employ these platforms to advocate their causes. Many of them are from the same social class. Therefore, this chapter employs Putman's (2000) definition that social capital is derived from 'connections among individual social networks and the norms of reciprocity and trustworthiness that arise from them' (19). These definitions of social capital have clearly identified this term as 'the resources available to people through their social interactions' (Phua and Jin 2011, 505). The term also implies that 'social capital' is a resource derived from social ties among people (Lin and Erickson 2008; Zúñiga et al. 2017). Here, we focus on social capital accrued from social networks without taking into consideration cultural, economic and social structure. This digression from Bourdieu's approach (1986) is based on recent studies of social capital on social media, which have also often adopted Putman's perspective (Claridge 2015; Mou and Lin 2017). These scholars have similarly ignored the influence of power in social structure, but merely examined the mobilization of social capital resource accumulated from both social ties and the capabilities of technologies to construct personal identity and to exchange information (Mou and Lin 2017).

Given the close connection between multi-platform technologies and social capital mobilization (Mou and Lin 2017; Zúñiga et al. 2017), recent literature has begun to explore how human interactions over the Internet and social media can lead to powerful networking effects and the cultivation of social capital (Hooghe and Oser 2015). Related to LGBTQIA+ topics, research concerning the links between social media and social capital has empirically established that social media can facilitate the exchange of social information to promote group membership, enhance a sense of camaraderie, reduce stigma and to foster mental health among sexual minorities (Chong, Zhang, Mak, and Pang 2015). Chong et al. (2015) claimed that social media is an important source of social capital for LGBTQIA+ groups. We argued that, while social media platforms allow the recreation, preservation and mobilization of social capital among marginalized LGBTQIA+ groups, these technologies have provided the same affordances and capabilities to mobilize the same resource (i.e. social capital) to achieve anti-progressive outcomes.

Social media enables anti-gay marriage groups to connect 'like-minded individuals, providing an infrastructure for communities and supporting their coordination' (Wilson and Peterson 2002, cited in Fieseler and Fleck 2013). Social media platforms have been used to help build a strong online community on the basis of 'shared reality' about the marriage institution, which strengthens shared beliefs in heterosexual marriage (Fieseler and Fleck 2013). Right and far-right rhetoric on the legalization of gay marriage often depicts a world full of 'perverted sexual behaviors' (Cole 2017). Many YouTube videos hosted in anti-gay marriage groups dramatize varied imagined realities of moral degradation and societal collapse once gay marriage is legalized. Interpersonal relationships and interactions are also facilitated through these networking technologies by creating bonds among individuals, which encourages the organization to host events and strengthen a sense of community (Zúñiga et al. 2017). According to Foster, Smith, Bell, and Shaw (2017), this type of *bonding social capital* is produced after linking together a group of people who have similar features and sturdy social ties among friends and family. For example, social media platforms such as YouTube and Facebook have been used by right and far-right groups to form coalition among people who similarly support anti-Muslim, anti-immigrant, and anti-LGBTQIA+ agendas (Ribeiro et al. 2019). For instance, the conservative YouTuber Steven Crowder shares his anti-LGBTQIA+ viewpoints among his 4.5 million subscribers (*TRT World* 2019) in the process forming a strong fan base to generate bonding social capital. In addition to creating social capital by bonding their geographically dispersed members, technologies such as crowd-funding also help these groups to recruit financial resources (ibid).

In addition to mobilizing bonding social capital among homogeneous individuals, technologies, both traditional and emerging, also contribute to the accrual of *bridging social capital* by linking people who are heterogeneous and often hold weaker social ties (Foster, Smith, Bell, and Shaw, 2017). Alongside using emerging multi-platform technologies, anti-gay marriage groups in Taiwan have employed traditional media, such as bus advertising and leaflets distribution, to reach out to heterogeneous demographic groups with otherwise weak social ties. In other words, the multi-platform strategies through both online and offline media enable many anti-gay marriage groups to disseminate their political agendas through mobilizing bridging social capital within individuals across society.

Bridging social capital involves information sharing and exchanging to gain new perspectives without incurring emotional bonds and attachment to the information source (Chung, Nam, and Koo 2016). Unlike bonding social capital created through close-knit social media groups through likes, sharing and subscriptions, bridging social capital can be built through the creation of mail distribution lists among members, the storage and archiving of photos and using the search function of anti-gay marriage websites. Access to these archived contents does not require users' emotional attachment. Social capital accrual from individuals with weak social ties can, however, still draw potential resources to help anti-gay marriage groups advocate their common agendas (Fieseler and Fleck 2013). For example, sharing campaign information through individuals' social networks, or word of mouth, may generate more powerful bonding than bridging social capital generated through less personal mass media advertising and email newsletters.

This chapter focuses on the technology-enabled mobilization of social capital resources through multi-platform technologies by examining what types of social capital resources these groups have mobilized, and what mobilization strategies they have employed to achieve their organizational objectives. This chapter aims to answer the following questions:

What are the resource mobilization strategies used by anti-gay marriage groups to accrue social capital to recruit volunteers and members and to mobilize support to accomplish their agendas?

What is the role of social capital resources that have been employed by anti-gay marriage groups to encourage civic participation and engagement?

RESEARCH METHOD

The Case Study Method

We employed a case study approach to examine and assess several campaigns by anti-LGBTQIA+ groups to oppose the legalization of gay marriage in Taiwan. On the basis of these case examples, we attempted to demonstrate how these multi-platform technologies have functioned as resource mobilization platforms to promote anti-LGBTQIA+ agendas in Taiwan. The rationale for this multi-organization case study is to explore to what extent these digital platforms have contributed to the success of their resource mobilization activities.

Yin (2009) has identified three types of case study research approaches: descriptive, explanatory and exploratory. In an exploratory case study, the focus is typically on the identification of patterns in the data. Instead, however, we have employed a descriptive case study method to provide a complete description of the selected anti-gay marriage groups to explain our two theoretically framed research questions. More specifically, this case study aims to describe the social capital mobilization strategies among four anti-LGBTQIA+ groups.

The Selection of Anti-LGBTQIA+ Groups in Taiwan

Civil society groups with strong anti-gay marriage agendas were included in this case study. In particular, we examined the following four anti-gay marriage groups that have made the most of new multi-platform technologies to mobilize social capital resources to support their agendas. These groups include Protection of Family Value Students Organization, The Coalition for the Happiness of Our Next Generation, Family Guardian Coalition, and Stability of Power/Stabilizing Force, all of which have been actively involved in the proposition of three referendums to oppose gay marriage (Agencies 2018; Wang and Chang 2018). Several of these civil society groups have also taken part in the 2020 Taiwan national election, but with limited success. For example, the newly formed Stabilizing Force Power Party received only 0.67% of the national political vote. The Coalition for the Happiness of Our Next Generation intended to recruit pro-family legislators, but failed to produce a large number of elected legislators and county officials to generate any significant political traction (Yeh 2018; refer to table 4.1).

Table 4.1. Anti-Gay Marriage Groups in Taiwan

	Chinese Names	*Multi-Platform Technologies*
Protection of Family Value Students Organization	捍衛家庭學生聯盟 (捍家盟) 中華家庭教育與權益促進協會	Facebook: https://www.facebook.com/PFVSO/?ref=ts&fref=ts
The Coalition for the Happiness of Our Next Generation	下一代幸福聯盟 (下福盟)	Facebook: https://www.facebook.com/Hope.family.tw YouTube: https://www.youtube.com/watch?v=ldiMzLMTIlk Internet: https://taiwanfamily.com/ LINE App: https://taiwanfamily.com/LINE
Family Guardian Coalition	台灣宗教團體愛護家庭大聯盟 (護家盟)	Facebook: https://www.facebook.com/familyguardiancoalition/
Stability of Power (now, Stabilizing Force Party)	安定力量聯盟/ 安定力量政黨	Facebook: https://www.facebook.com/StabilityOfPower/ Internet: https://sftaiwan.org/ YouTube: https://www.youtube.com/watch?v=_PW2N9ZH638 LINE App: https://line.me/R/ti/p/%40vfp2743g

Source: Compiled by the author.

FINDINGS AND DISCUSSION

Strategies to Mobilize Social Capital Resources among Anti-Gay Marriage Groups

Our analyses of these four anti-gay marriage groups have concluded that their mobilization strategies are based on interpersonal relationships, the strengths of social ties and information sharing and exchanging among members within or outside these social networks. Popular social media platforms have emerged as a frequently used technology among anti-gay marriage groups in Taiwan because of their capabilities to allow these organizations to set up these easy-to-access platforms, groups or pages to interact with current and potential members. For example, Protection of Family Value Students Organization (henceforth, PFVSO) has dedicated its Facebook presence to anti-gay marriage videos, 'educational' materials, commercials, past activity videos, public hearings, personal stories and so on (refer to figure 4.1 in the following). Its Facebook page has 17,399 likes and 17,656 followers. As a student-led

Figure 4.1. Facebook Page of Protection of Family Value Students Organization. ***Note*****: Video titles translated by authors; titles correspond to video positions in screenshot.**
Source: Screenshot of Public Page: Author.

Table 4.2. Video titles translated by authors; titles correspond to video positions in screenshot

'Agree or Disagree'	'Final Night before Pro-Family Referendum'	'At 12:00 today, Buddhism Leader Speaks for 3 Pro-Family Referendums'
'Come Down to Referendum. What does Each Side Say?'	'Flash Mob by Pro-Family Youngsters'	'I Support three Pro-Family Referendums. Taipei City Mayor Candidate, Ting, S.C. Campaign Video'

organization, its social media site includes videos created to target college students who are traditionally more supportive of marriage equity for LGBTQIA+ minorities (Ho 2018).

Setting up a Facebook page is an effective strategy to mobilize social capital resources by strengthening a sense of community among PFVSO's current members; this strategy could mobilize bonding social capital among current members who have already 'like(d)' the organization's Facebook page and established a virtual social tie with PFVSO and its members. Interpersonal relationships are established through PFVSO's Facebook among like-minded individuals whose demographic and religious background leads to their strong opposition of gay marriage in Taiwan. However, Facebook can function more than a community forum where sturdy social ties can be formed, fostered and maintained to generate bonding social capital for the organization (Williams 2006). The organization's members could also feel a sense of social support, either emotional or physical, that they are not alone in their beliefs, which also helps mobilize bonding social capital (Tian 2016).

In addition, Facebook can serve as the metaphorical bridge for reaching many ideologically heterogeneous participants, ensuring that anti-gay marriage messages will come into contact also with the general public. With its social media presence, PFVSO also aims to reach those who are not currently tied with the organization but might be persuaded once they read the Facebook contents the organization has archived. Bridging social capital can be mobilized through the diffusion of information (Tian 2016).

Another anti-gay marriage group, The Coalition for the Happiness of Our Next Generation (henceforth, CHNG), also employs a Facebook site to promote its agendas by linking the legalization of gay marriage with its claimed negative impacts on family values, the happiness of future generations, K-12 curriculum teaching tolerance and inclusiveness, and support of marriage as heterosexual unions only, as seen on its Facebook page (refer to table 4.1). CHNG's Facebook page also includes video archives to share with current and potential members about its previous public hearings, 'educational' videos on K-12 curriculum revisions, opposition to the gay marriage legalization law itself and campaign support for its endorsed candidates who also support its own anti-LGBTQIA+ agendas (refer to figure 4.2). The similarly eager intention to collaborate with other political entities can be found in the strategies adopted by *Stability of Power* (henceforth, SP) to promote its own candidates. In sum, CHNG's Facebook page mobilizes bridging social capital when information can be shared and exchanged among its members to strengthen their anti-gay marriage beliefs. With all resources stored in an easy-to-access Facebook site, the cost of information retrieval and sharing is reduced, contributing to the building and mobilization of bonding and bridging social capital as a result (Mou and Lin 2017).

Figure 4.2. Facebook Page of the Coalition for the Happiness of Our Next Generation. The Tagline reads: 'DDP Government Should Respect the Referendum Results of 7,650K Voters; Marriage Should Be Limited to between a Man and a Woman'. *Note*: Tagline translated by authors.

Source: Screenshot of Public Page: Author.

Unlike the student-led and resource-deficient PFVSO, CHNG's resource mobilization strategies go beyond its Internet website (https://taiwanfamily.com/). CHNG's website is used to share its organization's missions, recruit volunteers and supporters, establish a 'pro-family' virtual meeting place and maintain interpersonal relationships with its existing and potential members. In addition to ample video archives and searchable resource database to accrue bridging social capital from the general public who has not joined the organization, CHNG's website also has a link (https://donate.taiwanfamily.com/) to receive credit card donations. Donations are also received by a mobile-enabled QR code that users can scan to initiate the donation process. The inclusion of a donation link and a QR code function as affordances of these multi-platform technologies allow anti-gay marriage groups to mobilize different types of resources. CHNG's dedicated YouTube channel has 2.75K subscribers and includes over 100 videos of its 'educational' contents, public hearings on the definition of marriage and K–12 curriculum, constitutionality of the gay marriage law and so on. In addition to these social media pages, the popular mobile app Line is also used by CHNG to allow potential members to join geographic-specific forums and communities on the basis of their current residence (https://taiwanfamily.com/LINE; refer to figure 4.3). This is beneficial to the accrual of bonding social capital through community formation (Mou and Lin 2017). The inclusion of the Line on CHNG's Facebook page offers anti-gay marriage groups the opportunity to produce social capital by establishing social networks that can produce either strong or weak social ties. Once social ties are established through these technologies, users' sharing of personal stories, news reports, public hearings and podcasting videos enables members to collaborate in pursuing their anti-LGBTQIA+ beliefs and agendas. A mobile-enabled QR code is included on CHNG's Facebook page

Figure 4.3. Screenshot of the Coalition for the Happiness of Our Next Generation's Line App. Organization Icon and Official Name at the top. The Taglines read: 'The Happiness of Our Next Generation'; 'Join the Coalition for the Happiness of Our Next Generation's Line App@'; 'Select Which City and County You Want to Join'. *Note*: Chinese contents on the webpage translated by authors.

Source: Screenshot of Public Page: Author.

to allow easy and smooth membership sign-up for volunteers and members living in different cities and counties in Taiwan, making Family Guardian Coalition's mobilization strategies truly multi-platform.

Both PFVSO and CHNG have taken advantage of the networking effects of multi-platform technologies, but variations in their applications show that existing resources of civil society organizations could determine the extent of their technology-enabled strategies to mobilize various resources (Yang and Kang 2020). While both anti-gay marriage groups have used technologies to promote their agendas, CHNG is far more comprehensive in establishing virtual social ties with the organization and among members through social media, and mobile platforms. Strategic alliance with existing political parties can be done by listing them as 'Related Pages' on their Facebook pages (Kropczynski and Nah 2010). The 'Related Pages' feature further affords anti-gay marriage groups the ability to expand their social networks to other similar organizations.

Mobilizing Different Types of Social Capital to Encourage Civic Participation and Engagement

Recent literature has begun to explore the linkage between social capital, civic participation and political engagement (Choi and Shin 2017; Zúñiga et al. 2017). Scholars are interested in examining what mechanisms motivate

Figure 4.4. Screenshot of the Coalition for the Happiness of Our Next Generation's QR Code Donation Page. Slogans at the Top: 'Let's Care for Our Next Generation'; 'A Small Donation Can Help CHNG'; 'Donate through This QR Code'. Slogans at the Bottom: 'Support Pro-Family Culture'; 'Stipulate Pro-Family Policy'; 'Care for Young Children'. *Note*: Slogans translated by authors.

Source: Screenshot of Public Page: Author.

individuals to volunteer or commit their time or money (Mou and Lin 2017) 'to strengthen representative democracy, and help sustain a coherent society' as described by social movement groups (Choi and Shin 2017, 153). Anti-gay marriage groups anticipate that the mobilization of social capital resources could also lead to human and financial resources, which are critical to accomplish their agendas, as demonstrated in CHNG's website where donations can be made through a QR code (refer to figure 4.4 in the following).

An analysis of CHNG's website demonstrates how anti-gay marriage groups are able to transform their social capital to political engagement and civic participation. Endorsing and electing like-minded political candidates is an excellent example of how users are mobilized to 'strengthen representative democracy' to 'sustain a society' coherent with their own anti-LGBTQIA+ value systems (Choi and Shin 2017, 153). In these statements, the legalization of gay marriage is equated with the destruction of society and families, subsequently implying that mobilized persons that work against such legislation or movements are thereby 'strengthening' and 'sustaining' society. As shown in figure 4.5, the slogan of one of CHNG's mobilization campaign says, 'In 2020, Pro-Family Is the Key. Support Pro-Family Candidates. Reject Pro-Gay Marriage Candidates', 'Welcome Pro-Family', '(Ask Your Candidate to) Sign a Pledge to Support Pro-Family Agendas'. Political candidates in different electoral areas were listed to inform CHNG's supporters who to vote or who to reject. CHNG's list is also used to place pressure on candidates to sign and implement the pledge once they are elected.

Figure 4.5. Screenshot of the Coalition for the Happiness of Our Next Generation's Webpage. Slogans on the webpage: 'In 2020, Pro-Family Is the Key'; 'Support Pro-Family Candidates. Reject Pro-Gay Marriage Candidates'; 'Welcome Pro-Family'; '(Ask Your Candidate to) Sign a Pledge to Support Pro-Family Agendas'; 'Click Here to Read the Candidate List (We Endorse)'. *Note*: Slogans translated by authors.

Source: Screenshot of Public Page: Author.

Originally derived from the a far-right Christian Evangelical group Hope and Faith League, Stability of Power, later called the Stabilizing Force Party (henceforth, SP), also attempts to transform its social capital into political participation by electing its own pro-family candidates to promote anti-LGBTQIA+ agendas (*Christian Daily* 2015). Similar to CHNG, a multi-platform strategy has been used to mobilize social capital and other resources by sharing information about the party, recruiting new party members and mobilizing financial resources online (https://core.newebpay.com/EPG/sf/Lm04ZO). Interested donors can share the QR code through Line and Facebook link through their networks, to expand the size of social networks through which more social capital can be accrued. Line is also used to recruit new party members easily through users' mobile device. As seen in figure 4.6, SP's homepage can be used as a contact point to access its other multi-platforms to achieve its resource mobilization efforts.

Using mainly Facebook, Family Guardian Coalition (henceforth, FGC) has advocated its anti-LGBTQIA+ agendas, ranging from pro-family values, the exclusion of any sex education in K–12 curricula, resistance to gender fluidity designation in national identification cards and resistance to women's reproductive rights (refer to figure 4.7). FGC's social agendas mirror similar agendas of right-wing movements in the United States (Blee and Creasap 2010), even though women's rights to abortion have never been a contentious issue in Taiwan.

In 24 November 2018 local election in Taiwan, the strategic alliance of right and far-right pro-family groups and the so-called Pan Blue Union defeated the ruling liberal Democratic Progressive Party by winning in over fifteen counties and acquiring a landslide majority in both cities and counties.

Figure 4.6. Screenshot of Stabilizing Force Party's Website. Translation of horizontal menu buttons: 'Homepage'; 'About Stabilizing Force Party'; 'Small Amount of Donation'; 'News Updates'; 'Become a Party Member'; 'Our Candidates'; 'Facebook'. *Note*: Translation of horizontal menu buttons by authors.

Source: Screenshot of Public Page: Author.

Figure 4.7. Screenshot of Family Guardian Coalition's Facebook Page.

Source: Screenshot of Public Page: Author.

Furthermore, three anti-LGBTQIA+ referendums were passed to ban education on LGBTQIA+ issues in elementary and middle schools, to define marriage as a union between a man and a woman only and to limit gay couples' right to marry (Ellis and Lin 2018). Observers have attributed the success of right and far-right groups and their agendas to the use of traditional and emerging social media, which 'misinformed' the society by spreading fake news before the election (Aspinwall 2018; Steger 2018). One noteworthy example of this misinformation warfare includes the use of the communication app Line by anti-gay marriage groups to spread news that foreign AIDS patients will rush to Taiwan to marry a homosexual Taiwanese to take advantage of their universal health care system (Steger 2018, n.p.):

> 'Strange! Why do they want to rush to legalize same-sex marriage?' The message, whose source is unknown, claims that Taiwan – which offers universal health-care – will become a magnet for HIV-positive homosexual men, who will flock to the country and marry a Taiwanese man in order to use the health-care

system. Because of the high cost of treating HIV/AIDS, the ultimate beneficiaries will be drug companies while taxpayers and the health-care system will suffer, the message goes on to say.

Some advocates have also constructed false stories that 200,000 demonstrators in France have made the government to roll back its same-sex marriage laws – via Line, this viral fake news video led to a public debunking by the official Facebook page of *The Bureau Français de Taipei* (The French Taipei Office; Steger 2018, n.p.). However, the spread of fake news articles through Facebook and Line contributes to the mobilization of social capital among many anti-gay marriage advocates. Users were often willing and co-operative to share and exchange false, strikingly implausible information with others within and outside their networks (Mou and Lin 2017), resulting in the self-reinforcing cycle of social capital accrual for right and far-right groups through the recruitment of more members to join their organizations.

CONCLUSION

Multi-platform technologies are characterized by their capacity to accumulate, capitalize, operate and manage these important resources (Phua and Jin 2011). Social capital mobilized through social media (Mou and Lin 2017) and mobile platforms (Mazharul Islam, Habes, and Alam 2018) can generate financial resources for CNHG and SP, as well as human resources for all anti-gay marriage groups. Notably, in addition to Facebook, YouTube, Internet and Line, traditional media such as bus advertising and leaflets distribution were also used by these anti-gay marriage groups to communicate with individuals who are not part of the interpersonal networks. One leaflet was shown to spread fabricated information in voters' mailboxes during the 2018 campaign period to describe the legalization of gay marriage in Taiwan will ultimately 'make it legal to have sex with minors under 16' and 'pave the way for pedophilia' (Steger 2018, n.p.). Readers of this leaflet as well as the bus ad will be able to establish a social tie with these anti-marriage groups through their Facebook address, Line app or QR code to learn more about these organizations. These individuals, once persuaded by this kind of media content, can join their organizations, resulting in the mobilization of bonding social capital.

As an exploratory study of the resource mobilization strategies among anti-LGBTQIA+ groups to oppose the legalization of same-sex marriage in Taiwan, this study described mobilization strategies of bonding and bridging social capital resources. While scholars may interpret the success of marriage equality as a result of political process in Taiwan (Ho 2018), these analyses do not explain the backlash by right and far-right groups, and the dramatic losses by the ruling Democratic Progressive Party in 2018 local elections: the progressive party lost two-thirds of the county official seats, and three anti-LGBTQIA+ referendums were passed. Given that Taiwan is the first country in East Asia to legalize gay marriage (Horton 2016), the study of right and far-right anti-gay marriage groups can have some practical implications, offering civil society groups a chance to observe how other, more conservative countries may react or regress their policies in the future.

Though useful in understanding these particular examples, as a method the qualitative case study is inherently limited by the type and number of anti-gay marriage groups we have analysed. Resource mobilization strategies and types of resources mobilized by these groups are not generalized to those in other countries. This study focuses on the role of social capital resources, but other resources (such as human, financial, political and technology) may be equally important in terms of explaining the success or failure of anti-gay marriage groups in Taiwan.

Furthermore, the concept of social capital has been criticized for the lack of clarity to allow researchers to conduct useful analysis at both micro- and macro-level social issues (Lin 2001). Numerous criticisms are also summarized by Claridge (2018) that social capital has been overly stretched in different research contexts and may not be considered a form of capital as economists would argue. While the role of social capital has been found to encourage civic participation and political engagement (Choi and Shin 2017), its relationships with other variables (such as trust and media usage behaviours; Geber, Scherer, and Hefner 2016) may need further study.

Methodologically, the descriptive nature of a case study does not establish causal relationships among social capital, social relationship, and trust, among many variables in the literature (Choi and Shin 2017). Further studies using other methods may shed light on many important topics this chapter has yet to examine. Resource mobilization is an integral part of capacity-building for any civil society organization (Yang and Kang 2020). As described in this chapter, the technology-enabled mobilization of bonding and bridging social capital has been essential to the success of anti-gay marriage groups in Taiwan. Inevitably, we find that social capital mobilized through social interactions and interpersonal relationships (Phua and Jin 2011) proves valuable to these anti-gay marriage groups in Taiwan, enabling them to encourage civic participation and political engagement to implement their right and far-right agendas.

REFERENCES

Adamczyk, Almy, and Alice Y. H. Cheng. 2015. 'Explaining Attitudes about Homosexuality in Confucian and Non-Confucian Nations: Is There a "Cultural" Influence?' *Social Science Research* 51: 276–89. doi: 10.1016/j.ssresearch.2014.10.002.

Agencie. 2018. 'Taiwan Votes Down Same-Sex Marriage as China Welcomes Midterm Results'. *The Guardian*, 24 November. Retrieved on 1 March 2020 from https://www.theguardian.com/world/2018/nov/24/anti-gay-marriage-groups-win-taiwan-referendum-battle.

Aspinwall, Nick. 2018. 'Is Taiwan's Drive to Legalize Gay Marriage Descending Into Chaos?' *The Diplomat*, 6 November. Retrieved on 1 January 2019 from https://thediplomat.com/2018/11/is-taiwans-drive-to-legalize-gay-marriage-descending-into-chaos/.

Blee, Kahleen, and Kimberly Creasap. 2010. 'Conservative and Right-Wing Movements'. *Annual Review of Sociology* 36: 269–86. Retrieved on 11 June 2020 from https://doi.org/10.1146/annurev.soc.012809.102602.

Bourdieu, Pierre. 1986. 'The Forms of Capital'. In *Handbook of Theory and Research for the Sociology of Education*, edited by J. Richardson, 241–58. Westport, CT: Greenwood.

Büscher, Bram. 2014. 'Nature 2.0: Exploring and Theorizing the Links between New Media and Nature Conservation'. *New Media & Society* 18 (5): 1–18.

Butler, Lindsay. 2012. 'How Charities Can Use QR Codes'. *The Guardian*, 30 May. Retrieved on 29 July 2018 from https://www.theguardian.com/voluntary-sector-network/2012/may/30/using-qr-codes-charity-fundraising.

Cao, J., and X. Lu. 2014. 'A Preliminary Exploration of the Gay Movement in Mainland China: Legacy, Transition, Opportunity, and the New Media'. *Signs* 39 (4): 840–48. doi: 10.1086/675538.

Carroll, William, and Robert Hackett. 2006. 'Democratic Media Activism through the Lens of Social Movement Theory'. *Media, Culture, & Society* 28 (1): 83–104.

Chan, Kenneth. 2008. 'Gay Sexuality in Singaporean Chinese Popular Culture: Where Have All the Boys Gone?' *China Information* 12 (2): 305–29. DOI: 10.1177/0920203X08091548.

Cheng, Yen-Hsin, Felice Fen-Chieh, and Amy Adamczyk. 2016. 'Changing Attitudes toward Homosexuality in Taiwan, 1995–2012'. *Chinese Sociological Review* 48 (4): 317–45.

Choi, Doo-Hun, and Dong-Hee Shin. 2017. 'A Dialectic Perspective on the Interactive Relationship between Social Media and Civic Participation: The Moderating Role of Social Capital'. *Information, Communication & Society* 20 (2): 151–66.

Chong, Eddie, Yin Zhang, Winnie Mak, and Ingrid Pang. 2015. 'Social Media as Social Capital of LGB Individuals in Hong Kong: Its Relations with Group Membership, Stigma, and Mental Well-Being'. *American Journal of Community Psychology* 55: 228–38.

Christian Daily. 2015. 'New Political Platform, Faith and Hope League, to Break Blue and Green Political Boundaries'. *Christian Daily*, 11 September. Retrieved on 11 June 2020 from https://web.archive.org/web/20151211060634/ and http://www.cdn.org.tw/News.aspx?cate=14&key=6675.

Chung, Namho, Kichan Nam, and Chulmo Koo. 2016. 'Examining Information Sharing in Social Networking Communities: Applying Theories of Social Capital and Attachment'. *Telematics and Informatics* 33: 77–91.

Claridge, Tristan. 2015. 'Bourdieu on Social Capital Theory of Capital'. *Social Capital Research and Training*, 22 April. Retrieved on 6 August 2020 from https://www.socialcapitalresearch.com/bourdieu-on-social-capital-theory-of-capital/.

Claridge, Tristan. 2018. 'Criticisms of Social Capital Theory and Lessons for Improving Practice'. *Social Capital Research and Training*, 20 April. Retrieved on 6 August 2020 from https://www.socialcapitalresearch.com/criticisms-social-capital-theory-lessons/.

Cole, Michael J. 2013. 'The Perpetrator as Victim'. *Taiwan Sentinel*, 18 December. Retrieved on 1 March 2020 from http://fareasternpotato.blogspot.com/2013/12/the-perpetrator-as-victim.html.

Cole, Michael J. 2017. 'U.S. Hate Group Mass Resistance behind Anti-LGBT Activities in Taiwan'. *Taiwan Sentinel*, 2 January. Retrieved on 1 March 2020 from https://sentinel.tw/us-hate-group-anti-lgbt/.

Corte, Ugo. 2013. 'A Refinement of Collaborative Circles Theory: Resource Mobilization and Innovation in an Emerging Sport'. *Social Psychology Quarterly* 76 (1): 25–51.

Ellis, Samson, and Adela Lin. 2018. 'Taiwan Voters Reject Moves toward Legalizing Same-Sex Marriage'. *Bloomberg*, 25 November. Retrieved on 7 January 2019 from https://www.bloomberg.com/news/articles/2018-11-25/referendum-defeat-leaves-taiwan-same-sex-marriage-push-in-doubt.

Fieseler, Christian, and Matthes Fleck. 2013. 'The Pursuit of Empowerment through Social Media: Structural Social Capital Dynamics in CSR-Blogging'. *Journal of Business Ethics* 118: 759–75.

Foster, Kirk A., Richard J. Smith, Bethany A Bell, and Todd C. Shaw. 2017. 'Testing the Importance of Geographic Distance for Social Capital Resource'. *Urban Affairs Review* 55 (1): 1–26. DOI: https://doi.org/10.1177/1078087417714895.

Geber, Sarah, Helmut Scherer, and Dorothee Hefner. 2016. 'Social Capital in Media Societies: The Impact of Media Use and Media Structure on Social Capital'. *The International Communication Gazette* 78 (6): 493–513.

Hara, Noriko, and Zilia Estrada. 2005. 'Analyzing the mobilization of grassroots activities via the internet: A case study'. *Journal of Information Science* 31 (5): 503–14.

Hern, Alex. 2019. 'Facebook bans far-right groups including BNP, EDL and Britain First'. *The Guardian*, 18 April. Retrieved on June 9, 2020 from https://www.theguardian.com/technology/2019/apr/18/facebook-bans-far-right-groups-including-bnp-edl-and-britain-first.

Ho, Ming-Sho. 2018. 'Taiwan's Road to Marriage Equality: Politics of Legalizing Same-sex Marriage'. *The China Quarterly* 238: 1–22. DOI. https://doi.org/10.1017/S0305741018001765.

Hollingsworth, Julia. 2019. 'Taiwan Legalizes Same-Sex Marriage in Historic First for Asia'. *CNN* 17 May. Retrieved on 1 March 2020 from https://www.cnn.com/2019/05/17/asia/taiwan-same-sex-marriage-intl/index.html.

Hooghe, Marc, and Jennifer Oser. 2015. 'Internet, Television and Social Capital: The Effect of "Screen Time" on Social Capital'. *Information, Communication & Society* 18 (10): 1175–99.

Horton, Chris. 2016. 'Taiwan May Be First in Asia to Legalize Same-Sex Marriage'. *The New York Times*, 18 November, Retrieved on 18 May 2018 from https://www.nytimes.com/2016/11/19/world/asia/taiwan-gay-marriage-legalize.html.

Horton, Chris. 2017a. 'Taiwan Is Embracing Marriage Equality, and Refining Its Own Identity'. *Nikkei Asian Review* (7 December).

Horton, Chris. 2017b. 'Court Ruling Could Make Taiwan First Place in Asia to Legalize Gay Marriage'. *The New York Times*, 24 May. Retrieved on 15 May 2018 from https://www.nytimes.com/2017/05/24/world/asia/taiwan-same-sex-marriage-court.html.

Inagaki, Kana. 2016. 'Line App Looks to Export Asian Popularity to New Markets'. *Financial Times*, 4 June. Retrieved on 11 June 2020 from https://www.ft.com/content/3a37bcc4-2974-11e6-8b18-91555f2f4fde.

Kingston, Jeff. 2016. 'Same-Sex Marriage Sparks a "Culture War" in Taiwan'. *The Japanese Times*, 10 December. Retrieved on 23 June 2017 from http://www.japantimes.co.jp/opinion/2016/12/10/commentary/sex-marriage-sparks-culture-war-taiwan/#.WU2Z6GjyvIU,Opinion.

Kong, Travis. 2016. 'The Sexual in Chinese Sociology: Homosexuality Studies in Contemporary China'. *The Sociological Review* 64: 495–514. DOI: 10.1111/1467–954X.12372.

Kropczynski, Jessica, and Seungahn Nah. 2010. 'Virtually Networked Housing Movement: Hyperlink Network Structure of Housing Social Movement Organizations'. *New Media & Society* 13 (5): 689–703.

Lin, Nan. 2001. *Social Capital: A Theory of Social Structure and Action*. New York: Cambridge University Press.

Lin, Nan, and Bonnie Erickson, eds. 2008. *Social Capital: An International Research Program*. Oxford: Oxford University Press.

Mazharul Islam, Mohammed, Essam Habes, and Mohammed Mahmudul Alam. 2018. 'The Usage and Social Capital of Mobile Phones and Their Effect on the Performance of Microenterprise: An Empirical Study'. *Technological Forecasting and Social Change* 132: 156–64.

McCarthy, John, and Mayer Zald. 1977. 'Resource Mobilization and Social Movement: A Partial Theory'. *American Journal of Sociology* 82 (6): 1212–41.

Mou, Yi, and Carolyn Lin. 2017. 'The Impact of Online Social Capital on Social Trust and Risk Perception'. *Asian Journal of Communication* 27 (6): 563–81.

Phua, Joe, and Seung-A Annie Jin. 2011. 'Finding a Home Away from Home: The Use of Social Networking Sites by Asia-Pacific Students in the United States for Bridging and Bonding Social Capital'. *Asian Journal of Communication* 21 (5): 504–19.

Putnam, Robert. 2000. *Bowling Alone: The Collapse and Revival of American Community*. New York: Simon & Schuster.

Ribeiro, Manoel, Raphael Ottoni, Robert West, Virgílio Almeida, and Wagner Meira, Jr. 2019. 'Auditing Radicalization Pathways on YouTube'. *ARXIV*. Retrieved on 10 June 2020 from https://arxiv.org/abs/1908.08313.

Rich, Timothy, and Isabel Eliassen. 2019. 'Taiwanese Views on Homosexuality Based on Proximity of Relationship, Study Shows'. *Taiwan Sentinel*, 3 June. Retrieved on 1 March 2020 from https://sentinel.tw/taiwanese-views-on-homosexuality-based-on-proximity-of-relationship-study-shows/.

Smith, Nicola. 2016. 'Professor's Death Could See Taiwan Become First Asian Country to Allow Same-Sex Marriage'. *The Guardian*, 28 October. Retrieved on 1 March 2020 from https://www.theguardian.com/world/2016/oct/28/professors-death-could-see-taiwan-become-first-asian-country-to-allow-same-sex-marriage.

Steger, Isabella. 2018. 'How Taiwan Battled Fake Anti-LGBT News before Its Vote on Same-Sex Marriage'. *QUARTZ*, 22 November. Retrieved on 7 January 2019 from https://qz.com/1471411/chat-apps-like-line-spread-anti-lgbt-fake-news-before-taiwan-same-sex-marriage-vote/.

Tashman, Brian. 2015. 'Far-Right: Flee America before God Destroys Us for Gay Marriage!' *Right Wing Watch*, 26 June. Retrieved on 1 March 2020 from https://www.rightwingwatch.org/post/far-right-flee-america-before-god-destroys-us-for-gay-marriage/.

Tcheng, Jonathan. 2017. 'A First in Asia: Taiwan to Legalize Same-Sex Marriage: Court Ruling Opens the Way to Marriage Equality'. *Human Rights Watch*, 24 May. Retrieved 15 May 2018 from https://www.hrw.org/news/2017/05/24/first-asia-taiwan-legalize-same-sex-marriage.

Tian, Xiaoli. 2016. 'Network Domains in Social Networking Sites: Expectations, Meanings, and Social Capital'. *Information, Communication & Society* 19 (2): 188–202, DOI: 10.1080/1369118X.2015.1050051.

Today. 2020. 'Taiwan Gay Couples Urge Foreign Marriage Rights after Tsai Win'. *Today*, 21 January. Retrieved on 1 March 2020 from https://www.todayonline.com/world/taiwan-gay-couples-urge-foreign-marriage-rights-after-tsai-win.

TRT World. 2019. 'How Social Media and Tech Fuel the Far Right, Explained'. *TRT World*, 4 September. Retrieved on 10 June 2020 from https://www.trtworld.com/magazine/how-social-media-and-tech-fuel-the-far-right-explained-29517.

Wang, Amber, and Sean Chang. 2018. 'Anti-Gay Marriage Groups Win Taiwan Referendum Battle'. *AFP*, 24 November. Retrieved on 1 March 2020 from https://news.yahoo.com/taiwan-awaits-results-key-election-test-gay-marriage-110924346.html.

Williams, Dmitri. 2006. 'On and Off the "Net: Scales for Social Capital in an Online Era'. *Journal of Computer-Mediated Communication* 11: 593–628.

Wilson, Bruce. 2014. 'The National Christian Foundation Anti-LGBT Funding Encyclopedia'. Retrieved on 9 March 2020 from https://twocare.org/the-national-christian-foundation-anti-lgbt-funding-encyclopedia/.

Wilson, Scott. 2015. 'Mixed Verdict on Chinese Environmental Public Interest Lawsuits'. *The Diplomat*, 20 June. Retrieved on 31 May 2019 from https://thediplomat.com/2015/07/mixed-verdict-on-chinese-environmental-public-interest-lawsuits/.

Yang, Kenneth C. C., ed. 2018. *Multi-Platform Advertising Strategies in the Global Marketplace, Advances in Marketing, Customer Relationship Management, and Electronic Services (AMCRMES) Book Series*. Hershey, PA: IGI-Global Publisher.

Yang, Kenneth C. C., and Yowei Kang. 2020. 'Employing Digital Media Technologies for Environmental Communication Campaigns in People's Republic of China'. In *When the Local Meets the Digital: Implications and Consequences for Environmental Communication*, edited by Joana Pont, Pieter Maeseele, Annika Sjölander, Mishra Mishra, and Kerrie Foxwell-Norton, 49–67. Geneva: Springer Nature IMACR Palgrave Series. DOI: 10.1007/978-3-030-37330-6_3.

Yen, Steven, and Ernest Zampelli. 2017. 'Religiousness and Support for Same-Sex Marriage: An Endogenous Treatment Approach'. *Social Science Quarterly* 98 (1): 196–211. DOI: 10.1111/ssqu.12306.

Yin, Robert. 2017. *Case Study Research and Applications: Design and Methods (6th ed.)*. Thousand Oaks: Sage.

Zhang, Laney. 2019. 'Taiwan: Same-Sex Marriage Law Enters into Effect'. *Global Legal Monitor*,18 June. Retrieved on 1 March 2020 from https://www.loc.gov/law/foreign-news/article/taiwan-same-sex-marriage-law-enters-into-effect/.

Zúñiga, Homero Gil de, Matthew Barnidge, and Andrés Scherman. 2017. 'Media Social Capital, Offline Social Capital, and Citizenship: Exploring Asymmetrical Social Capital Effects'. *Political Communication* 34 (1): 44–68.

Part II

SOCIAL NETWORK, SOCIAL MOVEMENT AND THE GENDERED FAR-RIGHT

Chapter 5

Twitter as a Channel for Frame Diffusion? Hashtag Activism and the Virality of #HeterosexualPrideDay

JP Armstrong

On 29 June 2015, the #HeterosexualPrideDay hashtag first achieved trending status. In 2016, the self-declared creator of #HeterosexualPrideDay, @_Jack-NForTweets, encouraged users to employ the hashtag as a means of declaring and joining an online Heterosexual Pride celebration (Hanson 2016). Following this call, the hashtag resurfaced as a global trend on 29 June 2016 (and again on the same day in 2017). Rather than disparage LGBT Pride using explicitly anti-gay rhetoric, supportive tweets claimed Heterosexual Pride in the name of equality (co-opting the language of the mainstream LGBT movement), and claimed that opposition to the #HeterosexualPrideDay hashtag was both 'hypocritical' and 'heterophobic' (Armstrong 2021). Despite its popularity in 2016 and 2017, #HeterosexualPrideDay failed to gain traction and return as a trending topic in 2018. However, a year later the organizers of a seemingly disconnected offline Heterosexual Pride event employed similar rhetoric to that of the #HeterosexualPrideDay supporters. On 31 August 2019, a Straight Pride Parade was carried out by hundreds of supporters in Boston, Massachusetts (Garrison 2019). John Hugo, president of Super Happy Fun America (the organizers of the parade), says the following of Heterosexual Pride: 'Straight people are an oppressed majority. We will fight for the right of straights everywhere to express pride in themselves without fear of judgement and hate. The day will come when straights will finally be included as equals among all of the other orientations' (Super Happy Fun America n.d.).

Though these events were separate and had different organizers, and despite the availability of other rhetorical approaches to characterizing Heterosexual Pride (e.g. as explicitly anti-gay), the use of strikingly similar rhetoric between the online #HeterosexualPrideDay to the offline Straight Pride Parade in Boston calls for inquiry into a potential linkage between the two. Given that #HeterosexualPrideDay rose to popularity online, what role could Twitter have played in the circulation and increased public availability of the rhetoric shared between the two events?

In this chapter, I define the rhetoric shared between Twitter's #HeterosexualPrideDay and Boston's Straight Pride Parade as constitutive of a particular mode of framing Heterosexual Pride – a call for heterosexual equality. Collective action frames are interpretive schemas 'intended to mobilize potential adherents and constituents, to garner bystander support, and to demobilize antagonists' (Snow and Benford 1988, 198). However, the purpose of this chapter is not to dissect the equality framing strategy employed by either the users who tweeted in support of #HeterosexualPrideDay on Twitter or the organizers of the Straight Pride Parade in Boston – nor do I intend to merely describe the overlap in collective action frames. Instead, I explore the role Twitter may have played in frame diffusion: the spread of collective action frames and framing approaches from one episode of contentious collective action to another (Benford and Snow 2000). How did the cluster of collective action frames, which coalesced around #HeterosexualPrideDay, an online episode of contentious collective action, carry forward to Boston's offline Straight Pride Parade? This occurred even though the two episodes had different organizers and despite the availability of other means of framing Heterosexual Pride (e.g. as explicitly anti-gay). Rather than demonstrate 'the mere fact of diffusion' this approach attempts to offer some insight into 'the means by which it does' (McAdam and Rucht 1993, 3). McAdam and Rucht argue that diffusion involves four distinct elements: a transmitter, an adopter, the object of diffusion and a channel of diffusion (linking the transmitter to the adopter). I argue that the equality framing strategy (the object of diffusion) employed by supporters of #HeterosexualPrideDay (the transmitter) was widely circulated on Twitter (a potential channel of diffusion) increasing its public availability, thus, increasing the likelihood that it might be picked up and carried forward by others such as the organizers of Boston's Straight Pride Parade (the possible adopter). I suggest that the case of Heterosexual Pride illustrates Twitter's ample potential for channelling frame diffusion.

I centre this argument around socio-technical affordances or, put more simply, 'what material artifacts such as media technologies allow people to do' (Bucher and Helmond 2017, 235). Via a discussion of Twitter's features and resulting socio-technical affordances, I demonstrate the role the hashtag #HeterosexualPrideDay played in increasing the public availability of the equality framing of Heterosexual Pride. I argue that the use of hashtag activism – the 'act of fighting for or supporting a cause with the use of hashtags as the primary channel to raise awareness of an issue and encourage debate via social media' (Tombleson and Wolf 2017, 15) in which hashtags act as vehicles for collective action frames – contributed to this circulation. Given that a hashtag's likelihood of trending magnifies as its use increases, any employment of a hashtag, whether supportive or oppositional, contributes to its visibility. Thus, in the case of hashtag activism, repeated uses of a hashtag amplifies the hashtag itself as well as its associated frame(s) by demanding attention from a broader set of users. The larger the audience, the higher the likelihood that a user with a compatible belief system will find the collective action frame(s) resonant and re-employ the frame(s), whether it be online or offline.

A BRIEF HISTORY OF HETEROSEXUAL PRIDE EVENTS IN THE UNITED STATES (1990–2019)

A report authored by The Governor's Commission on Gay and Lesbian Youth (1993) indicates that in the United States Heterosexual Pride events have occurred as early as 1990. I provide a brief timeline starting with this event, documenting notable Heterosexual Pride events which occurred before the end of 2019. The 1990 Straight Pride Rally, organized by Young Americans for Freedom, occurred at the University of Massachusetts Amherst on 24 April, and featured the waving of both Bibles and American flags, as well as the 'vitriolic denouncements of lesbians, gays, and bisexuals' (21). *The New York Times* (1990) reports that 150 people attended the rally. However, about half of those present were counter-protesters decrying the event. The Lesbian, Bisexual, Gay Alliance responded to this event with an event of its own – which was disrupted by the Young Americans for Freedom. Theodore Maravelias, founder of the Straight-Pride Rally and one of the Young Americans for Freedom's leaders, had this to say: 'I'm against homosexuality because I think it is perverse. It goes against God's law. . . . I don't want my tax money subsidizing a gay week'. The Straight-Pride Rally returned to campus in 1991 as part of a larger Conservative Awareness Week organized by Young Americans for Freedom in cooperation with other conservative groups such as the Republican Club and the New Americans (*New York Times* 1991). Glen Caroline, president of the Republican Club, said the event would not consist of 'gay-bashing' and was organized for heterosexuals to 'proudly declare their sexuality'. Founder Theodore Maravelias argued that 'gay rights actions were distracting attention from more important issues, like the decline of the traditional family' and said this during the rally: 'They don't want rights, they want to force a sexuality on me. . . . Keep it in the closet!' Although the event drew a similar number of supporters as the year prior, about 500 counter-protesters showed up to decry the event (*New York Times* 1991).

The Heterosexual Pride mantra re-merged as a point of conversation when, on 27 June 2015, Anthony Rebello took to the Internet to criticize 'the whole gay marriage thing' (Sieczkowski 2015). This post followed the Supreme Court's 'decision to legalize same-sex marriage nationwide' and included a link to a Facebook event for a Heterosexual Parade in Seattle, Washington on 25 July 2015 'in the name of equality [and] equal rights' and in celebration of heterosexuality and the 'right to be heterosexual'. Rebello's 'Pride' post labelled marriage equality a 'trend' and 'a cry for attention', meanwhile employing anti-trans rhetoric:

> Gay Mafia? Maybe animals should be allowed to get married? Would they govern and tax them too? While they're at it, how about equal rights for insects? In my opinion, there is a difference between a man and a woman. If you can't appreciate those differences, you can't enjoy those differences. I don't agree with boys turning into girls, and I don't agree with girls turning into boys. The word/meaning of 'Pride' doesn't belong to the gay/lgbt community, it belongs to everyone. That includes us good old fashioned straight people. The way I see it, in my opinion, some boys never turn into men, and some girls never turn into women. What a shitshow. 'Welcome to the other side of the rainbow' Really? No thanks. (Rebello 2015)

Sieczkowski (2015) reports that Rebello was the only person to attend the Heterosexual Parade, 'marching with balloons and a cardboard sign reading "Straight Pride". On 31 October 31 2015, under a post labelled 'Double Standard', Rebello wrote that he has 'nothing against gay people', 'meant no harm to anyone' and 'thought it was funny'. Further, he suggested that people had misunderstood his stance on same-sex marriage. Rebello attempted to clarify his stance again on 25 July 2016, a year after the Heterosexual Parade, within a blog post titled 'Cross Examination'. He argued that the Heterosexual Parade was 'an event where heterosexual folks can find community and identity, a place for Heterosexuals to identify with other Heterosexuals and be #ProudToBe Heterosexual'. Further, Rebello identified as 'someone who supports #EqualRights' and stated: 'I figured the #LGBTQ would support the fact that I was just as happy to be Heterosexual as they are to be gay/transgender/bi'. However, he explicitly re-endorsed the anti-trans rhetoric within his original post.

On 29 June 2015, two days after Rebello's 'Pride' post announcing the Heterosexual Parade (but before the event itself), the #HeterosexualPrideDay hashtag began trending on Twitter at the town level in Dallas-Fort Worth, Texas. Despite this timing, there are no clear connections between these two events. Hanson (2016) credits Twitter user @_JackNForTweets as the first to mark 29 June as Heterosexual Pride Day using the hashtag. On the same day the next year, the self-declared creator of #HeterosexualPrideDay encouraged users to employ the hashtag as a means of declaring and joining a Heterosexual Pride celebration. Later tweets from @_JackNForTweets suggest that the hashtag was satirical in nature. However, given that the proposed date of the Heterosexual Pride Day celebration fell on a date associated with the Stonewall riots, #HeterosexualPrideDay might be better seen as an attempt at trolling (to 'cause disruption and/or to trigger or exacerbate conflict' [Hardaker 2010, 237] for amusement). Since @_JackNForTweets' use of the hashtag in 2015, the presence of #HeterosexualPrideDay has surged. On 29 June in both 2016 and 2017, the hashtag returned and became part of a global Twitter conversation as a worldwide trend. In another work, I analysed a subset of tweets containing the hashtag from 29 June 2016 and 29 June 2017 – all of which are from users in the United States (Armstrong 2021). I found that most supportive tweets are not explicitly anti-gay. Instead, they co-opt the language of the mainstream LGBT movement and frame Heterosexual Pride as an issue of equality. Supportive #HeterosexualPrideDay tweets argue that heterosexuals should also have a day to celebrate their sexuality. These tweets consider establishing a Heterosexual Pride day a step towards equality via the argument that, if equality is the true aim of LGBT Pride, Pride is equally deserved by heterosexuals. Any criticism of this argument from opponents – highlighting the privileges the heterosexual community enjoy and the oppression the LGBT community faces – is labelled as 'hypocritical' by Twitter users in support of #HeterosexualPrideDay and used as 'evidence' of the 'heterophobia' heterosexuals face. However, most tweets are oppositional; hijacking the hashtag as a means of decrying Heterosexual Pride. As pointed out by some tweets, the irony inherent to this distribution is that oppositional tweets fuelled the #HeterosexualPrideDay hashtag's global trend. Despite its popularity in prior years #HeterosexualPrideDay failed to return as a trending topic (at any level) in 2018.

Though the #HeterosexualPrideDay hashtag disappeared from the public conversation, there is evidence of continued interest in the concept of Heterosexual Pride offline. Three Straight Pride Parades (one in Modesto, California, another in Boston, Massachusetts, and a third in Dallas, Texas) made headlines in 2019. Wigglesworth (2019) reports that the event in Modesto, California, did 'not appear to be affiliated' with the other two events. The Straight Pride Parade in Modesto was organized by Don Grundmann (the originator of the National Straight Pride Coalition, Citizens Against Perversion and the American Warrior Ministry), Mylinda Mason as well as others who sought to protect 'the values that made America great' (Valine, Rowland, and Holland 2019). According to its website, the National Straight Pride Coalition seeks to prevent 'the current and future generations of all races and colours from being destroyed by the inherent malevolence of the Homosexual Movement':

> 'Straight Pride' is hence on the frontline of the Religious War between Christianity and its Satanism/Humanism opponent. Our standard bearer is Jesus Christ

> while the standard bearer of Satanism/Humanism is the Marquis De Sade. We represent the Culture of Life while our Satanist/Humanist opponents represent the Culture of Death.
>
> The battle between these 2 completely opposing religious beliefs is hence for the souls of both all citizens and the nation as a whole.
>
> We appeal to our Creator for strength in the battle before us as we fight to both stop the Jihad of the LGBT War Machine upon the children of our nation and to protect all races from the genocidal attack of PP upon humanity.
>
> We welcome you to join us in this great Crusade to save countless souls and to defeat these great Enemies of Humanity. (National Straight Pride Coalition n.d.)

The Straight Pride Parade took place on 24 August 2019 and, after experiencing numerous venue-related difficulties, the Straight Pride supporters settled on staging the event in front of Planned Parenthood (Valine, Rowland, and Holland 2019). The event was attended by 'about 200 people' but only about 20 people were there supporting the event; the majority were counter-protesters:

> While some yelling matches ensued when the two sides met, no physical altercations were reported. Chants veered from 'Love not hate makes America great!' and 'Nazis go home!' to 'Four more years!' and 'Build the wall!'
>
> Straight Pride protesters also had signs including 'Planned Parenthood Harvests Baby Parts' and 'Lord, Forgive Us and Our Nation'.

In response to being outnumbered, organizer Don Grundmann had this to say: 'That does not change the truth of our message. They talk about diversity and attack us. So-called diversity and tolerance is a one-way street'.

A separate Straight Pride Parade was organized by Super Happy Fun America and carried out in Boston, Massachusetts, on 31 August 2019 (Garrison 2019). Organizers of this event employed much different rhetoric than the explicitly anti-gay rhetoric employed by organizers of the event in Modesto, California. Super Happy Fun America's website asserts that 'Straight Rights are Human Rights!' and encourages everyone, regardless of sexual orientation, to embrace the heterosexual community's 'diverse history, culture, and identity'. Further, the website features a petition 'asking the LGBTQ community to include the S for straight. Let's not exclude the women and men of this world that procreate. After all, without us there would be no LGBTQ. We are asking for fairness and total inclusion'.

The parade itself was advertised as being 'held to achieve inclusivity and spread awareness of issues impacting straights in Greater Boston and beyond'. Initially Super Happy Fun America promised a flag-raising ceremony. However, this was not approved by Mayor Martin Walsh (Cotter 2019). Organizers equated the decision with discrimination, accused administration of not being ‘committed to creating a supportive environment for straights’ and vowed to ‘continue to fight for equality until the Walsh administration embraces our community and a more progressive vision of the future’. The Straight Pride Parade started at Copley Square and ended at City Hall. The event was attended by ‘a few hundred’ supporters, as well as counter-protested by thousands of opponents, and featured prominent gay right-wing figure Milo Yiannopoulos as parade grand marshal (Garrison 2019). Mark Sahady, vice president of Super Happy Fun America (with ties to another right-wing group Resist Marxism), welcomed participants with this message: ‘Whether you are straight and part of the oppressed majority, or here as an ally supporting us, we welcome you to the greatest parade in the history of the world!’

Supporters were encouraged to ‘fight against heterophobia in our modern society’, and Teresa Stephens Richenberger, Super Happy Fun America’s spiritual advisor, was quoted as saying: ‘We’re standing up today because we’ve been told to sit down, to suck it up, be quiet. You can’t offend nobody. . . . I don’t want to offend no one. If you’re gay, go be gay. That’s OK. But I’m straight and I have a right to teach my son to be straight and to marry a woman when he gets older’ (Garrison 2019). Counter-protestors ‘shouted “Nazi scum!” Some greeted the straight-pride marchers with their middle fingers and yelled expletives’. Addressing the counter-protesters, Mark Sahady responded by saying: ‘Today, we are showing them that their hate cannot stop us. . . . We shall overcome. Free speech!’

Super Happy Fun America attempted to organize a subsequent event in Dallas, Texas, on 16 November 2019 (Nash 2019a). This time organization of the event was led by Teresa Stephens Richenberger. Advertising for this event was distinct from the Boston event, centring on ‘standing up’ for ‘Biblical values’. Topics to be discussed at the event included ‘Marriage values (One man and one woman)’ and ‘Ploys of the RADICAL left wing LGBTQ groups trying to shut down our businesses and churches’. The event was cancelled at the last minute because permits were not secured (Nash 2019b). Despite the cancellation, two supporters showed up from Boston – presumably affiliated with Super Happy Fun America (Sonoma 2019). These two supporters are documented as yelling, ‘We know there are only two genders’ at the twenty counter-protesters. They also claimed to be ‘part of the oppressed majority’. Police had to step in and separate the two groups.

COLLECTIVE ACTION FRAMES

Given this history, how do we characterize Heterosexual Pride? There is an important distinction between episodes of contentious collective action, which involve collective action 'when it is used by people who lack regular access to representative institutions, who act in the name of new or unaccepted claims and who behave in ways that fundamentally challenge others or authorities' (Tarrow 2011, 7), and social movements, which involve contentious collective action 'based on common purposes and social solidarities, in sustained interaction with elites, opponents, and authorities' (Tarrow 2011, 9). Some of these events can surely be characterized as contentious collective action due to the reactionary nature of Heterosexual Pride. Heterosexual Pride is a clear challenge to LGBT Pride. Politically significant social movements like the LGBT movement often provoke opposition from actors who perceive these movements' goals as a threat to their own interests or social position. Thus, the critical characteristic of these reactionary mobilizations is their 'dependence on and reaction to an initiating movement' (Meyer and Staggenborg 1996, 1632). But what of the other three empirical properties: does Heterosexual Pride meet the criteria to be considered a social movement? Seemingly not. These events had (nearly) completely different participant bases (save for the Boston and Dallas events) and were sporadic (as opposed to sustained). Further, claims were not coherent. In some instances, the Heterosexual Pride mantra was employed to carry forward explicitly anti-gay sentiments. In other cases, Heterosexual Pride was employed as a means of demanding the equal right to publicly announce pride in one's heterosexuality. Given the use of the Pride moniker, we should see both rhetorical approaches to Heterosexual Pride as reactionary responses to and, thus, counter-framings of LGBT Pride. However, this rhetorical diversity indicates a variety of different ways of framing Heterosexual Pride as employed by these actors.

Scholarly interest in collective action frames emerged from a growing recognition that interrogating the relationship between social psychological processes and structural and organizational factors is necessary for a better understanding of mobilization. Snow and his colleagues (Snow et al. 1986) highlight the role collective action frames play in inspiring 'support for and participation in' (Snow et al. 1986, 464) contentious collective action. More generally, frames work to 'render events or occurrences meaningful and thereby function to organize experience and guide action' (Benford and Snow 2000, 614). Collective action frames perform a similar function but are 'intended to mobilize potential adherents and constituents, to garner bystander support, and to demobilize antagonists' (Snow and Benford 1988, 198). This emphasis on frames and micromobilization developed in reaction to a critique of existing theories which focus on 'organizational and macromobilization considerations' (Snow et al. 1986, 466) but fail to adequately address 'that what is at issue is not merely the presence or absence of grievances, but the manner in which grievances are interpreted and the generation and diffusion of those interpretations' (Snow et al. 1986, 466). Snow and his colleagues argue that achieving frame alignment by rendering 'individual interests, values and beliefs' compatible with the 'activities, goals and ideologies' (Snow et al. 1986, 464) guiding contentious collective action is a necessary condition for mobilization. Framing often begins as a less conscious process. However, framing generally becomes 'more strategic as the battle is waged' (Noakes and Johnson 2005, 7). But whether users truly believe in the frames they employ or do so out of tact does not change the impact of said frames. Framing is an ongoing process and, thus, collective action frames evolve as time goes by. For example, conflicts with opponents trigger changes to framing approaches (Meyer and Staggenborg 1996). Supporters must reframe their concerns and calls for action in response to opponents' counterframes, which seek to 'discredit, undermine, rebut, and otherwise neutralize' (Benford 1997, 418) their collective action frames.

My analysis of #HeterosexualPrideDay provides insight into the collective action frames employed by supporters of the hashtag (Armstrong 2021). Employing Burke and Bernstein's (2014) concept of frame co-optation, I argue that #HeterosexualPrideDay supporters usurp the mainstream LGBT movement's equality frame (as well as the Pride moniker) – subverting its original intent. By distancing themselves from explicit prejudice, #HeterosexualPrideDay supporters avoid the anti-gay label (Browne and Nash 2017). Co-opting the equality frame allowed proponents of the hashtag to frame themselves as victims of 'heterophobia' and cite backlash as evidence of 'an 'intolerant left' (649). It also enabled supporters to frame #HeterosexualPrideDay opponents as 'hypocrites' who are not actually interested in the equality that they themselves seek. The rhetorical similarities between the support for #HeterosexualPrideDay and Boston's Straight Pride Parade indicate the use of the same equality framing strategy. Further, this overlap calls for the consideration of diffusion theory, which 'attempts to explain when and how practices travel' (Wood 2012, 6). While a causal relationship between the two episodes of contentious collective action is unverifiable, the re-emergence of #HeterosexualPrideDay's equality framing at the Straight Pride March in Boston poses an interesting theoretical question concerning the role Twitter may have played in spreading and, thus, increasing the public availability of this mode of framing Heterosexual Pride. In the sections that follow, I use the case of Heterosexual Pride to highlight the socio-technical affordances of Twitter and discuss its potential for channelling frame diffusion.

HASHTAG ACTIVISM AND THE VIRALITY OF #HETEROSEXUALPRIDEDAY

Sidney Tarrow asserts that 'perhaps the most dramatic change in social movement organizing in the last few decades has been the impact of the Internet and, more generally, of electronic communication' (Tarrow 2011, 137). Prior to the advent of the Internet, the news media exercised primary control over which issues were communicated to the public as well as how said issues were framed (Tufecki 2017). Activists and movements, seeking positive coverage as a means of garnering support from the public, were forced to develop strategies to work within this system. In some cases, political stunts have been used to attract news media attention. In others, formal organizations were developed to liaise with news media. However, both strategies presented unique risks. For example, the flamboyance of stunts could overshadow movement concerns resulting in trivialization. As well, professionalization could 'submerge the radical nature and dynamism that existed in grassroots movements' (Tufecki 2017, 205). Though these strategies still exist today, the evolution from basic one-on-one forms of electronic communication to sites that can connect innumerable users offers activists and movements the ability to bypass news media, 'act as their own media' (Tufecki 2017, xxvi), and spread their message broadly. Because social networking sites 'have lower barriers to access and participation, and thus penetrate wider social networks' (Juris 2012, 267), they can enable the rapid spread of information beyond insular activist communities.

Zeynep Tufecki suggests that this is one of the most effective uses of social networking sites, as they offer activists a means of increasing narrative capacity or enhancing 'the ability of the movement to frame its story on its own terms, to spread its worldview' (Tufecki 2017, 192). The latter component of this definition seems to be conceptually synonymous with the ability to diffuse frames. However, when attempting to make statements about the capacity-heightening potential of such sites, we must go beyond making blanket statements about all networking sites. Instead, we need to consider site-specific socio-technical affordances to fully understand how these various sites differently facilitate the spread of information. Socio-technical affordances are 'practices that technologies afford' (Schrock 2015, 1233) as a result of their material aspects or features. Understanding these features and resulting socio-technical affordances is essential if we are to understand the circulation of the equality framing of #HeterosexualPrideDay or, more broadly, Twitter's potential for channelling frame diffusion.

Twitter, a microblogging site, has become one of the most popular social networking sites in the world. Oltmann and colleagues (2020) assert that Twitter's features 'include the ability to retweet others' posts (RT), reply to other users (using the @ function), and hashtags (#)' (Oltmann et al. 2020, 3). They argue that two socio-technical affordances of the hashtag are spreadability and visibility. Illustrating the relationship between the two socio-technical affordances, popular hashtags can be broadcasted to Twitter's userbase if they trend: 'If a large number of people post tweets containing the same hashtag within a short space of time, that hashtag will be said to be trending, and current trends are available for users to browse and view in real time' (Scott 2015, 12).

Hence, as hashtags gain traction, their likelihood of trending (and, consequently, reaching others) magnifies. The use of a hashtag drives it further into the public, increasing the likelihood that others will pick it up and circulate it even further. In other words, the base of users who may potentially interact with and re-employ a hashtag grows exponentially with repeated use. These two socio-technical affordances enable hashtag activism which, in part, involves the 'act of fighting for or supporting a cause with the use of hashtags as the primary channel to raise awareness of an issue' (Tombleson and Wolf 2017, 15). Hashtags are employed as vehicles for collective action frames, carrying them forward into a larger audience with the potential of mobilizing support for an issue. This was the case in 2016 and 2017 when hashtag activism pulled attention towards the constellation of frames which surrounded supportive use of the #HeterosexualPrideDay hashtag. Data from Trendogate – a website that monitors and logs trending hashtags from Twitter – shows the rise in popularity of the #HeterosexualPrideDay hashtag (see table 5.1).[1] It records the number of times a hashtag's use passes the threshold for trending status at three different levels: town, country and worldwide. Additionally, Trendogate indicates both where and when the hashtag was trending.

#HeterosexualPrideDay trended for the first time in 2015. This trend was notably short-lived and isolated to Dallas-Fort Worth, Texas, on 29 June 2015. However, in 2016 #HeterosexualPrideDay reappeared, this time garnering much more attention and becoming a trend in numerous locations

Table 5.1. Trending History of #HeterosexualPrideDay Hashtag on Twitter

Year	*Level*	*Number of Times Trending on 29 June*	*Number of Times Trending on 30 June*	*Number of Times Trending on 1 July*	*Number of Times Trending on 2 July*	*Number of Times Trending on 3 July*
2015	Town	1	0	0	0	0
	Country	0	0	0	0	0
	Worldwide	0	0	0	0	0
2016	Town	577	392	42	0	0
	Country	61	77	6	0	0
	Worldwide	1	0	0	0	0
2017	Town	280	284	102	0	19
	Country	25	43	19	1	0
	Worldwide	2	0	0	0	0

Source: Author.

not only at the town level but also at the country level (see table 5.1). It remained trending at these levels from 29 June 2016 to 1 July 2016. On 29 June 2016, the hashtag was so widely tweeted that it even became a worldwide trend. The next year, in 2017, #HeterosexualPrideDay returned with a level of visibility similar to that of the prior year. The hashtag surfaced on 29 June 2017; this time occurring as a country-level trend until 2 July 2017 and a town-level trend until 3 July 2017. Just as in 2016, the hashtag was tweeted enough to become a worldwide trend on 29 June 2017 (this time twice). However, the successful trending of #HeterosexualPrideDay did not mean it was widely supported by Twitter's user base.

Another important socio-technical affordance offered by the hashtag is searchability (Oltmann, Cooper, and Proferes 2020). Hashtags act as hyperlinks on Twitter, allowing 'users to search for any content that includes the same tag' (Scott 2015, 12). This creates the opportunity for users globally to interact with one another around a similar topic. In the case of hashtag activism, this socio-technical affordance encourages discussion from a broad user base and creates space for debating the highlighted issue (Tombleson and Wolf 2017). However, bringing users together to negotiate the hashtag's associated cause provides political opponents with opportunities for disrupting the said cause. These hashtags can become intense sites of debate and can even be hijacked completely to promote the opposite of their original cause (Jackson and Foucault Welles 2015; Maireder and Schlögl 2014). This was the case with #HeterosexualPrideDay. As indicated in my other work on #HeterosexualPrideDay, the majority of tweets actually rejected rather than agreed with supporters' framing of Heterosexual Pride (Armstrong 2021). Complicating this, however, opposition seemed only to provide 'credibility' to supporters' argument that a 'hypocritical' and 'heterophobic' left is intent on diminishing the pride of heterosexuals. Further, because the hashtag affords spreadability and visibility, it is amplified with increased use (regardless of whether that use is in support of or in opposition to the associated hashtag). As a result, #HeterosexualPrideDay opponents predominately fuelled the hashtag's trending status.

In the case of Heterosexual Pride, hashtag activism worked to create a dilemma for progressive users. A dilemma action is 'a type of action in which opponents have to make a choice between two or more responses, each of which has significant negative aspects' (Sørensen and Martin 2014, 95). Opponents had the choice of refuting the equality framing of #HeterosexualPrideDay, risking accusations of 'hypocrisy' and 'heterophobia' as well as contributing to the hashtag's viral spread, or ignoring the reactionary hashtag 'to prevent inflated attention' (Zulli 2020, 211), leaving supporters' co-optation and bastardization of an equality frame unchecked. Ironically, by decrying the hashtag, opponents provided 'credibility' to the constellation of frames employed by #HeterosexualPrideDay supporters, which sought to highlight that opponents were 'hypocritical' and 'heterophobic', and facilitated the spread of this equality framing strategy beyond the social networks in which it was initially contained.

TWITTER AS A CHANNEL FOR FRAME DIFFUSION?

It is common for hashtag activism to be dismissed as slacktivism. Critics have dismissed activism on social networking sites such as hashtag activism as 'feel good' activism which requires little effort and has little political impact (see Morozov 2011). Though the idea that hashtags are politically inconsequential has been widely critiqued, the common misconception that hashtags have little political influence highlights the difficulty in recognizing their long-term effects (Mina 2019). Indeed, it would be incorrect, if not impossible, to declare that #HeterosexualPrideDay (the transmitter) directly caused the Straight Pride Parade in Boston, which followed its trending period. To do so would ignore the complex and relational interplay of structural and organizational processes which lead to this contentious collective action. However, I argue that when the #HeterosexualPrideDay hashtag trended in 2016 and 2017, largely due to the response by opponents, it brought widespread attention to the equality framing (the object of diffusion) employed by #HeterosexualPrideDay supporters. While trending hashtags such as #HeterosexualPrideDay may seem 'ephemeral', quickly rising in prominence before disappearing abruptly, hashtag activism (enabled by the socio-technical affordances of Twitter) amplified the constellation of collective action frames which coalesced around #HeterosexualPrideDay – bringing the frames more attention than could have been achieved otherwise. Thus, hashtag activism pushed said frames into the mainstream where they could be picked up by possible adopters with compatible core belief systems, demonstrating Twitter's strong potential for channelling frame diffusion.

This process – in which an adopter is mobilized by the collective action frames in question and proceeds to carry the framing approach forward as part of a separate episode of contentious collective action – marks the successful diffusion of a frame. However, achieving frame alignment is required for this mobilization to occur. Snow and colleagues (1986) argue that the main mode of alignment appears to be frame bridging, in which 'individuals who share common grievances and attributional orientations, but who lack the organizational base for expressing their discontents and for acting in pursuit of their interests' (Snow, Burke, Worden, and Benford 1986, 467) are connected to ideologically compatible collective action frames and called to action. Hashtag activism works by spreading a hashtag and its associated frames as widely as possible, increasing the likelihood that these frames will reach sympathetic users and frames will be bridged (as opposed to participation-related processes in which individuals or specific subpopulations are identified and targeted because they are assumed to have compatible belief systems). In other words, a wide net is cast to reach and engage new networks. A newly mobilized user might simply demonstrate support by using the hashtag and related supportive frames, thus contributing to the hashtag's trending status. However, this newly mobilized user might also carry the collective action frame(s) forward as part of a separate episode of contentious collective action (indicating successful frame diffusion). As demonstrated by this case study, the socio-technical affordances of Twitter facilitated the global circulation of the #HeterosexualPrideDay hashtag and, as a result, drew attention to the constellation of supportive frames which had coalesced around it. Increasing the public availability of this equality framing increased the likelihood that said frames might be seen by an agreeable user, resonate with the user and function as a call to action (possibly mobilizing separate instances of Heterosexual Pride contentious collective action). Theoretically, this demonstrates Twitter's potential for channelling frame diffusion.

CONCLUSION

Major right-wing ideologues such as Andrew Breitbart and Milo Yiannopoulos promote the idea that 'politics is always "downstream from culture"' (Nagle 2017, 40). The successful diffusion of regressive frames, as a means of spreading conservative ideology and mobilizing right-wing action, is central to this cultural change. There are striking similarities between the equality-framing approach I have described in this chapter and other right-wing rhetorics. Berbrier (1998) documents the call for White Pride as an example of what he refers to as new racist rhetoric:

> Embedded within this is the argument that whites and ethno-racial minority groups are comparable. The discussion of 'equivalence' more explicitly indicates how NRWS claim makers present whites as an ethno-racial minority group equivalent to all others on the American cultural landscape. As a result, those who would deny the discrimination that this putative minority group is said to experience are themselves stigmatized as racists. (Berbrier 1998, 444)

Further, consider the Nazi skinhead tactic of mobilizing young people to call for a white student union in the name of equality: 'the concept of the White student union appeals to the adolescent's need for fairness and balance. Without an understanding of cultural history, in which power has been slanted in the direction of straight, White males, the concept seems just' (Blazak 2001, 993). When said calls for white Pride or for white student unions are rightfully opposed or rejected, it can foster a victim mentality among the claimants making them susceptible to further mobilization efforts which target the said 'injustice'. 'This victim mentality is commonplace within right-wing ideologies which often 'regard whites as under attack' (Blee and Creasap, 2010, 275), and is strategically exploited to foster recruitment. Further, if we see Heterosexual Pride as reactionary, it can be likened to right-wing movements which seek 'to preserve the power and privileges of white Aryans' (Blee and Creasap 2010, 275). Indeed, it seems that the advances of marginalized groups are commonly framed as threats to a traditional way of life within right-wing political ideologies. These movements are made up of individuals who 'feel a great deal of strain as their traditional picture of the world and their place in it is threatened' (Blazak 2001, 988) by such activism. As a result, they seek to sustain the ideologies and structures underlying their social position of dominance and challenge these threats to the status quo.

Given the central role of social networking sites in right-wing movement activity, it is important that we ask how digital technologies are employed to facilitate this goal. Nagle (2017) argues that contemporary right-wing movements such as the alt-right often operate without the support of traditional media. Thus, without social networking sites, these movements would have a tremendously limited narrative capacity and, as a result, an equally limited ability to diffuse their frames. While this is not to employ a technological-determinist framework, which might declare that Twitter (or other social networking sites) is responsible for the success of such movements, this is to say that such technologies and their socio-technical affordances can be exploited to increase visibility (sometimes in unexpected ways). By strategically employing Internet technologies, these alt-right activists have been extremely successful in their goal to influence culture by 'spreading their ideas through their own alternative and almost exclusively online media content' (Nagle 2017, 53). This highlights the important role that social networking sites play in enhancing the narrative capacity of Internet-era right-wing movements and in facilitating the viral spread of conservative ideology. These political narratives are digitally circulated via socially coded text, photos and videos (e.g. memes) with the intent of reaching beyond the insular networks of right-wing activists and penetrating the broader public.

In this chapter I have highlighted the socio-technical affordances of Twitter which make it an exemplary tool for channelling frame diffusion. Via a discussion of hashtag activism and the case of Heterosexual Pride, I demonstrate that resistance to reactionary hashtags such as #HeterosexualPrideDay can serve not only as fodder for the proposition that the right is 'under attack' from an 'intolerant left' but can also propel the hashtag (and its associated collective action frames) into the spotlight. By increasing the public availability of these collective action frames, Twitter's trending feature also increases the likelihood that the said frames will reach and connect with users who are already susceptible to right-wing ideology and that the said users will carry them forward, online or offline. This dilemma, in which opponents must choose between refuting a regressive hashtag and contributing to its spread or leaving conservative ideology unchallenged, poses several questions for our future studies of right-wing mobilization tactics. For example, to what extent are progressive actors potentially implicated in the spread of conservative ideology online and resulting right-wing mobilizations? More importantly, what does this mean for possible ways of resisting Internet-era right-wing movements?

ACKNOWLEDGEMENTS

I thank the editors, Lesley Wood, Daniela Zuzunaga Zegarra and Jaye Garcia for their feedback on earlier drafts of this chapter.

NOTE

1. This data was captured from Trendogate (trendogate.com) on 1 January 2020. The website is no longer active as of 12 January 2021.

REFERENCES

Armstrong, JP. 2021. `Framing #HeterosexualPrideDay: Frame Co-optation and the Call for Heterosexual Equality'. Manuscript Under review, resubmitted on 21 April 2021.

Benford, Robert. 1997. 'An Insider's Critique of the Social Movement Framing Perspective'. *Sociological Inquiry* 67 (4): 409–30. https://doi.org/10.1111/j.1475-682X.1997.tb00445.x.

Benford, Robert, and David Snow. 2000. 'Framing Processes and Social Movements: An Overview and Assessment'. *Annual Review of Sociology* 26 (1): 611–39. https://doi.org/10.1146/annurev.soc.26.1.611.

Berbrier, Mitch. 1998. '"Half the Battle": Cultural Resonance, Framing Processes, and Ethnic Affectations in Contemporary White Separatist Rhetoric'. *Social Problems* 45 (4): 431–50. https://doi.org/10.2307/3097206.

Blazak, Randy. 2001. 'White Boys to Terrorist Men: Target Recruitment of Nazi Skinheads'. *American Behavioural Scientist* 44 (6): 982–1000. https://doi.org/10.1177/00027640121956629.

Blee, Kathleen M., and Kimberly A. Creasap. 2010. 'Conservative and Right-Wing Movements'. *Annual Review of Sociology* 36 (1): 269–86. http://dx.doi.org/10.1146/annurev.soc.012809.102602.

Browne, Kath, and Catherine J. Nash. 2017. 'Heteroactivism: Beyond Anti-Gay'. *ACME: An International Journal for Critical Geographies* 16 (4): 643–52. https://acme-journal.org/index.php/acme/article/view/1631/1298.

Bucher, Taina, and Anne Helmond. 2018. 'The Affordances of Social Media Platforms'. In *The SAGE Handbook of Social Media*, edited by J. Burgess, A. Marwick, and T. Poell, 233–53. London: SAGE. http://dx.doi.org/10.4135/9781473984066.n14.

Burke, Mary, and Mary Bernstein. 2014. 'How the Right Usurped the Queer Agenda: Frame Co-optation in Political Discourse'. *Sociological Forum* 29 (4): 830–50. https://doi.org/10.1111/socf.12122.

Cotter, Sean Philip. 2019. 'Straight Pride Parade Gets Permit to March in Boston – But Flag Won't Fly at City Hall'. *Boston Herald*, 27 June. https://www.bostonherald.com/2019/06/26/straight-pride-parade-receives-permit-to-march-in-boston-but-flag-wont-fly-at-city-hall/.

Dommu, Ron. 2019. 'Boston Straight Pride Parade Application Has Been Approved'. 26 June. https://www.out.com/news/2019/6/28/boston-straight-pride-parade-application-has-been-approved.

Garrison, Joey. 2019. 'Boston's Straight Pride Parade Draws Hundreds of Marchers and Even More Counter Protesters'. *USA Today*, 31August. https://www.usatoday.com/story/news/nation/2019/08/31/bostons-straight-pride-parade-here-after-months-debate/2167020001/.

Governor's Commission on Gay and Lesbian Youth. 1993. 'Making Colleges and Universities Safe for Gay and Lesbian Students: Report and Recommendations of the Governor's Commission on Gay and Lesbian Youth'. *Commonwealth of Massachusetts*. https://www.massresistance.org/docs/downloads/romney/CommReport_Making_Colleges_Safe_7-93.pdf.

Hanson, Hilary. 2016. '#HeterosexualPrideDay Is Trending: Here's How It Started'. *HuffPost*, 30 June.

Hardaker, Claire. 2010. 'Trolling in Asynchronous Computer-Mediated Communication: From User Discussions to Academic Definitions'. *Journal of Politeness Research* 6 (2): 215–42. https://doi.org/10.1515/jplr.2010.011.

Jackson, Sarah, and Brooke Foucault Welles. 2015. 'Hijacking #myNYPD: Social Media Dissent and Networked Counterpublics'. *Journal of Communication* 65 (6): 932–52. https://doi.org/10.1111/jcom.12185.

Juris, Jeffrey. 2012. 'Reflections on #Occupy Everywhere: Social Media, Public Space, and Emerging Logics of Aggregation'. *American Ethnologist: Journal of the American Ethnological Society* 39 (2): 259–79. https://doi.org/10.1111/j.1548-1425.2012.01362.x.

Maireder, Axel, and Stephan Schlögl. 2014. '24 Hours of an #Outcry: The Networked Publics of a Socio-Political Debate'. *European Journal of Communication* 29 (6): 687–702. https://doi.org/10.1177/0267323114545710.

McAdam, Doug, and Dieter Rucht. 1993. 'The Cross-National Diffusion of Movement Ideas'. *The Annals of the American Academy of Political and Social Science* 528 (1): 56–74. https://doi.org/10.1177/0002716293528001005.

Meyer, David S., and Suzanne Staggenborg. 1996. 'Movements, Countermovements, and the Structure of Political Opportunity'. *American Journal of Sociology* 101 (6): 1628–60. https://doi.org/10.1086/230869.

Mina, An Xiao. 2019. *Memes to Movements: How the World's Most Viral Media Is Changing Social Protest and Power*. Boston: Beacon Press.

Morozov, Evgeny. 2011. *The Net Delusion: The Dark Side of Internet Freedom*. New York: Public Affairs.

Nagle, Angela. 2017. *Kill All Normies: Online Culture Wars from 4chan and Tumblr to Trump and the Alt-Right*. Alresford, UK: Zero Books.

Nash, Tammye. 2019a. 'Straight Pride March Planned for Dallas'. *Dallas Voice*, 8 November. https://dallasvoice.com/straight-pride-march-planned-for-dallas/.

Nash, Tammye. 2019b. '"Straight Pride" Event in Dallas Being Scaled Back over Permit Fees'. *Dallas Voice*, 15 November. https://dallasvoice.com/straight-pride-event-in-dallas-being-scaled-back-over-permit-fees/.

National Straight Pride Coalition. n.d. 'Home'. https://nationalstraightpridecoalition.org/.

New York Times. 1990. 'Rallies Opposing Gay Students Disrupt Campuses'. *New York Times*, 6 May. https://www.nytimes.com/1990/05/06/style/campus-life-umass-mount-holyoke-rallies-opposing-gay-students-disrupt-campuses.html.

New York Times. 1991. 'Angry Gay Groups Drown Out Rally by Conservatives'. *New York Times*, 10 March. https://www.nytimes.com/1991/03/10/nyregion/campus-life-massachusetts-angry-gay-groups-drown-out-rally-by-conservatives.html.

Noakes, John, and Hank Johnston. 2005. 'Frames of Protest: A Road Map to a Perspective'. In *Frames of Protest: Social Movements and the Framing Perspective*, edited by H. Johnston, and J. Noakes, 1–29. Lanham: Rowman & Littlefield Publishers.

Oltmann, Shannon, Troy Cooper, and Nicholas Proferes. 2020. 'How Twitter's Affordances Empower Dissent and Information Dissemination: An Exploratory Study of the Rogue and Alt Government Agency Twitter Accounts'. *Government Information Quarterly* 37 (3): 1–10. https://doi.org/10.1016/j.giq.2020.101475.

Rebello, Anthony. 2015a. 'Double Standard'. Blog post, 31 October. http://smilemeariver.blogspot.com/2015/10/double-standard.html.

Rebello, Anthony. 2015b. 'Pride'. Blog post, 27 June. http://smilemeariver.blogspot.com/2015/06/pride.html?view=classic.

Rebello, Anthony. 2016. 'Cross Examination'. Blog post, 25 July. http://smilemeariver.blogspot.com/2016/07/cross-examination.html.

Schrock, Andrew. 2015. 'Communicative Affordances of Mobile Media: Portability, Availability, Locatability, and Multimediality'. *International Journal of Communication* 9 (1): 1229–46. https://ijoc.org/index.php/ijoc/article/view/3288/1363.

Scott, Kate. 2015. 'The Pragmatics of Hashtags: Inference and Conversational Style on Twitter'. *Journal of Pragmatics* 81 (1): 8–20. https://doi.org/10.1016/j.pragma.2015.03.015.

Sieczkowski, Cavan. 2015. 'This Heterosexual Pride Parade Could Not Have Failed Any Harder Than It Just Did'. *HuffPost*, 27 July. https://www.huffingtonpost.ca/entry/heterosexual-parade-anthony-rebello_n_55b63852e4b0224d8832b657?ri18n=true.

Snow, David, and Robert Benford. 1988. 'Ideology, Frame Resonance, and Participant Mobilization'. *International Social Movement Research* 1 (1): 197–218.

Snow, David, E. Burke Rochford, Jr., Steven Worden, and Robert Benford. 1986. 'Frame Alignment Processes, Micromobilization, and Movement Participation'. *American Sociological Review* 51 (4): 464–81. https://doi.org/10.2307/2095581.

Sonoma, Serena. 2019. 'Dallas Straight Pride Was the Biggest Flop of All'. *Out*, 17 November. https://www.out.com/news/2019/11/17/dallas-straight-pride-was-biggest-flop-all.

Sørensen, Majken, and Brian Martin. 2014. 'The Dilemma Action: Analysis of an Activist Technique'. *Peace & Change: A Journal of Peace Research* 39 (1): 73–100. https://doi.org/10.1111/pech.12053.

Super Happy Fun America. n.d. 'Home: About'. https://www.superhappyfunamerica.com/home/about/.

Super Happy Fun America. n.d. 'Home: Petition'. https://www.superhappyfunamerica.com/home/petition/.

Super Happy Fun America. n.d. 'Home: Straight Pride Flag'. https://www.superhappyfunamerica.com/home/straight-pride-flag/.

Super Happy Fun America. n.d. 'Our Team'. https://www.superhappyfunamerica.com/our-team/.

Super Happy Fun America. n.d. 'Straight Pride Parade: About'. https://www.superhappyfunamerica.com/parade/.

Tarrow, Sidney. 2011. *Power in Movement: Social Movements and Contentious Politics*. New York: Cambridge University Press.

Tombleson, Bridget, and Katharina Wolf. 2017. 'Rethinking the Circuit of Culture: How Participatory Culture Has Transformed Cross-Cultural Communication'. *Public Relations Review* 43 (1): 14–25. https://doi.org/10.1016/j.pubrev.2016.10.017.

Tufecki, Zeynep. 2017. *Twitter and Tear Gas: The Power and Fragility of Networked Protest*. New Haven: Yale University Press.

Valine, Kevin, Marijke Rowland, and John Holland. 2019. 'Modesto Protesters Outnumber Straight Pride Supporters at Tense but Peaceful Rally'. *The Modesto Bee*, 24 August. https://www.modbee.com/news/local/article234322637.html.

Wigglesworth, Alex. 2019. '"Straight Pride" Parade Seeks Approval in Modesto'. *Los Angeles Times*, 24 July. https://www.latimes.com/california/story/2019-07-23/straight-pride-parade-planned-in-modesto.

Wood, Lesley. 2012. *Direct Action, Deliberation, and Diffusion: Collective Action after the WTO Protests in Seattle*. New York: Cambridge University Press.

Zulli, Diana. 2020. 'Evaluating Hashtag Activism: Examining the Theoretical Challenges and Opportunities of #BlackLivesMatter'. *Participations: Journal of Audience & Reception Studies* 17 (1): 197–216. https://www.participations.org/Volume%2017/Issue%201/12.pdf.

Chapter 6

The Online Manosphere and Misogyny in the Far Right: The Case of the #thotaudit

Simon Copland

In November of 2018, a man called David Wu posted a poll on Facebook with the question: 'Is "sex-work" real work? How would you guys consider it?' The next day another user – Kuba Zucc'd – replied, stating 'I just use these polls to find self admitted [sex] workers and report them to the IRS [Internal Revenue Service] and local law enforcement'. The exchange seems insignificant. Yet, it sparked a short but intense online harassment campaign called #thotaudit.

Derived from the term 'thot', an acronym for 'that ho over there', #thotaudit was an online campaign during which participants, mostly men, reported self-employed sex workers to tax authorities, to the Internal Revenue Service in the United States, with the intent to have these sex workers audited. Carried out online on sites such as 4chan, Reddit and, in particular, Twitter, #thotaudit sparked a brief wave of misogyny and harassment targeting female sex workers, particularly those who used premium Snapchat to sell their services. Some participants built databases filled with the names and accounts of thousands of sex workers to report. Those participating in this campaign assumed that these women were not already abiding by laws governing income tax and sex work, an assumption based in misogynistic understandings of women as irresponsible, selfish and hypocritical.

While it is not possible to determine exactly how many women were harassed or reported to the IRS because of this campaign, in the context of a workforce that is already highly stigmatized and marginalized around the world, #thotaudit had potential severe impacts on its target. As Alptraum (2018) explains, #thotaudit was another example of ongoing incidents of dehumanizing harassment targeting women sex workers both off and online. Many online sex workers recognized that the threat of being reported to the IRS due to the #thotaudit was likely to be minimal (Dancyger 2018).

However, as Dancyger (2018) observes, some sex workers said the campaign had the potential to cause hurt and distress, and to potentially increase digital and physical violence directed at those engaged in sex work.

This chapter examines the recruitment and mobilization strategies that underpinned the development of this campaign by proposing #thotaudit as an example of networked harassment conducted by adherents to 'manosphere' ideologies (Marwick and Caplan 2018). I ask two separate but interlinked questions:

1. What was the ideological rhetoric that underpinned recruitment to the campaign?
2. How did members of the manosphere mobilize around the #thotaudit and how did digital platforms such as Twitter, YouTube and Reddit facilitate this mobilization?

I ask these questions to build further understanding of the relationship between the ideology underpinning manosphere ideas and mobilization around issues such as #thotaudit. I argue that the rhetoric behind the #thotaudit tapped into existent ideologies within the manosphere – a digital network that links people that have far-right/traditionalist beliefs, which 'others' certain sexualized, non-traditionalist women like sex workers. In the case of the #thotaudit this community was mobilized behind the campaign through the involvement of a number of key microcelebrities. From the analysis presented here, we understand that these platforms and microcelebrities are the major reason as to why this campaign was so intense. Yet at the same time, these factors are the reason that it did not last long. In the case of #thotaudit, digital platforms facilitated quick mobilization of these members, but the affordances of these sites are not enough to allow for ongoing engagement, as there were not enough social links to maintain the campaign's strength. While this does not mean that this campaign was not harmful, the chapter provides important insights into the genesis, spread and collapse of such campaigns, which can be used to analyse other such campaigns in the future.

I start this chapter by providing a background to the ideology that underpinned #thotaudit, connecting the campaign to the broader manosphere. I explore how the manosphere ideology was used to recruit people to participate in #thotaudit. From here, using the concept of networked harassment as a guiding framework, I study how participants mobilized around #thotaudit, examining specifically how #thotaudit developed through online platforms and the ways in which digital platforms facilitated this campaign. This study analysed data collected from Twitter, which was the largest platform on which this campaign was conducted. This chapter aims to provide a holistic view of networked harassment campaigns such as #thotaudit by offering an analysis of how different recruitment and mobilization techniques created, spread and inevitably fuelled the decline of this particular networked harassment campaign.

THE MANOSPHERE, OTHERING AND THE RHETORIC FOR RECRUITMENT

#thotaudit was an anti-sex worker campaign undertaken by an online community broadly defined as the 'manosphere', the ideology of which attracts ideal recruits for this campaign. The popular website, 'Know Your Meme' describes the manosphere as:

> a neologism used to describe a loose network of blogs, forums and online communities on the English-speaking web that are devoted to a wide range of mens' interests, from life philosophies and gender relations to self-improvement tips and strategies for success in life, relationships and sex. (Know Your Meme 2015)

Marwick and Caplan (2018: 546) argue that while containing a range of disparate groups, the manosphere is bonded by 'a central belief that feminine values dominate society, that this fact is suppressed by feminists and "political correctness", and that men must fight back against the overarching, *misandrist* culture to protect their very existence'.

The manosphere is part of a broader anti-feminist tradition that exists within a men's rights movement (Hodapp 2019), which itself is deeply connected to the far right (Marwick and Caplan 2018). As Ging (2017) argues, most manosphere discourse gains its rhetorical logic from evolutionary psychology and genetic determinism, ideas that rely heavily on essentialized biological understandings of men and women. Members of the manosphere argue that society is gynocentric, that is, that women have more social advantages and social value than men do. These men argue that traditional gender roles have given men purpose within social systems, but that the rise of feminism has broken this balance, further entrenching gynocentrism to the point that men have little to no purpose at all except to be subservient to these women. These groups believe that feminism and progressive social change in general have left men purposeless, leaving society unfairly advantageous for women.

This ideology aligns heavily with much of the far right and, more specifically, the alt-right[1] (Marwick and Caplan 2018), with both groups having a general disposition to expressing resentment about changing social norms and structures. Manosphere ideas tap into many of the gendered and, at times, race-essentialist assumptions behind alt-right ideology (Furtelle, 2017). The alt-right and manosphere both appeal to men who feel socially isolated and alienated, men who see themselves as left behind and oppressed by recent social changes and progress. This creates natural links between the two ideological groups.

The manosphere exists primarily online, with ideas and communities emerging and spreading on forum discussion sites such as 4chan and its more radical brother 8chan, as well as the social news and sharing site Reddit (Nagle 2017). Members of the manosphere have engaged in a range of online 'networked harassment' campaigns, of which #thotaudit is one clear example. Networked harassment describes coordinated campaigns, largely targeted at women. These campaigns also use the digital technologies as platforms for speedy recruitment and mobilization (Banet-Weiser and Miltner 2016; Marwick and Caplan 2018). Networked harassment campaigns, which are able to spread misogyny and violence due to the networking effects of far-right/manosphere online spaces, are usually short, but intense.

These campaigns are underpinned by an ideology which 'others' particular forms of working women, in control of their sexuality in a way that deviates from traditionalist gendered expectations. Lister (2004: 101) argues that othering is a 'process of differentiation and demarcation, by which the line is drawn between "us" and "them" – between the more and less powerful – and through which social distance is established and maintained'. Othering requires the construction of two groups – the 'in-group' and the 'out-group' (Harmer and Lumsden, 2019). Othering is a useful rhetorical tool as it allows people to coalesce around their in-group and in turn to blame the out-group for their, and society's, ills. Othering in turn justifies campaigns of harassment and other forms of violence.

Much of the ideology of the manosphere, particularly elements based in evolutionary psychology and genetic determinism, others women entirely as a group. This ideology separates men and women based on biological understandings, creating one broad 'in-group' and other 'out-group'. However, this doesn't mean that all women come under the ire of the manosphere. In fact many women – in particular conservative commentators – are highly celebrated within manosphere circles and play a prominent role in elements of the movement. Othering practices in the manosphere are instead focused on specific types of women – in particular progressive, sexualized and feminist working women. Othering rhetoric within the manosphere is based in identifying the 'wrong kind' of women, those in particular who challenge dominant social norms about gender.

We can see this practice of other particular types of women through the networked harassment campaign of #thotaudit. #thotaudit focused specifically around sex workers as non-traditional women, with men speaking of them as frivolous, emotional, irresponsible – destroying society because of their refusal to pay taxes and also their willingness to sell their body for sex, ruining what these men see as the traditional heterosexual, monogamous ideal structure. 'Thots' were framed as diametrically 'other' to socially minded men, in the process both validating the social position of men of the manosphere as traditional and defending society, and the 'thot' as destroying it. As one user on 4chan[2] posted:

> Imagine being a whore.
> Imagine how much it stings being told off my [by] fucking virgins.
> Proof God has a Wonderful Sense of Humor.
> After years of being shunned and degraded . . .
> INCEL:[3] 'One way or another I'm fucking you! #ThotAudit'

Through positioning themselves against the thot 'other', #thotaudit gave users a sense of collective identity. As another user on 4chan posted, 'Now I become #ThotAudit destroyer of whores', posting as if he was joining a band of brothers fighting a just cause. Users also connected with each other over the campaign. As one 4chan user posted: '#thotaudit. i fucking love you guys'.

Participants also argued that they were on the side of the majority of the population, at least online. Not only were they a community themselves, but they were one that represented the wishes of broader society. There is evidence as well from the discourse surrounding #thotaudit that members of the manosphere position themselves as having typical opinions, and on the side of the rest of the population. This makes it become easier for others to feel comfortable joining in. In this sense, manosphere rhetoric that positions themselves as typical folk in some ways works as a mobilizing mechanism for online harassment campaigns like this one. As one 4chan user said:

> Normies on twitter think #thotaudit is fucking hilarious. there is a lot of support for it. people really don't like hookers.

Here we can see an example of users on more non-normative sites such as 4chan talking about Twitter as spaces for mobilization around more extreme ideas. Platforms such as 4chan tend to host more extreme content, while Twitter, YouTube and Reddit tend to be more moderate in their tone and politics (Horta Ribeiro et al. 2020). However, material often spreads from one site to the other, with 4chan in particular acting as a source for a range of right-wing memes (Nagle 2017). Participants spoke about the #thotaudit as a justified campaign against sex workers. @stone_toss, for example, has a highly tweeted comment, in which they simply write '#ThotAudit' with a link to the cartoon featured on their website, as seen in figure 6.1. The message evoked by this cartoon links up with many of the othering sentiments of the far right. It suggests that women, especially non-traditional women like sex

Figure 6.1. [@]Stone_Toss Cartoon.
Source: @Stone_Toss. Image circulated on public Twitter, collected by author.

workers, are irresponsible and that they, and the leftists who defend them, are hypocritical – demanding to be respected as workers, but not wanting to take on the 'responsibilities' of 'real work', such as paying taxes.

Brought together, users expressed that #thotaudit provided a means in which they could find purpose, even in the short term.

The most prominent of these tweets was one from the prominent microcelebrity RooshV (whose role in #thotaudit I discuss further in the following) in which he writes: 'What if the purpose of autism was to one day defeat thots using the US tax code?'. Here, RooshV references a discourse about autism from within the incel community. Incels are a group of men who believe that due to their own genetic failures, alongside women's alleged desires to only date attractive men they call 'chads', they are unable to make any sexual and romantic attachments. Many incels themselves claim the community is dominated by men on the autism spectrum, with a belief that their autism stops them from being able to attract partners. Incels played a significant role in #thotaudit. Here RooshV is indicating that incels/autistic men's engagement in #thotaudit provides a way for them to finally find purpose in their lives. This is a way in which they can do something that is not only good for themselves, but also for society as a whole.

There are other examples of this as well. One commenter on 4chan, for example, said: 'Damn this is fucking amazing, /pol/ has finally found a righteous cause through which to purge thots and their untaxed income #thotaudit'. Similar to Reddit 4chan is comprised of themed channels, or 'boards'. The board /pol/ is notorious for its right-wing activism and engagement in trolling and harassment. This comment again taps into the notion of #thotaudit being a righteous campaign, with the user this time indicating it has finally provided a valuable activity for /pol/ users. Another campaigner makes a joke out of this, saying on Twitter: 'Yeah sex is cool but have you ever reported premium snapchats to the IRS so they get audited? #ThotAudit #Patrolled'. Tapping into a common meme on Twitter in which users tweet about things better than sex, this user is jokingly expressing the emotional high of reporting sex workers. This is a signal, primarily towards incels (who complain at a lack of sex) that this activity is even better than sex.

Another clear example of this was found on Reddit. #thotaudit featured primarily on the subreddit r/Braincels, the now-banned main subreddit for the incel community. A common feature of r/Braincels was men talking about mental health problems, with suicide notes appearing frequently on the channel. During #thotaudit one user posted about his desire to commit suicide and wondered whether he should go through with it. Another user replied, simply stating '#Thotaudit is the reason why you shouldn't'.

While the sincerity of such comments is impossible to discern, participants used a rhetoric of finding purpose in life to recruit participants to be involved in the campaign. This, at least indirectly, responds to the broader manosphere idea that feminism has taken purpose away from men, with that purpose now found in fighting against 'thots'.

#thotaudit therefore tapped into sentiments about men's role in society that exists within the manosphere. For participants, campaigns such as #thotaudit are less seen as campaigns of harassment, but instead as campaigns of just retribution. According to these men, #thotaudit provided a social-digital space to come together and find purpose in defeating what was posited to them as the opposition or 'other'. This is the ideological-political context in which #thotaudit, and the manosphere more broadly, flourishes. This ideology has provided a fruitful context in which to recruit members to manosphere ideas, and in this case to participate in the #thotaudit more specifically.

MOBILIZATION: MICROCELEBRITIES AND THE RISE AND DECLINE OF #THOTAUDIT

So far, this chapter has used a qualitative analysis of a selection of tweets taken from the #thotaudit campaign to highlight the ideology that underpins the manosphere as an online network, and which was used to justify #thotaudit. This rhetoric, which othered particular types of women and argued the campaign gave purpose to some men, underpinned recruitment, providing a justification for men to be involved. In this second part of this chapter,

I examine how users mobilized around #thotaudit, studying the genesis, spread and decline of this particular campaign.

Digital platforms provided a space for participants to mobilize around #thotaudit spontaneously, with the campaign escalating quickly. While #thotaudit developed quickly however, it de-escalated almost as fast. The campaign lasted approximately four days, with the hashtag first being used on 25 November, peaking on 26 November and dying out by 29 November. Here I examine why this was the case and what this tells us about networked harassment campaigns run by manosphere communities.

To examine how participants mobilized around #thotaudit, I have collected data related to the campaign from Twitter. While existent on other platforms, #thotaudit played out primarily on Twitter, with this space providing a substantial voice for members of the manosphere. It in turn made sense to sample data from this platform. Using the R package *rtweet*, I collected tweets that included the hashtag #thotaudit across seven days – from 24 November 2018 to 30 November 2018. I collected 22,487 tweets, including both original tweets and retweets. I used the tools *Tableau* and the network visualization software *Gephi* to analyse these data in order to create visualizations of the spread of #thotaudit on Twitter, as well as the social network that underpinned the campaign. As I will detail in the following, these tools provide a valuable understanding of how participants mobilized around #thotaudit, allowing us to examine the genesis of the campaign, its spread online and how users connected over the issue. By showing how users mobilized and de-mobilized around #thotaudit, I mean to reveal the core role that microcelebrities played in the development of the campaign.

Figure 6.2 shows the way in which users mobilized rapidly around #thotaudit through presenting a time-series graph of Tweets associated with the campaign. Figure 6.2 distinguishes between original tweets and re-tweets, with the original tweet represented by the grey line, and re-tweets represented by the black line. This shows how much more #thotaudit re-tweets appeared compared to original tweets for the majority of time during the campaign.

#thotaudit originated on Facebook around 22 and 23 November, at which time there was some discussion of the campaign on Twitter, although the #thotaudit hashtag had not yet been developed. Users started using the #thotaudit hashtag on 24 November, which is where this data set begins. Hashtags allow users 'to follow and contribute to conversations on particular topics of interest' (Bruns and Burgess 2011, 2), creating what Bruns and Burgess (2011) describe as *ad hoc publics* around particular issues. Use of the #thotaudit hashtag increases rapidly, with a jump from zero tweets per hour to approximately 500 tweets (original tweets and retweets combined) within a matter of two to three hours. Discussion then peaks on the second day of activity, with a peak of close to 600 tweets (original tweets and retweets combined) occurring in a single hour.

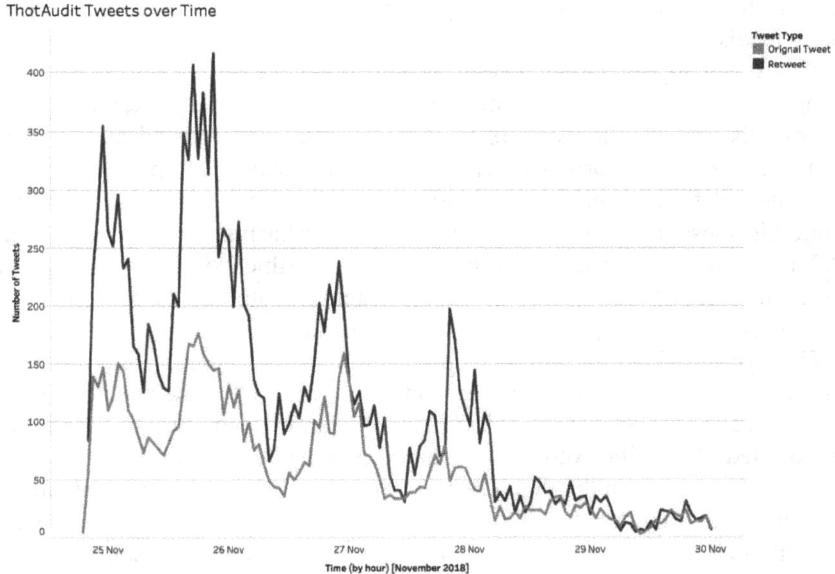

Figure 6.2. ThotAudit Tweets over Time.
Source: Author.

Importantly, while #thotaudit was originally started by regular members of the manosphere, it did not gain momentum until the engagement of two key manosphere *microcelebrities*. Microcelebrities are users who attain in-group fame because of their exposure and interaction within a group of niche users (Abidin and Brown 2019). Microcelebrities are particularly prevalent online (Khamis 2016), where the affordances of digital platforms allow users to coalesce around niche issues and for leaders to emerge from these spaces. Many microcelebrities, while focused on niche concerns, can therefore have hundreds of thousands or even millions of followers.

The manosphere has a number of well-followed microcelebrities, and two of these drove engagement in the #thotaudit. The first was RooshV, a well-known men's rights activist and former pick-up artist with over 48,000 followers on Twitter at the time of the campaign. On 23 November 2018 RooshV began tweeting about #thotaudit. His initial tweets did not contain any hashtags, and in turn do not appear in my tweet dataset. However, as previously mentioned, late on 24 November RooshV tweeted his 'autism tweet'. Figure 6.2 shows an immediate effect on the campaign from this tweet. RooshV's 'autism tweet' is one of the first to use the #thotaudit hashtag, and it sets off a significant spike in the use of the hashtag and of the number of tweets associated with the campaign. RooshV successfully tapped into insular incel humour in order to drive mobilization of the campaign, bringing attention to the issue and in bringing many incels into the fold.

This tweet in particular drove a growth in retweets associated with the campaign. Retweets play an important part of the spread of material on Twitter, as this feature allows users to share content from trusted and popular sources. The vast majority of retweets within the dataset are people retweeting material from RooshV. His 'autism tweet' has a total of 641 retweets, while his subsequent tweets using the #thotaudit hashtag have 586, 503 and 462 retweets. As a microcelebrity, RooshV's influence functions both in terms of endorsement, and to provide the actual material (the tweet) which other users can use to participate in the campaign.

The second far-right microcelebrity intervention came from the anti-feminist, Islamaphobic and former candidate for the UK Independence Party (UKIP) YouTuber *Sargon of Akkad* (Carl Benjamin), who posted a YouTube video titled 'The #ThotAudit Has Begun' on 24 November 2018 on his channel 'The Thinkery'. In the video, Sargon of Akkad describes the development of #thotaudit, running through some tweets and other posts related to the campaign. He, using an argument common within the manosphere, states that young women, and in particular online sex workers, have it easy, primarily through being able to take their clothes off for easy money. Examining a clause in the IRS tax code which says that whistle-blowers of tax fraud may be eligible to receive up to 30% of the taxes collected from their report, he then claims that #thotaudit has finally provided men an easy way to make money online. #thotaudit therefore balances the scales, giving men access to a privilege previously available only to women. Sargon of Akkad then calls for others to get involved saying: 'It is morally just that you report thots to the IRS for evading taxes. In fact morally just that you report anyone for evading taxes'. At the time of writing, this video has garnered over 900,000 views. Sargon of Akkad's intervention on YouTube then filtered through to his fans on Twitter, as the video was shared as a way to mobilize around the campaign. What we can see here therefore is both the needed influence of prominent microcelebrities to get this hashtag off the ground, as well as the spread of #thotaudit campaign from YouTube to Twitter.

From this analysis, it is evident that the genesis and mobilized spread of #thotaudit relied on the active participation of online far-right and anti-feminist microcelebrities, in this case RooshV and Sargon of Akkad. RooshV used his followership to spread the campaign on Twitter, while Sargon of Akkad provided further material on YouTube that was easily shared on other platforms. In their public endorsement of the campaign's sentiments, these microcelebrities gave authority and ideological validity to the campaign. Their use of digital technologies rapidly mobilized their followers to participate in the campaign, facilitating short bursts of activity across platforms.

WEAK NETWORKS AND THE DECLINE OF #THOTAUDIT

While #thotaudit developed quickly with rapid mobilization online, the campaign also declined nearly as fast. The #thotaudit hashtag lasted on Twitter for only approximately four days, indicating that participants quickly moved on from the campaign. This section aims to examine what led to this decline, particularly arguing that the campaign was unable to be sustained due to the relatively weak social network that underpinned it.

A central tenet of 'networked harassment' is the sociality that underpins it. This is a campaign of coordinated action, where users band together to identify targets, develop tactics and implement their actions. We can see very clear elements of these collective tactics at work in #thotaudit, which inevitably were a key factor in elevating the intensity of these attacks against women. For example, some participants compiled databases of sex workers, scraping data from platforms such as Chaturbate and other cam sites (in which sex workers perform live online for paying users), such as Kik and Twitter, in order to identify sex workers who could then be reported to the IRS (Cole 2018). These databases were likely developed using automated scripts, but they provided a collective resource for participating users to access. On Twitter, users shared information on how to report sex workers to the IRS. One user, @musashi_444, for example, tweeted a screenshot of an IRS form with relevant sections highlighted for those who wished to report sex workers (see figure 6.3).

However, despite these resources for easy mass participation, we can see from the tweet time series that #thotaudit tapered off almost as quickly as it began. While the two microcelebrities RooshV and Argon of Sakkad were central to mobilizing users around the campaign, I argue that this decline occurred because their involvement was not enough to create a strong social network in which participants could organize collectively to develop a sustained campaign. Rather, the 'collectivity' was based around a connection to the broad idea and bigger community of the manosphere, rather than based around specific social contacts related to #thotaudit. Given this, #thotaudit was one brief, intense moment which existed within the broader politics of the manosphere, indicating that the manosphere is more akin to a networked set of individuals attached to an idea rather than a social movement with significant political sway. Men participated due to their broader connections within the manosphere and their novel adherence to microcelebrities, as opposed to any recruited devotion to a political movement.

To further understand the technical elements of this network of individuals, it is useful to look at the structure of the digital network behind the campaign. A network refers to connections between users within a platform, expressed

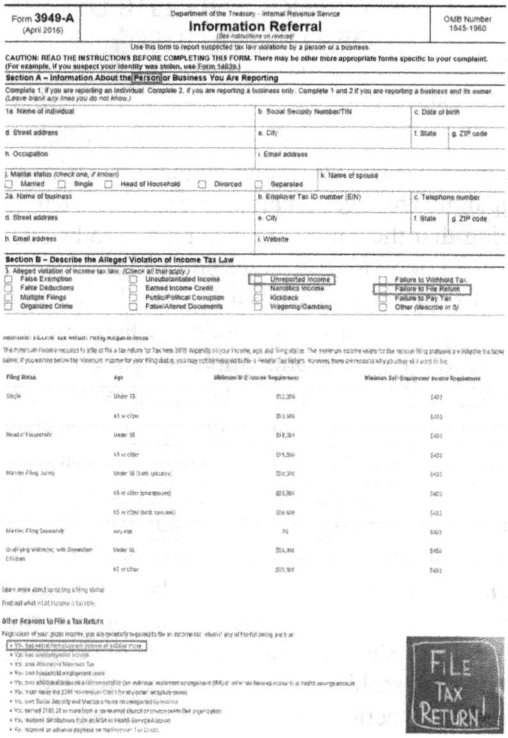

Form **3949-A** (April 2016) | Department of the Treasury - Internal Revenue Service | **Information Referral** (See instructions on reverse) | OMB Number 1545-1960

Use this form to report suspected tax law violations by a person or a business.

CAUTION: READ THE INSTRUCTIONS BEFORE COMPLETING THIS FORM. There may be other more appropriate forms specific to your complaint. (For example, if you suspect your identity was stolen, use Form 14039.)

Section A – Information About the Person or Business You Are Reporting

Complete 1, if you are reporting an individual. Complete 2, if you are reporting a business only. Complete 1 and 2 if you are reporting a business and its owner. *(Leave blank any lines you do not know.)*

1a. Name of individual	b. Social Security Number/TIN	c. Date of birth	
d. Street address	e. City	f. State	g. ZIP code
h. Occupation	i. Email address		
j. Marital status *(check one, if known)* ☐ Married ☐ Single ☐ Head of Household ☐ Divorced ☐ Separated	k. Name of spouse		
2a. Name of business	b. Employer Tax ID number (EIN)	c. Telephone number	
d. Street address	e. City	f. State	g. ZIP code
h. Email address	i. Website		

Section B – Describe the Alleged Violation of Income Tax Law

3. Alleged violation of income tax law. *(Check all that apply.)*

☐ False Exemption	☐ Unsubstantiated Income	☐ Unreported Income	☐ Failure to Withhold Tax
☐ False Deductions	☐ Earned Income Credit	☐ Narcotics Income	☐ Failure to File Return
☐ Multiple Filings	☐ Public/Political Corruption	☐ Kickback	☐ Failure to Pay Tax
☐ Organized Crime	☐ False/Altered Documents	☐ Wagering/Gambling	☐ Other *(describe in 5)*

Other Reasons to File a Tax Return

Figure 6.3. Sample IRS Form.

Source: Image circulated on public Twitter, collected by author.

through directed links such as the @ function on Twitter. While networks exist across platforms as well, this analysis considers these only when they are explicitly referred to by users. Using the network visualization tool Gephi, I have created a network graph of users from the Twitter data set (see figure 6.4). In this network the nodes (or dots) are individual Twitter users. Users are linked if one has mentioned the other in a tweet about #thotaudit, or if they have retweeted another user's tweet about #thotaudit. The initial dataset contained 22,487 tweets. Within this the network has a total of 11,817 identified users, with 17,000 edges, or links, between them. A majority of these links are likely retweets. The network has been colour-coded using a 'modularity' ranking. This modularity ranking identifies distinct sub-networks. These are often centred around an individual user, or particular conversations within a sub-group of users. Nodes within the network are then sized by 'in-degree', which measures those users who are mentioned the most by other users within the dataset. This gives us a stronger indication of who is central to the discussion.

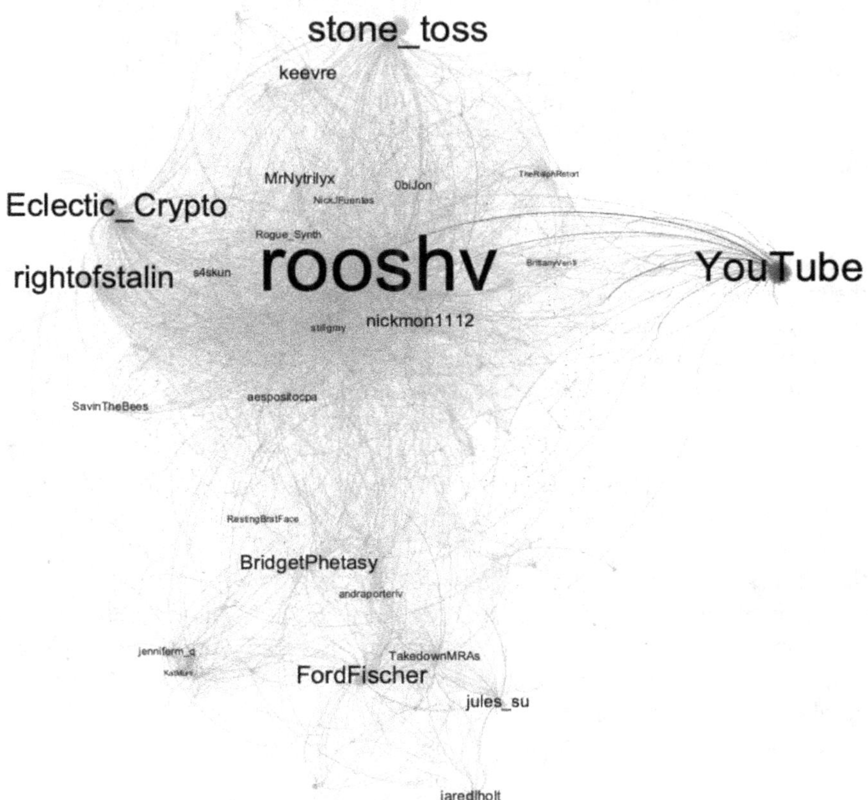

Figure 6.4. ThotAudit Twitter Network.
Source: Author.

There are some characteristics we can quickly identify with this network. The top of the network is dominated by participants within #thotaudit, including RooshV, who sits at the centre of the network, as well as a number of tweeters with highly retweeted content, the most prominent being @stone_toss, @eclectic_crypto and @rightofstalin. The bottom half of the network is filled with users who are critiquing or who oppose #thotaudit. These tweets represent a minority of the network. Interestingly, there is a distinct separation between those who are participating in the campaign and those who criticize it. This suggests little engagement between the two groups, meaning that the campaign of networked harassment did not entirely cross over to those criticizing it, and further that critiques of #thotaudit did not reach those participating.

Finally, on the right of the network we see YouTube appear as the second largest node within the network (only behind RooshV). This represents users who are sharing YouTube videos discussing the campaign, primarily Sargod of Akkad's video, as well as a video from the YouTube personality Philip DeFranco titled 'The Ridiculous #ThotAudit Tax Evasion Situation, GM's Massive Job Cut, & 2nd Amendment Controversy', which notably, provides a rebuttal to #thotaudit. Users cross-posted these videos on Twitter alongside the #thotaudit hashtag. As previously discussed, the discussion that surrounds the manosphere exists across a range of different social media platforms. Each of these platforms have different audiences, who engage in topics in different ways. Cross-posting is an effective means in which members of the manosphere spread messages and build campaigns despite not having ideological ownership of a certain platform like Twitter. Cross-posting is particularly effective across mainstream platforms such as YouTube and Twitter; YouTube's 'share' function allows users to quickly share YouTube material to Twitter, including standardized text that mentions YouTube in the Tweet. Across the period of my dataset, YouTube was mentioned a total of 737 times in this way. These mentions primarily involved the sharing of Sargon of Akkad's and DeFranco's videos. The prominence of YouTube within this network highlights the strong role that the sharing of these videos played in the discussion of #thotaudit on Twitter.

For the purposes of understanding the mobilization around #thotaudit, the most integral part of this network is the largely unstructured nature of the section of users who are participating in the campaign. While there are a large number of users who are part of this network, suggesting a high level of communication around the campaign, the network still centres on a few high-profile figures. These users, RooshV in particular, are central to the campaign, creating a core around which activity occurs. Here we can see the integral role that microcelebrities played in mobilizing people around #thotaudit.

Just as importantly, engagement within the network is primarily one-directional. While users are retweeting, replying or mentioning other users in their tweets, there is little back and forth. This means that users are tweeting at each other, but not having conversations *with* each other. One way to study the depth of engagement (i.e. the level in which participants are connected with a large number of other participants in long conversations) is by examining the density of the network graph. Measured in a scale of 0–1, the network density represents the number of network ties as a proportion of the maximum number of network ties (Ackland 2013). In a graph with a measure of one, each user in the network is connected to every other user, while in a graph with a measure of zero, no users are connected to each other at all. Graph density therefore represents a measure of connectedness in a network, with a higher connectedness suggesting stronger links between users. The density of this graph however is extremely low: 0.0001352005. Participants are therefore likely only connected to one, or maybe two, other users in the network.

This lack of deep connections provides some evidence to understand why #thotaudit was so short lived. In her seminal book on progressive organizing, *No Shortcuts: Organizing for Power*, for example, Jane McAlevey argues that social movements of previous eras gained their power through mass organizing, which requires the creation of deep social connections from a bottom-up perspective. This approach, she says, has recently been abandoned for a shallower form of mobilization and advocacy, which explains many of the failures of current progressive movements. While the context is obviously extremely different, the lessons are still the same, with a lack of deep social organizing making it difficult for #thotaudit to be sustained in the long run.

These lessons are particularly relevant in the online context. In a study of Facebook for example, Giraldi (2016) examines Granovetter's 'strength of weak social ties' theory to test whether Facebook users are motivated to social activism through their weak social ties on the platform. She instead however finds the opposite, stating that people are motivated to activism through Facebook but that it comes rather through those they already have strong social ties with. In a similar study, van Noort et al. (2012) look at the persuasiveness of viral campaigns on social media. They find that the strength of the response of social marketing is linked to the strength of the tie between the sender and the receiver of the campaign, with those receiving material from people they have stronger links with being more persuaded by campaigns overall. While social media can facilitate the spread of shallow advocacy campaigns, therefore, sometimes with great speed and intensity, they are likely to be sustained only if they involved deep social ties.

This does not however suggest that socializing was not an important part of #thotaudit. Socializing and building connection online can also include short engagement and even lurking (Han et al. 2013; Sun et al. 2014). These acts can still create a sense of community and communal purpose. In the case of #thotaudit, however, this socializing and community connection was driven primarily by a connection to the broader idea of the manosphere and the ideology which animates it.

Through the network underpinning #thotaudit we can see the existence of this broad community, which presented enough impetus for the campaign to spark and gather extensive and rapt attention. However, this did not present many deep links between users, meaning the campaign could not be sustained for long. Users mobilized around the campaign due to their links to high-profile manosphere figures such as RooshV and Sargon of Akkad. Many of these links to the microcelebrities were pre-formed, that is, participants already had some sort of knowledge of or followed these microcelebrities, and of the manosphere ideology of which they are proponents. However, most individual users did not have personal or social links with these figures, nor necessarily with other participants in the campaign, and in turn could not, and did not, create a campaign that spread past the attention span of these microcelebrities. With RooshV and Sargon of Akkad moving on relatively quickly from #thotaudit, there was not enough structured networks for other users to sustain an ongoing campaign.

While some users did use digital platforms to coordinate ongoing harassment, these were far fewer than the larger group of those who mobilized around the campaign briefly, and in turn these few committed users were unable to maintain momentum. The social ties provided by digital platforms simply did not provide a strong enough basis to maintain an ongoing, sustained campaign. #thotaudit was thus an opportunity for users such as RooshV or Sargon of Akkad to energize their fan base who were already primed to be sceptical of figures like the otherized sex worker, generating some short-term energy and controversy, before moving on to the next issue.

WHAT CAN WE LEARN FROM #THOTAUDIT?

The short-term nature of #thotaudit's targeting of sex workers does not diminish the impact it had upon its victims, nor does it necessarily suggest that we should not take it seriously as a mode of far-right mobilization.

Digital theorists have become increasingly interested in the role of speed of the Internet in spreading hateful material. Venturini (2019), for example, argues that the speed of the spread of information and other content has become an integral function of digital platforms. Platforms facilitate this speed in multiple ways, through the capacity of users to share content across platforms easily, functions such as 'retweets' which spread material quickly to new users, hashtags which allow other users to find new content and the capacity of microcelebrities to develop large followings that they can influence at speed.

The case of #thotaudit provides another example of the impact the speed of the Internet can have in fermenting a campaign of networked harassment which causes harm at a rapid pace, despite dying out quickly. Even if only for a brief period, #thotaudit allowed members to place themselves inside a collective, one which opposed an 'other' which was, as they claim, destroying their traditional, functioning society. In #thotaudit, the imagined enemy was the same as that of the contemporary far right, culturally owed to other anti-feminist campaigns like #gamergate: alleged radical feminists and progressives who seek to dismantle traditional gender roles from which men derive a sense of value and identity. Therefore, the campaign was seen as righteous, one which provided essential purpose for those involved. This rhetoric has proved useful in recruiting men into manosphere ideologies, in turn providing a strong user base to mobilize quickly around campaigns such as #thotaudit.

This particular campaign was spread through a range of online networks, boosted by high-profile members of the manosphere. However, the speed of this, driven by two key microcelebrities, did not create a strong or sustained social network to underpin the campaign, meaning that #thotaudit disappeared almost as quickly as it appeared. While users were connected to manosphere ideology, and the sense of connection and community that this brings, there were not enough deep ties within #thotaudit for it to be sustained as a campaign. While the sociality of this campaign was important to its spread, therefore, this sociality occurred primarily through short engagements and lurking. While there were some examples of men coordinating on things such as databases of sex workers to harass, in large there was little ongoing organizing or mobilizing around the issue.

This chapter has argued that networked harassment campaigns such as #thotaudit occur due to a combination of effective recruitment rhetoric and mobilization strategies. Digital technologies help facilitate the spread of hateful material, and in this case allowed manosphere users to mobilize around calls to action/harassment like the #thotaudit campaign at great speed. A core part of this process were the microcelebrities RooshV and Sargon of Akkad, who spread #thotaudit ideas to a large audience in a very short time. However, the Internet does not create or spread campaigns in a vacuum. #thotaudit was based in a broad sentiments of purposelessness and social alienation, which 'others' the sexualized, working women as the causes of these feelings. This rhetoric has been effective at recruiting members to manosphere ideologies overall and was then used again to mobilize people around #thotaudit. Without these underlying sentiments, far-right, anti-feminist and other harassment campaigns would not spread online in the way they do.

Understanding and addressing these campaigns require analysis of both mobilization and recruitment strategies. More research is required concerning these sorts of campaigns, including research that addresses the rhetoric that recruits participants into these ideologies, the means by which people mobilize online and the challenges they face in doing so, and finally, and most importantly, in effective strategies to reduce these sorts of campaigns of networked harassment.

NOTES

1. The alt-right, short for 'alternative right' is a new manifestation of American far-right ideologies (Koulouris 2018), one which 'emphasizes internet activism, is

hostile to both multicultural liberalism and mainstream conservatism, and has had a symbiotic relationship with Donald Trump's presidential campaign' (Lyons 2017: 2).

2. Comments from 4chan and Reddit were collected using the data collection tool 4cat.

3. Incels played a central role in the development and spread of #thotaudit. This community is described in further detail later in the chapter.

REFERENCES

Abidin, Crystal, and Megan Brown. 2019. *Microcelebrity around the Globe: Approaches to Cultures of Internet Fame*. London: Emerald.

Alptraum, Lux. 2018. '#ThotAudit Is Just the Latest Tactic People Are Using to Harass Sex Workers Online'. *The Verge*. 30 November. https://www.theverge.com/2018/11/30/18119688/thotaudit-sex-work-irs-online-harassment.

Banet-Weiser, Sarah, and Kate Miltner. 2016. '#MasculinitySoFragile: Culture, Structure, and Networked Misogyny'. *Feminist Media Studies* 16 (1): 171–4.

Bruns, Axel and Jean Burgess. 2011. 'The Use of Twitter Hashtags in the Formation of Ad Hoc Publics'. In *Proceedings of the 6th European Consortium for Political Research (ECPR) General Conference 2011*, edited by A. Bruns and P. de Wilde, 1–9. The European Consortium for Political Research (ECPR), United Kingdom.

Cole, Samantha. 2018. '#ThotAudit Is Compiling Massive Databases of Sex Workers and Reporting Them to PayPal'. *Vice*, 5 December. https://www.vice.com/en_us/article/gy7wyw/thotaudit-databases-of-sex-workers-and-reporting-them-to-paypal.

Dancyger, Lilly. 2018. 'Sex Workers Say Incel Campaign to Report Them to IRS Won't Work'. *Rolling Stone*, 27 November. https://www.rollingstone.com/culture/culture-news/sex-worker-irs-incel-mens-rights-thot-audit-760586/.

Furtelle, David. 2017. 'Men's-Rights Activism is the Gateway Drug for the Alt-Right'. *The Cut*, 17 August 17. https://www.thecut.com/2017/08/mens-rights-activism-is-the-gateway-drug-for-the-alt-right.html.

Ging, Debbie. 2017. 'Alphas, Betas, and Incels: Theorizing the Masculinities of the Manosphere'. *Men and Masculinities* 22 (4): 1–20.

Giraldi, Nichole. 2016. 'The Strength of Weak Social Ties: Social Activism and Facebook'. *Masters Thesis*. Old Dominion University.

Han, Jeong, Jiran Hou, Eunkyung Kim, and David Gustafson. 2013. 'Lurking as an Active Participation Process: A Longitudinal Investigation of Engagement with an Online Cancer Support Group'. *Health Communication* 29 (9): 911–23.

Harmer, Emily, and Karen Lumsden. 2019. 'Online Othering: An Introduction'. In *Online Othering: Exploring Violence and Discrimination on the Web*, edited by E. Harmer and K. Lumsden. Cham, Switzerland: Palgrave Macmillan.

Hodapp, Christa. 2019. *Men's Rights, Gender, and Social Media*. Lanham: Lexington Books.

Khamis, Susie, Ang, Lawrence, and Raymond Welling. 2016. 'Self-branding, "Micro-Celebrity" and the Rise of Social Media Influencers'. *Celebrity Studies* 8 (2): 191–208.

Know Your Meme. 2015. 'Manosphere'. https://knowyourmeme.com/memes/subcultures/manosphere.

Koulouris, Theodore. 2018. 'Online Misogyny and the Alternative Right: Debating the Undebatable'. *Feminist Media Studies* 18 (4): 750–61.

Lumsden, Karen. 2019. '"I Want to Kill You in Front of Your Children" Is Not a Threat. It's an Expression of Desire: Discourses of Online Abuse, Trolling and Violence in r/MensRights'. In *Online Othering: Exploring Violence and Discrimination on the Web*, edited by K. Lumsden and E. Harmer. Cham, Switzerland: Palgrave Macmillan.

Lyons, Matthew N. 2017a. 'CTRL-ALT-DELETE: The Origins and Ideology of the Alternative Right'. *Political Research Associates*. Accessed 30 May 2020. https://www.politicalresearch.org/sites/default/files/2019-05/Lyons_CtrlAltDelete_PRINT.pdf.

Marwick, Alice, and Robyn Caplan. 2018. 'Drinking Male Tears: Language, the Manosphere, and Networked Harassment'. *Feminist Media Studies* 18 (4): 543–59.

Massanari, Adrienne. 2017. '#Gamergate and the Fappening: How Reddit's Algorithm, Governance, and Culture Support Toxic Technocultures'. *New Media and Society* 19 (3): 329–46. https://doi.org/10.1177/1461444815608807.

McAlevey, Jane. 2016. *No Shortcuts: Organizing for Power*. New York: Oxford University Press.

Nagle, Angela. 2016. *Kill All Normies: The Online Culture Wars from Tumblr and 4chan to the Alt-Right and Trump*. Winchester, UK: Zero Books.

Sun, Na, Pei-Luen Rau, and Liang Ma. 2014. 'Understanding Lurkers in Online Communities: A Literature Review'. *Computers in Human Behavior* 38: 110–7.

van Noort, Guda, Marjolijn Antheunis, and Eva van Reijmersdal. 2012. 'Social Connections and the Persuasiveness of Viral Campaigns in Social Network Sites: Persuasive Intent as the Underlying Mechanism'. *Journal of Marketing Communication* 18 (1): 39–53.

Venturini, Tommaso. 2019. 'From Fake to Junk News, the Data Politics of Online Virality'. In *Data Politics: Worlds, Subjects, Rights*, edited by D. Bigo, E. Isin, and E. Ruppert. London: Routledge.

Chapter 7

'A Positive Identity for Men'?: Pathways to Far-Right Participation through Reddit's /r/MensRights and /r/TheRedPill

Luc S. Cousineau

Far-right ideologies are committed to defending particular conceptualizations of masculinity and male power, embedded in a certain type of Western traditionalism (Cornwall, Karioris, and Lindisfarne 2016; Pai 2016). When we think of the far right, most people imagine neo-Nazis, white nationalists/white separatists or the militia-focused second amendment enthusiasts in the United States: mostly white, sometimes armed, confrontational. Far-right groups are each of these things, and while women make up a small percentage of participants in their political and public activities (Dobratz and Shanks-Meile 2006), these groups are mostly made up of men (Gordon 2018; Ebner and Davey 2018). Far-right and alt-right communities have rooted and flourished online, and among them 'men's rights' groups have been particularly successful in community building and expansion (Hodge and Hallgrimsdottir 2019; Kelly 2017; Munn 2019). Using men's rights groups as an example, this chapter shows how Reddit provides affordances for the development of collectivity and community for people with harmful traditionalist and anti-feminist ideological values. These affordances are useful to this type of men's group – groups adjacent to the far-right in their obsessions with Western traditionalisms of gender and (in some cases) male supremacy – because they allow for the proliferation and radicalization of ideas within bounded and self-referential communities subject to limited censorship.

Men's groups that fall under the broad banner of 'men's rights' share much of the (Western) traditionalist and conservative rhetorical positioning of the far right and alt-right about gender; a 'natural' structuralist position where men should hold power and control over women and the 'Other' (Dragiewicz and Mann 2016; Jordan 2016; Messner 2016). Staunchly anti-feminist, these groups argue that gender equity has 'gone too far', and that it renders men (particularly white men) a disadvantaged class (Kalish and Kimmel 2010).

For the participants in these groups, and proponents of these ideologies (which include women), feminist-spurred social changes require a reset of public and moral values. As a larger movement composed of many different groups, the broader men's 'rights' community has expanded into a web of inter-related ideological constructs that share a common central message, then diverge from one another along different pathways. Ideology in this case is understood in Žižek's sense of both conscious and unconscious phenomena that, along with hiding how the world works for the purposes of control, serve themselves to shape the reality we live in. Men's 'rights' groups, while always being about sex, power and control, range in focus from perceived unfairness in fathers' custody rights cases (Crowley 2009), to the belief that the proper social orientation is a *Handmaid's Tale*-esque total domination of society, sexuality and culture by men (Jordan 2016). These groups have both shared and divergent ideological constructs.

Men's rights and aligned groups use similar tactics to other far-right groups when recruiting members. Using generalizable and unnuanced statements (e.g. 'white men have lower and decreasing employment prospects') and narrow interpretations of public controversies (e.g. the U.S. Supreme Court confirmation hearings for Brett Kavanaugh as an unfair witch hunt against a white, conservative man), these groups play on the latent desires and fears of their target audience (Willer et al. 2013; Munn 2019); which is (mostly) men. Then, through curated echo chambers, new participants are indoctrinated into the deeper recesses of these ideologies (Munn 2019; DeCook 2019). Using the website Reddit.com and the curated nature of its user interface as a backdrop, this chapter will explore how the Reddit user experience and platform design provide ideal spaces for the proliferation and dissemination of far-right rhetoric and ideology, and can serve as a pipeline toward more extreme views. I explore two groups that occupy different parts of the men's rights spectrum, /r/MensRights and /r/TheRedPill, both active on the website Reddit.com (reddit.com/r/MensRights and reddit.com/r/TheRedPill).

WHAT ARE MEN'S RIGHTS GROUPS AND WHY DO THEY EXIST?

Western culture is shaped by entrenched sex/gender systems (Rubin 2009) that dictate and regulate power, control and personal interactions (Foucault 1979; Connell 2005). Men and women are situated in particular ways through these oppressive systems, and formulations of meta-control, like hegemonic masculinity, patriarchy and systemic racism, which organize us into hierarchies that disproportionately give power and value to (white) men over others. Put simply, this type of valuation of one over others, or one group over others, leads to oppression of the individual or subordinate group through exploitation, marginalization, powerlessness, cultural imperialism and violence; these are Iris Marion Young's five faces of oppression (Young [1988] 2013). There is a deep body of literature that has explored elements of Young's five faces in online environments (e.g. Noble 2018), and as our use of networked technologies continues to proliferate, so too will egregious oppressive acts and opportunities to study them. These systems of social control and oppression are dynamic, and are subject, often with some latency, to changes in dominant social worldviews. The construct of masculinity, and in particular Connell's (2005) concept of hegemonic masculinity, provides a useful prism for examining how these flexible systems of control function.[1]

Conceptualized as the 'specific form of masculinity in a given historical and society-wide social setting that *legitimates* unequal gender relations between men and women, between masculinity and femininity, and among masculinities' (Messerschmidt 2018, 28, emphasis in original), Connell's *hegemonic masculinity* positions an 'ideal' masculinity as one that is difficult, if not impossible to achieve, that is enacted differently at different times and in different places, and that changes with cultural hegemony. For example, while an ideal masculinity of the 1990s would have excluded non-athletic, non-machismo forms of manhood such as the archetypical computer nerd, a new geek masculinity and 'techbro' masculine representation has emerged within the current world of app culture and the Internet of things (Reagle 2018; Braithwaite 2016). This change has opened up space in hegemonic masculinities for tech knowledge as masculine and appealing, but only if some more traditional expectations for masculine representations of the body are maintained (i.e. fit, white and handsome). The features of masculine interests may have changed, but relational power and control over others, including other men, remains (Connell and Messerschmidt 2005). The malleability of hegemonic masculinity (or any culturally hegemonic norm, gendered or otherwise) demonstrates that elements we often understand as static (like the 'ideal' man, or male dominance within relationships) are not immutable, and are themselves subject to change through cultural influence. For some, the types of cultural change that force evolutions in systems of social control and oppression are a threat to positions of power and dominance. For them, these shifts are a re-writing of a social contract that undermines their cultural capital, resulting in what Willer and colleagues (2013) called 'masculine overcompensation', or a set of feelings that Rachel Kalish and Michael Kimmel called 'aggrieved entitlement' (2010).

Like racist and other supremacist ideologies, discourses of masculinity and male dominance in men's rights groups extend from perceived entitlement (Martin 2004), and are rooted in North American institutions and social doctrines (Larkin 2007). Feelings of entitlement are derived from the perception of male historical dominance over women, and are perpetuated through the oppression of the rights and abilities of non-white, non-male figures (hooks 2003). Male entitlement to domination has been enshrined by the state and in our canons of laws (Rifkin 1980), the military and militarism (Howard and Prividera 2004), police and police states (Franklin 2005) and the Abrahamic religions (Condren 2009). Understanding this can help to expose why some men would feel entitled to power and control. The anger they feel from that loss finds many targets, among them immigrants, non-Christians or those who are not 'Christian enough', and some women (i.e. feminists and others who might eschew North American traditionalism). Some groups of men make these women their primary targets and scapegoats; these men make up part of the men's rights movement (see Copland, this Volume).

Ranging from simple disgruntlement to violent hatred, anti-feminism brings together otherwise diverse groups of online men's groups under a loose affiliation called 'the manosphere' (Ironwood 2013). The concept of the 'manosphere' as a distinct cultural entity first appeared in a blog in 2009, and was popularized by the book *The Manosphere: A New Hope for Masculinity* (Ironwood 2013). Debbie Ging (2019) describes the manosphere as a 'loose confederacy of interest groups [that] has become the dominant arena for the communication of men's rights in Western culture' (Ging 2019, 1). This confederacy of Internet groups shares an ideological standpoint that runs contrary to achieved discourses of gender equality.

Men's groups, including groups discussed in this chapter, are ideological offshoots of the 1970s women's and women's liberation movements (Messner 1998, 2016), and have developed in parallel with contemporary feminism. Men, who were themselves part of the feminist movement, began leveraging the theoretical structures of feminist theory to highlight men's experience as gendered beings. This was done with the intent of developing and promoting 'progressive personal and social change' (Messner 2016, 8). In their view, men were also repressed and oppressed by gendered structures, masculinity and sex/gender systems more broadly (Messner 1998). They acknowledged that men were privileged by social and sex roles, but argued that they were 'simultaneously dehumanized' by them (Pleck 2004). The contradictory notions of acknowledging privilege and situating themselves as an oppressed group divided the early men's activists into pro- and anti-feminist actors. The anti-feminist faction turned to the oppressive nature of sex roles, and co-opted the language of liberal feminists to refocus the critique of symmetrical sex-role oppression on men's experience.[2] This produced a narrative about men and male privilege that situated male privilege as a socially constructed myth that served to oppress men (Goldberg 1976).

Rather than a continuum of more or less radicalized versions of the same group, the modern manosphere consists of groups that share some core values, but diverge as they focus on different issues or aspects of men's experience. The philosophical underpinnings of these distinct groups 'manifest less as a continuum of ideologies (where on one end their work would be passive and contained, and on the other wild, aggressive, and militant)' (Cousineau 2021, 73), but instead like a sphere with filaments extending from the common core – like images of the coronavirus that causes Covid-19 – where the spikes and trees extending from the core represent different areas of focus and the extremeness of those views (figure 7.1).[3] For example, Men's Rights and Red Pill groups (along with other 'manosphere' groups like *incels*) share anti-feminist sentiments, but their solutions to the feminist 'problem' vary. Men's rights advocates generally favour legal and social reform through traditional means via governmental or judicial reform (less extreme), where incels have resorted to violence in an attempt to force change (very extreme; Humphreys and Edmiston 2018; Reeve 2018).

The introduction in the 1990s of widely available home Internet allowed groups with small numbers dispersed over wide geographical areas (including men's rights groups) to gather and grow (Turkle 1996; Wellman and Gulia 1999). A newly networked world allowed for the development of

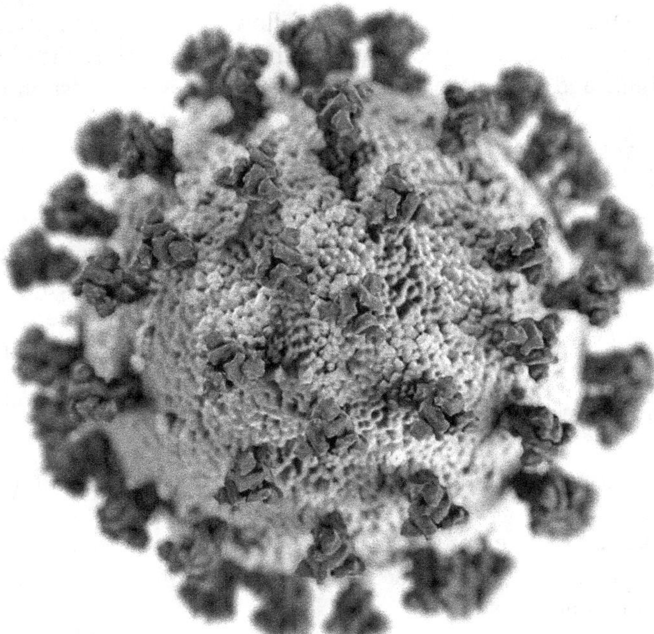

Figure 7.1. Covid-19 Coronavirus as Representation of Manosphere.
Source: Royalty free CDC image under the CC0 Public Domain license.

more active, larger and even more micro-focused communities (Thomas 2011). While touted as a new frontier for building socially just and equal spaces by early feminists and social theorists (Spender 1996; Rheingold 1993), the Internet has played an equally significant role in the proliferation of oppressive ideas and actions (Lumsden and Harmer 2019; Forscher and Kteily 2020). Men's groups used early text-only networked communication spaces (Bulletin Board Services), early websites (including organizations like National Coalition for Men (National Coalition For Men [NCFM] 2019),[4] and other forums to build community and grow their numbers. These were the precursors to current misogynist men's groups, and many of these digital discursive spaces (or versions of them) remain mainstays of these groups for communication and community action today. The proliferation of groups within the manosphere has been aided by websites and services that host content of individual users, or aggregate content from a variety of online sources. Blogging platforms have been used extensively by individual men's rights activists and men's groups to promote their messages (Ironwood 2013), but conversation and the development of specific subgroup ideologies have been best encouraged by websites like Reddit.com. On Reddit, authored content can be posted, can contain links from other content on the web, can be filtered by users in a variety of ways and views can be isolated into echo chambers (Auxier and Vitak 2019). The following section will give a primer on Reddit, its functionality and features. Then I will explore the elements of /r/MensRights and /r/TheRedPill communities as they manifest on Reddit.

WHAT IS REDDIT?

Reddit.com is a website where user posts and off-site content are aggregated for user consumption. Open communities can be accessed and read by anyone online, but to comment, use the website's voting system, or access quarantined communities (Carlson and Cousineau 2020), a unique username is required.

Reddit functions in five ways that are important for its success.

1. Users generate and/or share all of the content on the site, with the exception of ads and announcements from the company.
2. Users can curate the content they see by subject, limiting or expanding their experience to suit their needs, and coming together or building communities of shared interest.
3. Any user can vote on any Reddit content on the site.[5] Users may upvote (positive) or downvote (negative) content, and the number of votes associated with posts changes where they appear in the algorithmically mediated

pages of aggregated posts. Votes are logarithmically weighted, and users accrue points for their posts and comments in a sort of Reddit social credit called 'Karma'.

4. Users can comment and dialogue on any post or comment on the site. Discussion takes the form of asynchronous Bulletin Board System (BBS)–style threads where primary comments on a post become parent comments, and each parent may have a long and complex series of child comments/discussions associated with it.
5. Users have quasi-anonymity. The Reddit user can be as open or as anonymous as they want. As a user, I can be open about my name, where I live and my interests, or I can be a lurker/listener – never engaging or building a personal profile, and simply exploring and observing content.

The site is divided into 'subreddits' which allow for subject-based grouping of content (e.g. reddit.com/r/turtlefacts/ for photos and facts about turtles), and each subreddit has a set of unique rules moderated by volunteers from within that user community (Marwick 2017; Massanari 2015). This approach to content moderation allows Reddit to control the content available on the site, and maintain active users even if the content they are posting is contentious, such as with subreddits like /r/MensRights and /r/TheRedPill. These elements create a massive, mostly user-controlled, space for the sharing of content and opinion, and with so many communities, even users looking for niche content find space on the site.

New users are automatically subscribed to fifty subreddits selected by the site, but are able to remove all of those default subreddits and subscribe to any subreddits of their choosing. Doing so creates a personalized landing page when logged in that is unique to the user and aggregates content only from their subscribed subreddits.[6] Effectively, users create their own content filter bubble (Pariser 2011).

/R/MENSRIGHTS AND /R/THEREDPILL

www.reddit.com/r/MensRights
Created 19 March 2008
300, 855 subscribed members as of April 26, 2021

/r/MensRights and /r/TheRedPill provide good case studies for the exploration of the spread of men's rights content as afforded by Reddit specifically. These subreddits were chosen as they represent two different communities within the manosphere and how they approach gender and male power. They share deeply anti-feminist values, but discuss and act on them in very different ways (DeCook 2019). /r/TheRedPill, for example, regularly has posts about the differences between alpha (good) and beta (weak) men as a way of critiquing issues with the social order (/u/GayLubeOil 2019). /r/MensRights is more likely to post about current events, using them to highlight their perceptions of inequalities in the ways that men and women are treated in society (/u/Hibernia86 2019). While not the least or most extreme examples of manosphere thinking, they reveal contrast in the ways that different subgroups approach gender-linked social issues, but share some core values. They also demonstrate how Reddit's affordances allow groups to be driven by different kinds of content while espousing similar traditionalist values of the right.

The /r/MensRights subreddit is dominated by discussions of the misandry participants perceive in their lives. The users are mostly from Western democracies (e.g. United States, Canada, Australia and Western Europe),[7] and they craft narratives around specific issues to build a semi-coherent narrative of the oppression of men. The larger themes within this narrative include: statistically higher numbers of men are homeless or underhoused, murdered, incarcerated, die at work or die by suicide. They discuss issues of binary gender disparity between men and women in custody court proceedings; spousal support proceedings; allegations, convictions and relative severity of punishment for perpetrators in sexual assault and misconduct allegations; and the (United States) military draft. Posts and discussions most often begin with content from major news sources, national and local statistics, secondary news sources or social media that the user believes highlights one (or more) of the subreddit's core issues (e.g. men losing custody of children). They often include a catchy title and brief commentary from the original poster intended to promote discussion and/or frame the content as a men's rights issue in a particular way. Comments from users are generally agreeable, conversation is generally civil when there are disagreements and users are supportive of others who have been negatively affected by the issue highlighted in the post (e.g. users who feel they have been disaffected by the child custody court system). Almost all threads in the subreddit begin with or come back to being critical of feminism, and what they view as 'misandrist' public and judicial policy.

/R/THEREDPILL

www.reddit.com/r/TheRedPill
Created 25 October 2012
Quarantined September 2018
292,612 subscribed members as of September 2018[8]

/r/TheRedPill is dedicated to the 'Discussion of sexual strategy in a culture increasingly lacking a positive identity for men' (/r/TheRedPill 2019). What they mean by this is that they aim to help men (re)produce a specific type of masculinity, and leverage that masculinity to be dominant and sexually satisfied. Posts are largely divided between storytelling about sexual experience or lack thereof and the theoretical underpinning of their sexual and relationship ethos. Men are divided into successful (alpha) and unsuccessful (other – including beta, etc.) groups, and sexual strategy is discussed at length. Dominance and manipulation are paramount to the approach espoused by these men, and their understanding of male-female relationships is imbricated with ideologies of male supremacism. Discussion within the forum can be supportive and castigating, and while the tone is civil overall, users who challenge the red pill canon are quickly downvoted or banned.

CAN WE CALL THESE COMMUNITIES FAR RIGHT?

So, are /r/MensRights and /r/TheRedPill groups on Reddit far-right groups? Or do they occupy a kind of middle ground that can simultaneously expound or mobilize beliefs similar to those of far-right groups, but avoid the deleterious label associated with near-extremism? The work of Norberto Bobbio (1996) is useful here, as it provides a succinct way of discussing the difference between *left* and *right* as a representation of the 'original, essential dichotomy' (Bobbio 1996, 33) between opposing political viewpoints. The left, as Bobbio sees it, leans more towards the needs and benefits of the broader social group, and the right towards the needs and benefits of the individual. As Bobbio puts it, 'On the one hand, people who believe that human beings are more equal than unequal, and on the other, people who believe that we are more unequal than equal' (Bobbio 1996, 67). Citing Dino Cofrancesco, Bobbio explains that 'the soul of the right can be expressed succinctly in the motto "Nothing outside or against tradition, everything within and for the sake of tradition"' (Bobbio 1996, 46). Tradition here can mean a variety of things, including: as an archetype, the ideal of a past era, loyalty to a nation, a common destiny, historical memory, or as an awareness of the complexity of reality (Bobbio 1996). We can use Bobbio's interpretation of the binary between left and right (with the caveat that political ideology exists in spectrum, rather than binary) to evaluate whether /r/MensRights and /r/TheRedPill are in fact '*far-right*'.

For Bobbio, the fundamental question that separates the elements of this binary is the approach to equality, and whether a group works towards or away from equality. Understanding that Bobbio's conceptualization of equality is grounded in the Italian term *uguale* is essential, since this connotation makes the understanding of equality/inequality much closer to sameness/

difference, rather than having more of less of *something*. In the case of /r/TheRedPill, discussion is frequently and deeply entrenched in the concept of alpha and beta men (where alpha is always already different from and better than beta), and that men should be in charge of (most) spheres of society (see, e.g. Molten 2020).[9] While being problematically Western-centric and heteronormative, the crux of the belief is that there exists a permanent and socially solidified set of differences between men, and between men and women, and that given those differences (alpha) men should be in control. For the men of /r/TheRedPill, these standardized gender differences, and male domination as a result of them, are traditional in that they are archetypal, couched in a historical memory of male supremacy and hold gender ideals of a past era. They promote concepts of difference, and within the categories that separate people (i.e. gender, male hierarchies, etc.) humans are more unequal than they are equal. With these understandings in mind, we can certainly conclude that /r/TheRedPill is situated on the *right*, and the male supremacist content, centred on domination and control over the autonomy of others, makes for a compelling argument that we should consider them a potentially dangerous group on the far right of the spectrum.

/r/MensRights is slightly more complicated in this discussion of left and right. On the matter of equality, members of /r/MensRights would argue that the singular driver of their discussions and activism is to achieve Bobbio's equality-as-sameness. The men's rights movement of /r/MensRights believes that it is men who are widely disadvantaged in Western society, and therefore their agitation towards equality is meant to return men and women to parity in a world where feminist dogma has made women the privileged class. The difficulty of the disconnect between how you (the reader) might see the group politically, and how they (/r/MensRights users) might see themselves lies, then, in ontological and epistemological differences – fundamental differences in understanding how things are (ontology), and how we know what we know (epistemology). Members of /r/MensRights understand that we live in a world that is deeply unequal, which is true, but in their understanding it is men who are oppressed by this unequal system. Justification of this worldview comes in the form of personal anecdotes and posting of articles and content that serve to highlight the core issues listed in the community description earlier in this chapter. Wage disparity is a favourite topic, and community members use articles from popular press (/u/JohnKimble111 2020); social media posts they understand as feminist (/u/pritchie654321 2020); and statistics about benefits, work fatalities and injuries (/u/mhandanna 2020) to support the view that men are *the* subordinated class. Rarely are the assertions of male subordination challenged in the community, and this often leads to surface-level investigation of the resources and information the community uses to support its claims of male oppression.

On the surface, the counter-narrative presented by /r/MensRights should challenge our assumption that they are on the right, as they claim to stand in resistance to normative, gendered expectations of men. However, here too we can apply Bobbio's (1996) adherence to traditionalism as a mark of the right to help us establish their position. The rhetoric in /r/MensRights is deeply anti-feminist, and they use feminism as a foil and a scapegoat to demarcate their positions as advocates for men. They position their worldview as the alternative to feminist-influenced social structures – structures that they believe have made the world radically unequal in favour of women. They argue that feminism is, therefore, the reason for the male subordination they perceive in the world. Within their community, they agitate for reliance on meritocratic, neoliberal and capitalist ways of measuring value and social contribution; ways of knowing that disproportionately elevate and privilege (some) men and traditionally masculine ways of being over all others. In other words, when considered in relation to existing historical systems of oppression, they appear to push not for actual equality (sameness), but rather for a return to a system state that privileged men over women. One way they do this is through highlighting men's deeper engagement in dirty, dangerous or time-consuming professions and activities – roles traditionally taken on by men – without critical exploration about why these roles have historically belonged to men. They spend little time making arguments about opening up traditionally feminized professions to men (e.g. care work), nor changing traditionally male roles to be more inclusive to women (i.e. they don't seem interested in re-engineering tools and equipment to make them accessible to everyone, or changing the ways we work to make them more inclusive). This demonstrates that many of their arguments and intentions are steeped in a Western gendered traditionalism (both institutional and personal) and an historical memory of male privilege that would rather see the lives of men bettered, than strive for actual equality. There is also the implicit preference for an economic system that is fundamentally capitalist, where value is measured through time-at-work and 'production', at the expense of care work and other unpaid labour. While there are advocates within this group for more open emotional spaces for men, and an expanded role for men as fathers and mentors, the traditionalist undercurrents of gender and capitalist value orientation within /r/MensRights are enough to situate them on the *right.* The deeply anti-feminist discussion and calls for action are sufficient to place them on the far-right for the purposes of this chapter.

HOW REDDIT IS INVOLVED

Having positioned both /r/MensRights and /r/TheRedPill within the spectrum of anti-feminist far-right ideology, we can now consider how Reddit enables participation and recruitment to these groups, and provides space for expansion of far-right rhetoric and ideology. As a platform, Reddit builds community for its users in a number of important ways: (1) It brings groups together, either by allowing existing groups with low and geographically dispersed membership to gather online, or the formation of new groups of like-minded individuals (the de-coupling of shared experience from geography); (2) it allows those who would rather be listeners (lurkers) (Crawford 2011) to participate passively in group activities (it has an available spectrum of participation); (3) it acts as a safe haven for otherwise socially contentious groups (a free and open platform made up of communities of shared interest); and (4) provides the auspices of a legitimate and widely used site as a mode of connection (it feels cogent). Each of these affordances, as imbricated technological infrastructures and human agency (Leonardi 2011), are significant in their own way in the development of flourishing anti-feminist communities. Having an established meeting space helps build connection between community members, and allows low-participation members of the community to feel like part of the group (Glover and Sharpe 2020). Community sensibility helps groups better weather challenges (Kerwin et al. 2015), and community participation helps develop social capital and personal wellbeing (Glover 2016). Salazar (2018) argued that these concepts of personal and group gain through community should be applied to far-right groups, by positing the alt-right as a community of discourse. By doing so, Salazar helps us to understand the importance of community in the development and proliferation of the types of far-right anti-feminist ideology we see in /r/MensRights and /r/TheRedPill. These community elements, combined with Reddit's commitment to open speech, ease of use and the quasi-anonymity of users have allowed hate speech, misogyny and racism to proliferate on the site (Massanari 2017). Although much has changed on Reddit since it first introduced an actionable content policy in 2015, Reddit remains a place where individuals come to engage in contentious communities.[10]

Recruitment into /r/MensRights and /r/TheRedPill appears to follow the same types of trajectories identified in previous literature on the alt-right; work that is modelled on theories developed in the study of terrorism and extremist recruitment. Munn identifies three significant phases as individuals move from introduction of socially controversial views to extreme versions of those views: normalization, acclimatization and dehumanization. Munn points out that each individual journey is different and, 'while these phases might be loosely mapped to the start, middle and end . . . they should not be seen as mutually exclusive or strictly linear. They may overlap or occur in more cyclical formations' (Munn 2019, para. 1). Described by Munn's participants as a 'gradual progression', initial exposure and internalization come when the individual is repeatedly exposed to content that, while problematic, does not push the user away. Through this repeated exposure, the user becomes acclimatized to the content, opening them up to more radical notions through another round of normalization. Through this process, users move slowly towards ideological extremes, and other forms of (often more radical) content.

We can see a simplified version of this process within manosphere men's groups. /r/MensRights content is unrestricted on Reddit, and so it occasionally makes its way into the /r/all feed, or into the suggested subreddits of users. With over 288,000 members, participants are active in many parts of Reddit, and other users are likely exposed to /r/MensRights content through their comments, user pages and post histories. /r/TheRedPill has a different path, as content from the subreddit no longer appears in the /r/all feed or other non-subscribed aggregate feeds since being quarantined in 2018. Users who come to this group post-quarantine must be told about it in order to find it and participate – something that occurs from other men's rights subreddits, like /r/MensRights. Other than having predominantly male users, the closest connection between the two communities is their disdain for feminism and feminists. This disdain, within the /r/MensRights community, drives some users to seek out other models for building and maintaining relationships with women, and this exploration leads (through shared content, or the other affordances of the Reddit platform) to communities like /r/TheRedPill.

WHY THIS ALL MATTERS

The combination of the users' ability to specifically curate their own exposure to content, the sense of community within individual subgroups, Reddit's algorithmic and user vote–based sorting mechanisms and the permissive orientation of the platform to many kinds of speech makes Reddit an ideal platform for sustaining undercurrents of masculinist far-right ideology, and developing new users for these groups. Like Munn's (2019) pipeline to extremism, the men's rights communities on Reddit have both introductory spaces for first contact of new initiates and deeper, more intense discussion spaces as breeding grounds for more radical action and thought. Where /r/MensRights leverages examples of men's potential social subordination and provides examples of popular cultural 'misandry', /r/TheRedPill takes these issues to be self-evident and instead engages in a type of male superiority socio-sexual warfare where women are to be treated as a subordinated class in all aspects of life; especially sexually. While it is possible to move directly to the extremes of ideological thought and action relatively quickly (e.g. going full 'red pill'), adherents to extreme ideologies are far more likely to move through more socially palatable (mainstream) critiques and ideological standpoints before committing to strong extremist viewpoints (Munn 2019; Walklate and Mythen 2018). In this example, finding /r/MensRights, then moving on to /r/TheRedPill demonstrates this process. Reddit provides the type of scaffolded affordances required to carry new users into problematic ideological spaces and to mobilize misogyny.

If we can demonstrate the same kinds of inter-referential community patterns within men's groups as have been identified with far-right ideological development, then we must conclude that similar types of radicalization are occurring. Indeed, acts such as the murder of Daniel Anderl, son of New Jersey U.S. federal judge Esther Salas, by Roy Den Hollander (Marcotte 2020; Haworth et al. 2020) demonstrate that one end point of the ideological progression within men's groups is the murder of those who oppose their views. Den Hollander was involved in several federal lawsuits in the United States alleging discrimination against men, and was a known 'men's rights' troll' online (Marcotte 2020, para. 1). While acts of violence like Den Hollander's, or the murder of ten people by self-proclaimed incel Alek Minassian in Toronto, Canada (Humphreys and Edmiston 2018), are often positioned in the media as lone wolf attacks or stochastic terrorism, they link back to involvement in men's groups online – a phenomenon that demonstrates the interconnectedness of these misogynist murders (Marcotte 2020; DiBranco 2020). This should alarm us! While discussions within these men's groups are about the place of men and masculinity within modern (Western) society, they also push users to the ideological right and alt-right. This should be frightening, and participants in men's communities have demonstrated the ability to act on their feelings about gender and the social order with violence (Baker 2020; Humphreys and Edmiston 2018; Nasser 2020; Scaptura and Boyle 2019). Perhaps even more insidious is their less overt and non-violent push back against cultural and social justice movements. The embeddedness of sex role and gender traditionalism seen across the men's rights movement (overtly in places like /r/TheRedPill and more covertly in spaces like /r/MensRights), places them in lock-step with other far- and alt-right groups, while the absence of the same types of overt or obsessive racism or nationalism sets them apart.

While these men clearly see the progress achieved by feminism as an affront to male power and social order, the outcome of that sense of grievance has active and daily repercussions in civil society. Posts from /r/MensRights and /r/TheRedPill link to outside articles, YouTube videos and other forum platforms, and contain millions of words of topic comments and discussions. In many cases these outside links and comments direct the user further to the right, and deeper into the cultural and ideological spectrum of men's group participation discussed earlier. Reddit is designed to permit and encourage this aggregation of content, and creates focused ideological wind tunnels that carry information and users towards more radical viewpoints.

NOTES

1. Hegemony, throughout this chapter, can be understood through Halberstam's (2011) definition as 'multilayered system[s] by which a dominant group achieves power not through coercion but through the production of an interlocking system of ideas which persuades people of the rightness of any given set of often contradictory ideas and perspectives' (p. 17).
2. See the evolution of the writing of Warren Farrell (1975, 1996, 2005, 2012).
3. This chapter was authored during the Covid-19 pandemic, so this image is familiar to many; the image of the virus that causes the Covid-19 illness provides an excellent representation of how we can visualize the construction of the manosphere.
4. The earliest iteration of the NCFM website available is from the web archive of 1996 (National Coalition of Free Men 1996), but the copyright on that site reads 1995, indicating that the site was active at that time.
5. There are some exceptions to this rule, as users can be banned from posting or voting on content from a given subreddit if they are found to be in violation of the community rules of that sub-community.
6. Users can still navigate to /r/all to see content from the entire site if they choose, or set /r/all as their landing page.
7. There is a small but notable presence of users in this community from India and Pakistan, and although there are some women who participate in this subreddit community, the vast majority of users appear to be men.
8. This number is highly misleading and likely contains a high number of bots. In June 2019 the subscriber count was just over 400,000, and 292,612 subscribers at the time of quarantine in September 2018.
9. /r/TheRedPill also has an entire sorting category for posts labelled 'Red Pill Theory' which contains much of the group's discussion of topics of social order and men's positioning within that order.
10. There are signs that this may be slowing as Reddit has moved in significant ways to limit hate speech and harassment on the platform. Reddit's harassment policy has undergone some significant revisions since October 2019 that have resulted in the banning of a large number of communities, including /r/The_Donald and /r/Gender Critical, and in significant changes to what the site deems harassing behaviour (Allyn 2020; u/spez 2020).

REFERENCES

Allyn, Bobby. 2020. 'Reddit Bans The_Donald, Forum of Nearly 800,000 Trump Fans, over Abusive Posts'. *NPR.Org*. 29 June 2020. https://www.npr.org/2020/06/29/884819923/reddit-bans-the_donald-forum-of-nearly-800-000-trump-fans-over-abusive-posts.

Auxier, Brooke E., and Jessica Vitak. 2019. 'Factors Motivating Customization and Echo Chamber Creation within Digital News Environments'. *Social Media + Society* 5 (2): 1–13. https://doi.org/10.1177/2056305119847506.

Baker, Carrie N. 2020. 'Misogyny, Murder and the Men's Rights Movement – Ms. Magazine." *Ms.* 27 July 2020. https://msmagazine.com/2020/07/27/misogyny-murder-and-the-mens-rights-movement/.

Berbrier, Mitch. 2000. 'The Victim Ideology of White Supremacists and White Separatists in the United States'. *Sociological Focus* 33 (2): 175–91. https://doi.org/10.1080/00380237.2000.10571164.

Bobbio, Norberto. 1996. *Left and Right: The Significance of a Political Distinction*. Chicago, IL: University of Chicago Press.

Boehme, Hunter M., and Deena A. Isom Scott. 2020. 'Alt-White? A Gendered Look at "Victim" Ideology and the Alt-Right'. *Victims & Offenders* 15 (2): 174–96. https://doi.org/10.1080/15564886.2019.1679308.

Braithwaite, Andrea. 2016. 'It's about Ethics in Games Journalism? Gamergaters and Geek Masculinity'. *Social Media + Society* 2 (4): 1–10. https://doi.org/10.1177/2056305116672484.

Carlson, Caitlin Ring, and Luc S. Cousineau. 2020. "Are You Sure You Want to View This Community? Exploring the Ethics of Reddit's Quarantine Practice'. *Journal of Media Ethics* (September): 35 (4): 202–213. https://doi.org/10.1080/23736992.2020.1819285.

Condren, Mary. 2009. 'Suffering into Truth: Constructing the Patriarchal Sacred'. *Feminist Theology* 17 (3): 356–91. https://doi.org/10.1177/0966735009102364.

Connell, R. W. 2005. *Masculinities*. 2nd ed. Book, Whole. Berkeley: University of California Press.

Connell, R. W., and James W. Messerschmidt. 2005. "Hegemonic Masculinity: Rethinking the Concept." *Gender and Society*, no. 6: 829.

Cornwall, Andrea, Frank G. Karioris, and Nancy Lindisfarne, eds. 2016. *Masculinities under Neoliberalism*. Zed Books Ltd.

Cousineau, Luc S. 2021. 'Sex, Power, and Body Control: Men's Rights Leisure Participation and Neoliberal Discourses of Power and Control'. In *Promiscuous Perspectives: Explorations of Sex and Leisure*, edited by Diana C. Parry and Corey W. Johnson, 73–90. New York: Routledge.

Crawford, Kate. 2011. 'Listening, Not Lurking: The Neglected Form of Participation'. In *Cultures of Participation*, edited by Hajo Greif, Larissa Hjorth, and Amparo Lasén, 63–74. Berlin: Peter Lang.

Crowley, Jocelyn Elise. 2009. 'Fathers' Rights Groups, Domestic Violence and Political Countermobilization'. *Social Forces* 88 (2): 723–55. https://doi.org/10.1353/sof.0.0276.

DeCook, Julia. 2019. 'How Deep Does the Rabbit Hole Go? The "Wonderland" of r/TheRedPill and Its Ties to White Supremacy'. *Boundary 2* (blog). 8 November 2019. https://www.boundary2.org/2019/11/julia-decook-how-deep-does-the-rabbit-hole-go-the-wonderland-of-r-theredpill-and-its-ties-to-white-supremacy/.

DiBranco, Alex. 2020. 'Male Supremacist Terrorism as a Rising Threat', February. https://icct.nl/publication/male-supremacist-terrorism-as-a-rising-threat/.

Dobratz, Betty A., and Stephanie L. Shanks-Meile. 2006. 'The Strategy of White Separatism'. *Journal of Political and Military Sociology* 34 (1): 49–79.

Dragiewicz, Molly, and Ruth M. Mann. 2016. 'Special Edition: Fighting Feminism – Organised Opposition to Women's Rights; Guest Editors' Introduction'. *Inter-*

national Journal for Crime, Justice and Social Democracy 5 (2): 1. https://doi.org/10.5204/ijcjsd.v5i2.313.

Ebner, J., & Davey, J. 2019. How Women Advance the Internationalization of the Far-Right (Perspectives on the Future of Women, Gender, & Violent Extremism, p. 8) [Commissioned Paper]. George Washington University Program on Extremism. https://extremism.gwu.edu/sites/g/files/zaxdzs2191/f/How%20Women%20Advance%20the%20Internationalization%20of%20the%20Far-Right.pdf.

Farrell, Warren. 1975. *The Liberated Man: Beyond Masculinity: Freeing Men and Their Relationships with Women*. New York: Bantam Books.

Farrell, Warren. 1996. *The Myth of Male Power*. Berkley Books.

Farrell, Warren. 2005. *Why Men Earn More: The Startling Truth behind the Pay Gap – and What Women Can Do about It*. American Management Association. New York: AMACOM.

Farrell, Warren. 2012. 'Why Men Are the Disposable Sex'. 1 (2): 30.

Forscher, Patrick S., and Nour S. Kteily. 2020. 'A Psychological Profile of the Alt-Right'. *Perspectives on Psychological Science* 15 (1): 90–116. https://doi.org/10.1177/1745691619868208.

Foucault, Michel. 1979. *Discipline and Punish: The Birth of the Prison*. Vintage Books.

Franklin, Cortney A. 2005. 'Male Peer Support and the Police Culture: Understanding the Resistance and Opposition of Women in Policing'. *Women & Criminal Justice* 16 (3): 1–25. https://doi.org/10.1300/J012v16n03_01.

Ging, Debbie. 2019. 'Alphas, Betas, and Incels: Theorizing the Masculinities of the Manosphere'. *Men and Masculinities* 22 (4): 638–57. https://doi.org/10.1177/1097184X17706401.

Glover, Troy D. 2016. 'Leveraging Leisure-Based Community Networks to Access Social Capital'. In *Leisure Matters: The State and Future of Leisure Studies*, edited by Gordon J. Walker, David Scott, and Monika Stodolska, 277–85. Champaign, IL: Sagamore Publishing.

Glover, Troy D., and Erin K. Sharpe. 2020. *Leisure Communities: Rethinking Mutuality, Collective Identity and Belonging in the New Century*. Routledge.

Goldberg, Herb. 1976. *The Hazards of Being Male: Surviving the Myth of Masculine Privilege*. Wellness Institute, Inc.

Gordon, Glenna. 2018. 'American Women of the Far Right'. *The New York Review of Books* (blog). 13 December 2018. https://www.nybooks.com/daily/2018/12/13/american-women-of-the-far-right/.

Halberstam, Judith. 2011. 'Introduction: Low Theory'. In *The Queer Art of Failure*, 1–25. Durham: Duke University Press.

Haworth, Jon, Aaron Katersky, Mark Crudele, and Ivan Pereira. 2020. 'Salas Shooter Linked to California Murder of Men's Rights Attorney: FBI'. ABC News. 22 July 2020. https://abcnews.go.com/US/salas-shooter-targeting-female-judge/story?id=71892702.

Hodge, Edwin, and Helga Hallgrimsdottir. 2019. 'Networks of Hate: The Alt-Right, "Troll Culture", and the Cultural Geography of Social Movement Spaces Online'. *Journal of Borderlands Studies* (February): 1–18. https://doi.org/10.1080/08865655.2019.1571935.

hooks, bell. 2003. 'Feminism: A Movement to End Sexist Oppression'. In *Feminist Theory Reader: Local & Global*, edited by Carole McCann and Seung-Kyug Kim, 50–56.

Howard, John W., III, and Laura C Prividera. 2004. 'Rescuing Patriarchy or Saving "Jessica Lynch": The Rhetorical Construction of the American Woman Soldier'. *Women and Language* 27 (2): 89–97.

Humphreys, Adrian, and Jake Edmiston. 2018. 'Toronto Van Attack Suspect Alek Minassian's Interest in "Incel" Movement the Latest Sign of Troubled Life | National Post'. *The National Post*, 25 April 2018. https://nationalpost.com/news/alek-minassian.

Ironwood, Ian. 2013. *The Manosphere: A New Hope for Masculinity*. First Kindle Edition. Red Pill Press.

Jordan, Ana. 2016. 'Conceptualizing Backlash: (UK) Men's Rights Groups, Anti-Feminism, and Postfeminism'. *Canadian Journal of Women and the Law* 28 (1): 18–44.

Kalish, Rachel, and Michael Kimmel. 2010. 'Suicide by Mass Murder: Masculinity, Aggrieved Entitlement, and Rampage School Shootings'. *Health Sociology Review* 19 (4): 451–64. https://doi.org/10.5172/hesr.2010.19.4.451.

Kelly, Annie. 2017. 'The Alt-Right: Reactionary Rehabilitation for White Masculinity'. *Soundings* 66: 68–78. https://doi.org/10.3898/136266217821733688.

Kerwin, Shannon, Stacy Warner, Matthew Walker, and Julie Stevens. 2015. 'Exploring Sense of Community among Small-Scale Sport Event Volunteers'. *European Sport Management Quarterly* 15 (1): 77–92. https://doi.org/10.1080/16184742.2014.996581.

Larkin, Ralph W. 2007. *Comprehending Columbine*. Temple University Press.

Leonardi. 2011. 'When Flexible Routines Meet Flexible Technologies: Affordance, Constraint, and the Imbrication of Human and Material Agencies'. *MIS Quarterly* 35 (1): 147. https://doi.org/10.2307/23043493.

Lumsden, Karen, and Emily Harmer, eds. 2019. *Online Othering: Exploring Digital Violence and Discrimination on the Web*. Cham, Switzerland: Springer International Publishing. https://doi.org/10.1007/978-3-030-12633-9.

Marcotte, Amanda. 2020. 'Feminists Have Warned Us – and Now Another "Men's Rights Activist" Turns to Murder'. *Salon*. 21 July. https://www.salon.com/2020/07/21/feminists-have-warned-us--and-now-another-mens-rights-activist-turns-to-murder/.

Martin, Patricia Yancey. 2004. 'Gender as Social Institution'. *Social Forces* 82 (4): 1249–73. https://doi.org/10.1353/sof.2004.0081.

Marwick, Alice E. 2017. 'Scandal or Sex Crime? Gendered Privacy and the Celebrity Nude Photo Leaks'. *Ethics and Information Technology* 19 (3): 177–91.

Massanari, Adrienne L. 2015. *Participatory Culture, Community, and Play: Learning from Reddit*. New York: Peter Lang.

Massanari, Adrienne L. 2017. '#Gamergate and the Fappening: How Reddit's Algorithm, Governance, and Culture Support Toxic Technocultures'. *New Media & Society* 19 (3): 329–46. https://doi.org/10.1177/1461444815608807.

Messerschmidt, James W. 2018. *Hegemonic Masculinity: Formulation, Reformulation, and Amplification*. Rowman & Littlefield.

Messner, Michael A. 1998. 'The Limits of "The Male Sex Role": An Analysis of the Men's Liberation and Men's Rights Movements' Discourse'. *Gender & Society* 12 (3): 255–76.

Messner, Michael A. 2016. 'Forks in the Road of Men's Gender Politics: Men's Rights vs Feminist Allies'. *International Journal for Crime, Justice and Social Democracy* 5 (2): 6–20. https://doi.org/10.5204/ijcjsd.v5i2.301.

Molten, M. 2020. 'Learned Betaness: A Reflection on Societies Failure to Produce Alpha Males'. *Reddit.Com/r/TheRedPill*. 4 February. https://www.reddit.com/r/TheRedPill/comments/eyd42r/learned_betaness_a_reflection_on_societies/.

Munn, Luke. 2019. 'Alt-Right Pipeline: Individual Journeys to Extremism Online'. *First Monday* 24 (6). https://doi.org/10.5210/fm.v24i6.10108.

Nasser, Shanifa. 2020. 'Terror Charges in Alleged "Incel"-Inspired Stabbing Could Force Reckoning of Canada's Terrorism Laws: Experts'. CBC. 20 May. https://www.cbc.ca/news/canada/toronto/incel-canada-terrorism-1.5577015.

National Coalition of Free Men. 1996. 18 October. *National Coalition of Free Men Official Website* https://web.archive.org/web/19961018050013/; https://www.ncfm.org/.

National Coalition for Men (NCFM). 2019. 18 October. National Coalition of Free Men Official Website. https://web.archive.org/web/19961018050013/;https://www.ncfm.org/.

Noble, Safiya Umoja. 2018. *Algorithms of Oppression: How Search Engines Reinforce Racism*. New York: NYU Press.

Pai, Hsiao-Hung. 2016. *Angry White People: Coming Face-to-Face with the British Far Right*. Zed Books Ltd.

Pariser, Eli. 2011. *The Filter Bubble: What the Internet Is Hiding from You*. Penguin Books Limited.

Pleck, Joseph H. 2004. 'Men's Power with Women, Other Men, and Society: A Men's Movement Analysis'. In *Feminism and Masculinities*, edited by Peter Francis Murphy, 57–68. Oxford Readings in Feminism. Oxford, New York: Oxford University Press.

Reagle, Joseph. 2018. 'Nerd vs. Bro: Geek Privilege, Idiosyncrasy, and Triumphalism'. *First Monday* 23 (1). https://doi.org/10.5210/fm.v23i1.7879.

Reeve, Elle. 2018. 'This Is What the Life of an Incel Looks Like'. *Vice News* (blog). 2 August. https://news.vice.com/en_us/article/7xqw3g/this-is-what-the-life-of-an-incel-looks-like.

Rheingold, Howard. 1993. *The Virtual Community: Finding Connection in a Computerized World*. Addison-Wesley Longman Publishing Co., Inc. Reading, Massachusetts.

Rifkin, Janet. 1980. 'Toward a Theory of Law and Patriarchy'" *Harvard Women's Law Journal* 3: 83–96.

/r/TheRedPill. 2019. 'R/TheRedPill'. Reddit. 3 October. https://www.reddit.com/r/TheRedPill/.

Rubin, Gayle. 2009. 'The Traffic in Women: Notes on the "Political Economy" of Sex'. In *Feminist Anthropology: A Reader*, edited by Ellen Lewin, 87–106. New York: John Wiley & Sons.

Salazar, Philippe-Joseph. 2018. 'The Alt-Right as a Community of Discourse'. *Javnost – The Public* 25 (1–2): 135–43. https://doi.org/10.1080/13183222.2018.1423947.

Scaptura, Maria N., and Kaitlin M. Boyle. 2019. 'Masculinity Threat, "Incel" Traits, and Violent Fantasies Among Heterosexual Men in the United States'. *Feminist Criminology*, December, 155708511989641. https://doi.org/10.1177/1557085119896415.

Spender, Dale. 1996. *Nattering on the Net: Women, Power and Cyberspace*. Spinifex Press.

Thomas, Bronwen. 2011. 'What Is Fanfiction and Why Are People Saying Such Nice Things about It?' *Storyworlds: A Journal of Narrative Studies* 3: 1. https://doi.org/10.5250/storyworlds.3.2011.0001.

Turkle, Sherry. 1996. 'Virtuality and Its Discontents Searching for Community in Cyberspace'. In *The Wired Homestead: An MIT Press Sourcebook on the Internet and the Family*, edited by Joseph Turow and Andrea L. Kavanaugh, 385–402. Cambridge, MA: MIT Press.

/u/GayLubeOil. 2019. 'R/TheRedPill – The Unknowability of Beta Turd'. Reddit. 2019. https://www.reddit.com/r/TheRedPill/comments/a9qpbt/the_unknowability_of_beta_turd/.

/u/Hibernia86.2019. 'R/MensRights'. Reddit. 2019. https://www.reddit.com/r/MensRights/comments/ae25fl/prostitute_murders_sleeping_man_robs_him_serves/.

/u/JohnKimble111.2020. 'Great News, Ladies: The Gender Pay Gap Is a Myth – r/MensRights'. *Reddit*. 1 April. https://www.reddit.com/r/MensRights/comments/fsuof2/great_news_ladies_the_gender_pay_gap_is_a_myth/.

/u/mhandanna. 2020. 'The Work Place Gender Equality Agency Get Asked "What about the Gender Workplace Hours Gap?" And They Don't Know the Answer! I Wonder If Thet Know about Overtime, Holidays, Sick Leave, Work Place Fatalities and Injuries Etc (Hint: No but Oh MY GaWWad WyMyNN NoT PAiD EquALLy) – r/MensRights'. *Reddit*. 20 July. https://www.reddit.com/r/MensRights/comments/huc3xu/the_work_place_gender_equality_agency_get_asked/.

/u/pritchie654321.2020. 'Blatantly False Information, the Worst Part Is the Comments Seem to Think the Wage Gap Is Real. – r/MensRights'. *Reddit*. 16 March. https://www.reddit.com/r/MensRights/comments/fjxd7a/blatantly_false_information_the_worst_part_is_the/.

u/spez. 2020. 'R/Announcements – Upcoming Changes to Our Content Policy, Our Board, and Where We're Going from Here'. *Reddit*. 5 June. https://www.reddit.com/r/announcements/comments/gxas21/upcoming_changes_to_our_content_policy_our_board/.

Walklate, Sandra, and Gabe Mythen. 2018. 'The Problem with Radicalization: Overlooking the Elephants in the Room'. In *Routledge Handbook of Critical Criminology*, edited by Walter S. DeKeseredy and Molly Dragiewicz, 2nd ed., 213–21. Abingdon, Oxon UK: Routledge.

Wellman, Barry, and Milena Gulia. 1999. 'Virtual Communities as Communities: Net Surfers Don't Ride Alone'. In *Communities in Cyberspace*, edited by Marc A. Smith and Peter Kollock, 167–94. New York: Routledge.

Willer, Robb, Christabel L. Rogalin, Bridget Conlon, and Michael T. Wojnowicz. 2013. 'Overdoing Gender: A Test of the Masculine Overcompensation Thesis'. *American Journal of Sociology* 118 (4): 980–1022. https://doi.org/10.1086/668417.

Young, Iris Marion. 2013. 'Five Faces of Oppression'. In *Readings for Diversity and Social Justice*, edited by Maurianne Adams, Warren Blumenfeld, Carmelita Castaneda, Heather W. Hackman, Madeline L. Peters, and Ximena Zuniga, 4th ed., 35–49. New York, NY: Routledge.

Part III

PLATFORMS AND ALT-TECH COLLECTIVITY

Chapter 8

Soldiers of 4chan: The Role of Anonymous Online Spaces in Backlash Movement Networks

Andrey Kasimov

The growing popularity of radical right-wing movements and parties has led to a renewed interest by social movement scholars in studying how far-right movements use the Internet for the purposes of mobilization and recruitment. However, extant research on the digital far right is focused on online spaces that have an explicit agenda including but not limited to anti-Semitism, Islamophobia, anti-Black racism, misogyny and fascism. Consequently, this research mostly focuses on groups and individuals who have already been recruited into a movement, even if their participation is limited to an online context inhabited by like-minded users whose collective identity is loosely constructed around far-right ideology. As such, social movement scholars have overlooked a considerable population of young people who may share ideologies of the far-right and involve themselves in collective action guided by these ideologies, without necessarily pledging allegiance to specific movements and online communities. This chapter offers a systematic content analysis of a space that facilitates this type of participation: 4chan/pol/ – an enormous online community known for its racist and misogynist vitriol, its transgressive culture of trolling and perhaps less so for its ability to incite collective action among its members (Tuters and Hagen 2019). While early movements that formed on 4chan tended to organize around progressive causes (Watts 2018), over the past decade it has rapidly developed into a hub for proponents of radical right-wing ideology (Tuters 2020). This study will establish 4chan/pol/ as part of an online social movement scene of the far-right by identifying its connection to far-right movements and its attempts at recruitment, and then demonstrating the prevalence and effectiveness of calls to action motivated by far-right ideology.

SOCIAL MOVEMENTS OF THE FAR RIGHT

Social movement research has revealed much about how social movements function, why they form and disband and most importantly, what makes them appealing to potential recruits (Gamson 1995; McAdam, Tarrow and Tilly 2003; Polletta and Jasper 2001). Unfortunately, much of this research has been limited to progressive movements of the left and centre-left (although see: Blee and Yates 2015; Simi and Futrell 2015). Frequently, researchers have assumed that what is true for progressive movements on the left in terms of processes and operations must also hold for movements on the right (Blee 2017). Moreover, academics have historically avoided engaging in research with right-wing movements for a slew of methodological and practical reasons.

One such reason is studying radical right-wing movements, like the far-right, the so-called alt-right, and other reactionary groups with a reputation for violence, can sometimes be dangerous for the researcher (Simi and Futrell 2015). It is also often difficult to gain the trust of members of such movements when they are often highly mistrusting of authority figures and mainstream publics (Blee and Creasap 2010). Even in such cases where trust is acquired, interviewing members of such movements can be a great source of dissonance and even trauma for researchers (Glaser, Dixit and Green 2002; Wintrobe 2002). However, a lack of empirical, qualitative research on far-right or right-wing movements has left researchers struggling to answer pivotal questions pertaining to recruitment and mobilization on the far right at a time when such movements seem to be on the rise globally (Bessant 2018).

The limited research that exists on far-right movements has focused on groups that rally around a singular cause. A list of such movements might include the Ku Klux Klan (KKK) (Schmitz 2016), Skinheads (Valeri, Sweazy and Borgeson 2017), Neo-Nazis (Burris, Smith and Strahm 2000) and Christian Identity (Bailey 2010), among others. While such research is insightful, information and communication technologies have facilitated the growth of online spaces where adherents of each of these movements regularly interact and exchange ideas. Hitherto, there has not been as much research focusing on online communities that attract individuals from different segments of the far right, including individuals who are not aligned with any specific movement's cause. More recently researchers have begun to study how such movements are using the Internet as a 'safe space' where they are free to discuss contested views among like-minded individuals (Caren, Jowers and Gaby 2012; Futrell and Simi 2004). With features like anonymity and levels of censorship much lower than found in public spaces as well as traditional broadcast media, the Internet offers arenas for far-right movements to discuss strategic considerations, plan events on- and offline, build collective identity, incite individual or collective action and recruit new members into the movement (Marwick and Lewis 2017; Massanari 2017; Brown 2018; Daniels 2009; Jakubowicz 2017; Rohlinger and Bunnage 2018).

Caren, Jowers and Gaby (2012) extend Taylor and Whittier's (1992) concept of *social movement communities* to the virtual domain. Social movement *communities* were described by Taylor and Whittier (1992) in ways that emphasized their difference from social *movements* in their larger focus on establishing and maintaining a collective identity among their constituents. They consist of members with various levels of involvement and are often locally organized via conferences, events and media. When applied to the radical right, social movement communities often act as 'free spaces' for individuals who normally hide their espousal of far-right ideas in public (Futrell and Simi 2004). However, the attempts at making a distinction between social movements and movement communities have also faced criticism as it is often difficult to draw a strict boundary between the movement community and the movement itself (Dubet 2004).

One such space where the boundaries between movement and community are blurred is Stormfront.org, an online network for self-proclaimed white separatists that has existed for over two decades. Caren et al. (2012) argue that Stormfront is a social movement online community that exists and operates almost entirely digitally. Caren et al.'s conclusions are important because they demonstrate that an online setting changes the scope of social movement communities from local to global, thereby massively increasing their reach. For example, Stormfront currently has over 350,000 members worldwide, in comparison, there were approximately 600 people who showed up in Charlottesville for the 'Unite the Right' rally in 2017. However, this research begs a lot of unanswered questions regarding how online spaces are used for the purposes of mobilization and recruitment.

Social movement scholars have argued that a more effective outreach and recruitment strategy would be one where the movement can be advertised in areas that see significantly more traffic in order to (1) raise awareness about the movement to recruit individuals who may already sympathize with the movement ideologically but are unaware of its existence (Taylor and Whittier 1992) and (2) introduce the movement's ideologies to individuals who may be unfamiliar with them by broadcasting in a densely but heavily populated space (Leach and Haunss 2009). Online social movement communities like Stormfront seem to satisfy the former but not the second of these conditions.

SOCIAL MOVEMENT SCENES

Extant research on social movements has identified environments that are far more conducive than communities like Stormfront in the recruitment of new members into movements (Haunss and Leach 2007). These are referred to as *social movement scenes*. Social movement scenes are spaces with fluid boundaries where people sharing a common identity, beliefs, values and norms congregate regardless of whether they are already an affiliated participant in a movement or not (Leach and Haunss 2009). Importantly, social movement scenes often attract a mixture of people who range from apolitical to those highly involved in political causes (Creasap 2012). For example, Futrell, Simi and Gottschalk (2006) have studied the white power movement's music scene, where individuals initially came for music and to socially bond, only to be recruited into the movement and adopt its ideological framework later on.

Simi and Futrell (2015) reveal that scenes on the far right function differently compared to the left because of gatekeeping practices that are necessary to deter imposters, such as keeping names and addresses secret or requiring members to get tattoos of highly stigmatized hate symbols. Such studies demonstrate that the concept of social movement scenes is crucial to gaining a better understanding of the far right because it deals specifically with spaces that facilitate mobilization and recruitment. However, examples of far-right social movement scenes set in physical spaces are rare and are often difficult for outsiders to access. This is because most far-right communities have been associated with overt expressions of hate and violence within the mainstream, leading to their relegation to online, arguably less mainstream, spaces (Schmitz 2016; Simi and Futrell 2006).

While Leach and Haunss (2009) define *social movement scenes* as a network of physical locales, this definition proves limited when it comes to studying far-right movements that have developed an enormous online presence. Instead, my aim in this chapter is to extend the concept of *social movement scenes* to include *online social movement scenes*. While the added visibility and reach are one of the biggest benefits of hosting a scene online, rather than on the ground, they also leave it vulnerable to opponents of the movement who are free to analyzse discussions and mobilization attempts in an effort to thwart them. Thus, studying if and how members of online scenes adapt to this vulnerability has the potential to teach us something new about the function of Internet-based far-right communities. Sites like 4chan, 8chan and GAB, have been used by far-right groups in lieu of on-the-ground movement scenes because of their capacity to enable the recruitment and mobilization of a geographically diverse, uninitiated base of individuals on a massive scale (Marwick and Lewis 2017).

4CHAN AND /POL/

Given its staggering popularity and alleged positive impact on Donald Trump's presidential campaign (Beran 2019; Wendling 2018), 4chan remains an understudied phenomenon among social movement scholars. 4chan is unique when it comes to online communities because unlike other similar websites such as Reddit and Tumblr, users aren't required to register an account before posting. As a result, almost all posts on 4chan are made anonymously by users or 'Anons' as they are known on 4chan. Rather than a username, each post is authored by 'Anonymous'. This means that there is no way to track a user's posting history or readily establish if any two posts were made by the same individual (Knuttila 2011). The website also possesses an element of ephemerality because threads that do not get responses quickly disappear off the front page and eventually the website. This ensures that only posts that receive large amounts of engagement from other users have any sort of longevity on 4chan.

The website consists of over forty different message boards, each focusing on a different topic. Each board is more commonly known by an abbreviated name (usually between one and four letters long placed between two forward slashes like this: /name/). The diverse list of topics covered on each board includes Japanese animation (/a/), finance (/biz/), music (/mu/), pornography (/hc/), video games (/v/), among others. However, 4chan is best known for the content that gets posted on its biggest board: *politically incorrect* or /pol/ (Siegel 2015) which according to 4stats.io (as of June 2020) accounts for approximately 20% of all traffic to the site. This makes /pol/ the most popular board on 4chan. The stated purpose of /pol/ is to be a place for the discussion of politics and news around the world. Over the past decade however, /pol/ has developed into a space where violent and hateful content is posted daily (Hine et al. 2016). In order to limit the scope of this study towards social movements, I focused on collecting and analysing data from the 4chan/pol/ board alone.

THE PRESENT STUDY

Social movement scenes are prime environments for recruiting new members into social movements (Creasap 2012). The purpose of my study is to identify whether 4chan/pol/ fits the criteria of an online social movement scene, in order to use this diagnosis as a way of uncovering their recruitment and mobilization tactics. One common method for recruiting members into the far right is the spread of information that either directly or indirectly supports far-right ideology by targeting specific groups (Bessant 2018; Gerstenfeld, Grant and Chiang 2003; Marwick and Lewis 2017). In this chapter I have identified and analysed the prevalence of discussion threads on 4chan/pol/ that adapt this type of recruitment strategy on the board. Specifically, I performed mixed-methods content analysis on all threads posted to /pol/ between

September 2018 and October 2019. First, I counted the number of threads that supported far-right ideology. The content of these threads usually involves targeting groups based on ethnicity, religion, gender and/or sexuality. This targeting can be direct (through the use of slurs and vitriol) or indirect (by claiming these groups are a threat to the Western way of life). Threads that targeted another group were qualitatively analysed for which group was targeted. I also counted threads that promoted far-right ideology (i.e. white or male supremacy, eugenics) and coded these as recruitment threads. I then categorized these threads based on the medium of recruitment (i.e. far-right social media, publications, links to far-right communities). Once the threads were categorized, I conducted a qualitative analysis to identify specific examples of media used for recruitment. Finally, I counted the number of far-right images (i.e. swastikas, lynching) present in each thread.

Social movement scenes also provide opportunities for individuals to participate in individual and collective action. Thus, I analysed the prevalence of 'calls to far-right action' on 4chan/pol/. I qualified 'calls to far-right action' as threads that attempted to incite some sort of individual and/or collective action from users. I define posts that incite individual or collective action as threads that tell users that they should take a certain action in pursuit of a far-right cause. Any thread that calls upon users to act – regardless of engagement – qualified as a call to far-right action for the purposes of this study. While it is possible that the authors of these posts are merely posting such violent political calls for their shock value (Phillips 2015), previous studies confirm multiple instances of successful attempts at inciting collective action by 4chan users (Coleman 2014; Tuters and Hagen 2019). For example, past research has identified threads on /pol/ that successfully mobilized 4chan users to post hateful comments on YouTube videos in phenomenon known as *raids* (Hine et al. 2016). Raids serve as a tactical repertoire of 4chan users who call upon others to disrupt a community on another website. Hine et al. 2016 found a significant correlation between the time a link to a YouTube video was posted and the timing of hateful comments appearing in the comment section of that video. Thus, I posit that the main purpose of such posts is to introduce users to far-right ideology, entice interested members into joining far-right movements and/or act to help their cause. Subsequently, this chapter asks: what can we learn about far-right recruitment and mobilization by analysing 4chan as an *online social movement scene*?

FINDINGS

While conducting preliminary analyses for this study, my analysis confirmed colloquial knowledge about 4chan that groups targeted most on /pol/ are racialized people, women and LGBTQ groups. Unsurprisingly, these groups had an overwhelming amount of hateful and violent posts directed at them (see figure 8.1). Such posts frequently included images depicting violence against a member of the targeted group and/or discussed how and why members of one group are inferior relative to another. Anecdotal experiences of user's alleged encounters depicting members of minority groups as uncivilized and dehumanized were commonplace. Such posts are not banned or discouraged on 4chan because of its active commitment to anti-censorship and anonymity (Knuttila 2011).

My analysis of recruitment posts on 4chan/pol/ over the span of one year revealed the prevalence of links to other far-right communities, links to far-right social media, links to far-right propaganda blogs and links to pseudo-scientific books and articles that are used to support far-right ideas. These make up 62% of all posts linking out of 4chan/pol/. In total, there were 4,551 topic threads that linked to far-right pages in the topic post. The total number of links to far-right pages was 81,655. This data set also contained 1,088,122 images containing far-right imagery that ranged from swastikas to lynchings. The use of far-right symbolism and violent imagery is a well-documented tactic of far-right movements used with the intention of inducing fear in their detractors (Blee 2017). There were 23,009 threads targeting specific groups; Jewish people were the most common target of hate speech with a total of 5,959 posts (see figure 8.1). About one in fourteen posts contained at least one racial slur.

Out of the links to far-right pages, 42% linked to dubious, or misread, scientific books and articles that were used to support far-right ideology. For

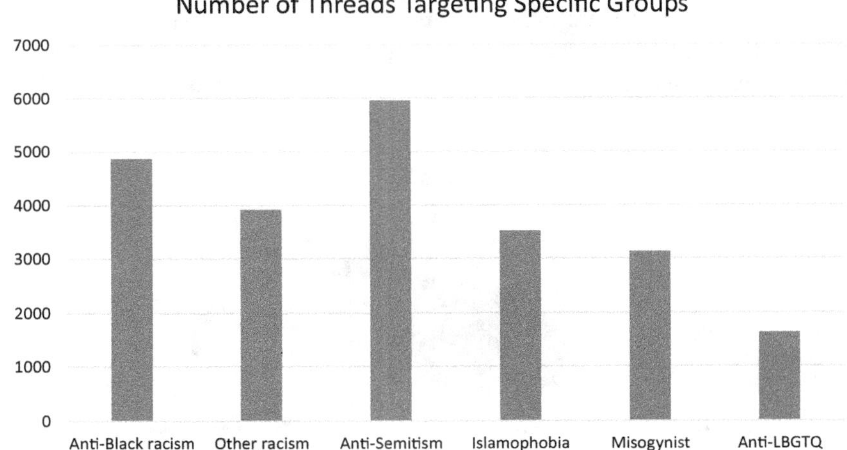

Figure 8.1. Graph of Number of Threads Targeting Specific Groups.
Source: Author.

example, the U.S. Federal Bureau of Investigation's crime statistics showing that Black and Latinx individuals are responsible for the majority of crimes were used to discuss white supremacy, given that such statistics are never paired with an analysis of underlying social, economic issues alongside racist policing and sentencing systems which account for such discrepancies (Alexander 2010). Articles and books on hereditary pseudo-science were also commonly discussed. These were used to support ideas that intelligence and aggression are genetic traits that prove that non-whites are inferior to whites and women are inferior to men, conclusions extensively disproven by studies within the social sciences (Fraser 2008). Some posts contained a collage of Wikipedia excerpts that reveal the Jewish religious affiliation or ethnicity of various influential figures. Another 33% linked to far-right propaganda blogs. Some of these were blogs by members of specific far-right movements such as James P. Wickstrom of the Christian Identity movement and Rick Wiles of TRUNews, a racist, homophobic, anti-semitic conspiracy theorist who has amassed a lot of followers. Another 12% linked to discussion boards similar to 4chan (i.e. 8chan, the *Daily Stormer*). Many of these communities differ from 4chan because they are more explicitly far-right as expressed by their mission statement, and thus are much more like Stormfront than 4chan. Finally, 9% linked to far-right social media accounts including Tweets by Richard Spencer and David Duke, and the Spotify podcast of Mike Enoch (see figure 8.2 for this breakdown).

The efforts to disseminate links to far-right communities, social media, blogs and pseudo-scientific propaganda are reminiscent of *leafleting* practices of on-the-ground movements which is a well-documented, low-involvement form of political activism (Taylor and van Dyke 2007). Just like leaflets, many posts on /pol/ were persistent, repetitive and their main purpose was to spread political dis-information in hopes of recruiting new members to their cause. Disseminating information is a tactic used to bolster the human

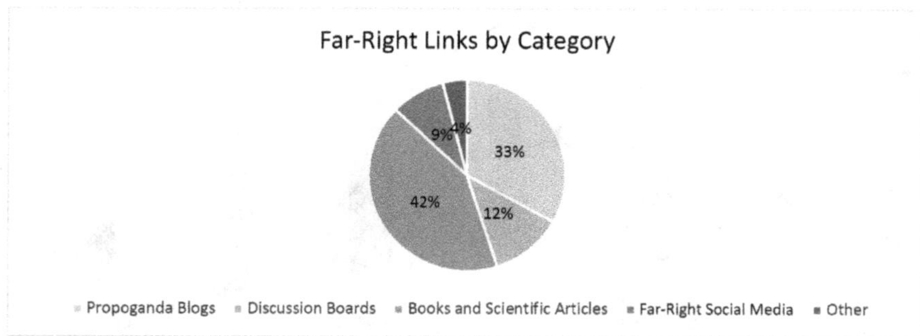

Figure 8.2. Pie Chart of Far-Right Links by Category.
Source: Author.

resources of social movements through consciousness raising (Turner and Killian 1987). Where there are leaflets, there are social movement constituents that are recruiting and potential new members they expect to recruit.

4chan/pol/ is also full of rampant praise for violent lone-wolf misogynists and white supremacists who have committed racialized or anti-women mass killings such as Dylan Roof, Elliott Rodger and Brenton Tarrant (among many others). In total, 71% of posts that mention an attacker inspired by some form of far-right ideology offered some sort of praise for the individual and his actions. Another 10% of posts discussing such attacks were neutral in that they neither praised nor admonished the attacker. However, almost half of these were posts questioning whether the attack had occurred at all, or if rather it was a 'psy-op planted by the state to continue pushing a liberal agenda'. Notably, such routing to conspiracy theories likely represents an attempt to dismiss culpability for their proximity to an attacker that resembles their own political behaviour (Devries 2021, this volume). Similarly, 19% of posts admonished the attacker and/or his actions, but about half of these lamented the fact that the attack did nothing to further far-right goals or ideology, and that it may even turn out to be a setback for the far-right.

While such posts neither provided links to far-right communities and websites nor called upon users to act on behalf of the far-right, the overwhelming support and notoriety given to lone-wolf attackers on 4chan's /pol/ board is nonetheless important to establishing 4chan/pol/ as an online social movement scene of the far-right. Several of these attackers have posted a 'manifesto' referencing 4chan (e.g. Alex Minassian, perpetrator of the Toronto Van Attack) prior to committing an attack, or had their manifesto re-posted on 4chan after first posting it on 8chan. This implies that they expected 4chan to be sympathetic to their ideas and actions (Glaser 2019). Furthermore, 4chan's commitment to anti-censorship, no matter the content, makes it one of the only places that is guaranteed to provide these individuals a platform for manifestos. During the data collection phase of this project, I observed how a leaked video of the New Zealand Christchurch Mosque massacre circulated around 4chan for weeks despite being banned everywhere else. The situation got so dire that the Australian government had to request Internet service providers to ban access to 4chan while it tried fruitlessly to contain the viral spread of the video.

4chan is rife with posts that attempt to recruit members by exposing them to far-right ideology via pseudo-science, propaganda, social media feeds, blogs and decontextualized statistics. These threads combined with overwhelming support for lone-wolf attackers inspired by far-right ideology suggest that 4chan/pol/ satisfies at least one criterion of an online social movement scene. It acts as a space where new members can be recruited by becoming exposed to far-right ideology and culture.

Calls to Far-Right Action and Responses

Social movement scenes foster an environment in which political goals and collective and/or individual action are more likely to be discussed and supported relative to other spaces (Leach and Haunss 2009). I analysed how prevalent 'calls to far-right action' are on 4chan's /pol/ board, what form they take and what type of these calls are most successful. A high prevalence of calls to action on 4chan satisfies the second criterion of what constitutes an online social movement scene. In addition, analysing them reveals how far-right movements are using online movement scenes like 4chan to accomplish their goals. Over the course of one year, I found that 3.1% of all topic posts could be classified as a call to action. Meanwhile, there was not a single instance of a call to action that propagated a progressive cause. In total, one in thirty-three threads urged users to take some sort of action on behalf of a far-right movement or ideology. These calls to far-right action primarily took three forms: online, offline and hypothetical/informative (see figure 8.3).

Online Calls to Action

Online calls to action were the most common, making up 58% of all such threads. Such posts requested 4chan users to engage in action over the Internet. In total, I identified 2,094 of these threads. These threads urged users to post comments on mainstream media websites (i.e. comments supporting Trump, or that would cause in-fighting within the left); send spam emails to various individuals and businesses; spam far-right memes on targeted

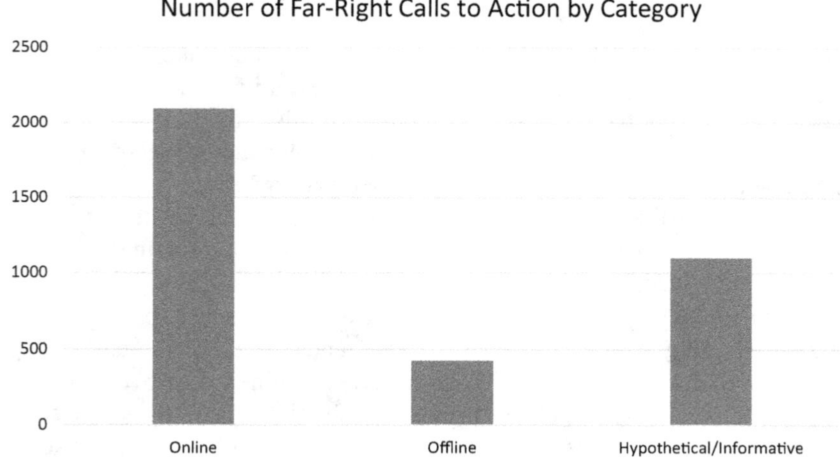

Figure 8.3. Graph of Number of Calls to Action by Category.
Source: Author.

individuals' social media on popular platforms like Twitter, YouTube, and Facebook; and post limited personal information of former romantic partners in order to get others to harass these individuals via private or public messages, among other things. Such posts often included ideological and political undertones, including anti-feminist and homophobic rhetoric, whereby the post would suggest that by targeting a specific individual, users would be doing their part to 'prevent the feminist and Jewish agenda [from spreading]'. However, most online calls to far-right action were broader in nature and did not target specific individuals for personal reasons, rather, their targets almost solely consisted of identity groups. These were the same groups that were persistently implicated in violent and hateful posts that I identified earlier. Thus, the othering that occurs via these posts eventually leads to calls for mobilization against the targeted groups. An excellent example of what such threads look like can be observed in figure 8.4. The subject line of the post reads: 'How to stop the rise of oestrogen and socialism to secure republican votes. This will also increase the birth of whites in the USA by upping testosterone level for males'. The author of the thread then calls on 4chan/pol/ users to act by writing, 'We need to spread propagandistic memes that expose how this increases mental/health problems to decrease liberals and leftwing in the USA'. The post concludes with links to two news articles, one suggesting that teen hormones are being altered to increase testosterone through tap water plastics, and another link to a study that suggests 'estrogen makes you liberal or left-wing'. The post also provides an image file that serves as an example of a meme that users are meant to 'spread' in order to achieve the objective of securing more republican votes and white births in the United States. The goal of this post is to mobilize readers into spreading political memes that target liberals, to aid the Republican party.

Memetic antagonism is a popular form of political dissent and participation in young adults (Huntington 2016; Milner 2013). Memes are prominent means of online political participation often for those on the left (Shifman 2013) as well as the right (Beran 2019; Ross and Rivers 2017). However, alt-right aligned individuals and groups have been able to tap into memetic affordances such as anonymity and virality to spread hateful rhetoric on popular social media platforms that avoid the detection algorithm on these platforms

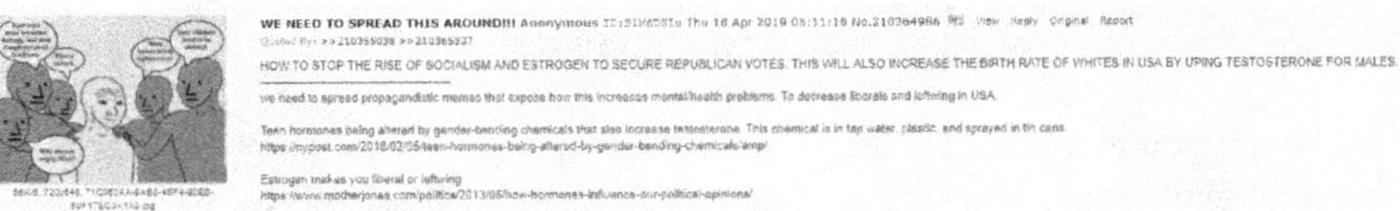

Figure 8.4. Thread Post on Socialism and Oestrogen.

Source: Screenshot of public post from 4/chan. Original creator anonynous: Author.

(Tuters and Hagen 2019; Wiggins 2020). The persistent attempts at mobilization via online calls to action demonstrate that 4chan is more than a board for posting shocking content. Just like a classic social movement scene, 4chan/pol/ provides a space where users regularly attempt to mobilize one another into supporting far-right causes.

Hypothetical/Informative Calls to Action

The second category of calls to far-right action on 4chan's /pol/ board accounted for 30% of all such threads. I identified 1,098 of these threads. Qualitative analysis revealed that authors of these threads adapted a unique strategy towards inciting far-right action on 4chan/pol/. Rather than suggesting that users take action online, they instead proposed a hypothetical scenario and asked users to answer what they would do in the event the scenario took place. Such posts can be categorized as calls to far-right action because they use a confirmed strategy adopted by members of far-right movements to avoid self-incrimination when inciting action. Purportedly, should an individual be inspired by a post on 4chan/pol/ to commit a crime, the original poster of the thread would not be held liable if the post was worded as a hypothetical scenario rather than a full-on call to action. While it is outside the scope of this chapter to verify if this belief is warranted, according to numerous posts I analysed, 4chan/pol/ users seem to hold this belief to be true and act accordingly. Throughout this research I discovered multiple posts that recommended this approach.

Threads featuring hypothetical/informative calls to action often prompted questions and subsequent suggestions on how to start a far-right movement or political party. Other threads once again focused on identity groups asking, for example, how to 'keep Black[people] and Brown people away from white women' or asked for methods for convincing white women that racialized men are sexual predators. These threads were often supplemented with links to dubious news stories about rape committed by racialized men. Other examples included threads proposing suggestions on how to legally make the lives of racialized people and women more difficult, and even threads requesting help with cultivating a virus and 'learn(ing) disease warfare'. A popular type of informative/hypothetical thread was a variation of 'How to prepare for the coming race war' post. One such post (figure 8.5) reads:

> How are you preparing for the inevitable [race] war? We all know the basics, ammo, guns, food, water. Any other useful advice? I'll start. Bury some guns and plant food off property. Only you know about it; It can't be confiscated and/or stolen; You become less of a target.

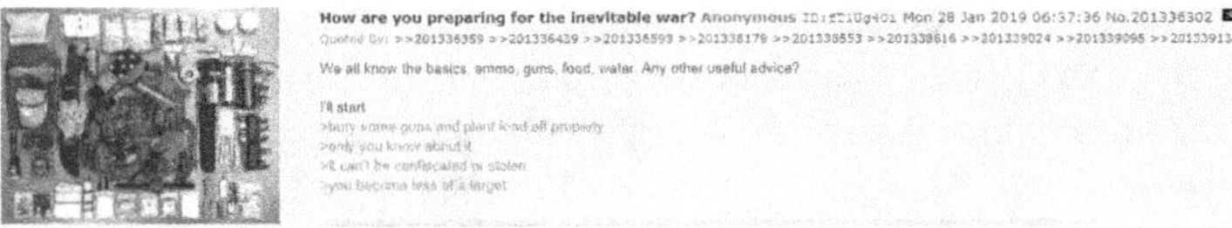

Figure 8.5. Thread Post, 'How Are You Preparing for the Inevitable War?'
Source: Screenshot of public post from 4/chan. Original creator Anonymous: Author.

These threads are often accompanied by an image of a survival kit that includes various weapons, like handguns, hunting knives, duct tape, rope, bullets and other military-grade survival gear. These posts always consisted of two parts: (1) A hypothetical scenario with a question about what actions must be taken to prepare for or respond to such a scenario and (2) a list of actions the author of the thread has already taken and encouragement for others to take similar action in anticipation of such a scenario. Such threads demonstrate attempts to incite more meaningful action that is no longer limited to the confines of the Internet. The downside for users of this strategy is that it provides somewhat vague instructions and depends on a high level of initiative from 4chan/pol/'s userbase. For this reason, some attempts at inciting offline action scale down on the suggested act in favour of providing more direct instructions. I present one such case in the next section.

Offline Calls to Action

Offline calls to far-right action were the least common of the three categories I identified. These were the threads that requested users to take action in the physical world rather than on the Internet and provided specific instructions on what to do. In total, 12% of all calls to far-right action took this form. I identified 425 of these threads which included, but were not limited to, calls to distribute pamphlets and posters, harass members of various minority groups in public, start all-white Christian organizations on university campuses and take part in rallies and 'crusades'. Some of these calls to far-right action shared similarities with certain progressive movements such as the idea of 'taking the fight to the elites' and to 'avoid civilian casualties'. However, such objectives would also be accompanied by statements like 'Israel and the Jews are part of the problem' and 'Get most of Islam out of Europe'. An example of an offline call to action that received a lot of engagement was a post telling users to hang up posters that read: 'IT'S OKAY TO BE WHITE. Million Poster Pinup' The topic post (figure 8.6) in the thread states:

> Do Not Alter the Message or Flyers. Its Okay to be white. 5 words. Simple, elegant, effective. Stick to the plan. There is no phase 2. Do not trespass or vandalize. Do not do anything illegal. Anons have confirmed with local law

> enforcement and lawyers that it is perfectly fine. DO NOT CONFRONT ANY LEFTIST PSYCHOS. Just walk away and put up posters elsewhere. Our message of tolerance is enough to further unhinge an already badly unhinged left. The goal is to expose the media's anti-white bias through their reaction to a harmless flyer. Stick to the plan. On Halloween post the fliers EVERYWHERE legally possible to post stuff. [Universities], car windshields, bulletins, posts, walls, etc. Wear a costume to disguise yourself. THIS IS NOT HATE.

Such posts take extra care to explain exactly what they want others to do while emphasizing that such action is legal, straightforward, not a form of hate or violence and effective at making the left look bad in the eyes of mainstream observers. While it is impossible to state where this movement originated from, it was disseminated and advertised heavily on 4chan well before the mainstream media outlets started reporting on stories of such posters appearing all over Canada and United States. Given 4chan's enormous reach on the Internet, it would not be unreasonable to assume that its users played an important role in encouraging widespread collective action across the country. The purpose of posting these flyers was to spread a purportedly inoffensive statement that would be interpreted as racist by the media. By interpreting the poster in a negative light, the media would essentially provide a platform for the discussion of why such an allegedly simple message is viewed as racist. Doing so would, in theory, expose 'normies' (anyone who does not use 4chan) to the alleged fact that liberalism and progressive politics are a threat to the survival of white culture and identity in the West.

Calls to action on 4chan/pol/ regularly called for coordinated instances of collective action, but these almost always fell short of developing into a full-fledged movement. Calls to action threads almost never referenced or followed up on other call-to-action threads, irrespective of engagement. A lack of follow-up prevented such coordinated efforts by loosely organized groups of individual actors from developing into any semblance of a movement. A quick analysis of the post reveals this was in fact the intention of the author of the post. The line 'there is no phase 2' (figure 8.6) makes it clear that this call to far-right action was not meant to be a part of a more elaborate movement or connected to any particular far-right group. This is one of the reasons why online social movement scenes are conceptually effective at studying far-right phenomena. They facilitate research on the far-right in instances where studying the movements themselves becomes impossible, since many of these movements dissolve almost as quickly as they form (Blee 2017).

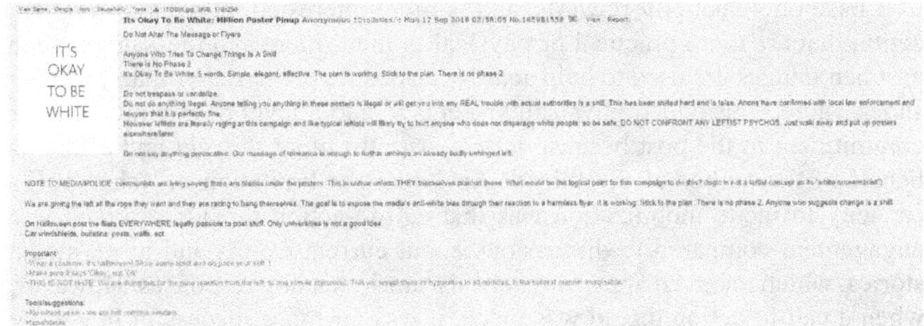

Figure 8.6. Thread Post, 'It's Ok to Be White'.
Source: Screenshot of public post from 4/chan. Original creator Anonymous: Author.

Responses to Calls to Action

In addition to documenting the prevalence and content of call to action threads on 4chan/pol/, I also identified what type of threads were most effective at getting engagement from other users. This finding is important because it reveals whether persistent attempts at mobilization are successful at capturing the attention of other users, as well as revealing what tactics are being used by the authors of these threads to increase engagement. To measure effectiveness, I counted the number of responses to each thread. As mentioned earlier, 4chan differs from most other online communities due to its ephemeral structure. Due to a high volume and frequency of posts, threads that do not get a high number of responses within a relatively short amount of time, disappear from the website. As such, a response to a thread on 4chan has the effect of increasing the longevity and visibility of the thread irrespective of whether the responder agrees or disagrees with the thread's content.

In total, 3,617 call-to-action threads were analysed. First, I wanted to know whether the images posted alongside each thread influenced the threads' engagement. An image-incongruent post is when a poster provides a colloquial image or meme that is not directly or tangibly related to the physical call to action. This differs from the image-congruent post, where a call to action is accompanied by an image that is useful or directly relevant to the demanded action. An example of an image-congruent call to action was the 'It's okay to be white' poster in figure 8.5 or the image of a propaganda meme that was meant to be spread over the Internet in figure 8.4. In both cases, the image in the thread served a purpose towards completing the goal of the call to action. Image-congruent calls to action were almost twice as popular as image-incongruent calls to action ($t = 2.33$, $p < 0.05$). This suggests that the user base on 4chan/pol/ rewards, and is more interested in, calls to far-right action that are more practical or physical in their intent and messaging, such as when images are used to help achieve a specific cause rather than for mere shock value. This added physicality seems to add a level of intentionality or commitment to the post because it demonstrates more thought and effort on behalf of the author of the thread. An important limitation of 4chan/pol/'s capacity to incite mobilization was that call-to-action threads received less engagement compared to discussions about current events and news media stories, which received approximately six times as many responses. However, when a call-to-action thread was made, it was far more successful in getting engagement when the image accompanying it was purposeful (congruent).

Call-to-action threads also received differing engagement depending on whether a specific group or groups were targeted or not. Targeting any specific group increased thread response rate by 47% ($t = 2.02$, $p < 0.05$). However not all groups had the same effect on response rate. Call-to-action threads that received the most responses were posts containing anti-Semitism ($F = 4.80$, $p < 0.05$), anti-Black racism ($F = 5.53$, $p < 0.05$) and Islamophobia ($F = 11.1$, $p < 0.01$). Call-to-action threads containing misogyny, homophobia and other racism did not have a significantly different response rate compared with non-targeted call-to-action threads (see figures 8.7 and 8.8). These findings establish that 4chan/pol/ is an online social movement scene where attempts to target identity groups and mobilize users reinforce one another. Attempts at recruitment occur via persistent links to the v/blogs and social media of prominent far-right personalities and the spread of false information and pseudo-science about various identity groups, framing them as a cause of

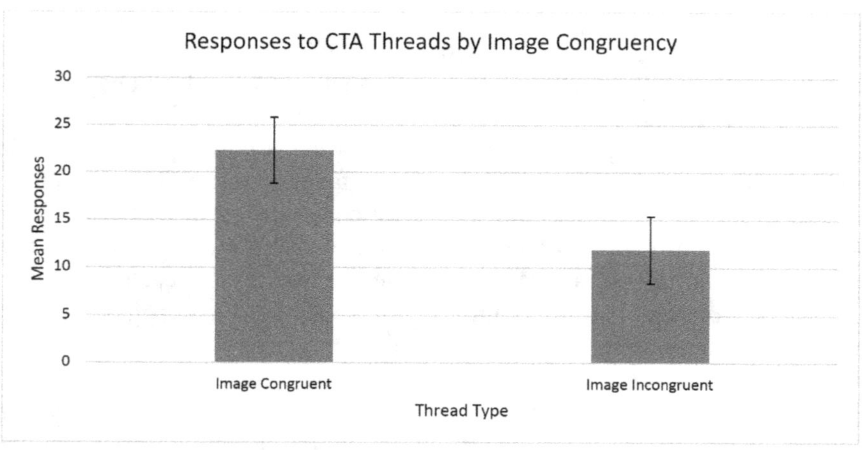

Figure 8.7. Graph on Responses to CTA Threads by Image Congruency.
Source: Author.

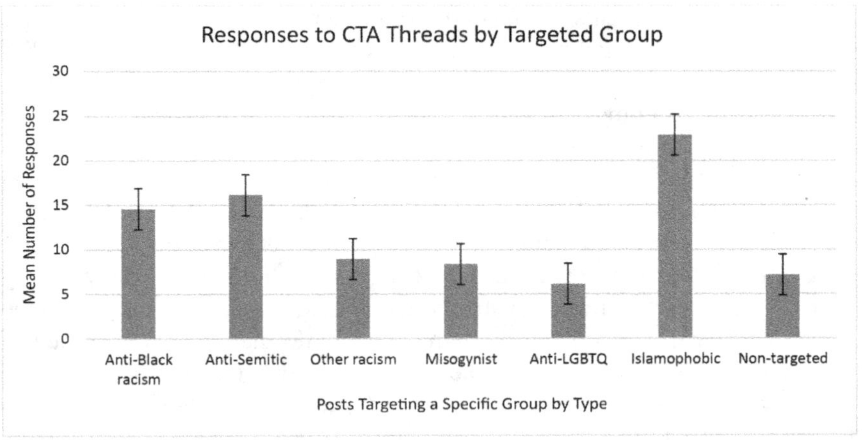

Figure 8.8. Graph on Responses to CTA Threads by Targeted Group.
Source: Author.

some problem that needs to be solved. This misinformation is then followed up by threads that incite mobilization against these groups as a solution to this purported problem.

THIS IS A SCENE, AND AN ARMS RACE

The combination of links to far-right websites, communities and social media, along with pervasive calls to far-right action inspired by far-right ideology establish 4chan/pol/ as an online social movement scene of the far right.[1] Online scenes are like traditional movement scenes because they act as a pseudo-political network of locales (physical or digital) where individuals can be recruited and mobilized by social movements. This pseudo-political property is crucial to maintain a steady in-flow of potential recruits and a growing audience for various movements. This is possible on 4chan/pol/ where anonymity, ephemerality and uncompromising commitment to free speech (even when it is hate speech) provide a digital environment that is ripe for assimilation by far-right ideologues and movements looking to recruit and mobilize new members. Unlike traditional movement scenes of the far-right whose borders are tightly controlled (Creasap 2012), online scenes allow for highly porous boundaries that facilitate recruitment and mobilization. However, this lack of gatekeeping does not come without a cost.

The accessibility of online scenes presents more of a risk for movements attempting to mobilize others for the simple reason that mobilization threads are visible to opponents of far-right movements (i.e. police, progressive movements) who can archive and analyse these threads. In contrast, the police are far less likely to get access to private conversations held in physical locations like bars or homes, as within a traditional movement scene (Simi and Futrell 2006). Three categories of calls to far-right action reveal strategic adaptations to this heightened visibility. Online calls to action focus on inciting action that is mostly legal and provides a relative level of safety, because they allow the users to maintain anonymity and physical distance from targets and law enforcement. However, online calls to action are limited by their relatively minimal capacity for impact. Threads that call for more decisive and often borderline illegal action adapt the hypothetical/informative style to establish alleged plausible deniability for the authors of such threads. This type of strategy has its own limits because a lack of specific instructions makes coordinated offline action difficult. Furthermore, calls to far-right action that target specific groups and provide digital artifacts such as images and documents to aid in accomplishing the goal of the act seem to get more engagement than threads lacking these features. To minimize risk, the authors of threads calling for more coordinated offline action stress the importance of staying within the confines of the law so much so that they consult with lawyers and even include a message to law enforcement. This demonstrates that the authors of these threads are aware that the relative accessibility of 4chan to new recruits also leaves the scene exposed to opponents. They strategically call for liminal collective action whereby movements start, and end almost instantaneously as seen in the 'It's okay to be white: Million poster pin up' example.

There are several important limitations to these findings. For one, measuring engagement does not tell us how many users on 4chan/pol/ actually become inspired to act as a direct result of such threads. However, the fact that several 4chan campaigns have received national coverage suggests to us that calls to far-right action on /pol/ have mobilizing potential that deserve scholarly attention. Another important limitation of our study is it was impossible to tell how successful digital leafleting is at recruiting new members into far-right movements. The persistence and prevalence of such threads are nonetheless alarming and suggest that their authors view 4chan/pol/ as a viable scene for recruitment into the far-right.

Online movement scenes allow far-right movements to exploit Internet features such as anonymity and low social or organized censorship to amass a global presence without having to worry about hate speech legislation and physical borders. This research has shown that calls to far-right action are strategically constructed to allow for mobilization at various levels of commitment from online to offline spaces. Digital affordances such as 4chan's ephemeral structure, where shocking content is rewarded with user engagement, are highly conducive to a cultural milieu where free speech rhetoric is used to justify hateful and violent language and imagery. The combination of these digital features and their strategic deployment generates an online social movement scene where domestic terrorists driven by far-right ideology get positive reinforcement and achieve a notoriety they could never hope to get in a classical social movement scene, even on the far-right (Simi and Futrell 2015). Don Black, the founder of Stormfront, hails the Internet as the single most important invention for the proliferation of the far-right, claiming that he's 'accomplished more on the Web than in 25 years of political activism [on the ground]'. Hence, it is pertinent that social movement scholars engage with how information technologies are changing the landscape of far-right politics. While this chapter provides important insights into the use of technology to aid far-right mobilization and recruitment, many questions remain unanswered about 4chan/pol/'s capacity to consistently attract new users and whether they believe 4chan/pol/ has the means to create social change. Future research that focuses on how 4chan/pol/ users view their own participation may offer valuable insight into what attracts users to online social movement scenes of the far-right, and just how effective the strategies are for political recruitment and mobilization.

NOTE

1. The ephemeral nature of the posts on 4chan/pol/ makes it hard to generalize over longer periods of time. While 4chan/pol/ may act as a space of far-right recruitment for a large section of folks, its ephemerality and anti-censorship ethos will always attract a diverse variety of users some of whom merely wish to joke around or provoke people, as well as others that are seriously committed to their politics and beliefs, and to using 4chan/pol/ as a far-right recruitment space.

REFERENCES

Alexander, Michelle. 2020. *The New Jim Crow: Mass Incarceration in the Age of Colorblindness*. New York: The New Press.

Bailey, Julius. 2010. 'Fearing Hate: Re-examining the Media Coverage of the Christian Identity Movement'. *Journal for the Study of Radicalism* 4 (1): 55–73.

Beran, Dale. 2019. *It Came From Something Awful: How a Toxic Troll Army Accidentally Memed Donald Trump into Office*. New York: All Points Books.

Bessant, Judith. 2018. 'Right-Wing Populism and Young "Stormers": Conflict in Democratic Politics'. In *Young People Re-generating Politics in Times of Crises*, 139–59. London: Palgrave Macmillan.

Blee, Kathleen. 2017. 'How the Study of White Supremacism Is Helped and Hindered by Social Movement Research'. *Mobilization* 22 (1): 1–15.

Blee, Kathleen, and Kimberly Creasap. 2010. 'Conservative and Right-Wing Movements'. *Annual Review of Sociology* 36: 269–86.

Blee, Kathleen, and Elizabeth Yates. 2015. 'The Place of Race in Conservative and Far-Right Movements'. *Sociology of Race and Ethnicity* 1 (1): 127–36.

Brown, Alexander. 2018. 'What Is So Special about Online (as Compared to Offline) Hate Speech?'. *Ethnicities* 18 (3): 297–326.

Burris, Val, Emery Smith, and Ann Strahm. 2000. 'White Supremacist Networks on the Internet'. *Sociological Focus* 33 (2): 215–35.

Caren, Neal, Kay Jowers, and Sarah Gaby. 2012. 'A Social Movement Online Community: Stormfront and the White Nationalist Movement'. *Research in Social Movements, Conflicts and Change* 33: 163–93.

Creasap, Kimberly. 2012. 'Social Movement Scenes: Place-Based Politics and Everyday Resistance'. *Sociology Compass* 6 (2): 182–91.

Daniels, Jessie. 2009. *Cyber Racism: White Supremacy Online and the New Attack on Civil Rights*. Lanham: Rowman & Littlefield.

Dubet, François, and Henri Lustiger Thaler. 2004. 'Introduction: The Sociology of Collective Action Reconsidered'. *Current Sociology* 52 (4): 557–73.

Fraser, Steven, ed. 2008. *The Bell Curve Wars: Race, Intelligence, and the Future of America*. New York: Basic Books.

Futrell, Robert, and Pete Simi. 2004. 'Free Spaces, Collective Identity, and the Persistence of US White Power Activism'. *Social Problems* 51 (1): 16–42.

Futrell, Robert, Pete Simi, and Simon Gottschalk. 2006. 'Understanding Music in Movements: The White Power Music Scene' *The Sociological Quarterly* 47 (2): 275–304.

Gamson, William. 1995. 'Constructing Social Protest'. In *Social Movements and Culture*, 85–106. Minneapolis: University of Minnesota Press.

Gerstenfeld, Phyllis. Diana Grant, and Chau-Pu Chiang. 2003. 'Hate Online: A Content Analysis of Extremist Internet Sites'. *Analyses of Social Issues and Public Policy*. 3 (1): 29–44.

Glaser, April. 2019. '8chan Is a Normal Part of Mass Shootings Now'. *Slate*, 4 August. https://slate.com/technology/2019/08/el-paso-8chan-4chan-mass-shootings-manifesto.html.

Glaser, Jack, Jay Dixit, and Donald Green. 2002. 'Studying Hate Crime with the Internet: What Makes Racists Advocate Racial Violence?' *Journal of Social Issues* 58 (1): 177–93.

Haunss, Sebastian, and Darc Leach. 2007. 'Social Movement Scenes: Infrastructures of Opposition in Civil Society'. In *Civil Societies and Social Movements*, edited by R. Lipschutz, 85–101. Abingdon: Routledge.

Hine, Gabriel Emile, Jeremiah Onaolapo, Emiliano de Cristofaro, Nicolas Kourtellis, Ilias Leontiadis, Riginos Samaras, Gianluca Stringhini, and Jeremy Blackburn. 2017. 'Kek, Cucks, and God Emperor Trump: A Measurement Study of 4chan's Politically Incorrect Forum and Its Effects on the Web'. In *Eleventh International AAAI Conference on Web and Social Media*. arXiv:1610.03452 [cs.SI].

Huntington, Heidi. 2016. 'Pepper Spray Cop and the American Dream: Using Synecdoche and Metaphor to Unlock Internet Memes' Visual Political Rhetoric'. *Communication Studies* 67 (1): 77–93.

Jakubowicz, Andrew. 2017. 'Alt_Right White Lite: Trolling, Hate Speech and Cyber Racism on Social Media'. *Cosmopolitan Civil Societies: An Interdisciplinary Journal* 9 (3): 41–60.

Knuttila, Lee. 2011. 'User Unknown: 4chan, Anonymity and Contingency'. *First Monday* 16 (10). https://firstmonday.org/article/view/3665/3055.

Leach, Darcy, and Sebastian Haunss. 2008. 'Scenes and Social Movements'. In *Culture, social movements, and protest*, edited by H. Johnston, 255–76. Abingdon: Routledge.

Marwick, Alice, and Rebecca Lewis. 2017. 'Media Manipulation and Disinformation Online' *New York: Data & Society Research Institute*. https://datasociety.net/pubs/oh/DataAndSociety_MediaManipulationAndDisinformationOnline.pdf.

Massanari, Adrienne. 2017. '# Gamergate and the Fappening: How Reddit's Algorithm, Governance, and Culture Support Toxic Technocultures'. *New Media & Society* 19 (3): 329–46.

McAdam, Doug, John McCarthy, and Mayer Zald, eds. 1996. *Comparative Perspectives on Social Movements: Political Opportunities, Mobilizing Structures, and Cultural Framings*. Cambridge: Cambridge University Press.

Milner, Ryan. 2013. 'Pop Polyvocality: Internet Memes, Public Participation, and the Occupy Wall Street Movement'. *International Journal of Communication* 7: 2357–90.

Phillips, Whitney. 2015. *This Is Why We Can't Have Nice Things: Mapping the Relationship between Online Trolling and Mainstream Culture*. London: MIT Press.

Polletta, Francesca, and James Jasper. 2001.'Collective Identity and Social Movements'. *Annual review of Sociology* 27 (1): 283–305.

Rohlinger, Deana, and Leslie Bunnage. 2018. 'Collective Identity in the Digital Age: Thin and Thick Identities in Moveon.Org and the Tea Party Movement'. *Mobilization* 23 (2): 135–57.

Schmitz, Rachel. 2016. 'Intersections of Hate: Exploring the Transecting Dimensions of Race, Religion, Gender, and Family in Ku Klux Klan Web Sites'. *Sociological Focus* 49 (3): 200–214.

Shifman, Limor. 2013. *Memes in Digital Culture*. Cambridge: MIT Press.

Siegel, Jacob. 2017. 'Dylann Roof, 4chan, and the New Online Racism'. *The Daily Beast*, 14 April. https://www.thedailybeast.com/dylann-roof-4chan-and-the-new-online-racism.

Simi, Pete, and Robert Futrell. 2006. 'Cyberculture and the Endurance of White Power Activism'. *Journal of Political and Military Sociology* 34 (1): 115–42.

Simi, Pete, and Robert Futrell. 2015. *American Swastika: Inside the White Power Movement's Hidden Spaces of Hate*. Lanham: Rowman & Littlefield.

Taylor, Verta, and Nancy Whittier, 1992. 'Collective Identity in Social Movement Communities: Lesbian Feminist Mobilization'. In *Frontiers in Social Movement Theory*, edited by A. Morris and Carol Mueller, 104–29. New Haven: Yale University Press.

Turner, Ralph, and Lewis Killian, 1987. *Collective Behaviour*, Englewood Cliffs: Prentice-Hall.

Tuters, Marc. 2020. 'Esoteric Fascism Online: 4chan and the Kali Yuga.' In: *Far-Right Revisionism and the End of History*, edited by L. Valencia-Garcia, 286–303. London: Routledge.

Tuters, Marc, and Sal Hagen. 2019. '(((They))) Rule: Memetic Antagonism and Nebulous Othering on 4chan'. *New Media & Society* 22 (12): 1–20.

Valeri, Robin Maria, Nicole Sweazy, and Kevin Borgeson. 2017. 'An Analysis of Skinhead Websites and Social Networks, a Decade Later'. *Michigan Sociological Review* 31: 76–105.

Watts, Rob. 'New Politics: The Anonymous Politics of 4chan, Outrage and the New Public Sphere'. In *Young People and the Politics of Outrage and Hope*, edited by P. Kelly, P. Campbell, L. Harrison, and C. Hickey, 73–89. Leiden: Brill.

Wendling, Mike. 2018. *Alt-right: From 4chan to the White House*. London: Pluto Press.

Wiggins, Bradley. 2020. 'Boogaloo and Civil War 2: Memetic Antagonism in Expressions of Covert Activism'. *New Media & Society* 1–27. https://doi.org/10.1177/1461444820945317.

Wintrobe, Ronald.2002. 'Leadership and Passion in Extremist Politics'. In *Political Extremism and Rationality*, edited by A. Breton, G. Galeotti, P. Salmon. and R. Wintrobe, 23–43. Cambridge: Cambridge University Press.

Chapter 9

The Internet Hate Machine: On the Weird Collectivity of Anonymous Far-Right Groups

Sal Hagen and Marc Tuters

In attempting to make sense of the 2016 Trump insurgency, there was a great deal of popular discussion in the United States about 'alt-right trolls' manipulating public opinion and stoking discord online. The political scientist George Hawley, among others, has recognized the alt-right as a 'genuinely new phenomenon' on the American right (2017, 50). The perceived novelty of the alt-right was largely due to the effective appropriation of a subcultural style of 'trolling' associated with anonymous online discussion boards and used to launder a very old form of white supremacist politics (Ganesh 2020). One common practice of this style involved tricking journalists into generating the coverage of the alt-right and thereby amplifying their reach – or in their vernacular, 'memeing' their ideas into reality. While examples of these trolling exploits were abundant, some of the most remarkable included the claims that drinking milk and using the 'ok' hand sign in public were both signifiers of white supremacism (Harmon 2018; Noor 2019). Despite the fact that these tactics took the form of media hoaxes, for a period they also succeeded in becoming the symbols that they jokingly purported to be, thereby drawing mainstream audiences into the radicalized nether regions of the 'deep vernacular Web' (De Zeeuw and Tuters 2020).[1]

One subcultural online locale closely linked to the alt-right is the anonymous imageboard 4chan. While its users tend to resist the alt-right label, with its provocative mixture of subcultural ephemera and far-right ideology, 4chan's political discussion board '/pol/' was central to the alt-right's rise, as well as inspiring documented acts of far-right terror (Thompson 2018). As our past research has shown, 4chan posters use memes and other forms of subcultural capital to negotiate a sense of belonging to an essentially chaotic and disorganized community, which results in strong and often highly antagonistic group dynamics (Tuters and Hagen 2020). Despite this chaos as well as the aforementioned alt-right technique of hiding extremism behind a veil of supposed irony, 4chan/pol/ has in fact functioned as a zone for recruitment and mobilization of white supremacists, neo-Nazis and various newer forms on extreme-right ideology referred to as 'idiosyncratic terrorism' (Norris 2020). In this sense, 4chan/pol/ at first sight seems to serve a role similar to that of the neo-Nazi web forum *Stormfront* in an earlier era (Hawley 2017, 19). However, the fact that 4chan users are *anonymous* and their posts are *ephemeral*[2] complicates a straightforward conception of how /pol/'s far-right recruitment works. Whereas Stormfront brought like-minded extremists in personal contact with each other – even featuring an Aryan dating service (Backwood 1999) – *direct and personalized contact on 4chan is actively discouraged* by its design as well as its 'mask culture' (De Zeeuw 2019), which frowns on individuals identifying themselves by name. It thereby effectively undermines most efforts at organized leadership. Moreover, unlike Stormfront, whose founder's explicit objective was 'to recruit everyone that is interested in our point of view' (Backwood 1999), 4chan's current owner Hiroyuki Nishimura appears peculiarly uninterested in the politics that take place on his site, seeming to primarily value 4chan as a source of subcultural amusement (Beran 2019, 148).

The objective of this chapter is to understand how exactly far-right mobilization works on 4chan/pol/, a site whose design and culture appear quite different from traditional online recruitment forums. To do so, this chapter argues that in order to understand how 4chan/pol/ works as a far-right recruitment site, one needs to understand *the role of ingroup/outgroup thinking in the construction and maintenance of a collective sense of group identity*. The goal here is thus to understand how 4chan/pol/ users negotiate a sense of collective group identity in continuous dialogue with representations of themselves in the media. To that end, the chapter empirically redescribes the dynamics of 'weird collectivity', by which a cohesive ingroup identity results primarily from an antagonistic dialogue with representations by an outgroup. We outline how, in the case of /pol/, weird collectivity holds together a far-right movement (albeit loosely) in the absence of many of the features normally associated with movement politics in general, and far-right politics in specific.

While previous scholarship has recognized the transformative impact of social media platforms and of memes on the 'connective logic' of social movements (Bennett and Segerberg 2012), the specific collective dynamics of anonymous online groups nevertheless remain understudied. As the site of innovation of a number of extremely successful far-right memes that subsequently spread to mainstream platforms, such as 'Pepe the Frog' and conspiracy theories like 'Pizzagate' and 'QAnon' (Tuters et al. 2018; Tuters and Hagen 2020; de Zeeuw et al. 2020), a specific understanding of how collectivity works on 4chan/pol/ promises to be of more general value as well.

In the first section we outline some broad sociological debates on group formation and import the term *entitativity*, a psychological concept referring to the perceived coherence of groups, be it by outsiders or insiders. In the second section, we use a dataset of journalistic articles that mention 4chan to sketch a brief history of why and how often the imageboard was covered in the news since 2005. We then extract the dominant journalistic descriptions of 4chan in 2017 – a particularly eventful year for the alt-right – to show how 4chan *as a whole* has largely become associated with the far right or alt-right. The third section uses this same dataset of journalistic accounts about 4chan to pinpoint salient reactions to these portrayals by the ingroup: 4chan/pol/ users, also known as 'anons'. We specifically close-read comments from users that reflect on the journalistic frames of 4chan, and argue that these feed back into the strategic construction of anons as a coherent group. Through this combined analysis, we aim to illustrate how /pol/ can form an effective recruitment space despite its ephemeral content and absence of personal ties, the latter of which has been traditionally considered of central importance to the radicalization process (Daniels 2009).

ENTITATIVITY AND WEIRD COLLECTIVITY

Unlike the highly personalized style of political engagement that motivates 'connective action' via social media platforms (Bennet and Segerberg 2012), the type of coordination that occurs via anonymous message boards tends to be distinctly impersonal, often while imagining the community as a single, faceless and homogeneous entity (De Zeeuw 2019; Coleman 2014, 114–5). Sociological theory has long emphasized the relevance of such shared and symbolic imaginaries, for instance in symbolic interactionism (Blumer 1969). Similarly, the internalization of a 'generalized other' and how this affects the perception of group coherence have long been a topic of sociological concern, both broadly pertaining to the question of what makes a 'society' as well as the specific sociology of subcultures (Brake 2014, 17). However, the question of how the perception of groups as imagined and generalized *wholes* affects group-making processes gains an increased and somewhat different significance for online groups whose anonymity actively invites such generalizations.[3]

This reinvigorates an old concept that explicitly addresses the perception of groups as wholes: *entitativity*. Originally coined by the social scientist Donald Campbell, entitativity was defined as 'the degree of having the nature of an entity, of having real existence' (1958, 17). Campbell argued for an empirical method of analysing how social entities are perceived by individuals based on various 'degrees of consistency' which he saw as 'analogous to the permanent relations among the parts of a living body' (1958, 15). Although Campbell initially conceptualized entitativity as applying to humans as well as non-humans – a village community would be less 'entitative' than, say, a stone – the concept was revitalized in the 1990s by several psychological studies of the *perception* of human groups. This was done to understand how humans arrive at a 'theory of common origin' vis-à-vis other social ensembles, whether it be that of a distant outgroup or that of direct peers (Brewer et al. 2004, 19).[4] Scholars in this field thus used it to study what elements are important in the perception of the 'groupiness' of groups, and tied the degrees of this to behavioural traits, for instance, by observing that a group member's perception of an outgroup as highly coherent or 'entitative' can elicit stronger emotional or even aggressive reactions as compared to when it is perceived as incoherent (Lickel et al. 2006).

Entitativity goes to the heart of a fundamental sociological question: what makes a society a society? While scholars like Émile Durkheim answered this by considering a society as a sui generis entity, as an inseparable structure of systems, his contemporary Gabriel Tarde considered a society as networks of imitations that are never 'more than the sum of its parts' (1903). This problem directly translates to the study of anonymous online communities, since they confront the researcher with how to distinguish the individual from the group and how to conceptualize the 'whole' of the object of study. How, for instance, does one conceptualize structural notions like 'the alt-right'? As a thing in itself or simply as emerging as a concept to describe millions of interactions?

Instead of defining a group's *essence*, entitativity shifts the emphasis towards the *perception* of groups, be it as self-reflection by its members or as perceived by outsiders. This is a worthwhile endeavour since the conceptualization of the 'whole' of a group is not just a methodological hurdle but also affects group members themselves. For instance, 4chan users often express how they imagine themselves as part of a group with a shared history through many self-referential memes, instead of a materialized and stable group of followers or friends you would find on Facebook and Twitter (see Hagen 2020; de Zeeuw and Tuters 2020). Furthermore, in highly antagonistic communities like 4chan/pol/, above all, entitativity binds together an ingroup against an outgroup perceived as tight-knit yet nebulous (Tuters and Hagen 2020).

Tracing what we call *expressions of entitativity* is arguably best served with a neo-Tardean approach. Notably, Bruno Latour has outlined how communications technology has effectively rendered visible and traceable Tardean social ties (2010). Latour's provocative argument is that the digital traceability of social media effectively overcomes and obviates any divide between the micro-scale and macro-scale (Latour et al. 2012). This approach represents a general shift within the new field of digital sociology from theory-driven and causal explanation to a method of 'empirical re-description'

(Marres and Lezaun 2011).[5] By tracing minute expressions of entitativity on 4chan/pol/, the point of this chapter is therefore not to engage in a structural discussion on /pol/ or the alt-right, or to debate the finer points of how far-right ideology manifests on 4chan, as many others have already done (see Nagle 2017; Thompson 2018; Beran 2019). Rather, the point is to follow *the role of the idea* of 4chan as a singular entity, and in this case of /pol/ in particular, and how this idea can play into the mobilization and manifestation of tight-knit extremist groups.

Long before the supposed 'extremist turn of the Trump-era Internet' around 2016 (Phillips 2019), studies of 4chan had already touched on how its community constitutes itself as a single entity or 'undifferentiated mass' (Auerbach 2011). Thanks in particular to Gabriella Coleman (2014) and Whitney Phillips (2015), the early history of 4chan's collective identity formation is quite well researched. Coleman's work considers the 'hacktivist' collective Anonymous, noting how it was seen as 'an amorphous and formless entity existing in some mythical and primordial jelly-like state of non-being' by both outside commentators as well as by some within the group itself (2014, 114). Phillips offers a subcultural history of trolling and considers how media hoaxes helped anons to develop a sense of collective identity, emphasizing how Fox News, which portrayed 4chan as an ominous space for dangerous hackers, 'helped legitimize the development of a discrete, deliberate, and highly recognizable trolling identity' (Phillips 2015, 61). Similarly, de Zeeuw outlines how the logic of anonymous imageboard culture plays into the imagination of the collective as part of an imagined singular 'grotesque Media body' (2019). What binds these cases is an emphasis on how expressions of entitativity play into 4chan's collectivity, be it as journalistic generalizations or ironic self-imaginations.

Much of the research on 4chan mostly concerns the /b/ 'Random' board, whose users tended to revel in nihilism while lacking a clear ideology (Phillips 2015, 147). However, the largely white supremacist /pol/ – at the time of writing 4chan's most active board – raises the question on entitativity's relation to extremist politics. Conveniently, beyond its value in understanding perceived group coherence more generally, entitativity is also helpful in making sense of the discourse and rhetorical strategies of extremists. Notably, Berger (2018) summarizes how extremist groups benefit from the discursive construction of *high group entitativity*, both regarding the in- and outgroup. Presenting the ingroup as tight-knit offers the idea of internal homogeneity, common goals and fraternity, while doing so for the outgroup helps constructing them as dangerous and organized antagonists. This can in turn feed into the dramatic narrative of two tight-knit groups intertwined in an apocalyptic struggle. Such narratives are particularly appealing to individuals uncertain about their own identity (Hogg 2007). As we explore in the following, all of these qualities also describe the type of community that one observes on /pol/.

While part of 4chan's oppositional stance arises from an absolutist dedication to free speech and resistance to 'data extractivist' practices by large social media platforms (Colley and Moore 2020; de Zeeuw and Tuters 2020), much discussion on /pol/ concerns extremist fantasies of white supremacists in an existential battle with a Jewish cabal, sometimes expressed in seemingly 'ironic' terms (Finkelstein et al. 2018; Tuters and Hagen 2020).[6] Entitativity thus helps us to understand the 'weird' rhetorical strategies that seem to make 4chan appealing to so many more generally, as well as offering more specific insights into the dynamics of /pol/ as an extremist forum.

While most quasi-coherent groups can to some extent be defined by who or what they are *not*, a defining collectivizing feature for others is a continuous dialectic between an outgroup's perception of the group and the ingroup's response to this. We refer to this process as *weird collectivity*. Defining 'weirdness' here as 'an eruption of something from the outside' (Fisher 2016), *weird collectivity* thus refers to how representations 'from the outside' are incorporated ouroboros-like into a group's own self-image, which subsequently feeds back into how the group can be seen by outsiders as a cohesive 'entity'. In the case of 4chan, inseparable from the site's unique affordances is an antagonism towards 'the other' – be they journalists, researchers or Reddit users – so consistent that weird collectivity figuratively functions as an 'infrastructure of being' (Peters 2015, 10). Along these lines, what John Durham Peters refers to as 'weird media theory' rejects the conventional view of communications media as means by which to convey messages in favour of an ontological approach in which 'wiring precedes being', and wherein [ontology, whatever else it is, is usually just forgotten infrastructure' (Peters 2015, 27, 38). *Weirdness* also refers to the way in which the group members' self-perception as a coherent entity is connected to a quasi-religious experience of their individual identities being subsumed by something greater than themselves – a particularly common sentiment amongst 4chan anons, for instance, expressed by mythologizing their collective efforts as 'meme magic'.[7] In the next section we will operationalize this weird media theory framework by applying a mixture of distant and close reading techniques, first to analyse the consideration of 4chan by 'the outside' – in this case, description of the space in media reports – followed by an analysis of how those representations are in turn discussed on 4chan/pol/.

THE VIEW FROM OUTSIDE: WHO IS THIS HACKER 4CHAN?

A striking example of how an outside view of 4chan as a singular entity directly affected the self-perception of its group members comes from Phillips's (2015) account of how a Fox News affiliate once described the site as an 'Internet Hate Machine'. The ensuing ridicule directed at Fox highlighted anons' long-standing antagonism towards an essential outgroup: the media. Moreover, the 'Internet Hate Machine' label provided a powerful means with which 4chan anons could mythologize themselves as a coherent entity – ironically or not. Since Phillips profiled 4chan/b/ from the mid-2000s to early 2010s, this antagonism towards the media was already in place prior to /pol/ and the alt-right, which brought overt racists to the fore.[8] But while the media thus remained a consistent opposing factor to 4chan's anons, how did media reports consider 4chan over time? What sort of 'entity' has been conceived of by journalistic accounts, and which subsequently function relationally with the group itself? To engage with this, we first trace the emergence of the journalistic frame of 4chan generally, before going on to consider how /pol/ anons reacted to this.

We used *Nexis Uni*, an online database of historical news articles, to acquire a corpus of articles that mentioned 4chan.[9] This returned articles from 1,703 different news outlets.[10] To filter out irrelevant sources, we kept articles only from news outlets with at least five appearances and deleted those from niche sources.[11] After removing duplicate texts,[12] this process resulted in 10,243 articles mentioning 4chan. With these, we first map the volume of articles over time to identify which events animated journalists to write about 4chan. Afterwards, we consider more closely all articles from 2017 because it was a particularly eventful year in relation to the alt-right online. From all articles in the three largest spikes in 2017, we manually extracted all the sentences in which 4chan was described and analysed what sort of 'entity' the imageboard was framed to be.[13]

To first sketch general trends in media coverage of 4chan over the years, figure 9.1 shows the number of articles per month, starting in December 2005.

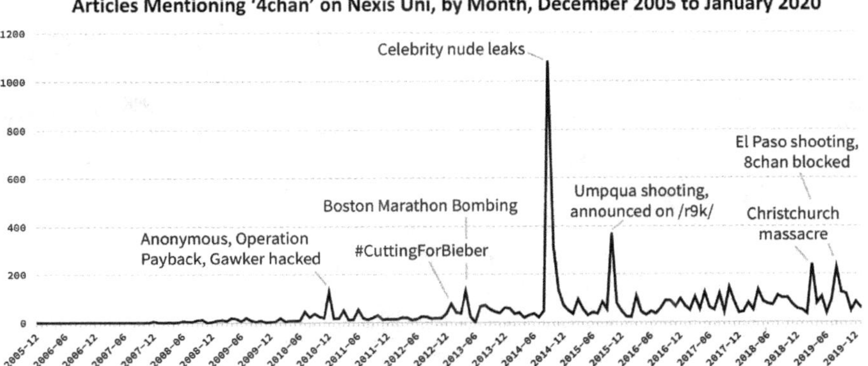

Figure 9.1. Articles Mentioning '4chan' on Nexis Uni, by Month, December 2005 to January 2020.
Source: Author.

In her discussion of the 'golden years' of trolling on 4chan, Phillips (2015) argues that between 2008 and 2011, 4chan's /b/ board engaged in numerous high-profile media hoaxes, which helped to generate its aforementioned reputation as an 'Internet Hate Machine'. However, the Nexis Uni dataset shows articles about 4chan only appearing sporadically during this period. The first notable increase came in 2010, when 4chan became a breeding ground for Anonymous. However, this spike and subsequent ones in 2013 pale in comparison to the one in September 2014. Following an iCloud breach, a link was posted to 4chan/b/ leading to nude pictures of A-list celebrities (Massanari 2017), prompting many articles to mention the imageboard. While many of these frame 4chan quite ambivalently, it was also in this period that a CNN presenter would ask 'Who is this hacker 4chan?'. This ignorant statement would enter 4chan folklore as an ironic metonym for 4chan whose weird collectivity so often depends on such mistaken media representations.

The next major spike in coverage shows a clear shift towards 4chan as a space for far-right extremism. It came in October 2015, when a shooter opened fire at Umpqua Community College near Roseburg, Oregon, killing ten and injuring eight. Prior to the killing, the perpetrator had posted a foreboding message on 4chan's /r9k/ board. After this event, the overall number of articles mentioning 4chan gradually increased from 2016 onwards, peaking twice more in 2019, corresponding to two shootings in a Mosque in Christchurch, New Zealand, and in a Walmart in El Paso, Texas. Although both killers posted manifestos on the sibling imageboard 8chan, many news articles referred to 4chan in some way.

Having sketched this brief timeline, we now zoom in on the journalistic descriptions of 4chan during three spikes in 2017, a particularly eventful year

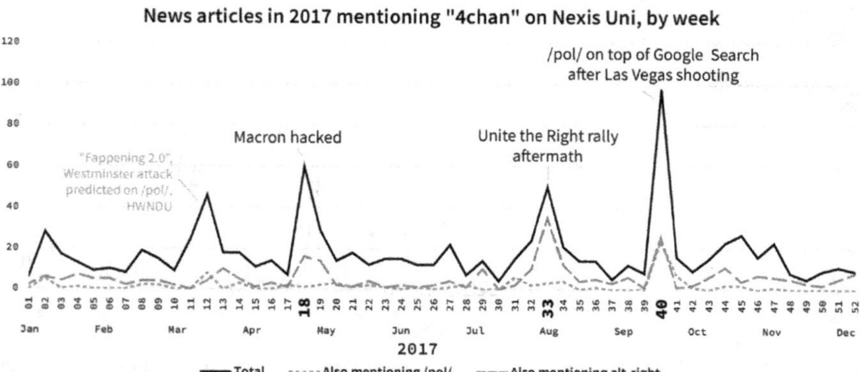

Figure 9.2. Articles Mentioning 4chan on Nexis Uni in 2017. Articles from the weeks in bold are analysed further and taken as an input for the 4chan/pol/ data collection

Source: Author.

for the alt-right (figure 9.2). The first one in week 18 (1–7 May) concerns a breach of the email servers of the French presidential candidate Emmanuel Macron. A file containing some 20,000 emails was posted to 4chan/pol/ (Morenne 2017). Within the thirty-six articles in this week, 4chan is described as either a home to 'trolls' and 'hoaxers' (e.g. Buncombe 2017; MacLaughlin 2017; Satter 2017), or the 'far-right', 'white nationalists', 'alt-right' and 'political extremism' (e.g. Scott and Morenne 2017; Delesalle-Stolper 2017; Erickson 2017). While the aforementioned articles all concerned activities taking place on /pol/, with only one exception (Mills 2017), none mention the board by name – which as we will see in the following relates to anon's critique of the media's tendency to mischaracterize and generalize their community. The second spike comes in week 33 (14–20 August) due to coverage of the Unite the Right rally, which saw neo-Nazis and other far-right activists take to the streets of Charlottesville, Virginia. While some articles addressed the relationship between Anonymous and 4chan (Grierson and Gibbs 2017; Rose 2017), others continued to frame the site as a hub for alt-right and white supremacists' activity, with 'alt-right' being mentioned in almost all of the articles (Johnson 2017; Willingham 2017).

The last and largest 2017 spike occurs in week 40 (2–8 October) following a mass shooting in Las Vegas, Nevada. Here, the reason for the increased coverage was not because the Las Vegas killer was connected to 4chan, but because Google temporarily placed a /pol/ thread at the top of its search results page, in which anons had incorrectly claimed the perpetrator to be a registered Democrat. In contrast to the previous articles relating the entirety of 4chan to the alt-right or white supremacism, the Las Vegas articles frame 4chan in quite technical and ominous terms as an 'anonymous anarchic forum' and a 'shady online forum' (Ians 2017; Nakashima 2017). To summarize, then, in 2017 journalists typically described 4chan either ambivalently as merely a 'forum' or otherwise as a space for various strands of the far-right.

THE VIEW FROM WITHIN: 4CHAN IS NOT /POL/

Shifting the perspective, we now explore these journalistic descriptions in dialogue with anons' own self-perception and mythologization as a singular entity. We gathered an 'ingroup dataset' consisting of posts to 4chan/pol/ *linking to* the articles mentioned earlier. We extracted all posts on /pol/ containing at least one URL leading directly or indirectly to any of the articles from the weeks of the three spikes in 2017 (labelled 'blue' in figure 9.2).[14] We did so using 4CAT (Peeters and Hagen 2018), a tool that extracts data from a variety of sources, including virtually all posts on /pol/ since November 2013. With 4CAT, we found fifty-one posts linking to twenty-eight stories published during the three spikes.[15] From these, we then picked so-called opening posts, meaning they started a new conversational thread, and took the *three* threads that garnered the most replies.

Although the corpus is relatively small (three threads with a total of 233 comments), we call here on the anti-structuralist approach as originally proposed by Tarde and applied within contemporary Latourian digital sociology. Following from Tarde's theory of imitation, this approach attempts to draw out those social ties by which the community is held together. Of particular interest are instances in which actors express conceptions of 'the "whole" in which they are said to reside' (Latour et al. 2012, 604–5). While Latour considers this metaphor as epistemologically flawed, he nevertheless recognizes that 'panoramic' conceptions of a 'whole' often serve an important function of binding groups together (Latour 2005, 189). This is an especially important function to the anonymous and ephemeral environment of 4chan, where, as we mentioned, this wholeness cannot be fixed as semi-permanent networks of 'friends' or 'followers'. We argue that the highlighted threads articulate four aspects that underpin the role of entitativity in 4chan/pol/: a homogenization of and hostility towards the outgroup, a strategic rhetoric of ingroup diversity, expressions of ingroup togetherness and self-mythologization.

To understand how anons manifest their weird collectivity in dialogue with media representations of 4chan, we first consider the most replied-to thread (100 replies) from 4 October 2017.[16] The thread links to a *Politico* article reconstructing the spread of misinformation in the aftermath of the aforementioned Las Vegas shooting. It specifically focuses on how 'false flag proclamations and conspiracy theories' emanated 'from the darkest corners of the internet and the likes of Alex Jones, 4chan and Reddit', framing /pol/ users as 'amateur sleuths' who willingly or unwillingly helped spread false stories (Straus and Robertson 2017). While a number of comments to this thread lament *Politico*'s characterization of /pol/ users as hoaxers instead of investigators, others are emboldened by the coverage, with one commenter stating, 'The fact that the [mainstream media] is even acknowledging conspiracy theories proves that we're /breaking the conditioning/'. Similar comments position 'the media' as a coordinated outgroup, working in league with other 'deep state' establishment institutions such as the FBI and CIA. Illustrative of this, one comment claims '(((they))) are trying to shut [the story] down'. Similarly, the opening post implies a conspiratorial association between Politico and 'THE (((FBI)))'. Replying to this, another reply shows this conspiratorial opposition as violent hostility: 'We know damn well why he [the shooter] did it, and until journalists are dealt with they will keep radicalizing the left'. While most of the thread slides into further conspiracy thinking, what we see here is a discursive homogenization of 'the media' as a tight-knit outgroup looking to silence /pol/ anons whose true aims, as one commenters states, are 'independently investigating claims made by the media'.

As mentioned before, a central technique by which anons manifest their weird collectivity is the anti-Semitic triple parentheses meme – '(((FBI)))' and '(((they)))' – by which /pol/ anons imagine their outgroup as part of a vast conspiracy including 'Jews' and other elites (Tuters and Hagen 2020).[17] In this sense, the thread exemplifies how /pol/'s mobilization does not operate through rigid membership, but rather by rhetorically offering a sense of unity through vigorously opposing an even more unified *other*. As Bourdieu noted, nothing unifies so effectively as a sense of 'visceral intolerance' towards the outgroup (1996).

In the second thread we find evidence of how /pol/ anons construct their weird collectivity in dialogue with media (mis)representations of their subculture's supposed diversity.[18] The strange and knotted conceptual structure at work here paradoxically aims at constructing the ingroup as in fact relatively *incoherent* and dispersed, as opposed to characterization as a hub for extremist activity online, in the manner that 4chan is often (correctly) framed in media accounts. Opening with a link to a *New York Times* story in which 4chan is described as 'a message board favored by white nationalists' (Rubin 2017), the thread starts with a poster lamenting: 'Is /pol/ really all of 4chan now? Is 4chan nothing more than a website for "white nationalists?"' (see figure 9.3). In the ensuing discussion, multiple anons argue that '4chan is always the home of contrarians' towards 'the established political elite' with a relatively diverse array of political viewpoints. When one takes into account that the site includes over seventy thematic discussion boards ranging from /a/ 'Anime' to /lit/ 'Literature', each with a distinct culture and many of which have little to do with far-right politics at all, then it is in fact technically incorrect to conflate 4chan as a whole with discussions on /pol/. Even within /pol/ itself, in which far-right activity is the norm, there are ongoing discussions dedicated to specific topics which function, for instance, to

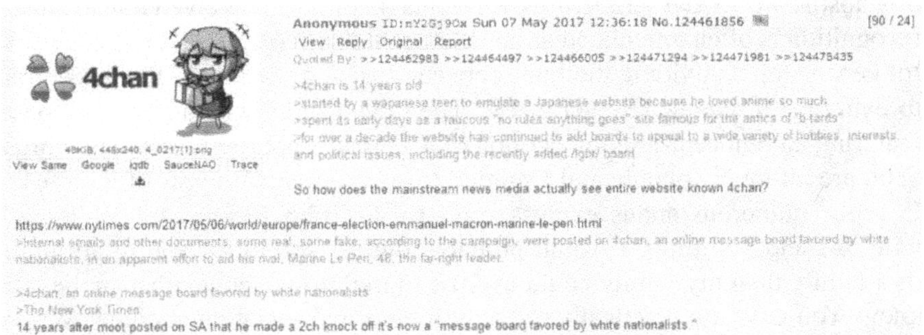

Figure 9.3. Screenshot Derived from 4plebs.org Showing the Opening Post of the Second Most Replied-to Thread Referencing One of the News Articles.

Source: Screenshot of public post from 4/chan. Original creator Anonymous: Author.

separate Trump supporters from those deeming him too mild (Jokubauskaitė and Peeters 2020). As with other articles in our dataset, the *New York Times* report quite understandably overlooks such nuances. The significance of this second thread thus lies in how /pol/ anons make strategic use of this journalistic generalization to negotiate a type of entitativity that is at once both tight enough to hold the collective together and also loose enough so they can distance themselves from one another. The latter is so common that it has even morphed into the memetic phrase '>/pol/ is one person', used to paraphrase and ridicule other poster's generalizing remarks and strategically manifest difference amongst the ingroup.[19] Often combined with the equally disingenuous 'trolling' argument – which posits that /pol/ anons are not actually serious – this double positioning offers a sense of deniability for users who do not want to be directly associated to the board's omnipresent white supremacist activity or the occasions when the site is tied to acts of real-world violence (Reitman 2018; Beran 2019). Considering radicalization often starts with gradually acclimatizing to content first thought to be too blunt (Munn 2019), these narratives can help soften initial encounters with extremist ideologies instead of immediately enrolling in rigid group membership.

The third most replied-to thread displays how ingroup entitativity functions on /pol/ as a weird form of collective affinity.[20] The thread is in response to another *New York Times* article, in this case concerning 4chan's role in the bloody Unite the Right rally in Charlottesville (Roose 2017). In considering the significance of this thread, it is important to understand that not only are discussions on /pol/ typically characterized by high levels of antagonism towards the outgroup, but anons also tend to attack one another and frown upon expressions of affect. It is against this context of ubiquitous mutual hostility and cynicism that the thread stands out as a surprising expression of ingroup solidarity. In particular, anons use the *New York Times* article as an excuse to express a sense of togetherness and mutual understanding in the face of a hostile world that serially misrepresents them. The perceived outside misrecognition is often articulated as an existential threat (e.g. with constant fears 'of censorship'), dividing the lines between 'us' and 'them' – a theme central to extremist discourse (Berger 2018). The thread starts with an opening post featuring an innocent-looking cartoon of a Trump supporter next to the words 'You are all lovely people and I'm glad to spend time with you' (figure 9.4). In reply, numerous anons express similarly heartfelt feelings of belonging, with one anon writing: 'I would probably die for you guys. You're all more of a family than my family could ever be to me', to which another replies, 'I know. You guys are practically my only friends and social interaction'. While these statements do need to be read through the complex and knotted ironic language games that characterize imageboard culture (De Zeeuw and Tuters 2020), the public displays of affection are remarkable given 4chan's cultural

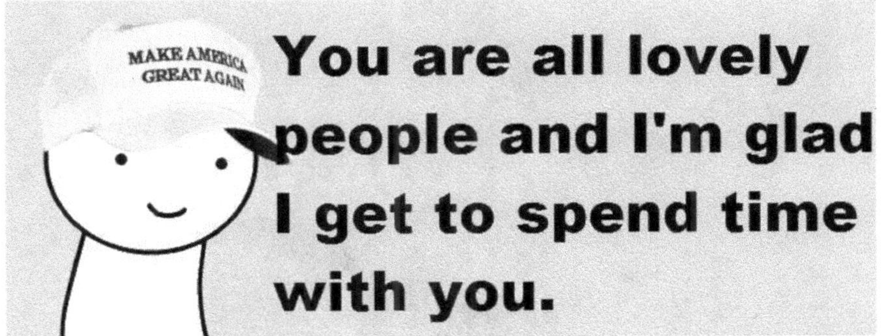

Figure 9.4. Image from the Opening Post of the Third Most Replied-to Thread, Responding to a *New York Times* Article about the Charlottesville Unite the Right rally and 4chan's Role Therein (Anonymous).
Source: Image from public 4/chan post. Original creator Anonymous: Author.

norm of hostility, even towards other posters. From this thread, we can thus deduce a crucial affective dimension to /pol/ anons' weird collectivity as a seemingly innocent expression of togetherness which could not be further from those images we normally associate with far-right mobilization. As summarized in another reply: 'The shills will never understand our bonds of friendship. The brotherhood that runs through this board is what makes it fun'.

A final crucial element in 4chan anons' construction of their weird collectivity may be referred to as their *self-mythologization* as a highly entitative 'body'. A telling image from the second thread captures this paradox (figure 9.5). Reacting to the aforementioned characterization by the *New York Times* (4chan as 'a forum favored by white nationalists'), the image depicts a variation of the *Rhodes Colossus*, an iconic cartoon showing British colonialist Cecil Rhodes as a giant standing over Africa. Here, Rhodes's head is substituted with the word */pol/*. In the outline of Africa, we see 4chan's landing page with the names of other boards. The manifest intention of this image suggests that /pol/ has conquered and subjugated the diverse inhabitants of 4chan under its boot and, crucially, that /pol/ has become 4chan. Indeed, anons in the same thread express how 'the media only cares about /pol/' since /pol/ is 'the only one that matters in global politics'.

Sensationalistic or otherwise, off-the-mark reporting has long been incorporated by anons in constituting an ironic collective self-identity. While Phillips et al. (2017) warn journalists to eschew exaggerations on the historical continuity of 4chan's collectives, on 4chan itself, teleological histories are typical to its weird collectivity. While it would be relatively unusual for the users of larger social media to engage in discussions about the history of their favourite platform's ideological essence, the 4chan anons' 'meta awareness'

Figure 9.5. Image Found on 4chan/pol/ in Response to a *New York Times* Journalist's Characterization of 4chan as a 'White Nationalists' Forum (Anonymous).
Source: Image from public 4/chan post. Original creator Anonymous: Author.

(Auerbach 2011) is frequently expressed in vernacular historiographies of the space. Amongst others, this can be seen in a category of images that present 'timelines of 4chan', with figure 9.6 drawing the historical line from the 'trolling years' of /b/ to the '/pol/ Reich' in the 2010s and beyond. While

Figure 9.6. Image Found on 4chan/pol/ Depicting the 'Six Ages of 4chan' (Anonymous).
Source: Image from public 4/chan post. Original creator Anonymous: Author.

the cultural capital of such objects will always be 'contested' (Nissenbaum and Shifman 2017), the imagined continuity of 4chan as a whole arguably works in tandem with its weird collectivity since it endows its ever-evolving set of users with a sense of partaking in an ongoing legacy. As one anon of the aforementioned threads reminisces, 'Remember the good old days when it was /b/? The "internet hate machine" filled with "hackers on steroids?"'. Combining this sentiment with those described before, 4chan's weird collectivity can be seen as being upheld by a perpetual duality of imagining the ingroup as both unified and dispersed, ever-changing yet compressible into simplistic timelines. This in turn rhetorically offers social leeway between a range of far-right publics that are nonetheless unified in their shared subcultural practices and hatred for common enemies.

CONCLUSION

In 2016–2017, 4chan/pol/ functioned as a key site of far-right recruitment and mobilization for the alt-right, a new far-right movement whose protean identity was entangled with the 'deep vernacular Web' subcultures that also found a home on the site (De Zeeuw and Tuters 2020). Of all the many topics of threaded discussion that take place on 4chan/pol/, in this chapter we chose to focus on those weirdly self-referential threads in which 'anons' discuss journalistic accounts about 4chan. Our objective was to analyse how such accounts feed into this oppositional subculture's own self-imagining as a collective entity. To this end we combined the concept of 'entitativity' from social identity theory with the bottom-up approach or neo-Tardian digital sociology, which aims at 'fine-grained description of social life on the granular level, as well as extrapolations towards wider "patterns of living"' (Marres 2017). Our contention has been that such a fine-grained analysis offers insights into how /pol/ anons perceive themselves and at the same time constitute themselves as a singular 'us' in opposition to a nebulous yet coordinated outgroup.

4chan's technical affordances impede personal ties or reputational capital to demonstrate belonging, unlike social media platforms or other objectively white supremacist forums like *Stormfront*. However, as we have shown, this does not impede the mobilization of like-minded groups. Instead, 4chan/pol/'s collectivity is constituted by engaging in vernacular expressions, mythologizations and antagonisms towards the outgroup. Rather than person-to-person recruitment, this process happens through a tangled knot of complex (yet regressive) conceptual structures, in which media hoaxing practices and 'casually' racist humour become entwined and can lead inexorably, if only 'incrementally', towards far-right radicalization (Munn 2019). Despite protestations to the contrary, most of /pol/'s activity is indeed white supremacist, and its subculture has formed the foundation for far-right terrorist activity (Thompson 2018). As such, we should take seriously the self-reflexive practices of /pol/ anons, however absurd they might appear, in order to understand how the far-right have weaponized the 'weird collectivity' of anonymous imageboards – already a feature at the time of /b/'s heyday around 2010 – towards the end of generating memetic antagonisms and viral conspiracy theories (Tuters and Hagen 2020; Tuters et al. 2018; de Zeeuw et al. 2020).

As an oppositional subculture, /pol/ anons are united by a sense of being misunderstood by the mainstream 'parent culture', against whom they violently struggle for independence and recognition. While their organizational techniques in this struggle appear emergent and non-hierarchical, their political ideology is the exact opposite. Returning to the edited image of the Colossus of Rhodes, perhaps there is also a latent meaning to be found that speaks further to the weird collectivity of anons. As a metonym for the British Empire, the image is visually similar to the famous cover of Hobbes's *Leviathan*, in which a giant crowned figure emerges from the landscape, his torso and arms composed of a multitude of individual bodies. The drawing may be seen to represent the essence of Hobbes's argument that a strong, undivided government was the only means by which to avoid the brutal 'war of all against all'. We may thus say that, united only by their incidental articulations of togetherness, irony and purist white identity politics (Beran 2019), the omnipresent antagonisms of 4chan/pol/ similarly demonstrate its users' view of human life as profoundly Hobbesian: 'solitary, poor, nasty, brutish and short' (Hobbes 1651).

NOTES

1. As Whitney Philips (2018) argues, even journalistic exposés of the alt-right that sought to reveal these tactics could ironically help them to gain more visibility.

2. Imageboard software deletes posts after a certain amount of activity – sometimes after weeks, sometimes after minutes (Hagen 2018).

3. Note that we are not claiming that these depersonalized generalizations offer suitable models to properly understand movements arising from 4chan or their

organizational structures (or lack thereof). For such literature, see, e.g. Wiedemann (2014) or Uitermark (2017). Rather, the attempt here is to emphasize the relevance of generalized self-imagination within group-making processes.

4. In these later studies, Campbell's original use of the term was criticized for its conceptual ambiguity (Hamilton et al. 2002, 141), but nonetheless proved useful under the new umbrella of *social identity theory* (Tajfel and Turner 1979).

5. Acknowledging the concern that the more descriptive approach here contrasts structural debates and critical normative lenses on a problematic space like 4chan/pol/, our research should be understood in dialogue with such more normative approaches to the issue of online extremism.

6. For instance, at the start of 2018 a staggering number of 4% of all monthly posts on /pol/ contained the word 'Jew' (Hagen 2020).

7. Instead of using Durkheim's (1965 [1912]) concept for this type of phenomenon – 'collective effervescence' – a neo-Tardean approach calls for a different nomenclature.

8. This assumption does not mean 4chan anons' antagonisms towards the media remained consistent over time: /b/'s grievances were largely concerned with ridiculing news media sensationalism (Phillips 2015) while on /pol/ (as we will see), the antagonisms acquire a reactionary political valence.

9. We set the source language to English and queried for the word '4chan' in the entire historical record until 20 February 2020. We refrained from querying the board names (e.g. /b/, /r9k/ or /pol/) because '4chan' would allow us to study the popular understanding of 4chan as a whole. We queried only for '4chan' and not the misspellings '4 chan' or '4-chan' since they gave many false positives. Errors in capitalization, for example, '4Chan', were allowed.

10. A few relevant online-only sources are missing, such as Vox, as are articles from some mainstream media, like Fox.

11. We kept articles from international or renowned news outlets, newswires, regional news, university papers and specialist websites, and removed those from blogs, fringe websites and transcripts from radio and TV shows.

12. Nexis Uni data often return duplicates. To mitigate this, we automatically removed entries featuring an identical title and body text. Since duplicates with minor body variations remained, we also removed entries with both the same title and the same source.

13. The annotated dataset of news articles within the three spikes can be found on http://doi.org/10.5281/zenodo.3678199.

14. We also queried the article URLs in archive.is, the most popular archiving site on /pol/. For the articles that had been archived, we also searched for comments with these archive.is links. Note that other archiving sites are also used, as are screenshots of an article, so some references could be missing.

15. The full dataset with the 4chan/pol/ post referring to the articles in the 2017 spikes can be found on http://doi.org/10.5281/zenodo.3678199.

16. See http://archive.4plebs.org/pol/thread/144007541/.

17. The triple parantheses meme has well known anti-Semitic connotation and origin, initially developed as a technique for harassing journalists with Jewish-sounding surnames on Twitter. Although it is relatively rarely used in this originally explicit form on /pol/, the purpose is that anons know who (((they))) really are.

18. See http://archive.4plebs.org/pol/thread/124461856/.

19. See http://archive.4plebs.org/pol/search/text/%22pol%20is%20one%20person%22/.

20. See http://archive.4plebs.org/pol/thread/143516060/.

REFERENCES

Auerbach, David. 2011. 'Anonymity as Culture: Treatise by David Auerbach'. *Triple Canopy*.

Bennett, W. Lance, and Alexandra Segerberg. 2012. 'The Logic of Connective Action'. *Information, Communication & Society* 15 (5): 739–68.

Beran, Dale. 2019. *It Came from Something Awful: How a Toxic Troll Army Accidentally Memed Donald Trump into Office*. New York: All Points Books.

Berger, John. 2018. *Extremism*. Cambridge: MIT Press.

Blumer, Herbert. 1969. *Symbolic Interactionism: Perspective and Method*. Berkeley: University of California Press.

Bourdieu, Pierre. 1996. *Distinction: A Social Critique of the Judgement of Taste*. (Translated by R. Nice). 8th ed. Cambridge, MA: Harvard University Press.

Brake, Michael. 1980. *The Sociology of Youth Culture and Youth Subcultures*. London: Taylor & Francis.

Brewer, Marilynn, Ying Yi Hong, and Qiong Li. 2004. 'Dynamic Entitativity: Perceiving Groups as Actors'. In *The Psychology of Group Perception*, edited by V. Yzerbyt, C. Judd, and O. Corneille, 19–29. New York: Psychology Press.

Buncombe, Andrew. 2017. 'Anti Defamation League Says "OK" Hand Sign Not a White Supremacist Hate Symbol'. *The Independent*, 4 May.

Campbell, Donald T. 1958. 'Common Fate, Similarity, and Other Indices of the Status of Aggregates of Persons as Social Entities'. *Behavioural Science* 3 (1): 14–25.

Coleman, Gabriella. 2014. *Hacker, Hoaxer, Whistleblower, Spy: The Many Faces of Anonymous*. New York: Verso Books.

Colley, Thomas, and Martin Moore. 2020. 'The Challenges of Studying 4chan and the Alt-Right: "Come on in the Water's fine"'. *New Media & Society* https://doi.org/10.1177/1461444820948803 1-26.

Daniels, Jessie. 2009. *Cyber Racism: White Supremacy Online and the New Attack on Civil Rights*. Lanham: Rowman & Littlefield.

Delesalle-Stolper, Sonia. 2017. 'MacronLeaks Is Final Twist in Surreal French Election Campaign'. *The Guardian*, 6 May. https://www.theguardian.com/commentisfree/2017/may/06/macronleaks-french-election-campaign-hackers.

Durkheim, Émile. 1965 [1912]. *The Elementary Forms of the Religious Life*, London: The Free Press.

Erickson, Amanda. 2017. 'Macron's Emails Got Hacked: Here's Why French Voters Won't Hear Much about Them before Sunday's Election'. *The Washington Post*, 6 May.

Finkelstein, Joel, Savvas Zannettou, Barry Bradlyn, and Jeremy Blackburn. 2018. 'A Quantitative Approach to Understanding Online Antisemitism'. *The International AAAI Conference on Web and Social Media (ICWSM 2020)*. arXiv:1809.01644.

Fisher, Mark. 2017. *The Weird and the Eerie*. London: Repeater.

Ganesh, Bharath. 2020. 'Weaponizing White Thymos: Flows of Rage in the Online Audiences of the Alt-Right'. *Cultural Studies* 58 (3): 1–33.

Grierson, and Gibbs. 2017. 'Message Showing Apparent Hack Appears on Neo-Nazi Daily Stormer Website'. *The Guardian*. 15 August. https://www.theguardian.com/technology/2017/aug/14/anonymous-hackers-take-over-neo-nazi-website-daily-stormer-charlottesville-heather-heyer.

Hagen, Sal. 2020. ' "Trump Shit Goes into Overdrive": Tracing Trump on 4chan/pol/'. *M/C Journal* 23 (3). https://journal.media-culture.org.au/index.php/mcjournal/article/view/1657.

Hamilton, David, Steven Sherman, and Luigi Castelli. 2002. 'A Group by any Other Name: The Role of Entitativity in Group Perception'. *European Review of Social Psychology* 12 (1): 139–66.

Harmon, Amy. 2018. 'Why White Supremacists Are Chugging Milk and Why Geneticists Are Alarmed'. *The New York Times* 11 October. https://www.nytimes.com/2018/10/17/us/white-supremacists-science-dna.html.

Hawley, George. 2017. *Making Sense of the Alt-Right*. New York: Columbia University Press.

Hobbes, Thomas. 1651. *Leviathan: Or the Matter, Forme and Power of Commonwealth, Ecclesiasticall and Civill*. London: Andrew Crooke.

Hogg, Michael. 2007. 'Uncertainty–Identity Theory'. *Advances in Experimental Social Psychology* 39: 69–126. https://doi.org/10.1016/S0065-2601(06)39002-8.

Ians. 2017. 'Las Vegas Massacre: Google, Facebook, Twitter Failed to Curb Fake News'. *The Indian Express*, 3 October. https://www.newindianexpress.com/world/2017/oct/03/las-vegas-massacre-google-facebook-twitter-failed-to-curb-fake-news-1666081.html.

Johnson, Bridget. 2017. 'The Hate Spewed in Charlottesville Helps ISIS and al-Qaeda'. *Observer*, 16 August. https://observer.com/2017/08/anti-semitism-charlottesville-terrorism/.

Jokubauskaitė, Emilija, and Stijn Peeters. 2020. 'Generally Curious: Thematically Distinct Datasets of General Threads on 4chan/pol/'. *Proceedings of the Fourteenth International AAAI Conference on Web and Social Media* 14 (1): 863–7.

Latour, Bruno. 2005. *Reassembling the Social: An Introduction to Actor-Network-Theory*. Oxford: Oxford University Press.

Latour, Bruno. 2010. 'Tarde's Idea of Quantification'. In *The Social after Gabriel Tarde: Debates and Assessments*, edited by Mattei Candea, 145–62. London: Routledge.

Latour, Bruno, Pablo Jensen, Tommaso Venturini, Sébastian Grauwin, and Dominique Boullier. 2012 'The Whole Is Always Smaller than Its Parts – A Digital Test of Gabriel Tardes' Monads'. *The British Journal of Sociology* 63 (4): 590–615.

Lickel, Brian, Norman Miller, Douglas Stenstrom, Thomas Denson, and Toni Schmader. 2006. 'Vicarious Retribution: The Role of Collective Blame in Intergroup Aggression.' *Personality and Social Psychology Review* 10 (4): 372–90.

MacLaughlin, Sinead. 2017. 'Pokemon Go Gamer Pleads Guilty to Child Porn Charges after Vile Images Were Spotted by a Work Colleague and He Is Surprised Images Are Illegal'. *The Daily Mail.* 5 May. https://www.dailymail.co.uk/news/article-4475606/Pokemon-gamer-pleads-guilty-child-porn-charges.html.

Marres, Noortje. 2017. *Digital Sociology: The Reinvention of Social Research.* London: Wiley.

Massanari, Adrienne. 2016. '#Gamergate and the Fappening: How Reddit's Algorithm, Governance, and Culture Support Toxic Technoculture'. *New Media & Society* 19 (3): 329–46.

Mills, Chris. 2017. 'French Election Campaign Hit by "Massive Hacking Attack". *BGR* 5 May. https://finance.yahoo.com/amphtml/news/french-election-campaign-hit-massive-hacking-attack-223906120.html.

Munn, Luke. 2019. 'Alt-Right Pipeline: Individual Journeys to Extremism Online'. *First Monday* 24 (6). https://doi.org/10.5210/fm.v24i6.10108.

Nagle, Angela. 2017. *Kill All Normies: Online Culture Wars from 4Chan and Tumblr to Trump and the Alt-Right.* London: Zero Books.

Nakashima, Ryan. 2017. 'False News of the Vegas Attack Spread on Google, Facebook'. *AP News*, 3 October.

Nissenbaum, Asaf, and Limor Shifman. 2017. 'Internet Memes as Contested Cultural Capital: The Case of 4chan's /b/ Board'. *New Media & Society* 19 (4): 483–501.

Noor, Poppy. 2019. 'How the Alt-Right Co-Opted the OK Hand Sign to Fool the Media'. *The Guardian*, 3 October. https://www.theguardian.com/world/2019/oct/03/ok-sign-gesture-emoji-rightwing-alt-right.

Norris, Jesse J. 2020. 'Idiosyncratic Terrorism: Disaggregating and Undertheorized'. *Perspectives on Terrorism* 14 (3): 2–18.

Peeters, Stijn, and Sal Hagen. 2018. *4CAT: Capturing and Analysis Toolkit.* Computer software. Amsterdam: University of Amsterdam. https://github.com/digital methodsinitiative/4cat.

Peters, John. 2015. *The Marvelous Clouds: Toward a Philosophy of Elemental Media.* Chicago: University of Chicago Press.

Phillips, Whitney. 2015. *This Is Why We Can't Have Nice Things: Mapping the Relationship between Online Trolling and Mainstream Culture.* Cambridge MA: MIT Press.

Reitman, Janet. 2018. 'All-American Nazis: Inside the Rise of Fascist Youth in the U.S.' *Rolling Stone*, 2 May. https://www.rollingstone.com/politics/politics-news/all-american-nazis-628023/.

Roose, Kevin. 2017. 'This Was the Alt-Right's Favorite Chat App. Then Came Charlottesville'. *The New York Times*, 15 August. https://www.nytimes.com/2017/08/15/technology/discord-chat-app-alt-right.html.

Rose, Eleanor. 2017. 'Daily Stormer Hack: 'Anonymous' Group Take Control of Far-Right Website after Vile Heather Heyer Post'. *Evening Standard*, 14 August. https://www.standard.co.uk/news/world/anonymous-hackers-take-control-of-farri ght-site-the-daily-stormer-after-it-mocks-heather-heyer-a3610936.html.

Rubin, Alissa J. 2017. 'France Chooses a Leader, and Takes a Step into the Unknown'. *The New York Times*, 6 May. https://www.nytimes.com/2017/05/06/world/europe/france-election-emmanuel-macron-marine-le-pen.html.

Satter, Raphael. 2017. 'In Long-Feared Twist, Online Leak Rattles French Campaign'. *AP News*, 7 May. https://apnews.com/article/0dc066bde11b409d98c9608 86cdda905.

Scott, Mark, and Benoit Morenne. 2017. 'Far-Right American Activists Promote Hacking Attack on Macron'. *The Independent*, 6 May. https://www.independent.co.uk/news/world/europe/far-right-activists-america-us-macron-hack-emails-france-election-le-pen-latest-a7722111.html.

Straus, Ben and Derek Robertson. 2017. 'Misinformation Is the New Normal of Mass Shootings'. *Politico*, 2 October. https://www.politico.com/magazine/story/2017/10/02/las-vegas-shooting-fake-news-guns-215670.

Tajfel, Henri, and John Turner. 1979. 'An Integrative Theory of Intergroup Conflict'. In *Organizational Identity: A Reader*, edited by: M. Schultz and M. Hatch, 33–47. Oxford: Oxford University Press.

Tarde, Gabriel. 1903 [1890]. *The Laws of Imitation*. (Translated by E. Parsons). New York: Henry Holt and Company.

Thompson, Andrew. 2018. 'The Measure of Hate on 4Chan'. *Rolling Stone*, 10 May. https://www.rollingstone.com/politics/politics-news/the-measure-of-hate-on-4chan-627922/.

Tuters, Marc. 2019. 'LARPing & Liberal Tears: Irony, Belief and Idiocy in the Deep Vernacular Web'. In *Post-Digital Cultures of the Far Right Online Actions and Offline Consequences*, edited by M. Fielitz and N. Thurston, 37–48. London: Transcript Verlag.

Tuters, Marc, and Sal Hagen. 2020. '(((They))) Rule: Memetic Antagonism and Nebulous Othering on 4chan'. *New Media & Society* 22 (12): 2217–27.

Tuters, Marc, Emilija Jokubauskaitė, and Daniel Bach. 2018. 'Post-Truth Protest: How 4chan Cooked Up the Pizzagate Bullshit'. *MC Journal* 21 (3). http://journal.media-culture.org.au/index.php/mcjournal/article/view/1422.

Uitermark, Justus. 2017. 'Complex Contention Analyzing Power Dynamics within Anonymous'. *Social Movement Studies* 16 (4): 403–17.

Wiedemann, Carolin. 2014. 'Between Swarm, Network, and Multitude: Anonymous and the Infrastructures of the Common'. *Distinktion Journal of Social Theory* 15 (3): 309–26.

Willingham, Alexandra J. 2017. 'Trump Made Two Statements on Charlottesville. Here's How White Nationalists Heard Them'. *CNN*, 15 August.

de Zeeuw, Daniël. 2019. *Between Mass and Mask: the Profane Media Logic of Anonymous Imageboard Culture*. PhD Thesis. Amsterdam: The University of Amsterdam.

de Zeeuw, Daniël, Sal Hagen, Stijn Peeters, and Emilija Jokubauskaitė. 2020. 'Tracing Normiefication: A Cross-Platform Analysis of the QAnon Conspiracy Theory'. *First Monday*: https://doi.org/10.5204/mcj.1422.

de Zeeuw, Daniël, and Marc Tuters. 2020. 'The Internet Is Serious Business: On the Deep Vernacular Web and Its Discontents'. *Cultural Politics* 16 (2): 214–32.

Chapter 10

Gab as an Imitated Counterpublic

Greta Jasser

Computer scientist Megan Squire describes the emergence of the 'Alt-Tech' movement and its social media platforms: 'Imagine you have a playground at school and there is a bully on your playground. The teacher keeps putting the bully in time out, so the bully gets his dad to build a brand-new playground. . . . That's alt tech' (Letson and Squire 2019).

Social media platforms such as Gab and Voat have sprung up in response to perceived censorship by Facebook and Twitter. Large social media firms have been under political and social pressure to adjust and enforce their terms of service, especially in the wake of (live-broadcast) far-right terrorist attacks, such as the Christchurch Massacre in New Zealand and violent right-wing protests in the United States, most notably the 'Unite The Right' Rally in Charlottesville in 2017 (Donovan, B. Lewis, and Friedberg 2019). Following the death of counterprotester Heather Heyer and the ensuing backlash against the violent manifestations and the means of the far-right to organize them online, several platforms, including Facebook and Twitter, updated and enforced their terms of service. After these events, users who violated the terms were banned in larger numbers than ever before (Donovan, Lewis, and Friedberg 2019, 49–50). After the storming of the U.S. Capitol by Trump supporters, and the permanent suspension of Donald Trump from Twitter in January 2021, Alt-Tech platforms experienced an unprecedented influx of users.

Anticipating social media bans in 2017 Alt-Tech founders decried 'the status quo in the technology industry', claiming it was controlled by left-wing big tech companies, and began to position themselves as 'the defenders of free speech, individual liberty, and truth' (Alt-Tech Alliance 2017, cited in Donovan, Lewis, and Friedberg 2019, 56). This rhetoric has become an integral part of the Alt-Tech business model, and Alt-Tech founders welcomed far-right and other users who were banned from large social networks on their nascent platforms (Zannettou et al. 2018). The loss of direct communication channels of right-wing groups and movements towards their followers made a shift in movement communication necessary and encouraged the emergence of a variety of Alt-Tech platforms, which initially mirrored their larger counterparts like Twitter or Reddit.

The term *Alt-Tech* (short for *alternative technology*) refers to two things: a right-wing, libertarian tech-movement and the conglomerate of social media platforms this tech movement has yielded. After being forced off or voluntarily leaving Twitter and other large platforms, far-right actors found a friendly environment on these platforms. Most of them do not openly endorse the far-right, claiming instead to simply offer a space for 'free speech'. Alt-Tech platforms quickly evolved from being copies of their larger counterparts to social media spaces with distinct target populations, audiences and affordances (Squire 2019). The most prominent Alt-Tech platform is Gab.com – a micro-blogging platform which resembles Twitter.

When Alt-Tech in general and Gab.com in particular gained traction in 2017 and 2018, a number of studies (Zannettou et al. 2018; Fair and Wesslen 2019) documented the origins, uses and levels of toxicity and hate speech that characterized these platforms. They found that Gab 'users rang[e] from alt-right supporters and conspiracy theorists to trolls', and that the platform is mainly used for discussing 'news, world events, and politics-related topics' (Zannettou et al. 2018, 7), as well as offline events related to U.S. president Donald Trump or white nationalism. Quantitative studies find Gab to be a politically oriented system with predominantly conservative, male and Caucasian users. Some prominent users are known right-wing extremists (Lima et al. 2018). Ebner and Davey determined that users join Alt-Tech platforms because they are frustrated about the enforcement of terms of service by large social media platforms against extremists, and because they see their freedom of speech impaired (Davey and Ebner 2018).

Following this research, in this chapter I address the question: What motivates users to use right-wing, Alt-Tech platforms?

As an example of these alternative network technologies, I scrutinize the Alt-Tech platform Gab.com. I analyse how the platform is built, what it affords to its users and how the platform's self-presentation is tied to right-wing grievances. I argue that Gab acts as an *imitated counterpublic* mediated through network technology. It affords a familiar user-experience as well as a predominantly right-wing user base, establishing its place in the far-right (social)media ecosystem. It promotes signing up as an act of political defiance.

The concept of *counterpublics* highlights the simultaneous existence of several publics. These publics are either hegemonic and align with dominant power structures, or they are counterpublics in the traditional sense: speaking outside of or against existing systems of oppression. Some – like Gab – claim an unwarranted status of oppression for themselves, as well as for their users.

I find that traditional far-right fears and perceptions of persecution by, for example, big tech political opponents, or a diffuse elite, motivate users to join, support and find solidarity in far-right or fringe spaces like Gab. It facilitates an identity formation in opposition to a variety of shared enemies, most importantly big tech, which is perceived as hegemonic, and liberal/left-wing. Gab is a social network that is marketed to users who see themselves as victims of 'liberal' (i.e. progressive or left-wing) content regulation. While it is promoted as a space which functions like a counterpublic, it is neither counter-hegemonic, nor a public, as publics typically facilitate diverse deliberation. I argue that Gab therefore functions as what we can refer to as an *imitated* counterpublic (Sik 2015; Tischauser and Musgrave 2019).

The platform community is brought together by a shared perception of victimization, an outcast identity and a sentiment of defiance produced by joining the social network. This sense of victimhood and defiance are crucial for the identity formation that occurs on the platform.

In this chapter, I first delineate the concept of imitated counterpublics and highlight their role in identity-formation. Second, I explicate the concept through a case study of Gab AI Inc. – that is, the social network itself and the adjacent websites belonging to the enterprise. I analyse two sets of data, employing a qualitative content analysis – the corporate blog and Gab posts wherein users gave reasons for why they joined the platform. In this case study, I first provide an overview and analysis of the platform affordances, establishing the network character of Gab.com and its branches. I then detail how Gab.com is positioned as an imitated counterpublic by scrutinizing the way the website is marketed and presented by its owner, Andrew Torba, particularly on the 'Gab News' Blog. Third, I prove the efficacy of this presentation, by analysing the reasons why people are motivated to join the platform. I conclude that typically users join because they perceive the platform as providing some form of counterpublic space, where they are free to communicate what they conceive of as subversive ideas.

COUNTERPUBLICS, IMITATED COUNTERPUBLICS AND IDENTITY FORMATION

This section outlines the concept of publics and their centrality to identity formation. I describe imitated (or parasitic) publics and imitated counterpublics. The concepts I employ highlight the importance of politically tailored affordances when considering who is part of a (counter)public and why.

These concepts illuminate the results of the counterpublic's structures and motivations.

Formation of Collective Identities Online

As Nancy Fraser (1992) argues, publics 'are among the most important and underrecognized sites in which social identities are constructed, deconstructed, and reconstructed'. She identifies 'public spheres as loci of identity reconstruction' (Fraser 1992). Positioning oneself in opposition to others is central to the formation of collective identities, of a 'we' opposed to 'them' (Polletta and Jasper 2001). Collective identities are actively produced, 'invented, created, reconstituted or cobbled together' (Snow 2001) – offline, as well as on the web. The Internet and its communication technologies are:

> not only a tool or resource for individuals to disseminate ideas and products but also a site of important identity work, accomplished interactively through the exchange of radical ideas. Online discussion forums have become an essential conduit for the extreme right to air their grievances, bond and form a collective identity by othering their "common enemies" '. (Scrivens, Davies, and Frank 2020)

Gaudette et al. (2020) equate the many-to-many interactions – that is, networked interactions – facilitated through network technology with the face-to-face interactions that are pivotal in establishing collective identities. 'As a result, the internet's many online platforms have facilitated extreme right-wing identity work' (Gaudette et al. 2020). Alt-Tech platforms are no exceptions to this observation, as (counter)publics, imitated or not, are crucial for this development.

Networked Imitated Counterpublics

When using the term *networked imitated counterpublic*, I refer to spaces that claim marginalization for themselves and their users – in this way appropriating the language and tactics of de facto marginalized communities and movements. In contrast to actual counterpublics, their claims to the status of victimhood have no material grounds. Additionally, unlike proper counterpublics, these imitated counterpublics of the far-right do not enable deliberation or critical engagement. Instead, they are self-referential and based on the ritualized repetition of negative sentiments (Sik 2015, 151).

Nancy Fraser developed the concept of the *counterpublic* when she critically engaged with Habermas's (Habermas [1962] 1999) conceptualization of the public sphere. She defines counterpublics as 'parallel discursive arenas where members of subordinated social groups invent and circulate counter discourses to formulate oppositional interpretations of their identities, interests, and needs' (Fraser 1992, 123). Fraser's counterpublics are subaltern spaces (though not necessarily always pro-democratic or pro-egalitarian) which aid in developing oppositional identities. They have critical potential to influence the dominant public realm in favour of subaltern groups that are not typically represented by the liberal, bourgeois public sphere as defined by Habermas. The question of whether counterpublicity is applicable only to the subaltern, as Fraser argues, has generated plenty of scholarly debate (for a short overview, see Larson and McHendry 2019).

On the question of whether racists and ultra-nationalists can claim to be a counterpublic, Larson and McHendry put it simply: 'If one can use "counterpublic" to identify [both] Black feminist publics and white nationalist publics, then the conceptual framework lacks sufficient recognition of power, privilege, and oppression' (2019, 520). In working to differentiate between the subaltern counterpublic and fringe publics that align with oppressive societal structures, Larson and McHendry introduce the concept of a 'parasitic public'. A 'parasitic Public' 'holds a privileged symbiotic relationship with dominant power structures, while not necessarily being central enough to be a "dominant public"' (Larson and McHendry 2019, 519). Importantly, far-right publics display a counterpublic *style*, while residing in a place of relative societal privilege given their alignment with oppressive systems of power. In a similar conceptualization, Tischauser and Musgrave (2019) identify the replacement of deliberation with ideological closure and repetitive reinforcement of a far-right worldview as central features of an imitated counterpublic. Both parasitic and imitated (counter)publics are aligned with dominant societal forces. Tischauser and Musgrave (2019) find that – as opposed to the Habermasian public sphere – the imitated counterpublic is defined by two features: the ideological closure of discursive space and the 'disavowal of dialogue and deliberative engagement with broader publics' (3).

The concept of *ideological closure* was coined by linguist John Hartley (1982). Hartley wanted to show how readers of a text characterized by ideological closure were 'guided toward a dominant, "preferred meaning" by institutionalised "performative rules"' (Strauss 2014, 257). When translated to the online sphere, this guidance towards a dominant preferred meaning can be found in a variety of online spaces, including those of the far-right. Tischauser and Musgrave find ideological closure in the self-referential nature of the webspace they examine. This space solely links to itself, to ideologically congruent news outlets, or for example, to news stories about crimes where the suspect is a person of colour (Tischauser and Musgrave 2019, 5), ensuring ideological closure for their readers. This works to constantly reinforce a far-right, racializing viewpoint, as opposed to encouraging the deliberation Habermas and Fraser imply as a necessary characteristic of a democratic public. Imitated (counter)publics are characterized by 'ritualized communicative acts lacking any potential of mutually understanding the world' (141), that is, inhibiting deliberation. Further, they are 'based on negative sentiments. . . . [They are] grounded by the feeling of being threatened on [an] individual and collective level' (Sik 2015, 151).

The concept of imitated counterpublics better enables the analysis of spaces that were built for the purpose of conveying a sense of brave defiance and identity formation (Fraser 1992, 140) in the face of perceived injustices and aggrieved entitlement. The individual members of the said groups might very well be marginalized or victimized by individuals around them or by factors of class. Yet, they are not, as they claim, marginalized or victimized on the basis of belonging to the specific group (Ganesh 2019, 2020) such as whiteness, conservatism or free speech absolutism. Alt-Tech users claim these features for themselves to synthesize their marginalization from big tech. This considered, I argue that we can use the concept of the *imitated counterpublic* to understand the far-right's positioning of themselves as a victimized group, despite their alignment with dominant systems of power such as patriarchal white supremacy.

GAB AI INC.

Gab AI Inc. is one of the most prominent instances of Alt-Tech platforms and has been described as a 'safe haven' for the far-right (Hope not Hate 2018). Gab gained notoriety when the perpetrator of the deadliest attack against the Jewish community in U.S. history – the attack on the Tree of Life Synagogue in Pittsburgh in 2018 (McIlroy-Young and Ashton 2019) – posted anti-Semitic statements there.

Gab.com was introduced as a social network that combined Twitter-like micro-blogging, with a voting feature akin to that of Reddit. It now offers a news hub (Gab Trends), a blog (Gab News), a web browser (Dissenter), an online shop and, most prominently, a social media platform. At the time of writing, Gab.com appears to be one of the largest Alt-Tech platforms, claiming 3.7 million monthly visitors in 2019, according to its annual report (GAB AI Inc. 2020). Gab's 2018 claim of having had 800,000 visitors was said to be inflated (Dougherty and Edison 2019), which has cast doubt on the 2019 numbers.

When the platform gained traction in 2017, its logo was a cartoon frog that harkened back to the Alt-Right mascot Pepe the Frog (ADL 2019). It has since changed to a letters-only logo, yet the initial recognition value of Pepe for the Alt-Right and sympathetic movements should not go unnoticed. From the start Gab very clearly catered to the Alt-Right. Donovan et al. point out that it 'stood out as one [platform] that adopted a public stance on the issues of free speech, technological design, and white nationalism' (2019, 55). Gab provided the Alt-Right with a social network of medium reach (Jasser and Wankmüller 2020). It has a lower threshold for joining than more explicitly far-right forums like Stormfront, an openly white supremacist, but openly accessible online space. Yet, it has a more conservative to right-wing user base than larger social media platforms (Zannettou et al. 2018, 4). It also affords the familiarity of larger platforms like Twitter, rather than the anonymity and distinct subcultural code of platforms like the message board 4chan (Tuters 2019).

Platform Affordances, Network Structure and Identity Formation on Alt-Tech Platforms

The far-right was an early adopter of the web and recognized the potential of digital technologies. The Internet serves it as 'a space in which they could create their own ideological publishing frames' (Albrecht, Fielitz Maik, and Thurston 2019). The development of Alt-Tech is merely another instance of the far-right reacting to quickly changing possibilities and circumstances online.

Regarding Alt-Tech websites, Stern notes that 'shadow sites of Gab and BitChute . . . are more than springboards for the dissemination of alt-right propaganda; they constitute . . . a "networked public", a porous yet cohesive online community whose connectivity is enabled by posting, re-posting, sharing, and commenting' (Stern 2019).

The options to post, re-post and share function as platform affordances. They are embedded in the architecture of the social media platforms. As the affordances encourage sharing and connection with other users, Gab (or any social media with these features) can be constituted as what boyd refers to as a 'networked public' (boyd 2010): 'Networked publics are publics that are restructured by networked technologies. As such, they are simultaneously (1) the space constructed through networked technologies and (2) the imagined collective that emerges as a result of the intersection of people, technology, and practice' (boyd 2010, 39). In this sense, networked publics are spaces and imagined collectives, mediated by the underlying platform architecture. Unlike traditional publics, networked publics do not simply occur, but rely on programming and platform architecture. These digital architectures produce the affordances of social media platforms. They allow, encourage or inhibit certain behaviour, like presenting oneself through a profile, or forming groups corresponding to the users' interest.

Gab.com is first and foremost a social network. Users can create profiles, see a catered feed of accounts they follow, join groups and message one another. Furthermore, like most Alt-Tech platforms, Gab.com is very limited in its moderation policies (Donovan, Lewis, and Friedberg 2019). Any speech except illegal content, impersonation and 'doxing' is free from content moderation (GAB AI Inc. 2019). The micro-blogging function, that is, the posts, replies and re-posts, as well as the (now defunct) opportunity to vote on posts foster engagement and networked connection between users. On far-right subreddits, the voting feature in particular encourages ideological closure, and 'facilitates identity work among its members by creating an environment wherein extreme right views are continuously validated' (Gaudette et al. 2020, 1). It stands to reason that it had a similar effect on Gab.

Another important way users can build their network on the platform, and which highlights the mass communication aspect of web 2.0 social media, is to join groups, where users gather around shared interests. The most popular groups on Gab in February 2020 were 'Free Speech' (74,200 members), 'Breaking News' (62,200), 'Memes, memes and more memes' (41,600) and 'Guns of Gab' (38,400).

The popularity of groups like Free Speech as well as News, Memes and Guns can be considered as reflective of Gab's user base, supporting previous research that the platform is politically engaged and conservative to far-right leaning. Both gun owner's rights and free speech are highly ideologically charged topics that are claimed by the U.S.-right (Melzer 2009; A. R. Lewis 2017) and allow users to interact with like-minded individuals on the platform.

Since the storming of the Capitol and the sharp increase in users, the most prominent groups changed to 'Trump 2020' (181,000 members), 'News' (178,800), a replacement group of The_Donald Subreddit '/g/The_Donald' (167,400) and 'Qanon and the Great Awakening' (162,000) – illustrating yet a stronger orientation towards Trumpism (Jasser and McSwiney 2020) and conspiracy beliefs.

THE IMITATED COUNTERPUBLIC CHARACTER OF GAB

Gab claims counterpublicity and displays a counterpublic rhetorical style amongst its users, despite being wrapped up in far-right and right-wing politics. It displays a counterpublic style, while residing in a place of relative societal power. This means that most of the politics promoted on the platform are not currently or historically under any threat from mainstream systems of power. Anti-socialism, whiteness, coloniality, imperialism and heteronormativity remain the organizing structures of contemporary global systems.

Yet, Gab's owner and CEO Andrew Torba claims that 'the oppressed' – that is, Gab users – 'need voices' and that 'as censorship undertaken by and at the behest of major platforms like Twitter and Facebook grows, marginalized people from every background . . . need a safe place to engage in public' (GAB AI Inc. n.a.), that is, on his platform. They appropriate the language and tactics of marginalized groups and imitate their place in society. Yet, it does not affect their hegemonic position in a material way. Gab is therefore *marked* as a counterpublic. It is characterized by ideological closure and ritualized forms of communication. Its uniting feature is a perception of an existential threat and a negative coalition against a constructed array of malevolent opponents. It is a negative coalition, united, not primarily in a shared goal, but in a diffuse sense of grievance and resentment (Rucht 1982).

I set out to determine why users join Gab, and how it is presented to potential users. I therefore analyse two sets of data, employing a qualitative content analysis. The blog belonging to Gab.com, 'Gab News', as well as the motivations expressed by users themselves to join the platform, was analysed to this end. In the selection of this data, the founder's perspective and marketing approach is complemented by users' perspectives of the platform.

The format of 'Gab News' is that of a corporate blog, in which members of the company write about relevant news and promote their product, that is, Gab's platforms. In total, 130 posts published on the platform between May 2019 – the first available entry – and the end of June 2020 were analysed. The second dataset consists of posts gathered leveraging the Gab Pushshift API (Baumgartner 2019). It contains posts between August 2016 and February 2020. I analysed over 2,000 posts, though including re-posts, containing either 'I am on Gab' or 'I'm on Gab'. This helped compile posts where users discussed their reasons for being on the site.

Marketing a Counterpublic

On the corporate blog, the site's owner Andrew Torba regularly posts about news stories he deems relevant, as well as about news impacting Gab. Additionally, he posts about new products, software or features on Gab. Most of the entries focus on stories criticizing tech companies like Google, Facebook and Twitter. At times, they consist of news articles from other outlets, with a short introduction; some entries are longer posts detailing what Torba deems problematic in, for example, tech companies' conduct.

Torba frequently criticizes what he calls 'Big tech tyranny' (Torba 2020b). His general critique is that large tech companies censor their users and invade their privacy. In addition, Torba questions the effects of the market power of Silicon Valley and points to cases in which tech companies have worked with authoritarian regimes. While Torba touches on some broader concerns that motivate Gab, like privacy issues, his main focus is what he perceives as censorship of conservatives. The main motives he sees behind the behaviour of big tech companies are material gains, claiming, for example, that 'Silicon Valley giants continue to put profit before principles in bowing to the Communist Chinese government' (Torba 2019a).

Simultaneously, Torba sometimes also ascribes a liberal or 'social justice' ideology to the companies or their employees, which he claims leads to an anti-free speech bias. This framing of tech giants as liberal advocates of social justice follows the terminology of right-wing 'culture warriors', thereby appealing to a specific far-right political audience already familiar with such rhetoric (Tuters 2019). Notably, however, he contrasts these claims with his own opinion on speech and its limitations. Torba makes it clear that he does not believe 'hate speech' is a valid concept and thus does not see it as a legitimate reason to moderate or de-platform users or companies. In one post, Torba synthesizes the profit motive and the ideological motive in an anti-elitist remark:

> Big Tech 'leaders' think they have a moral responsibility to protect people from themselves and from information on the internet. They believe that they are the anointed warriors of justice for the 'oppressed'. Yet the central irony here is that they understand nothing about real people and their concerns. They can't relate to them and won't ever be able to with their Stanford education, eight figure homes, and their nihilistic technocratic 'beliefs'. These people don't care about you. They don't care about the 'collective health and civility of public conversation'. They care about control. (Torba 2019c)

Here, Torba firmly pits an elite against the 'common people' – a known right-wing populist rhetoric – and alleges a somehow malevolent desire for control by big tech leaders. In this, he constructs this array of opponents, with other tech companies being at the forefront of the attacks. Other adversaries Torba identifies are Democratic politicians, media companies and outlets who he claims are distorting facts and demonizing Gab due to their alleged political bias. While his antagonistic focus lies primarily with Democrats, he denotes some Republicans as members of a 'gatekeeper right'. These Republicans are, Torba claims, pitted against the 'dissident America First-right', which 'represents the values, principles, and ideals of hundreds of millions of Americans' (Torba 2019b). He describes these establishment Republicans as 'the beltway gatekeeper Conservative Inc right, which represents the interests of big business among other globalist elites while pretending to represent The People' (Torba 2019b), using the same rhetoric that is used on more openly far-right blogs and websites (Tischauser and Musgrave 2019). The adoption of this far-right jargon is congruent with the overall worldview conveyed on all branches of the enterprise. What Tischauser and Musgrave detail for the openly white nationalist website VDare is thus simultaneously applicable to the Gab News blog. VDare reinforces the belief that white people are under threat; in the case of Gab, the threat, too, is pre-detected for its (potential) users. They are viewed as being 'under attack by not only liberals, Marxists, and social justice warriors, but also from neoconservatives, market libertarians, and liberal Republicans – what many on VDare refer to as "Conservative Inc."' (6).

These attacks, Torba claims, are not just directed at users of social media platforms, but also at Alt-Tech as a whole. Torba frequently bemoans the de-platforming of Gab, sometimes in drastic, threatening language. In one instance, he claims a pervasive anti-Christian bias and persecution at work in Silicon Valley and that 'they are coming for us. Just as communists always do' [10]. Torba aims at generating a sense of existential threat. This rhetoric of threat and victimization is of course not new in far-right propaganda and is often used to justify far-right actors' own aggression (Adorno et al. 1950).

Evoking such threats is constitutive for imitated counterpublics, given that they are 'based on negative sentiments. . . . [They are] grounded by the feeling of being threatened on [an] individual and collective level' (Sik 2015, 151). The reiteration of threatening scenarios connects users by (a) establishing a threatened ingroup (note Torba's use of 'us') and a predatory outgroup; and by (b) uniting users as those who recognize the threat and are willing and equipped to fight back. As an answer to these attacks, Torba positions his platform as the solution to this threat, and himself as being at the forefront in the battle against the outgroup. He explains that he 'started Gab as an alternative [platform] to defend free speech' (Torba 2020a). And, employing religious rhetoric, he claims in another post: 'Thankfully God moved me to build what would become a digital Noah's arc [sic] of sorts, although I didn't realize that at the time back in 2016' (Torba 2020d). This religious and apocalyptical impetus is a common theme of the far right (Miller-Idris 2020). It creates urgency and demands action, selling the space as a persecuted counterpublic. Consequently, Torba urges people to join Gab, and advertises his platform accordingly: 'We can tell you from experience that no one is coming to save us from Big Tech tyranny. It's on us to save ourselves. . . . We welcome everyone with open arms to escape the Big Tech panopticon and join a community of millions of people who cherish freedom' (Torba 2020b).

Welcoming everyone with open arms, that is, acquiring new members and eventually donations and subscriptions, of course, sustains Torba's business. Marketing towards a target group that is disillusioned with social media and perceives itself as threatened is a business strategy (GAB AI Inc. 2019) with political impact. It is in Gab's financial interests to use its blog to promote the notion of victimhood which attracts users to its platform. In this sense, the corporatization of social networking encourages the propulsion of sentiments of 'oppression' and 'victimhood identities'.

Gab is also quick to capitalize on bans imposed by other social media platforms. For example, when Reddit banned over 200 subreddits in June 2020, including the highly active and increasingly infamous subreddit r/TheDonald for constantly breaking rules and breaching the terms of service (Roose 2020), Gab reacted. Within hours, Andrew Torba announced that its users had set up The_Donald group with 14,000 members on Gab.com (Torba 2020c). He repeated the same procedure when Twitter announced a ban of Qanon-related posts in September 2020; followed by Facebook, Instagram and YouTube a month later (Jasser 2020). Torba synthesizes an ideological project with a business project. Gab's character as such a synthesis is reflected in the rhetoric used on 'Gab News'.

In tune with prominent Alt-Right talking points and a conception of the importance of culture and its influence on politics (Hawley 2017), Torba emphasizes the impact of online activism facilitated through his platform: 'We can surface new ideas and powerful plans of action that have a measurable impact on our culture. . . . They can't control me, they can't control Gab, and they know it. Gab is a place for people and ideas to challenge the establishment. Not a place for the establishment to control and solidify their power' (Torba 2020e).

This marketing technique appears to attract and resonate with Gab's users. My analysis shows that for the majority of users in the sample, signing up to Gab is a political act. Users' participation in a social media platform for this reason sets Gab apart from the other social media platforms which are not part of Alt-Tech. Specifically, this analysis suggests that it is an act of political defiance and emancipation from the supposed oppression of the liberal mainstream. This can manifest in clear expressions of self-identification like 'I am a White Nationalist, therefore I am on Gab', mentioning the U.S. constitution or their political stance ('Woo hoo! I'm on Gab! I'm [a] huge Trump/Pence supporter! Looking to connect with like-minded Conservatives who believe in Freedom of Speech and o[u]r Constitution! #MAGA'), to reiterations regarding the value of free speech ('I'm on #gab because #freespeech is a reality here, unlike ALL OTHER social media platforms').

One of the most prevalent grievances for users in the sample is the dissatisfaction with large social media platforms, especially Twitter. The reasons for this dissatisfaction, however, are manifold: the impression that there are double standards for left- and right-wing users that disadvantage the latter is expressed frequently as is the suspicion that mainstream platforms have a leftist agenda and are purposefully pushing conservatives off the platforms. As one user put it, 'I'm on Gab because I believe in free speech! And i'm tired of Facebook and twitter and google controlling what others see because of there [sic] leftist agendas!"

A sense of injustice often goes hand in hand with an assertion that the users themselves didn't do anything wrong, when they were banned from large platforms: 'At least you still have your Twitter, I got suspended indefinitely back in February for being a conservative, that's why I'm on Gab instead. . . . my appeals fall on deaf ears because Twitter is run by liberals and leftists, it's f****n' sickening'.

Brought together by resentment about these social media companies, users form an identity around this resentment. One user writes: 'I'm on Gab because I believe in free speech. I guess I had too many arguments with people who disagree with free speech on Twitter, so they banned me again. Let's be outcasts together'. This particular comment aggregated a number of reasons people give for being on Gab:

(1) the perceived curtailment of free speech – the main grievance named by the users in the sample
(2) treatment by mainstream platforms and their users that is perceived as unfair, and
(3) the motivation of 'being outcasts together'.

This outcast identity is often paralleled by a sense of superiority. The implication in a comment such as this is that Gab offers itself as a superior platform, reflected in its platform architecture, but first and foremost because it has 'better' users who are more rational', and that do not need any corporate policy or company to censor or 'babysit' them. These statements indicate the effectiveness of Torba's marketing of the platform as a counterpublic. It imitates and effectively appropriates a sense of persecution on the part of members, which functions as a strong method of mobilization for users' subscription to Gab. Notably, while these users claim to be open for 'real debate', they opted to join a space that has a significantly more conservative and far-right audience and that exhibits ideological closure, rather than exposure to different opinions. As one user declares, 'I'm on Gab because it's the only place where I feel safe to express my opinions freely as a White man'.

On Gab, users express anti-Semitic, homophobic, Islamophobic, transphobic and/or racist sentiments. Expressing them without repercussions is often given as an explicit reason for joining the platform. It should be noted that a number of users in the sample distance themselves from white nationalist or anti-Semitic views, yet agree that these worldviews and expressions of freedom of speech should be protected. Nicknames are commonly employed by users in this sample to describe other large social media companies, such as 'FascistBook', 'Fakebook' or 'Nazi-Twitter', as well as the anti-Semitic 'Jewbook'. Following this logic, one user states: 'I'm on Gab because the Jews shut down the Daily Stormer'. This illustrates the perception that tech companies, ranging from Internet service providers to social media platforms, are seen to have a malevolent, and/or 'Jewish agenda' – a common anti-Semitic trope that is often combined with another conspiracy theory also alluded to by Torba on his blog: 'Cultural Marxism'. This 'conspiracy holds that a small group of Marxist critical theorists have conspired to destroy Western civilisation by taking over key cultural institutions' (Busbridge, Moffitt, and Thorburn 2020). Conspiratorial thinking, as found on both the blog and in the sample of users, is one of the core elements of far-right ideology.

Self-Perception and Identity Formation

While the counterpublic image of Gab is palpable throughout, and indeed constitutive for the self-presentation of the enterprise, the imitative character of the platform becomes apparent in the content users share. The imaginary persecution of users as described is accompanied by an ideological closure of the discursive space. This also shows in the political leaning of news sources shared on Gab. Zannettou et al. (2018), for example, have documented the extensive use of right-wing and far-right news sources among the URLs that are shared on the platform. Among the top ten URL shares of their dataset are Breitbart, The Gateway Pundit and InfoWars, though major news sources like *The Daily Mail* or *FoxNews* are shared less (rank 16 and 19, respectively; Zannettou et al. 2018, 5). The media ecosystem Gab users are offered is that of (far)right-wing news perpetuating a right-wing worldview. Tischauser and Musgrave establish that 'the function of far-right media is not so much to change public opinion, but to participate in a collective process of myth-making that legitimates claims of marginalization for white Americans' (2019, 2). Some user comments indicate that joining Gab has influenced their worldview, pushing them further towards fringe beliefs and further away from feeling as a part of the political mainstream: 'That is totally insane. The longer I am on Gab and the more I see and read, the stronger my belief system that the globalist [sic] are an evil bunch and this is a Holy War'. The expression that the social environment on Gab led this user to consolidate a conspiratorial, far-right belief system is further evidence for a relatively closed ideological imitated counterpublic.

The analysis of Gab (the social network platform as well as the adjacent sites) shows the construction of a space of essentialized belonging, anchored in perceived victimization and defiance. It serves a narrow discursive space (as described by Tischauser and Musgrave 2019, 4) on the political right, providing a space where hateful speech goes unmoderated and oftentimes uncontested. It is presented as a counterpublic, giving a room to supposedly suppressed voices. The users are united in a sense of aggrieved entitlement

(Kimmel 2017), a perceived existential threat and the conviction that signing up to this Alt-Tech platform is a political act of defiance.

Positioning themselves as marginalized or as victims is a common rhetorical trope used throughout the far-right historically and contemporarily (Berbrier 2000; Daniels 2016, 2009). Such tactics reach way beyond notorious far-right media outlets. The notion that white men supposedly have lost their rightful place in society and are therefore entitled to be 'righteously angry' is a common conception. This 'righteous anger' is emblematized in popular books like Kimmel's *Angry White Men* (2017) and Hochschild's *Strangers in Their Own Land* (2016). These authors describe a process of disenchantment with society, of not getting what one felt entitled to, and the resulting resentment about the loss of this entitlement. As mentioned in the discussion of imitated counterpublics, their members might indeed have experienced real loss resulting from the economic precarity and class oppression typical in capitalist societies. However, their understanding of said loss is shaped through cultural and racialized discourse rather than through coming to terms with economic and systemic or structural causes. Their aggrieved entitlement is shaped by and created by their identity as (predominantly) white men rather than by their experience of loss. To grasp the motivational energy that emerged from aggrieved entitlement, Ganesh engages the Platonic concept of 'thymos'. Thymos is 'the part of our souls that desires recognition of injustices done to us' (Ganesh 2020, 2); and especially weaponized white thymos: 'a complex of pride, rage, resentment, and anger that is created through informational and affective circuits that create the perception of a loss of white entitlement' (Ganesh 2020, 3). It is weaponized (online), as 'users that are connected in their rage against the purported marginalization and oppression of white people and the channelling of this rage by pundits and radical right populists to advance their own aims' (3). It is this aggrieved entitlement, and sense of white/male victimization that is reflected in online forums and on social media (e.g. Crosset, Tanner, and Campana 2019). It is particularly palpable on Alt-Tech platforms, where the perception of being victimized is extended to conservatives and free-speech absolutists.

CONCLUSION

In this chapter, I sought to answer the following question: 'How are new, alternative network technologies wrapped up within the process of identity building for the far-right?' As an example of these alternative network technologies, I have scrutinized the Alt-Tech platform Gab.com. Alt-Tech platforms create their own affordances, which provide the familiarity of large social media sites and encourage identity-building. They also offer ideological support and reinforcement of far-right positions and foster an ideological closure.

I have argued that Alt-Tech social media platforms, that is, social networking sites created by and for far-right actors are imitated counterpublics, mediated through network technology. Notably however, Gab isn't a counterpublic, because its users don't occupy counter-hegemonic social groups or positions. The imitation character of Gab lies in the perceived existential threat that motivates the users to join – they form a negative coalition, seemingly pitted against an array of perceived adversaries. Gab's character as an imitated counterpublic, then, is evidenced both by the platform's user content and by the statements of the platform's founder, Andrew Torba.

However, Gab is marketed as a right-wing counterpublic and safe haven, where users can gather and take a stand against their perceived victimization and join a like-minded political community. Perceiving oneself as part of a defiant counterpublic works to form user identity as persecuted by the liberal mainstream and big-tech, further mobilizing their participation on Gab and other Alt-Tech sites. The counterpublic style itself is part of the appeal of Alt-Tech. That is, alternative network technologies encourage building a shared identity and hence mobilization potential. The users themselves are united by a perception of an existential threat and by a sense of unjustified persecution.

Users joining Gab either did so after being banned from large social media platforms – usually on their own account for violating the terms of service – or joined to find an audience they consider different to that of large social media platforms. They also express great disappointment with the companies running these platforms and seek out Gab so that their hateful speech can be published unmediated and uncontested. The ideological closure and shared experiences confirm the impression of persecution by offering a constant stream of (relatively) coherent ideological content. Additionally, Alt-Tech platforms help to build a far-right community online by facilitating exchange between those who feel persecuted for their political views on other platforms, motivating these users to join Alt-Tech social media. For these users, joining the platform and posting on Gab become an act of political activism in supposed resistance to the mainstream. Through these features, the networked, imitated counterpublic that Gab has created caters to the needs of the contemporary far-right. That is, it provides a space in which right-wing users can express, share and reinforce a sense of victimhood, of being wronged and of defiance.

REFERENCES

ADL. 2019. 'Hate on Display: Hate Symbols Database'. 1–60. https://www.adl.org/hate-symbols.

Adorno, Theodor W., Else Frenkel-Brunswik, Daniel J. Levinson, Nevit Sanford, and Peter E. Gordon. 1950 [2019]. *The Authoritarian Personality*. London/New York: Verso Books.

Albrecht, Stephen, Fielitz Maik, and Nick Thurston. 2019. 'Introduction'. In *Post-Digital Cultures of the Far Right: Online Actions and Offline Consequences in Europe and the US*, edited by Fielitz and Thurston, 7–22. Columbia University Press.

Baumgartner, Jason. 2019. 'Pushshift API: Gab_Mastodon: Pushshift'. https://github.com/pushshift/gab_mastodon.

Berbrier, Mitch. 2000. 'The Victim Ideology of White Supremacists and White Separatists in the United States'. *Sociological Focus* 33 (2): 175–91. doi:10.1080/00380237.2000.10571164.

boyd, danah. 2010. 'Social Network Sites as Networked Publics: Affordances, Dynamics, and Implication'. In *A Networked Self: Identity, Community and Culture on Social Network Sites*, edited by Zizi Papacharissi, 39–58. New York: Routledge.

Busbridge, Rachel, Benjamin Moffitt, and Joshua Thorburn. 2020. 'Cultural Marxism: Far Right Conspiracy Theory in Australia's Culture Wars'. *Social Identities* 26 (6): 722–38. doi:10.1080/13504630.2020.1787822.

Crosset, Valentine, Samuel Tanner, and Aurélie Campana. 2019. 'Researching Far Right Groups on Twitter: Methodological Challenges 2.0.' *New Media & Society* 21 (4): 939–61. doi:10.1177/1461444818817306.

Daniels, Jessie. 2009. *Cyber Racism: White Supremacy Online and the New Attack on Civil Rights*. Perspectives on a multiracial America series. Lanham: Rowman & Littlefield Publishers.

Daniels, Jessie. 2016. *White Lies: Race, Class, Gender and Sexuality in White Supremacist Discourse*. Abingdon, Oxon, UK, and New York: Routledge, Taylor and Francis Group.

Davey, Jacob, and Julia Ebner. 2018. 'The Fringe Insurgency: Connectivity, Convergence and Mainstreaming of the Extreme Right'. Report. Institute for Strategic Dialogue.

Donovan, Joan, Becca Lewis, and Brian Friedberg. 2019. 'Parallel Ports: Sociotechnical Change from the Alt-Right to Alt-Tech'. In *Post-Digital Cultures of the Far Right: Online Actions and Offline Consequences in Europe and the US*, edited by Fielitz and Thurston 2019, 49–66. Columbia University Press.

Dougherty, John, and Michael Edison. 2019. '"No Way" Gab Has 800,000 Users, Web Host Says'. *Southern Poverty Law Centre*. 14 February. https://www.splcenter.org/hatewatch/2019/02/14/no-way-gab-has-800000-users-web-host-says.

Fair, Gabriel, and Ryan Wesslen, eds. 2019. 'Shouting into the Void: A Database of the Alternative Social Media Platform Gab'. *Proceedings of the Thirteenth International AAAI Conference on Web and Social Media* 13.

Fielitz, Maik, and Nick Thurston, eds. 2019. *Post-Digital Cultures of the Far Right Online Actions and Offline Consequences in Europe and the US*. Bielefeld: Transcript Verlag.

Fraser, Nancy. 1992. 'Rethinking the Public Sphere: A Contribution to the Critique of Actually Existing Democracy'. In *Habermas and the Public Sphere*, edited by Craig J. Calhoun, 109–42. Studies in Contemporary German Social Thought. Cambridge: The MIT Press.

GAB AI Inc. n.a. 'What Is Gab?' https://news.gab.com/what-is-gab/.

GAB AI Inc. 2019. 'Annual Report 2018'. https://www.sec.gov/Archives/edgar/data/1709244/000114420419021378/tv519744_annualreport.pdf.

GAB AI. 2020. 'Annual Report 2019'. Accessed 15 June 2020. https://www.sec.gov/Archives/edgar/data/1709244/000110465920067852/annual_report.pdf.

Ganesh, Bharath. 2019. 'How the Swarm of White Extremism Spreads Itself Online'. *The Spin-Off*. https://thespinoff.co.nz/media/28-03-2019/how-the-swarm-of-white-extremism-spreads-itself-online/.

Bharath, Ganesh. 2020. 'Weaponizing White Thymos: Flows of Rage in the Online Audiences of the Alt-Right'. *Cultural Studies* 58 (3): 1–33. doi:10.1080/09502386.2020.1714687.

Gaudette, Tiana, Ryan Scrivens, Garth Davies, and Richard Frank. 2020. 'Upvoting Extremism: Collective Identity Formation and the Extreme Right on Reddit'. *New Media & Society* (September): 146144482095812. doi:10.1177/1461444820958123.

Habermas, Jürgen. [1962] 1999. "The Structural Transformation of the Public Sphere: An Inquiry into a Category of Bourgeois Society". *Studies in Contemporary German Social Thought*. Cambridge, MA: MITPress.

Hartley, John. 1982 [1995]. *Understanding News: Studies in Culture and Communication*. Abingdon. Oxon, UK: Routledge.

Hawley, George. 2017. *Making Sense of the Alt-Right*. New York: Columbia University Press.

Hochschild, Arlie R. 2016. *Strangers in Their Own Land: Anger and Mourning on the American Right*. New York and London: The New Press.

Hope not Hate. 2018. 'Alt-Tech: Far Right Safe Spaces Online'. https://www.hopenothate.org.uk/2018/11/04/alt-tech- far right-safe-spaces-online/.

Jasser, Greta. 2020. 'The Social Media Platform That Welcomes QAnon with Open Arms: QAnon Conspiracy Followers Have Turned to Gab.Com as a Safe Space for All Manner of Right-Wing Online Communities'. *Open Democracy*. https://www.opendemocracy.net/en/countering-radical-right/social-media-platform-welcomes-qanon-open-arms/.

Jasser, Greta, and Jordan McSwiney. 2020. 'Gab.Com: The Pro-Trump Alternative to Social Media'. *VOX-Pol*. https://www.voxpol.eu/gab-com-the-pro-trump-alternative-to-social-media/.

Jasser, Greta, and Agnes Wankmüller. 2020. 'Alt-Right, Alt-Tech, Alt-Internet? Rechte Online Plattformen Und Ihre Funktion'. *Forschungsjournal Soziale Bewegungen* 33 (2): 506–12. doi:10.1515/fjsb-2020-0042.

Kimmel, Michael. 2017. *Angry White Men: American Masculinity at the End of an Era*. Third trade paperback edition. New York: Bold Type Books.

Larson, Kyle R., and George F. McHendry. 2019. 'Parasitic Publics'. *Rhetoric Society Quarterly* 49 (5): 517–41. doi:10.1080/02773945.2019.1671986.

Letson, Al, and Megan Squire. 2019. 'Hate in the Homeland'. *Reveal*. https://www.revealnews.org/episodes/hate-in-the-homeland/.

Lewis, Andrew R. 2017. *The Rights Turn in Conservative Christian Politics: How Abortion Transformed the Culture Wars*. Cambridge University Press.

Lima, Lucas, Julio C. S. Reis, Philipe Melo, Fabricio Murai, Leandro Araujo, Pantelis Vikatos, and Fabrício Benevenuto. 2018. 'Inside the Right-Leaning Echo

Chambers: Characterizing Gab, an Unmoderated Social System'. In *2018 IEEE/ACM International Conference on Advances in Social Networks Analysis and Mining (ASONAM)*, 515–22.

McIlroy-Young, Reid, and Anderson Ashton. 2019. 'From "Welcome New Gabbers" to the Pittsburgh Synagogue Shooting: The Evolution of Gab'. *Proceedings of the Thirteenth International AAAI Conference on Web and Social Media (ICWSM 2019)*. https://ojs.aaai.org/index.php/ICWSM/article/view/3264/3132.

Melzer, Scott. 2009. *Gun Crusaders: The NRA's Culture War*. New York: New York University Press. http://site.ebrary.com/lib/alltitles/docDetail.action?docID=10347238.

Miller-Idriss, Cynthia. 2020. *Hate in the Homeland: The New Global Far Right*. Princeton University Press.

Polletta, Francesca, and James M. Jasper. 2001. 'Collective Identity and Social Movements'. *Annual Review of Sociology* 27 (1): 283–305. doi:10.1146/annurev.soc.27.1.283.

Rucht, Dieter. 1982. 'Neue soziale Bewegungen oder: Die Grenzen bürokratischer Modernisierung'. In *Politikwissenschaft und Verwaltungswissenschaft*, edited by Joachim J. Hesse, 272–92. Politische Vierteljahresschrift 13/1982. Wiesbaden: VS Verlag für Sozialwissenschaften.

Scrivens, Ryan, Garth Davies, and Richard Frank. 2020. 'Measuring the Evolution of Radical Right-Wing Posting Behaviors Online'. *Deviant Behavior* 41 (2): 216–32. doi:10.1080/01639625.2018.1556994.

Sik, Domonkos. 2015. 'The Imitated Public Sphere: The Case of Hungary's Far Right'. In *Digital Media Strategies of the Far Right in Europe and the United States*, edited by Helga Druxes and Patricia A. Simpson. Lanham, MD: Lexington Books.

Snow, David. 2001. 'Collective Identity and Expressive Forms'. CSD Working Paper. https://escholarship.org/uc/item/2zn1t7bj.

Squire, Megan. 2019. 'Alt-Tech and the Radical Right: Part 1: Why the Shift?' *Centre for Analysis of the Radical Right*. https://www.radicalrightanalysis.com/2019/08/09/alt-tech-and-the-radical-right-part-1-why-the-shift/.

Stern, Alexandra M. 2019. *Proud Boys and the White Ethnostate: How the Alt-Right Is Warping the American Imagination*. Boston: Beacon Press.

Strauss, Dafnah. 2014. 'Ideological Closure in Newspaper Political Language during the U.S. 1872 Election Campaign'. *JHP* 15 (2): 255–91. doi:10.1075/jhp.15.2.06str.

Tischauser, Jeff, and Kevin Musgrave. 2019. 'Far Right Media as Imitated Counterpublicity: A Discourse Analysis on Racial Meaning and Identity on Vdare.Com'. *Howard Journal of Communications*, 1–15. doi:10.1080/10646175.2019.1702124.

Torba, Andrew. 2019a. 'Gab's Policies, Positions, and Procedures for Unlawful Content and Activity on Our Social Network'. *Gab*. https://blog.gab.com/2019/08/23/gabs-policies-positions-and-procedures-for-unlawful-content-and-activity-on-our-social-network/.

Torba, Andrew. 2019b. 'The America-First Right vs the Gatekeeper Right'. https://news.gab.com/2019/10/30/the-america-first-right-vs-the-gatekeeper-right/.

Torba, Andrew. 2019c. 'The Smug and Out of Touch Elitism of Silicon Valley's Sultans'. https://news.gab.com/2019/08/12/the-smug-and-out-of-touch-elitism-of-silicon-valleys-sultans/.

Torba, Andrew. 2020a. 'Anti-White, Anti-Trump: Welcome to Facebook'. https://news.gab.com/2020/06/25/anti-white-anti-trump-welcome-to-facebook/.

Torba, Andrew. 2020b. 'Big Tech Tyranny Is Here'. https://news.gab.com/2020/06/18/big-tech-tyranny-is-here/.

Torba, Andrew. 2020c. 'Reddit Purges 2,000+ Communities Including The_Donald'. Accessed 30 June. https://news.gab.com/2020/06/29/reddit-purges-2000-communities-including-the_donald/#more-1638.

Torba, Andrew. 2020d. 'Then They Came for Christians: A Warning'. https://news.gab.com/2020/06/24/then-they-came-for-christians-a-warning/.

Torba, Andrew. 2020e. 'Why Conservative "Influencers" Aren't on Gab'. https://news.gab.com/2020/06/23/why-conservative-influencers-arent-on-gab/.

Tuters, Marc. 2019. 'LARPing & Liberal Tears: Irony, Belief and Idiocy in the Deep Vernacular Web'. In *Post-Digital Cultures of the Far Right Online Actions and Offline Consequences in Europe and the US*, edited by Fielitz and Thurston, 37–48.

Zannettou, Savvas, Barry Bradlyn, Emiliano de Cristofaro, Haewoon Kwak, Michael Sirivianos, Gianluca Stringhini, and Jeremy Blackburn. 2018. 'What Is Gab? A Bastion of Free Speech or an Alt-Right Echo Chamber?' *Companion Proceedings of the Web Conference 2018*. International World Wide Web Conferences Steering Committee.

Part IV

ASSEMBLAGES AND ASSEMBLED TOOLS: FROM THEORY TO RESISTANCE

Chapter 11

Moments of Political Gameplay: Game Design as a Mobilization Tool for Far-Right Action

Noel Brett

STUDYING GAMES RELATIONALLY

'Do video games cause violence?' This famous and hotly debated question is notoriously difficult to answer given that it assumes a dualist framework in which individuals and bits of culture exist as *separate, discrete objects* that interact separately from each other (Elias 1978; Dépelteau 2013; Powell 2013). Thinking about the interactions between humans, technology and culture in a way that discusses what effects consuming a specific form of culture has on individual behaviour sees pieces of technology as stubborn, impervious to changing. In other words, the debate implied by this question assumes that technology unilaterally affects the human, or vice versa.

Proponents of relational theory claim that using relational theory offers several advantages over more dualist approaches where we see the *connections* rather than the *separations* between humans, culture and technology, where they are constantly acting, interacting and affecting each other (Latour 1992; Barad 2007). Building on this, radical relationalism says that all objects, even humans themselves, are made up of relations and all action takes place through relations (Powell 2013, 191). Importantly, in this model, relations become not only our basic unit of social analysis but also a process or transformation (194). In this chapter, I propose that we shift gears into radical relationalist thought, so that we can frame the interaction between players, games and political artefacts as a relational process of exchange (188–9). In this way, our question about technology and humans interacting is no longer 'how does technology affect the human?', but rather 'what are the effects or exchanges that occur when humans and technology come together?' In the case of people playing political games, 'what political outcomes arise from the figuration created between human, political and game?'

In this chapter, I define 'moment of gameplay' as the moment when the effects of the human-game relation take shape.[1] In political gameplay, it is at the 'moment of political gameplay' where the political effects of the relation surface within the human-game-political relation. Directing our attention in this way, I argue that we can investigate the agency or efficacy of moments of political gameplay as these moments appear in and circulate through their relational network (Latour 1992). I develop this concept using an approach informed by radical relationism, microethnography and performativity, in order to produce detailed readings of how video games and their players reproduce (far-right) political action. This concept does not consider video games as technologies that produce *new violence* on its players. Rather, this framework argues that in order to map the stages of gameplay that affect players, we must see political gameplay as made up of the coming together of multiple ingredients: the human, the technological and the political. Each ingredient is fundamental in creating a final output: a racist, misogynist or anti-progressive moment of gameplay. Hence, the object of study here is the *processes* by which players *reproduce a political worldview* from their involvement in gameplay. In doing so, I outline how spotting moments of political gameplay allows us to trace the processes which produce political features of play, mobilize the player to digitally enact and perform far-right play, reconfigure the political identities of its player and outline the breadcrumbs that lead the player towards far-right recruitment.

For the purposes of this chapter, I define 'political practice' as practices that forward the beliefs and values which are undeniably political, dealing with markers of political rhetoric or engaging with political themes (feminism, racial terrorism, inequality, etc.). Further, I define far-right practices as actions which cultivate and forward three general characteristics: racial and gender essentialism, racialized nationalist protectionism, and traditionalist, anti-progressive values. Additionally, I propose that, for the purposes of this study, we consider political mobilization in video games as a *process* of *political gameplay*. When either games or players bring in (right-wing) political elements into their relationship, the participants within the relationship end up leaving in altered states (Powell 2013) by performing (Butler 1993, 1998) the politics at play. More specifically, through each instance of gameplay, there is a transaction between the actants of the relation which reconfigures each other if ever so slightly (Powell 2013, 196–7; see also Devries in this volume). While these games don't *explicitly* act as a recruitment mechanism, conceptualizing political practice as the coming together of political elements with game and human elements implies that playing these games acts as a form of *digital mobilization*, where players enact or perform far-right politics regardless of their intent.

I form the concept of *moments of political gameplay* through two qualitative case studies from two seemingly different games: *Angry Goy II* (AG2; Wheel

Maker Studios 2018), a game developed with politics at its forefront; and *Red Dead Redemption 2* (RDR2; Rockstar Games 2018), an open world game which allows its players to approach objectives freely. I uncover moments of political gameplay for AG2 via an auto-ethnographical and personal research interactions with the game. Whereas, for RDR2, I use moments of political gameplay to extract detailed readings out of YouTube videos where players of RDR2 influence the game to react politically. Moments of political gameplay of AG2 showcase how the game and its technological and design affordances have more pull to influence the player to play politically. While an analysis of RDR2 shows the reciprocal relational processes of how the social and political elements of the player shape the gameplay relationship. Combining analysis of AG2 with that of RDR2 helps showcase the potentiality of political gameplay within varying gameworlds, whether intended to be spaces of far-right gameplay or not.

IT'S ALL RELATIONS

Taking up this radical relationalism has implications for our qualitative methodologies, since our new object of study is not objects themselves, but the relations (or figuration [Elias 1976]) between human and non-human actors (Latour 1992; Bennett 2010; McFarlane 2013) that produce objects or entities as such. Microethnography provides a methodology that aligns with this theoretical approach.

Giddings describes gameplay as a phenomenon which brings together multiple human and non-human actors (Giddings 2009). Adams's diagram of a gameplay mode in figure 11.1 (Adams 2013) speaks to this coming together of human and non-human actors[2] that make up a moment of gameplay, that is, the relational meaning-making that occurs through the reciprocal interaction

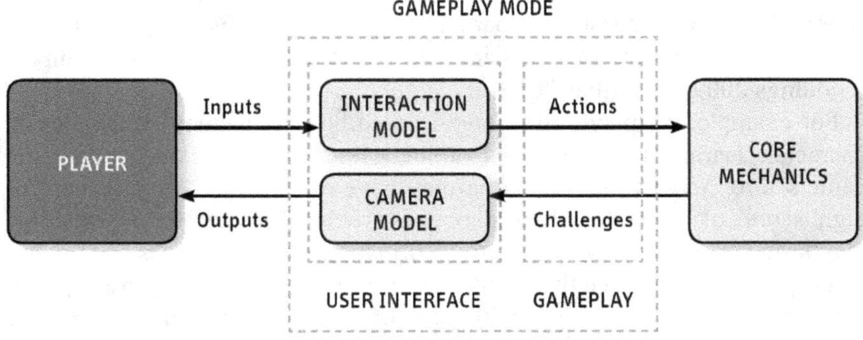

Figure 11.1. Adams's Model of Gameplay.
Source: (Adams 2013).

between human and machine (Haraway 2006, Giddings 2009). Players participate in gameplay with input technologies (often a keyboard and mouse, or game controller). The user interface links the input devices from the world of the player to actions that take place within the gameworld. As Adams notes, 'Actions refer to events in the gameworld directly caused by the user interface interpreting a player input' (276). The game answers the player's actions by providing the player with *game challenges* – non-trivial tasks the player must perform in order to progress in the game, which often require either some mental or physical effort (10). The player must understand (or *learn to understand*) the game challenges provided so they can act accordingly and satisfy the game's goals. Game challenges often restrict the player such that there are only certain possible actions for the player to do, thereby directing the player to complete the game. These challenges, by design, guide the player experience onto the next step in the game. The interface translates the game challenges for the player by showing the feedback of the communication on screen.

For example, the game Super Mario Bros. (see figure 11.2) presents a set of platforms and enemies, and the player must get to the end of the level without losing a life. Here, the game challenge is to not get hit by enemies and jumping over the holes formed by the platforms without falling. Simultaneously, the player actions are moving and jumping (and subsequently jumping on enemies or over the holes).

In this (apolitical) moment of gameplay, a cyclic exchange occurs between player, technologies and game from player actions and game challenges. This exchange is spurred by both player actions and game challenges occurring together near instantaneously. This results in a near-conversational interactive moment between the game and the player, where both affect or have agency upon each other and shape the output: gameplay. This considered, we can resist conceiving of video games as discrete or 'whole' objects. Games are not only used for play; we play *with* games, in a mutual and cyclic interaction. The games' constituent parts are constantly configuring the player's experience, responding to and changing from the player's actions and inputs (Giddings 2009; McArthur 2019).

For example, the player may have learned how to manoeuvre their game character, learned the mechanics of the game or even learned about the game's lore. Meanwhile, the game may have obtained a new safe state or high score, or perhaps unlocked new playable character for consecutive playthroughs. In other words, a transformation of both parties' states has taken place via their relational interaction with each other, where parts of the game entangle themselves with parts of the player, and visa-versa. This perspective aligns with a radically relational approach; describing radical relationalism, Powell notes that 'one might say [one] makes [oneself], but

Figure 11.2. Gameplay of Super Mario.
Source: Google images, original author unknown. Image of Super Mario (Nintendo, 1985), publicly available game.

under conditions not of [one's] own choosing, through relationships [one] can influence but not control' (Powell 2013, 193). These actions and interactions work to 'produce differences'; human and non-human actors within the relation experience *change*, even if that change is minimal or maintaining an equilibrium (196–7). In other words, a radically relational approach proposes that relations between objects compose the very qualities of the objects, as opposed to a traditional relationalism, which proposes networked interaction between whole entities (187–8).

MOMENTS OF POLITICAL GAMEPLAY

Building from these perspectives, I propose the concept of *moments of political gameplay* as a means of highlighting how games and users come together, transforming each other in ways that produce political outcomes. I argue that when adding political elements to the gameplay relation, other actants in the relation are *mobilized* to practise the political actions encoded by the game's political design. Political elements are able to participate in the relation by either game design (*politically encoded game challenges*) or by the player (*politically charged actions*) via the political positionality of the player. This means that the actants participate in arranged ways set by the game's design. In this way, the amalgamation of player elements, game elements and political elements form moments of political gameplay. In other words, when we spot a moment of political gameplay, we are spotting the *coagulation* of the *relations between game, player, and political.*

I use the expression 'moment'[3] because it allows us to tag the (micro-) temporal periods when the human-game-political relation happens, enabling us to label the exchange or transformation between all actants. In moments of political gameplay, the recreation of violent, racist, misogynist or otherwise anti-progressive gameplay practices emerges from the involvement of both game and player. The process of participating in moments of political gameplay is a performative *way of doing* far-right politics (Butler 1988, 1993; Devries, this volume), where the political practice (i.e. the moment of political gameplay) is *dependent* on the product of the relation.

By using the concept of moments of political gameplay to focus on these co-constitutive relations between human and non-human actors like games, we can bypass individualistic perspectives that reduce analysis of human actions to *intentions*.[4] Rather than concerning ourselves entirely with whether a gamer or designer is actually racist, misogynist and so on, we can focus instead on what individuals *contribute to an outcome* which is political, whether they *intended* to or not. Shifting our focus this way becomes especially important when considering the racist or violent actions that happen in open-world games that aren't necessarily political, but that carry the affordances for political play.

In what follows, I use this relational framework to spot the moments of political gameplay in the game Angry Goy II, and following this, Red Dead Redemption 2. This provides two opposite examples where we can consider relational moments of political gameplay at work. In the first, the game asserts more political action onto the player, while in the second, the player is able to assert more political force on the gameworld.

ANGRY GOY II AND ENCODING POLITICAL VIOLENCE

A voice clip of PewDiePie[5] plays the following message: 'You know, Hitler was right. I really opened my eyes to White power. And it's about time we did something about it'. I click on the glowing red 'Start' button to attempt another playthrough of the video game *Angry Goy II* (Wheel Maker Studios 2018). The game prompts me with a character select screen titled: 'The Right-Wing Death Squad'. This screen is reminiscent of classic arcade video game aesthetics and paired with a synth track. I elect to play as Christopher Cantwell, a self-described White nationalist who took part in the Charlottesville 'Unite the Right' rally in 2017, and click 'continue' to begin the game. My character spawns on a street near a familiar park. I follow a pixel walkway to the centre of the park where I find a statue of a man riding a horse with a plaque that reads 'Robert E. Lee', surrounded by purple pixel flowers (see figure 11.3). No doubt this resembles the park where the bronze equestrian statue of Robert E. Lee sits, located in Charlottesville's Market Street Park, formerly known as Lee Park.[6]

Shortly after arriving at the foot of the statue, a horde of digitized people rush towards my character. Among these people are characters marked as 'Black Lives Matter' supporters, people from the LGBTQ+ community, Jewish people, Muslim people 'Social Justice Warriors', as well as other minority and left-wing activist groups. As the hordes of non-player characters get closer, they start to throw various objects intended to hurt my character. My character is holding a weapon, and a target cross hairs follow my mouse position, the game invites me to shoot and kill the incoming attackers in order to protect my character. After several rounds of ammunition are used up, my character dies amongst a pile of digital corpses and the game transfers me to the title screen, where the game replays the PewDiePie voice clip and prompts me to replay the game once again.

Figure 11.3. A Christopher Cantwell Character in a Level Resembling Lee's Park.

Source: Screenshot from publicly available /pol/ archives game Angry Goy 2. Collected by author.

I try instead to explore the gameworld with my avatar. I bring my character towards the pixel flora hoping to interact with these instead of the minorities programmed to be aggressive. However, another ambush of protesters surround my character and I lose once more. Determined to explore the rest of the gameworld, I move my character away from the centre of the park. In no time, I reach impassable barriers and walls where protester hordes spawn. If I don't move quickly, they will steer towards my character to kill me. With impossible interaction between other mundane digital objects and restricted access outside of the digital park, the game tells me that my only possible action is to participate in shooting people that compose the political groups that are out to kill me. Or, if choosing to resist and play another type of politics, such as joining the digital activists, I must lose, over and over again.

At this moment, I think about how the game and me are working with each other, or rather, against one another. We, digital program and human, are locked together in a feedback loop of player actions and game challenges to see who has the most influence within the moment of gameplay. The game has provided a particular trajectory for me to take, and the many game challenges it introduces when I attempt to stray from this trajectory make it nearly impossible to pursue other options of my choosing. In this gameplay moment, the game has a higher influence on me than I can have on the game.

Games like Angry Goy II show how games and their affordances can affect or sculpt the actions and logics of the player: the two enter a relationship in which both the game and the player affect each other. The game affects the player by limiting the player's in-game possibilities in order to coax the player to digitally perform the political narratives of the game. And, the player reconfigures the game by playing and progressing through the game's story, in turn changing the game's internal state.

Political elements find themselves in game either by the encoding of (far-right) politics as a means for playing the game, or through the player's realization of political affordances in a game. In the former, the player must be able to read and understand the politically encoded *game challenges* in order to learn from them. In other words, they must not only learn how to play the game, but also learn what political practices are playable from the game – for the latter, the player's social relationships with right-wing politics visualize the *possibilities* or *experimentations* for political play. And, if the game is able to react to the political inputs via its technological features, then the relationship between player and game is able to *produce* a *moment of political gameplay*. In both of these instances, each playthrough reformulates the political worldview of the player from their *participation* with the game and the political features of the gameplay moment. In what follows, I dive into the design details of AG2. As these will show how the political elements participate in the gameplay relationship *by design* of far-right game developers.

Figure 11.4. One of Angry Goy II's Title Screen.
Source: Screenshot from publicly available game Angry Goy 2. Collected by author.

Wheel Maker Studios produced the games *Angry Goy* (2017) and *Angry Goy II* (2018) (see figure 11.4), which were designed to include far-right elements as a means of game progression. In both games, the player must fight journalists, racial minorities, communists, Jewish people, queer people and other political minority groups in order to move through the game. The titles of the games refer to the word *Goy*, 'a term in modern Hebrew and Yiddish to refer to a gentile or a non-Jewish person now part of white nationalists' antisemitic discourse' (Verhoef 2019). In other words, the games' far-right coding is explicit; if a player who is anything less than an avowed white supremascist stumbles across these games, it will inevitably carry a heavier far-right influence on gameplay than the player themselves.

The real Christopher Cantwell, pictured here as a playable character, promoted AG2 on his website and podcast *Radical Agenda*. Here, Cantwell describes it as 'the season's hit game for White males who have had it with Jewish bullshit' where 'instead of taking out your frustrations on actual human beings, you can fight the mongrels and degenerates on your computer!' (Verhoef 2019). Aside from playing as Christopher Cantwell, the players of AG2 have the option of choosing to play as other right-wing political figures such as 'The Golden One' (a Swedish white nationalist YouTuber), 'Moon Man' (a far-right meme figure), TayAI[7] and Hitler (see figure 11.5).

Before arriving to the start screen, the player must agree to the license agreement, which states that 'by playing this game you agree not to hold the creators of this game responsible for any harm or injury that could possibly

Figure 11.5. 'Right Wing Death Squad'.
Source: Verhoef 2019.

result from the use of this game. . . . All violence is meant for entertainment purposes only. These are merely exciting plot elements'. The gameplay of AG2 heavily borrows from the top-down shooter (or shoot-em-up) genre popularized in 1980s arcade games (Verhoef 2019). All NPCs (non-player characters) in AG2 have distinct themes and differ only in terms of visual design, mechanics and verbal expression. As Verhoef (2019) notes, 'From being labelled a piece of "cisgender heterosexual scum" by rainbow flag waving LGBTQ activists, to being called a "white male" by a group of feminists the next – the enemies encountered throughout the game consistently ascribe amoral qualities to the player's character'.

The game consists of two different game modes. In the campaign mode, the player must save President Donald Trump who has been kidnapped by left-wing terrorists (Palmer 2018). The second mode is the *Survival* mode, which the game describes as 'Defend your Right to Free Speech and Fight off Hordes of Leftists'. Aesthetically, this mode functions as a recount of the Unity the Right rally in Charlottesville. In campaign mode, the player must go through several levels, each consisting of multiple stages, leading up to a mini-boss. The player completes each stage once they kill multiple waves of enemies. The win condition for each level is met once the player defeats the mini-boss. This formula repeats until the player reaches the final boss, with each level having distinct thematic design and narratives.

The first level is situated within 'The Communist Headquarters'. The enemy hordes are comprised of Antifa, feminists and Black Lives Matter characters. The first mini-boss fight of the game is with 'The Red Terror', stylized after the 'Happy Merchant' – a historic meme which portrays a caricature of a stereotypical Jewish man based on anti-Semitic views, characterizing the figure as greedy, manipulative and striving for world domination (see figure 11.6).

In the second level, the player must shoot people inside a gay club called 'LGBTQP+ Agenda and HQ'[8]. A poster outside of the club reads 'Children Welcome' suggesting that gay clubs are nothing more than spaces for paedophiles, an established homophobic trope used historically by right-wing folks to resist civil rights advances for LGBTQ+ people. The level strongly resembles the 2016 Pulse Nightclub mass shooting in Orlando, Florida, during which the shooter killed forty-nine attendees. The player finds and rescues Mike Pence in this level, who was kidnapped and brought to the LGBTQP+ HQ. The mini-boss, 'Progress Master', resembles Canadian's current prime minister Justin Trudeau; the mini-boss threatens to 'make sweet love' to the player since Trudeau is construed by the far-right as 'weak' for his neo-liberal progressive and multiculturalist policies. In this sense, even passive progressive politics are vilified as a threat to the white nationalist.

Level three takes the player to 'The Diverse Urban Area', where the player meets Officer Darren Wilson (Darren Wilson is the police officer who murdered Michael Brown, Jr., an eighteen-year-old African American, which prompted the Ferguson unrest of 2014). The digitized Wilson tells the player that 'n**** brought crime and poverty'[9] to America's once-thriving white suburbs. Wilson then gives the player extra health before the player shoots Black, Mexican and Muslim Americans. Eventually, the player rescues

Figure 11.6. 'The Red Terror' Mini-Boss and 'Happy Merchant' Anti-Semitic Meme.
Source: Left: Screenshot from publicly available game Angry Goy 2; Right: *Know Your Meme: Happy Merchant,* original creator unknown. Both collected by author.

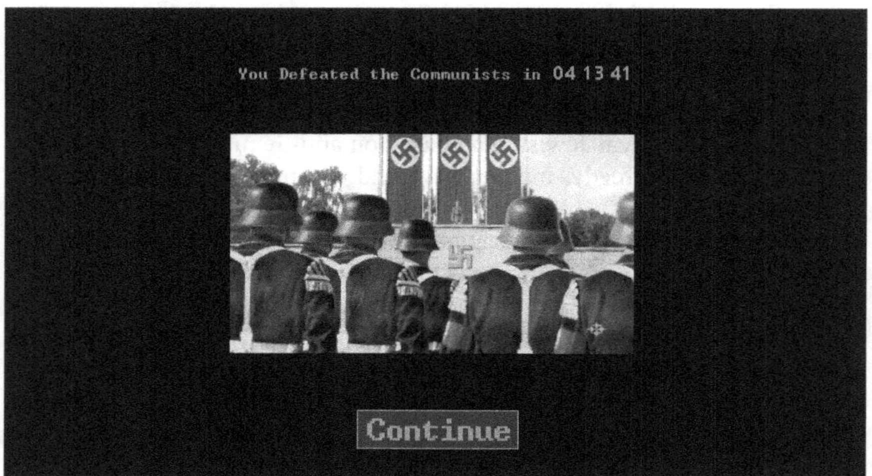

Figure 11.7. Nazi Speech Video between Levels.
Source: Screenshot from publicly available game Angry Goy 2. Collected by author.

PewDiePie in this level. The fourth and final level takes place in the 'Fake News Network' studio, tapping into 'anti-mainstream media' discourses prevalent in new right circles. AG2 perpetuates the myth that the media is not independent, but controlled by 'the left' and influenced by Jewish interests, which explains why the media censors right-wing commentary (Verhoef 2019). The player fights and kills a character resembling David Hogg (an American gun control student activist who survived the Stoneman Douglas High School shooting in 2018) before moving onto the mini-boss of the level: 'Media Boss Shill'. Finally, the player is presented with 'Rootless Cosmopolitan', the final boss resembling another caricature of the anti-Semitic image of the happy merchant.

Before each new level is loaded, the player is presented with a screen that plays videos of pro-Nazi Germany speeches, or of elderly people and veterans reminiscing about their lives in Nazi Germany (see figure 11.7). Whenever the player runs out of lives, a fail screen is loaded up which has the caption 'You have failed to save the West' This screen presents a random video to the player which underlines the threat that trans lives, multiculturalism and Jewish culture pose to Western civilization. As Verhoef (2019) notes in his analysis of AG2, 'This communicates anti-Semitic conspiracy theories about the cultural hegemony of Jewish people, popular in white nationalist's discourses'. This fail-screen sequence also further communicates to players what exactly would happen if white Americans fail to maintain whiteness and 'Western culture'. As such, in both the play and narrative elements of *Angry Goy II*, political violence is contextualized as necessary in order to win and complete the game (Verhoef 2019).

VIDEO GAMES AS A MOBILIZATION TOOL

Through these mechanics and qualities, the game pushes political content for the player to interact with by including *politically charged game challenges*. Undeniably, the player is changed by their interaction with the game, regardless of where they are on the political spectrum. If they were playing the game 'just for a laugh' for example, or because they were curious about the far right, after playing they would leave the interaction with a much more extensive knowledge of far-right ideology and symbolisms, who its enemies are and so on. When players recognize what the game asks them to do, that player is mobilized to perform digital political practices – they read and enact political narratives that make the game progression make sense. This contrasts my attempted play, described at the beginning of this section, where I attempt to engage with non-politicized elements of the game world, but am nevertheless forced to fight the leftist mobs.

After my own playthroughs, I did not instantly become violent, nor did I have the urge to bring these practices offline. In fact, I felt my own leftist politics concretizing. This is because of my own relational elements and political inclinations that I as a player bring to the game experience, and how those interact with the political elements of the game. After my many digital interactions with the game, I leave the interaction with new knowledges of right-wing figures, for example. However, playing the game by itself may not be enough to recruit someone who has leftist inclinations. If I was a centre-leaning player, with no inclinations towards the left or right or with no knowledge of recruitment or mobilization practices, it is likely I may be left changed in a rightward direction; having new knowledges of far-right ideologies and narratives, and who we (other players) consider violent enemies, online *and* offline. The extent of this always depends on all the micro-features the player brings to the game interaction.

In other words, playing the game works not only to re-establish the features of far-right political ideology but also to bring these features onto the player to the extent that their political worldview is mixed with the heavy messages of far-right ideology presented in these levels. As Giddings and Kennedy note:

> Games configure their players, allowing progression through the game only if the players recognize what they are being prompted to do, and comply with these coded instructions. The analysis of the pleasures of gameplay must take [into consideration the work done by] the players and the game technologies as central, as well as those between players and the game. (Giddings & Kennedy 2008)

By participating in the politically encoded game challenges presented by the game, and by acting them out in embodied gameplay moments, players relationally *become* part of the type of politics that such involvement implicates (Devries, this volume). In this sense, gameplay becomes a type of *transformative process* as spoken of by relational theorists. Through repeated interactions, playthroughs constitute a change in state for each of the actants (human or non-human) in the relation, even if slight or unnoticeable (Powell 2013, 196–7). Notably, as players learn the game system and achieve mastery over it, they experience mastery is the source of enjoyable gameplay (Giddings and Kennedy 2008). For AG2, the actions required by the player encodes the same right-wing ideologies that they may enact offline. In other words, playing AG2 reinforces players' political worldview in the same way that attending a rally like Unite the Right might, or as watching or reading white supremacist literature might. Here, media and the user enter an interactional relationship – with games like AG2, however, political narratives are enacted through digitalized actions and interactions with game parts, scripts and characters. By either re-enacting far-right mass shootings or murdering minority figures, the player's actions re-enact the material violent actions conducted by actual far-right mass shooters In this interaction, since the game enforces stronger political influence than the player, the player's political self must come to terms with what this interaction means for them. Through mobilization then, pathways for recruitment are potentially made more accessible.

From my own playthroughs, the game pushed me towards one type of play: the practice of killing political targets. To achieve mastery of the game, I have to not only learn the game mechanics (i.e. *how* and *when* to shoot), but I must also understand why I must kill these politically charged digital targets in order for the game progression to make sense, to resonate with me, the player, and thus for the experience to be enjoyable (i.e. *what* and *why* to shoot). Otherwise, the gameplay is unenjoyable (which, it certainly was). In this moment of political gameplay, I am mobilized to learn, act and practice far-right politics. This echoes with Ian Bogost's work on *persuasive games*: 'video game players develop procedural literacy through interacting with the abstract models of specific real or imagined processes presented in the games they play. *Video games teach biased perspectives about how things work*' (Bogost 2007). Hence, games like these can serve as powerful mobilizing mediums (if not necessarily recruiting ones) where players learn or practice right-wing politics.

By looking for moments of political gameplay in games like AG2, we can see that players, including those that do not share the same political identities with the game and those who are 'apolitical', undergo the same relational process that outputs the following effect:

1. Participating and recreating far-right digital (game) action.
2. Entanglement of political elements with player elements.
3. The reformulation of political identity in relation to the interaction enabled both by the design of the game and the player's initial positionality.

Moments of political gameplay allows us to see how political elements find themselves within games from game design practices, which allow the player to participate in processes that mobilize them to reproduce far-right digital action. If it's the case that AG2 shows how politics have more pull than the player, can we find moments of political gameplay where the player has more political pull? From where do politics emerge in these interactions? To investigate this, I turn to the game *Red Dead Redemption 2* (RDR2), a game which, unlike AG2, has not been packaged or sold as a far-right game, but whose system has allowed the possibilities for players to find moments of right-wing political practice. I argue that this result is both the product of the game's affordances, and the player's own political features which, like the game, afford certain interaction.

RED DEAD REDEMPTION 2: GAMES AND THE POTENTIAL FOR POLITICAL VIOLENCE

RDR2 is a video game set circa 1899 in a fictionalized representation of the Western, Midwestern and Southern United States. The game follows the protagonist and his position in a notorious gang. The protagonist must deal with the decline of the *Wild West* whilst attempting to survive against government forces, rival gangs and other enemies. RDR2 has been highly praised for its writing, themes, characterization and its high-fidelity graphics and physics. But, most importantly, the game is highly cherished as completely open-world, affording players the freedom to do nearly anything they want. This style of game contrasts sharply with the type of scripted gameplay dynamics that players experience in a game like AG2, where users cannot explore worlds and must follow the (political) objectives of the game. In RDR2, players can play poker, get a haircut, play in knee-deep snow, give money to homeless NPCs, visit the remains of a pagan ritual, kidnap civilian NPCs and admire digital miles of beautifully rendered landscapes. For many players, the pleasure of playing RDR2 'is to test the boundaries of what is possible within its elaborate simulation' (Hernandez 2019).

However, players have used this unboundedness to recreate racial and misogynist violence, inevitably bringing certain political practices into the game-world. For example, a series of YouTube videos of gameplay show a compilation of violence against an NPC suffragette. These videos are dedicated specifically to violence against the suffragette, and show her being punched, stamped on, tied up and shot (see figure 11.8), and even kidnapped, tied to a horse, dragged around the game world, and thrown to be devoured by an alligator. Whatever the real intent of those posting the videos, these videos frame the violence as political actions through their reactionary titles like: 'Annoying Feminist Fed to Alligator.'

Figure 11.8. Player Tying Up a Suffragette Right before Killing Her.
Source: Shirrako, YouTube video: "Red Dead Redemption 2 - Annoying Feminist Fed To Alligator", Posted 31 Oct. 2018. Screenshot by author.

The video depicts a broken and disjointed set of interactions, as the game struggles to keep up with the player's unanticipated political actions. In the video, the player makes many attempts to lasso the suffragette; the suffragette flees but then stops, almost as if she has forgotten why she was running in the first place. Meanwhile, the alligator's eating animation consists of the 3-D model lunging and clipping through the woman, but not actually eating her. Since this attempt at her demise did not work, at the end of the video, the player stomps on her head until she stops moving (Martin 2018). While the player intends to produce a certain political experience with the game, the game is complicit only to an extent; these particular actions have not been completely predicted by game designers.

Consider another interaction between player and game: another YouTube video depicts an RDR2 player searching for and kidnapping a Black man to bring to a Ku Klux Klan (KKK) meeting in the woods (see figure 11.9). The player tries to lasso a Black man driving a horse carriage. The player's character sends out a long lasso and wraps it around the driver's neck, and a forceful pull on the rope propels the driver out of his seat and onto the ground. The game calculates that this blow will kill the driver. So, the player is made to search for another Black person in the gameworld. The player finds another Black person at a farm, ties him up and brings him to the KKK gathering,

Figure 11.9. Player Bringing a Black Man to the KKK.
Source: Skirrako, YouTube Video: "Red Dead Redemption 2 - What Happens If You Bring Black Man To KKK?", Posted Nov 11, 2018. Screenshot by author.

where the player then lets him down and unties him. However, instead of running away, the now untied man tries to fight the player in front of the members of the KKK group, since the game tells the NPC that he has been captured and kidnapped. The KKK figures do not notice the brawl between the player and the man, as they are preoccupied by their robes caught aflame from burning the cross, a scene intentionally encoded by game designers. In other words, the game was unprepared to render the social and political ramifications of the player's intentionally inflammatory and undeniable political actions. In this case, the game has allowed players to exert some political symbology onto itself, but assumes a sort of apolitical passivity by attempting to create only a 'historically accurate online game world'.

However, in both of these moments of political gameplay, the player observes a potential for experimenting with political play, and in the end renders the game a space for excessively violent, digital action. The player inputs *politically charged actions* and it is up to the game to understand and reply. Even though the game often struggles to keep up with the far-right actions of the player (evident in 'unrealistic' moments such as when the suffragette acts as if she was never attacked), the player can still guide the game to political violence in other ways, such as via shooting or torturing of political targets like suffragettes or people of colour. In this case, the moment of political gameplay – the moment at which the player and game together produced a far-right action – is enabled by design affordances that allow for the game to adjust to player's inputs, and outputs new politically encoded game challenges back to the player.

Here, both technological and ideological political elements have considerable influence over the rest of the actants in the relation. The game play-acts extreme violent and graphic far-right practices via the influence of the ideological elements brought in by the player, and the player engages in the politically charged game challenges generated by the game's technological elements. This reveals a *reciprocal process* at work through moments of political gameplay, where the players influence the game to reply politically, and the game provides gameplay content for the player to continue re-producing their political actions. A moment of political gameplay in the case of RDR2 is thus the instance where the player asserts their political force, and to which the game abides. Together, the player and game create a reciprocal political conversation, composed of many moments of political gameplay.

In the case of RDR2's moments of political gameplay, the player seems to assert much more political force on the game than the game does upon them, especially compared to AG2, where the game asserts much more restrictive politics on the players. However, in both cases, interactive processes from both games and players mobilize the production of far-right digital action. Both player and game are transformed, if slightly, by this exchange in innumerably various ways. While we cannot necessarily yet track the extent of these transformations on players – humans who act in the physical world – it is important to note that the mobilization of far-right digital practice is *not neutral* or *benign*. Apart from the political affordances or features of games, the affordances of sharing platforms like YouTube provide further potential for these gameplay moments – like the violent scenes from RDR2 – to act amidst larger far-right networks, exacerbating their potential affect as political actions. Rebecca Lewis states that 'by connecting to and interacting with one another through YouTube videos, influencers with mainstream audiences lend their credibility to openly white nationalist and other extremist content creators' (Lewis 2018).

CONCLUSION

As Deleuze and Guattari say, bodies refer *not necessarily to human bodies* but to a multiple and diverse *series of connections* which *assemble* as a particular spatial and temporal moment (Deleuze and Guattari 1987). Similarly, we can consider a moment of political gameplay to be like a Deleuzian body where and when the player, game and political or ideological elements assemble, intermingle and connect. Participating in gameplay is a way to *embody* and *feel* the *effects* of the *political (gameplay) body*.

In this chapter, I have defined 'moments of political gameplay' as the moment when the player, game and political relations coagulate into a solidified entity. I analysed the moments of political gameplay that arose from playing the game *Angry Goy II*, a game whose design elements bring politically charged game challenges for the player. Following this, I examined RDR2, a game not designed with a far-right narrative in mind, but where the player has to work hard to construct one by using politically charged actions. With this, the game's affordances allows for the possibility for any player to play and experiment with politics.

Notably, in either case we did not have to prioritize either humanist determinism or technological determinism. Using the theoretical concept of moments of political gameplay works to highlight the interchange between game and player which produces the end result – politicized gameplay – allowing questions of intentionality to take a back seat. Instead, this model brings our attention to the relational formations that produce political gameplay. This change in analytical approach opens up avenues for further investigation and conclusions about political mobilization through gameplay, and the implicit politics of video games generally.

Moments of political gameplay does not dismiss more essentialist claims as false. Rather, my hope is that the framework of *moments of political gameplay* (or more generally, *moments of gameplay*) can provide a qualitative tool to help game studies researchers conceptualize our relational transformation with the physical world and with games. This is because the concept of moments of political gameplay enables us to answer 'what political outcomes arise from the figuration created between human, political and game' by tracing the political exchange and transformation that happens from the human-game-political relation. In the gameplay moments described in this chapter, political elements are found within the gameplay body through game design – either from deliberate design choices to guide the player, or through the affordances of the gameworld and the player's own political inclinations.

Additionally, in this chapter, I have shown the capacity this framework has to highlight the relations that *mobilize* a player to enact and perform right-wing politics, allowing for new ways of studying digital mobilization. In both AG2 and RDR2, addressing moments of political gameplay is essential in order to foreground the effects and outcomes of the relation: the player and game *participate* in processes that mobilize them to reproduce far-right digital action. Each actant participates in the relation through the actions they take. From politically charged actions and challenges enacted through the moments of gameplay, political transformation becomes effective in mobilizing these various actants in a relationship to re-enact right-wing practices. In other words, the player and the game *become political* through their constant interaction with one another.

In this way, I believe this framework has the potential to describe and conceptualize relational recruitment processes that come from the assembling of games, humans and other cultural phenomena. For example, moments of political gameplay could be used to highlight and outline the microrelations or interactions that lead any player further towards actual far-right recruitment. Schlegel states that games could increase the susceptibility of recruitment processes for individuals (Schlegel 2020). Players concretize their own political identity by participating in political gameplay and, sometimes, later become involved in larger political networks such as #Gamergate,[10] the manosphere, the proudboys, QAnon and so forth. Spotting and dissecting moments of political gameplay in these contexts could work to uncover the relational ties between gameplay, other platforms and far-right subcultures.

ACKNOWLEDGEMENTS

I'd like to thank Melody Devries for the many enlightening exchanges, and as well for the encouraging words and collaboration during the writing process. I'd also like to thank Dr. Christopher Powell for providing me with detailed feedback and suggestions on this chapter.

NOTES

1. Akin to an *event* proposed by Seth Giddings (2009).
2. Other gameplay models exist (e.g. see MDA [Hunicke et al. 2004] and A.G.E. [Dillon 2010]). In game studies and game design research, it is often debated what type of model is more 'appropriate' for designing and critiquing games. However, my argument here is not in favour of one model over another. Rather, I hope to illustrate how gameplay *is* a relationship between player, the game and game technology. All other models are illustrated to reflect a relational process, however, with certain emphasis on different parts or actants.
3. Giddings uses the term 'event'.
4. This is to say that a player intending to play politically (or more generally perform any political practice) will of course contribute to a moment of political gameplay.
5. A famous YouTube personality whose channel is largely devoted to humour and video games. However, PewDiePie has been accused of anti-Semitic or anti-Muslim bigotry (Munn 2019).
6. The game mentions the intentional link between the game level and the real-world park on a warning screen prior to entering the digital park.
7. This is an infamous chatbot that became racist after 'learning' from Twitter for several hours (Neff and Naggy 2016).
8. The game designers have deliberately included a 'P' in the LGBTQ+ acronym to insinuate that pedophiles are part of the queer community.
9. Safiya Noble advises against the re-printing of this slur in her book *Algorithms of Oppression: How Search Engines Reinforce Racism* (2018).
10. A group dedicated to defending video games against the evils of feminist and progressive views (Gray et al. 2017; Salter 2018).

REFERENCES

Adams, Ernest. 2013. 'Fundamentals of Game Design'. 3rd ed. Berkeley, CA: New Riders.

Barad, Karen. 2007. *Meeting the Universe Halfway: Quantum Physics and the Entanglement of Matter and Meaning*. Durham, NC: Duke University Press.

Bennett, Jane. 2010. *Vibrant Matter: A Political Ecology of Things*. Durham, NC: Duke University Press.

Bogost, Ian. 2007. 'Persuasive Games: The Expressive Power of Video Games'. Cambridge: MIT Press.

Butler, Judith. 1988. 'Performative Acts and Gender Constitution: An Essay in Phenomenology and Gender Theory'. *Theatre Journal* 40 (4).

Butler, Judith. 1993. 'Bodies that Matter: On the Discursive Limits of Sex'. New York: Routledge.

Deleuze, Gilles, and Felix Guattari. 1987. '*A Thousand Plateaus: Capitalism and Schizophrenia*, translated by Brian Massumi. London and New York: Continuum.

Dépelteau, François. 2013. 'What Is the Direction of the "Relational Turn"?'. In *Conceptualizing Relational Sociology*, 163–85. New York: Palgrave Macmillan.

Dillon, Roberto. 2010. 'On the Way to Fun: An Emotion-Based Approach to Successful Game Design'. Florida: AK Peters/CRC Press.

Elias, Norbert. 1978. *What Is Sociology?* New York: Columbia University Press.

Giddings, Seth. 2009. 'Events and Collusions: A Glossary for the Microethnography of Video Game Play'. *Games and Culture* 4 (2): 144–57.

Giddings, Seth, and Kennedy, Hellen. 2008. 'Little Jesuses and *@#?-Off Robots: On Cybernetics, Aesthetics, and Not Being Very Good at Lego Star Wars'. In *The Pleasures of Computer Gaming: Essays on Cultural History, Theory and Aesthetics*, 13–32.

Gray, Kishonna L., Bertan Buyukozturk, and Zachary G. Hill. 2017. 'Blurring the Boundaries: Using Gamergate to Examine "Real" and Symbolic Violence against Women in Contemporary Gaming Culture'. *Sociology Compass* 11 (3): e12458.

Haraway, Donna. 2006. 'A Cyborg Manifesto: Science, Technology, and Socialist-Feminism in the Late 20th Century'. In *The International Handbook of Virtual Learning Environments*, 117–58. Dordrecht: Springer.

Hernandez, Patricia. 2019. 'Playing Red Dead Online as a Black Character Means Enduring Racist Garbage'. *The Verge*. Accessed 12 November 2019. https://www.theverge.com/2019/1/15/18183843/red-dead-online-black-character-racism.

Hunicke, R., M. LeBlanc, and R. Zubek. 2004. 'MDA: A Formal Approach to Game Design and Game Research'. In *Proceedings of the AAAI Workshop on Challenges in Game AI* 4 (1): 1722.

Latour, Bruno. 1992. *Reassembling the Social: An Introduction to Actor-Network-Theory*. Oxford: Oxford University Press.

Lewis, Rebecca. 2018. 'Alternative Influence: Broadcasting the Reactionary Right on YouTube'. *Data & Society* 18.

Martin, Gareth Damian. 2018. 'The Cynical Politics of Red Dead Redemption 2's Symbolic Violence'. *Frieze*. Accessed 20 November 2019. https://frieze.com/article/cynical-politics-red-dead-redemption-2s-symbolic-violence.

McArthur, Victoria. 2019. 'Making Mii: Studying the Effects of Methodological Approaches and Gaming Contexts on Avatar Customization'. *Behaviour & Information Technology* 38 (3): 230–43.

McFarlane, Craig. 2013. 'Relational Sociology, Theoretical Inhumanism, and the Problem of the Nonhuman'. In *Conceptualizing Relational Sociology*, 45–66. New York: Palgrave Macmillan.

Munn, Luke. 2019. 'Alt-Right Pipeline: Individual Journeys to Extremism Online'. *First Monday*.

Neff, G., and P. Nagy. 2016. 'Automation, Algorithms, and Politics| Talking to Bots: Symbiotic Agency and the Case of Tay'. *International Journal of Communication* 10: 17.

Noble, Safyia. 2018. *Algorithms of Oppression*. New York: NYU Press.

Palmer, Ewan. 2018. 'Neo-Nazi Video Game Lets Users Murder LGBT People to Save Donald Trump'. *Newsweek*. Accessed 9 December 2019. https://www.newsweek.com/charlotesville-crying-nazi-hosts-video-game-allowing-users-kill-lgbt-people-1212855.

Powell, Christopher. 2013. 'Radical Relationism: A Proposal'. In *Conceptualizing Relational Sociology: Ontological and Theoretical Issues*, 187–207. New York: Palgrave MacMillan.

Rockstar Games. 2018. *Red Dead Redemption 2*. Multi-platform video game.

Salter, Michael. 2018. 'From Geek Masculinity to Gamergate: The Technological Rationality of Online Abuse'. *Crime, Media, Culture* 14 (2): 247–64.

Schlegel, Linda. 2020. 'Jumanji Extremism? How Games and Gamification Could Facilitate Radicalization Processes'. *Journal for Deradicalization* 23: 1–44.

Verhoef, Shannon. 2019. 'Play and Metapolitics in Angry Goy II'. *Diggit Magazine*. Accessed 16 December 2019 from https://www.diggitmagazine.com/papers/metapolitics-angry-goy-ii.

Wheel Maker Studios. 2017. *Angry Goy*. PC game.

Wheel Maker Studios. 2018. *Angry Goy II*. PC game.

Chapter 12

Mobilized but Not (Yet) Recruited: The Case of the Collective Avatar

Melody Devries

Anonymous /pol/ User 3/14/19: *I'm leaving this disgusting cesspool once and for all. /pol/ is no longer about edgy memes. It has become clear to me that this place radicalizes white men to do abhorrent things. This place is cancer. Goodbye and good riddance.*

Anonymous /pol/ User (3/14/19) (Reply): *Goodbye. See you in the morning.*

During the first hours of the morning on 15 March 2019, I scour 4chan from my Toronto apartment. On the other side of the world it is early evening, and Christchurch, New Zealand, reports tragic breaking news of the deadliest shooting in the nation's history. The exchange above between anonymous /pol/ users was part of a barrage of mixed and diametrically opposed expressions of confusion, denial, anger, disbelief, indifference, racial hatred and regretful heartache that emerged that night on 4chan's notoriously far-right board /pol/.

In that moment, practically every thread discussed New Zealand's tragedy. /pol/ was rapidly engaging in one of the things it does best: expressive and condescending banter. If just for that night however, whether posts were emotional, confessional, apathetic or celebratory, threads across the board were tinged with various forms of *panic*. While official news reports had released few details about the tragedy, 4chan users already had access to the video streamed live by the shooter himself. From the footage, later uploaded to *Liveleak*, it was obvious to /pol/ not only that the shooter's motives were white supremacist but that he was a user familiar with 4chan and its subculture of 'politically incorrect' memes, its colloquial discussion of anti-Semitic white genocide conspiracies and other recognizably racist, shock-worthy participation.

Years earlier in December 2017, I sat online watching another group interact. Here, nameless users swarmed other players in the virtual world VRChat using an identical digital avatar: a 3-D distorted rendering of the

Sonic the Hedgehog character *Knuckles*. To the uninitiated, the avatar's image – a bright red echidna – seems racially and politically innocuous. Yet, when playing the identical avatar, users yelled phrases in mock African accents. Through players' microphones, racial and colonial stereotypes about Ebola, witchcraft and tribalism rushed into the virtual space. This meme and all its associated practices – screaming racial obscenities, swarming others, dressing up the identical avatar in other racializing ways (i.e. giving it a Ugandan flag) or creating related image macros to circulate on other platforms – is widely known as *Ugandan Knuckles*. Despite the vividness of the racist caricature these users enact, many participants as well as folks across Twitter and YouTube denied that Ugandan Knuckles was racist. Users earnestly argued that in any case, *they* certainly weren't racist, and that while maybe others took it too far, their play with the meme was entirely innocent, conducted merely in good-intentioned humour.

4chan's everyday banter and VRChat's Ugandan Knuckles vary widely in manner and means of participation, severity of violence and technological and cultural accessibility. However, in both instances, users participate in racist actions while denying or disavowing the racist effects of their practice. In cases of forced confrontation with consequences like the night of the New Zealand massacre, users expressed shock, bafflement, remorse, and searched for an explanation for the proximity of their meme-actions to the meme-actions of a mass murderer. This implied that some were genuinely unaware of the 'seriousness' with which other users took these racist phrases. Still, others (whether 'jokingly' or not) aggressively condoned the violence, or reflected the indifference and skepticism that online participation classically affords. Hence one user's reply: 'Goodbye. See you in the morning'.

This variety of ambivalence, denial and remorse reminds us that online, we cannot 'prove' a user's true intent, that is, the extent of their intentional racism or lack thereof. In attempts to solve this, academics and journalists have tried to differentiate between the traditional trolling subculture of the 'weird' Internet, and the Internet-saavy culture of contemporary Western far-right politics. Often, this results in depictions of the online 'alt-right' as a cultural monolith composed of identical, like-minded users who are the product of a linear evolution from mean-trolling culture into something dangerously political. Still others delineate strict borders around movements like the Alt-Right, in effect rendering interactive relationships with cultural elements outside their ideological sphere as less important.

However, instances like VRChat's Ugandan Knuckles and /pol/'s mixed feelings on the night of the massacre reveal a complex, non-homogenous assemblage of users that, *nevertheless, collectively* produced harmful effects. I argue that these effects emerge not through the work of some ideological monolith of intentionally hateful politics, but, more insidiously, through ambivalent participation. If it is true that not everyone that contributes to racist or far-right action is ideologically converted to far-right belief, this raises several questions: How can we better account for instances when participants have moments of *doubt*, or even *regret* their political beliefs, practices or sentiments? How do we account for the far-right consequences of actions *despite* users' political uncertainty or indifference? Further, how can our models about the production of online far-right oppressive violence both address and *challenge* the individualizing logic often held by users: '*I'm* not racist, *I* was just playing around'?

This conundrum of 'true intent' can be resolved by moving past such inquiries entirely. I argue that the political intent behind online participation in problematic communities does not actually matter, because participatory action – *regardless of intent* – leads to the construction of political identities that script further violent or racist action. This occurs because participation is performative in Butler's (1988, 1993) sense, and therefore works to re-define and concretize a user's political identity and values in relation to the collective with which they participate.

This stance reverses typical contemporary logics about the far right, where users are recruited towards a cause and are then mobilized to pursue its goals. Here, I posit that mobilization *precedes* recruitment in online spaces like 4chan and VRChat. My development of the collective avatar is an attempt at using theoretical concepts to map this process of mobilization before recruitment, where users find themselves affiliated with political practice that goes above and beyond what they signed up for (figure 12.1).

The collective avatar is a character – a way of acting or being – collectively constructed by an online community. Users embody this character in order to participate effectively in a certain online space, in turn re-affirming its features and characteristics. I use the term *avatar* because it refers to a process of embodied, performative action or participation. When using an avatar, one becomes something other than themselves in terms of how they move about or exist relationally with the world. Yet a collective avatar is not a product of any one individual, as might be the case when a user designs a custom avatar in a game like *The Sims*. A collective avatar is instead the collective product of ongoing interactions between human users, technological platforms and sociological conditions.

This isn't what I signed up for Anonymous (ID: Yyz9JfTV) 03/14/19(Thu)23:36:15 No.206274549

Figure 12.1. A /pol/ Post Title: 'This Isn't What I Signed Up For' – Night of the New Zealand Massacre (EST).

Source: Screenshot of public post from 4/chan. Original creator Anonymous: Author.

When embodying a collective avatar, human users within these interactions do performative work (Butler 1988, 1993). In the process of participating in a certain way that abides by online cultural expectations, users not only re-build the features of the collective avatar but also re-build and concretize the features of their own (political) identity. In this sense, embodying the collective avatar is both a performative and relational process. In the moments that we shape and become an avatar through performative actions, the avatar also shapes and bends us. In fluid cyclicity, the collective informs the individual who helps inform the collective (Powell 2013). In this chapter I apply this concept to participation on both 4chan and VRChat in order to show how users built and concretized a collective avatar that prescribed, validated and mobilized further action by other users. In some cases, this further action was ultra-violent, or extensively racist. However, under the model of the collective avatar, the work of the far-right recruit is just as influential in producing far-right ends as the work of the not-(yet)-recruited user that acts 'just as a joke'.

Importantly, this is not to validate the alleged 'apoliticalness' or to 'let off the hook' users who say or do racist things online while claiming otherwise. On the contrary, it is to show how users' implicit involvement helps perpetuate racism and far-right ends in spite of their passivity. While these users would likely not describe themselves as racist, their performance of such acts implicates historically embedded racializing biases (Noble 2018). In this sense, I do not mean to say that these users are 'not racist', but instead that it is more accurate to describe them as participating in performative, racializing action that further concretizes their political position over time. This approach resists describing them as an objectively racist, bounded subject (Devries 2021). That is, a user is not *a* racist. Rather, a user *does* racism, and ends up *being racist*. This distinction shifts our analysis away from a non-relational, individualized subject that exists statically (*a* racist), towards an ongoing, materially enacted state of being or acting in the world (*being* or *acting* racist). This allows us not only to see how racism is actively re-produced by users that might occupy a wide variety of political positions, but also how it has the capacity to grow or change through time.

This framework encapsulated by the collective avatar allows us to take seriously the unstable moments of doubt, denial, regret, insincerity or confusion experienced by users who get caught up in mobilizing far-right ends. By taking seriously the ways that users participate in far-right practice without the explicit intention of being political or doing racism, we posit the far right not as some homogenous subject, group or pre-formed whole, but rather as something unsteady, non-static and performatively re-made through users' participation. Here, the far-right is something anyone can do, intentionally or unintentionally, to varying extents and yet with material consequences.

By showcasing what the collective avatar offers, I argue that more models that focus on "doing the far-right" are necessary to push studies of the far-right towards analysis of practice and material effects, as opposed to describing homogenous attributes of far-right subjects, groups, memes or movements. In the next section, I argue that this re-alignment is an important evolutionary step in digital-ethnographic work of far-right online spaces. I follow this with two different applications of the collective avatar, in order to show what a relational, unbounded approach might offer instead.

PART 1: THEORY AND CONTEXT

Expanding the Culturalist Approach

My goal in developing the collective avatar as a conceptual tool is to avoid more descriptions or explanations of the subcultural traits, rules or histories of the 'Alt-Right'. This important work has already been done by academics and journalists (Nagle 2017; Neiwert 2017; Hawley 2017, 2019; Wendling 2018). Generally, these studies have employed a qualitative or ethnographic methodology (Hughes 2019). This mode has provided critical insights; an ethnographically informed or investigative approach allows researchers to develop vivid images of what a cultural entity like the Alt-Right *is* (i.e. its beliefs, values, conceptual frameworks), where it came from or what its discursive histories and tropes are. This is necessary in order to recognize or identify when contemporary white nationalist groups or organizations attempt to make waves in media, parliamentary process or policy, or elsewhere. This methodological goal is captured well by Alexandra Stern (2019) when they state that they are interested in the Alt-Right 'ideas, concepts, and frameworks' that 'have migrated into everyday discourse, becoming imaginable and utterable' (8).

This approach works by using immaterial concepts, discourses and/or symbolic digital images to represent what composes a given cultural group. Analytical descriptions of 'the Alt-Right' thus conceptualize an ideologically unified political entity, and implicitly attempt to explain the behaviour of affiliated users via an understanding of the content of far-right ideology, memes and language. Brian Hughes (2019) has referred to this as a *culturalist approach*, explaining that digital ethnographies which outline cultural features, discourse and other ideological historiographies were a necessary response to the speed at which the Alt-Right grabbed global attention. However, while culturalist approaches to understanding the contemporary far-right provide important foundations for understanding the demands, beliefs or logics of the content and meme-material output by the amalgamate

'Alt-Right', they are less able to make claims about the variety of actual humans who act with, upon or amidst such concepts and discourses.

This was less of a problem in 2015–2017, when the Alt-Right was a very visible and categorizable political movement, as described explicitly by Hawley (2017, 2019). However, as 'the Alt-Right' that we've come to know as a tiki-torch-wielding collective of young white men in polo shirts dissolves (Weill 2018; McCoy 2018), this culturalist approach for describing a unified, Alt-Right 'movement' becomes unable to keep up with how contemporary online far-right culture rapidly dissipates, dilutes and yet still outputs harmful effects (Ellis 2019). While we have received many descriptive accounts of the 'Alt-Right', scholarship that provides a materialist analysis of the contemporary far right is in shorter supply. Rather than using discursive and ideological features to define or qualify the contemporary far right, a more materialist analysis might add to this literature by highlighting the political economy of conservative policy and institutions, far-right organizational histories and flows of capital, and/or mainstream material systems of oppression that afford the upkeep of contemporary far-right politics.

A materialist analysis of the contemporary far right can take a variety of forms. While Hughes (2019) notes it is worthwhile to be skeptical of the ability of ethnographically informed methods to provide a more traditional materialist account of the contemporary online far right, I argue that with theoretical tools like the collective avatar, ethnography is an important device for materialist analysis of ongoing political practice. Deeply qualitative methods which investigate the material interactions between actual users, technologies and online groups can provide necessary insight into how these users are mobilized into racializing action and thus, how the contemporary far right maintains an existence in a variety of unexpected forms or places.

The collective avatar's theoretical structure showcases that a revised, relational ethnographic approach with a re-alignment towards performative political *practice* provides a new framework for study of what we call the contemporary online far-right, one that does not assume the far-right to be a homogenous political movement. In this sense, I intend for the collective avatar to shift us from the 'level of culture' (Hughes 2019), where we analyse the symbolic or ideological content of posts and memes, towards instead the material practices of users and the far-right *effects* or *outcomes* of those practices. In order to show the collective avatar's place within this evolution of digital ethnographic methods of studying the far right, in what follows I present a quick tour of digital ethnography. From here, I locate the collective avatar and its qualitative, relational lens towards performative action as part of a pattern within ethnographic study which has moved from the culturalist towards the materialist, and from the bounded to the unbounded.

Where We've Been – Online Ethnography and the Bounded

Between 2008 and 2010, ethnographers popularized digital ethnography, spending years building their presence within online virtual game-worlds like *Second Life* and *World of Warcraft* in order to develop an emic understanding of how virtual worlds were built and experienced by inhabitants or players (Boellstorff et al. 2012). These texts spanned topics from community norms, love and friendship, to digital landscapes, gender and race. Via this approach, these texts mimicked the traditional features of anthropological ethnography, where the ethnographer immerses themselves in a geographically bound community and works to holistically describe its features, from kinship, ritual or other elements of its social structure. Like early ethnographies (i.e. Malinowski 1922; Evans-Pritchard 1940), these early digital ethnographies conceptualized (online) worlds as whole cultural entities with various, interacting parts. However, changing online communication technologies have allowed for online subcultures to exist outside of and between bounded virtual worlds, thus requiring online ethnographers to conceptually expand the digital field site. This expansion is similar to the expanded approach of many contemporary offline ethnographies that are neither entirely bounded by the geographical boarders of a certain field site (i.e. Desmond 2016; Gordillo 2014).

Coleman's (2014) ethnography of Anonymous – an ambiguous activist collective that formed across various websites and IRC channels – helped mark this turning point in online ethnography away from traditional, spatially bounded anthropological field sites and holistic accounts of cultural systems towards platforms and dispersed digital communities. Coleman effectively combines their depiction of Anonymous' slippery features with analysis of the 'weird Internet' culture in which the political/activist entity formed. In doing so, Coleman's work contrasted online ethnographies of a local virtual world or 'people', and encouraged further analysis of *how* or through what features and practices unbounded online culture *worked* to create the appearance or experience of cohesion in the form of Anonymous.

Digital ethnographies that followed not only described online worlds and norms but explained the function and cultural implications of their features outside of bounded subcultural categories. A prominent example is Whitney Phillips's (2015) text, which is less about trolls (as a people) and 'more about a culture in which trolls thrive' (168). Phillips's approach emphasizes the need not to paint Internet trolls as a distinct bounded group, a nefarious 'them' posited against innocent 'us'. Rather, everyone's actions online contribute to forming a cultural milieu of normalized tropes from which 'trolling' derives its toxic ingredients.

And so it was that digital ethnographic work mirrored the evolution of predominant online culture itself, transitioning from holistic accounts of bounded cultural locations like virtual worlds to unbounded qualitative mappings of how digital subcultures that spanned platforms worked. However, while discussing the use of political themes within memetic, participatory media (i.e. Milner 2018), these texts stop short of addressing the political outcomes of such participation. Their strategy acknowledges how online practice contributes to online subcultural life but does not yet account for the political ramifications of online play with politics. For example, Whitney Phillips and Ryan Milner (2017) have pointed out the function of uncertainty and ambivalence within weird Internet subcultures, arguing that meme content and online play are always deeply ambivalent: Internet content and participation are simultaneously celebratory and derogatory, generative and degenerative of community, playful and racializing. But in revealing the extent to which Internet content and play are ambivalent, we face an explanatory gap between play and political violence. What happens between the user 'just playing around', and serious material consequences?

Phillips and Milner's (2017) work usefully points in the direction that further study of the political Internet should go. The Internet's ambivalence shows us that studies of meme-meaning are perhaps not as pressing as further study of what online play and practice achieves, politically or otherwise. Regardless of user intent, what do participatory actions online *do*? And more pertinently, what do these actions do to users?

Texts like Coleman's (2014), Phillips's (2015) and Milner's (2018) establish the difference between, on the one hand, trolling and weird/mean Internet culture and, on the other hand, online far-right culture as represented by the Internet-savvy features of phenomena like the Alt-Right and #gamergate (Salter 2018). This latter phenomenon produced a new genre of texts. Nagle's (2017) *Kill All Normies* launched a trend of qualitative studies of online political communities in order to explain the emergence of Internet-based far-right movements. Explicitly connecting trending far-right political movements in the United States with campus culture debates, Nagle (2017) describes the growth of a new form of right-wing politics that purposefully denies the staunch traditionalism of its conservative predecessors.

But while forming a new genre, *Kill All Normies* and others that improved on Nagle's model with extensively researched dissections of online far-right culture and history are now in the same position as early digital ethnographies that holistically described bounded virtual worlds. Like those of classic digital ethnographies, Wendling's (2018) and Beran's (2019) tables of contents span many separate elements of the Internet far-right's cultural body, packing in examinations of meninists, 'channers', conspiracy theorists, the violent fringe, Neo-Nazis, 4chan's history and its protype forum *Something Awful* and other details pertinent to defining a whole cultural body. Importantly, this new genre of Internet studies more explicitly addressed contemporary online far-right subcultures, discussing who was and from where had emerged this extensively problematic subcultural community. Despite its descriptive richness, however, this approach tends to lack *explanatory* power and reduces such phenomena to a bounded, homogeneous entity that can be holistically described and traced. But how do users become affiliated with these spaces in the first place? Are all of these users committed to the same political and cultural beliefs?

I argue that more attention should be given to the complex variety of worldviews and political positions that compose far-right spaces, underneath what we perceive from the top down as a uniformly motivated group or subculture. Just as early digital ethnographies set the stage for more complex studies of non-bounded Internet culture, existing studies that delineate the features of the contemporary online far-right's cultural body must now be followed by qualitative analyses which complicate the supposedly stable or bounded features of such an entity. I position the collective avatar as providing one possible next step away from the 'culturalist' approach of contemporary studies of the Alt-Right which describe a holistic, spatially bounded and assumedly always already far-right entity. By focusing on the politicizing effects of material practice, qualitatively informed theoretical tools can instead conceptualize the contemporary online far right as something with fluid edges, constantly coming into existence through users' play with it.

Attempting this, I use the following two case studies to draw attention to the complex ambiguity, confusion and denial that exists behind objectively racist online practice. I apply the concept of the collective avatar in order to account for the work done by ambiguous participation in racist or far-right action. In these cases, the collective avatar marks not only how user participation scripts further racist action, but how it *prescribes and concretizes* political identity: developing recruitment via mobilized participation.

PART 2: APPLICATION

Ugandan Knuckles, Collective Avatar

In January 2018, there is a new PewDiePie YouTube video trending. At the time, #1 YouTuber PewDiePie has a video series called 'meme review', wherein he shows several examples of a trending meme and humorously rates the meme in terms of its unspoken, affective qualities. For this video, the meme is *Ugandan Knuckles*. As PewDiePie describes, Ugandan Knuckles is a sprinkling together of multiple ingredients: a clip from a Ugandan

Figure 12.2. Ugandan Knuckles Skins Placed Throughout the Virtual World. Video Screenshot: 'YOU DO NOT KNOW THE WAY | UGANDAN KNUCKLES TRIBE! VRChat'. *Source*: ooh Remix, YouTube, 7 January 2018.
Source: ooh Remix, YouTube, posted 7 Jan. 2018. Collected by Author.

film where a character asks 'why are you running?' at a screaming woman;[1] a shorter, wider animation of the original *Sonic the Hedgehog* Knuckles character, which first appeared in a YouTube game review; and VRChat: a free-to-play massively multiplayer online (MMO) virtual reality platform. A 3-D rendering of the altered Knuckles character was placed in VRChat, where (unlike other open worlds) other users can easily pick up and wear identical avatars (figure 12.2), moving around and interacting with other players either via a mouse and keyboard or a VR headset and handholds.

In late 2017 into early 2018, *Ugandan Knuckles* took over VRChat. Large groups of participants wearing the identical avatar would surround others, digitally touching them and loudly repeating phrases in an attempted Ugandan accent and making clicking noises meant to mock the phonics of some Southern African languages. In his meme review, PewDiePie shows clips of Knuckles swarms screaming, 'why are you running?' 'do you know the way of the devil?', 'she is not the queen', and 'he does not know the way'. The screen fills with Knuckles avatars, and the sound is overwhelming in your headphones (figure 12.3). This practice fits the definition of the colloquially termed 'ear rape', which describes an unwanted assault on the ears of an unsuspecting headphone wearer and implies the (often male-led) violence of such action.

In other popular YouTube streams of VRChat, users yell into their microphones about Ebola, aids, priests, rituals and the devil, sometimes letting their mock accent slide and dropping 'N–'[2] with the unmistakable hard 'r' pronunciation of a white teenager. In these and in the PewDiePie

Figure 12.3. Video Screenshot: DO U KNO DA WEI? [MEME REVIEW] 👏 👏 #6.
Source: PewDiePie, Youtube video, posted 11 Jan. 2018. Collected by Author.

Figure 12.4. Video Screenshot: DO U KNO DA WEI? [MEME REVIEW] O DA WEI? [MEME REVIEW] 👏 👏 #6.
Source: PewDiePie, Youtube video, posted 11 Jan. 2018. Collected by Author.

video, users make loud sniffing, clicking or spitting sounds, bow and yell 'our queen' or 'spit on the fake queen' at feminine avatars, all while embodying the Knuckles avatar (figure 12.4).

Objectively, these phrases, clicking phonics and other noises paired with scores of white users attempting a Ugandan accent render the meme action as a digitally mediated yet easily recognizable caricature of racist tropes. To add to PewDiePie's list of meme ingredients, *Ugandan Knuckles* is also the product of centuries' worth of colonial and white supremacist knowledge about Black Africans and Diasporas. White and European colonization has described and constructed Black peoples as permanently tribalistic, violent, hyper-sexual and involved with dark magic or voodoo (Hall 1992; Abrahams 1998; Sheller 2003). This colonially produced knowledge, while not explicitly discussed by users, finds its way into the actions users *do* as they work to join in on the meme and depict the *Ugandan Knuckles* character. This mass participation rapidly adds to and re-writes the meme, congealing into the set characteristics of *Ugandan Knuckles*, which can be enacted by others. That is, as users participate in the meme, who and what the Knuckles is and represents is further brought into existence.[3] These participatory actions form a *collectively produced* avatar with identifiable characteristics.

Critically, in order to participate effectively with a collective avatar like *Ugandan Knuckles*, even in creating variations, one's actions must match the avatar's most notable features. Users must not only wear or use the red Knuckles 3-D image, they must *embody* its expected actions so that their participation can coherently articulate with other users' participation. It is this coherent articulation that renders such participation with the meme effective as such. In this sense, the formation of the collective avatar through ongoing participation creates a script for further, continued participation, which recursively continues the coagulation of the collective avatar's character, or its expected 'way of being'. Even as the meme spread outside of VRChat, users on Reddit, Twitter and other meme-sharing spaces re-created the meme in images that followed suit of the original caricature (figure 12.5).

Before long, the meme rightly attracted criticism by progressive gaming publications and anti-racists. However, many Ugandan-Knuckles participants on YouTube and Twitter denied the presence of any racism in the meme, despite the colonialist qualities embedded in Knuckles's characteristics. Knuckles's racializing features were claimed as 'not intended' or 'just fooling around'. Stoking the outrage from regular users, far-right actors (e.g. Ian Miles Cheong) decried how easily 'the left' became 'hysterical' over what was clearly 'fun', or 'just a joke' (figure 12.6).

The Ugandan Knuckles meme thus presents us with a tricky phenomenon. Whether on VRChat or elsewhere, users' play and participation with Ugandan Knuckles simultaneously mobilizes a re-doing of racializing, colonial stereotypes. However, since meme practice like this does not require explicit claims of white supremacy or far-right ideological recruitment in order to mobilize participation, the Knuckles meme instigated widespread participation from a large political variety of users who due to their own social privilege and

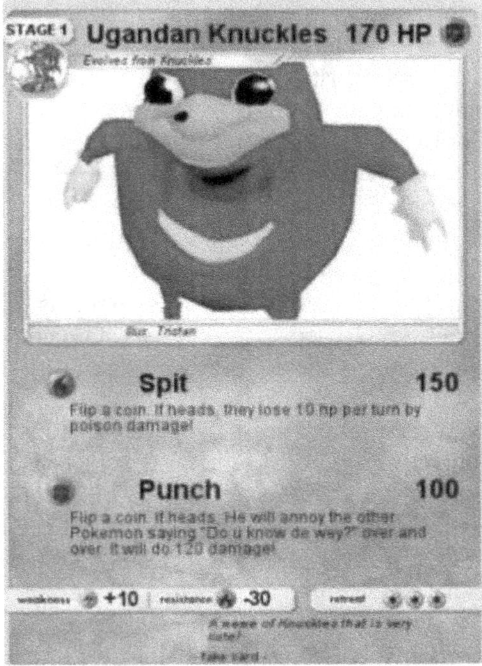

Figure 12.5. This Meme Re-does the Ugandan Knuckles as a Pokemon Card. Reads: 'Punch: Flip a coin. If heads, He will annoy the other Pokemon saying, "Do u know de wey" over and over. It will do 120 damage!'

Source: google images, original creator unknown. Collected by Author.

Figure 12.6. Public Twitter Discussion Concerning When Knuckles Is Racist.

Source: Public Tweets. Compiled by Author.

whiteness, do not recognize its racist qualities (Nakamura 1995). This spurred confused denial of racism from participants who might otherwise consider themselves apolitical or at least 'not racist' or 'not far right', despite their participation in such a meme.

It is difficult to prove the 'true intent' of these users, who may either deny or be sincerely oblivious to their hitherto unquestioned racist actions. Alternatively, an ethnographic-inspired analysis of meme content might attempt to typify the racist, anti-progressive, anti-feminist ideological qualities of a specific gaming culture in order to name the motives of participants. But this may construct subcultural boarders around a group that is sincerely diverse in beliefs and intent. Indeed, the network of users who come into contact with the Knuckles meme is vast – these can be centrist folks on YouTube who subscribe to PewDiePie, apolitical teens on VRChat or far-right spokespeople on Twitter. Instead, researchers of the far right can account for *how* the meme mobilized racist action, *regardless* of initial user intent. As a conceptual tool, the collective avatar attempts this by marking the effects of such participatory action irrespective of participants' politics. This is achieved through the model's emphasis on the theoretical concepts of relationality and performativity.

To review, we can consider this meme as a collective avatar because *Ugandan Knuckles* is a character that is collectively constructed and re-affirmed through ongoing participation, where a user must embody certain actions in order to effectively participate in the given online space. This creates further scripts for action required by prospective participants. The more a meme is engaged with, the more its features concretize and are validated as another form of normative online practice.

Importantly however, the collective avatar also marks a relational process. The collective avatar's features continuously come into existence through users' enactment of those features, but this relationship is not unilateral. As the user interacts with the collective avatar via their reading and embodiment of its features, their actions are shaped by the expectations and political characteristics of the avatar, and therefore take on a performative quality. Judith Butler's (1988, 1993) concept of *performativity* showcases how concepts like gender that seem fixed and located within the individual are collectively manufactured through a sustained set of articulative acts that congeal into what *appears to be* a stable concept or identity. In this process, repeated gestures and actions are erased and forgotten as they solidify into a comfortable reality or identity which feels natural and deeply personal to an individual (Butler 1993; Devries 2021).

The concretizing effects of performativity are not, however, limited to the constitution of the gendered self. I argue that similarly, with each participatory action, online users concretize an identity that is informed by the features of the collective avatar with which they participate. Looking to participate in the meme they have encountered, the user performs actions associated with its character; they embody the collective avatar. Over time, these performative actions shape what the user experiences or understands as their own political identity, subsequently affiliating them with whatever politics the collective avatar evokes. Like a gendered identity, a political identity constructed through mundane, playful and frequent online material action feels natural or deeply personal. Yet, in the same way that the performance of gender is a historical one, the features of the collective avatar that the user performs exist in relation with wider online communities, histories and practices. In this setting, regardless of users' intent or whether they identify as 'apolitical', participants have entered a reciprocal relationship with an objectively political collective avatar. The user's performative participation allows the collective avatar to entangle them in its outputs.

As the Ugandan Knuckles meme garnered critique for its racism, it was colloquially qualified as 'hated by liberals'. This feature itself became part of the collective avatar's character: pissing off 'the left' was a way of embodying the avatar. Because participants exist relationally with the avatar, continuing to perform the Knuckles meme concretized their own political identity as 'oppositional to liberals', 'anti-politically correct' or as 'not afraid of being called racist'. Evidence for this emerged in the widespread pushback to criticism of the meme by average or otherwise not-categorically 'far-right', or non-explicitly racist, users and gamers. While these accounts presented themselves as typically apolitical or not engaged with political debates, their participation with the Knuckles collective avatar implicated them in a political situation, effectively re-writing the features of their own political identity and position. In other words, continued performative participation – forgotten gestures and actions – with an objectively political (racist) collective avatar congeals into a political identity that is informed by its relation to the (racist) features of that embodied collective avatar. Considered this way, we see how the collective avatar marks a process of mobilization *before* recruitment, where playful and/or ignorant embodiment of the Ugandan Knuckles became part of a formative process of self-hood that is unavoidably politicized and racially harmful, whether users were willing to acknowledge this or not.

When applying the model of the collective avatar to phenomena like Ugandan Knuckles, we find that all participants – whether those joining in 'for fun', or with conscious far-right or racist political intent – are caught up in the *same process* that outputs the following effect:

1. The development of scripts which define further (racializing) actions by experienced and prospective participants.
2. The concretization of political identity in relation with the collective avatar and the politics it implicates.

The collective avatar thus allows us to call out intent-ambiguous meme practice as part of a politicizing, racism-producing process that moves from mobilization (enacting) towards recruitment (concretized political identity). However, visual avatars are not required for this process to function. In what follows, I discuss another collective avatar which links allegedly 'non-serious' users with serious consequences.

Collective Avatar, Anon

With an interface scarcely altered since 2004, 4chan easily overwhelms new users with its barrage of images and trailing comment threads, the frequent use of neologisms, and of course, the excessive use of sexual vulgarity, racism and otherwise offensive discussion on boards like /b/, /bant/ and /pol/. While there are no visual avatars to duplicate like in VRChat, 4chan's unchanged hyper anonymity – a lack of accounts and usernames – allows users to embody sameness by posting under the default title 'Anonymous' (Knuttila 2011).

Posting anonymously is just one of the ways users perform the *anon avatar*, just as acquiring the Knuckles skin is only one step in embodying the Knuckles avatar. 4chan users also refer to each other as 'anon', a figure imagined as the typical 4chan user. Anons are often described in the same way, as if the same person, through ambiguously real or imagined narratives about experiences with themselves or platform outsiders. Outsiders are conceptualized as liberals, normies (i.e. family, friends or others that don't use the platform), feminists, minorities and any other type of progressive or mainstream figure. As users participate with each other over time via their embodiment of anon, mutations of anon's characteristics result in a complex, often contradictory, yet predictable, collectively constructed character that interacts with the world in a specific way. While users might claim that 4chan is the only space for true debate and free speech, uncensored neither by political correctness nor conversational norms, even debate is done in an *expected way*, and about expected topics. For example, while /pol/ is defined as simply a 'politics' board, it is tacit knowledge that users will discuss and enact only white supremacist, racializing, anti-Queer rhetoric or extreme far-right conspiracy theories via their posts. There is *typically* no room for debating whether a conspiracy theory is true or not. Rather, users comment or post images with ambiguous seriousness, random or racially targeted violent videos, anger at otherized minority groups or progressives and racist humour while discussing the details or features of far-right conspiracies, such as how or to what extent 'globalists' or a Jewish elite control media narratives, contemporary protests or uprisings and so on.

Like posting anonymously, being ambiguous or acting as if one is 'just joking' *while nevertheless* forwarding racist, vulgar, or offensive concepts is a key feature of the anon collective avatar. As with the Ugandan Knuckles, performance of this collectively constructed avatar is simultaneously a mobilization of these users to conduct far-right practices, without necessarily recruiting these users within an identifiable far-right group or belief system.

When a platform community requires enactment of a collective avatar in order to participate effectively, the result is the *appearance* of a homogenous collective, all equally committed to the beliefs implied by their actions. However, on the night of the Christchurch massacre, I watched this collective avatar break down and expose its heterogenous innards. In this breakdown, evidence emerged of just how truly politically varied and uncertain 4chan's public is, despite its ability to collectively contribute to violent far-right outcomes.

Tragic Participation

On the night of the Christchurch massacre, I encountered an image of *Pepe the Frog*,[4] typically posted as a way to embody anon's smug play with far-right concepts. But tonight, Pepe sweats nervously. The image is paired with the caps lock phrase: EVERY POST I HAVE EVER MADE ON THIS BOARD IS SATIRE. Many replies follow suit, frantically denying their past participation. Amidst these replies, another user maintains the collective avatar's typical politics, and doubles down in extreme, violent racism while mocking the regretful sentiment of the previous posters. Another anon replies to this post, sharing an image that expresses smirking approval at its familiar enactment of hyperbolic racist violence (figure 12.7).

Below this thread, a user has posted a link to the livestreamed video of the attack, which reveals the assailant's violence alongside his own meme actions that resemble meme actions of the anon avatar. This had clearly

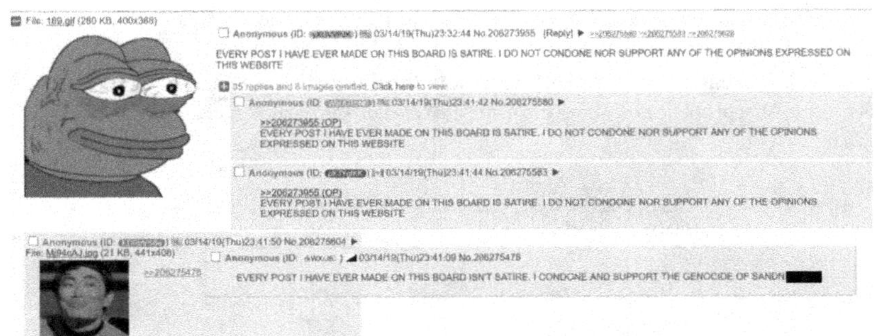

Figure 12.7. Regret, Panic, and Doubling Down on /pol/.
Source: Screenshot of public post from 4/chan. Original creator Anonymous: Author.

alarmed many users. Another user posts a crying Pepe in reply, dropping any remaining embodiment of anon and confessing: ‘I must have a weak heart, this video makes me sick. Just so sad’. In reply, an anon explains: ‘You are weak and have lived too comfy a life, leave the board’ (figure 12.8). This post emphasizes that this confessional action didn’t fit the features of the collective avatar, and thus disqualified their belonging.

In another reply to the video, a user correctly attempts to embody the politics of the collective avatar. But unlike some others, their faith in the avatar’s politics seems to be slipping. They ask the board with some urgency to explain how the massacre could be staged to make online far-right actors look bad in order to provoke forum shut down (referred to as a ‘false flag’), in the end asking if it is a false flag at all (figure 12.9). This provides a more avatar-compatible post than admission that 4chan racist practices had incited real-world violence, and incites several explanations and theories from other anons (not pictured).

In these posts and dozens of others, we do not see the usual seamless depiction of the expected features of the collective avatar. Anons have disagreed in the past, but in ways that are *prescribed*, and that do not challenge the political implications of the avatar’s racist, anti-progressive characteristics. Yet, as users read through the shooter’s manifesto laden with /pol/ memes and watched his livestream that revealed a slew of familiar racist phrases written on the shooter’s gun, and which showed the gunman repeating meme phrases and playing several racist meme songs (like ‘remove kabob’) in his car while

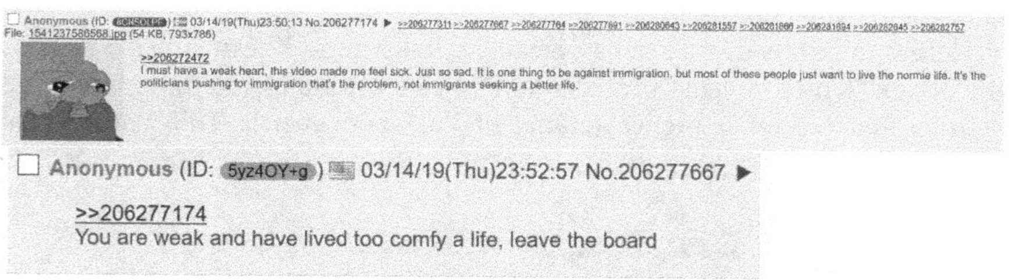

Figure 12.8. Heartache Does Not Resemble the Collective Avatar.
Source: Screenshot of public post from 4/chan. Original creator Anonymous: Author.

Anonymous (ID: qqqGY9Sa) 03/14/19(Thu)23:32:41 No.206273949
>>206266056
Someone explain how could this be a false flag? Is a false flag?

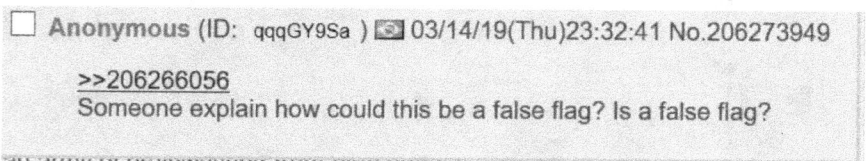

Figure 12.9. Anon Asks If This Is a False Flag.
Source: Screenshot of public post from 4/chan. Original creator Anonymous: Author.

driving to the mosque, many realized that while perhaps their actions were 'less serious' than the shooters, they were similar enough to create a resemblance between them. In other words, many of these users had been mobilized to *do* far-right practice, but not all were yet fully recruited into its ideology.

Regardless of their recruitment, users' action solidified a racist, far-right collective avatar whose characteristics composed a script for other users to embody in order to participate. As users enter a reciprocal relationship with the collective by embodying and re-writing these characteristics, their actions concretize a personal political identity in a process similar to the performativity of gender. Over time, material habitual gestures – posting comments, images, reading and posting assembled racist sentiments – concretize a political identity that feels deeply internal, personal and compellingly real. Yet, such remains a product of user's ongoing performative embodiment and relational existence *with* the collective avatar. This is not to say that all users will be radicalized like this shooter through continued use. Rather, this case reveals the vastly varied intentions and motivations that exist underneath the homogenous, edgy demeanour of the collective avatar, which some users will embody more violently or more 'seriously' than others, depending on other contextual factors. All users, however, are connected.

In this screenshot (figure 12.10), a user deflects collective responsibility for the memer's violence, while simultaneously admitting that the shooter exists along a spectrum with other 4chan users who can 'handle the memes'. Anon claims that it was just *this* user, *they* couldn't handle the memes; *they* took it too far. Here, we see an inkling of awareness that whether someone was 'just playing' with memes or 'taking them too far', all handle the same fire while embodying the anon collective avatar.

Ultimately, the New Zealand shooter was the product of serious, violent racializing ideologies as well as far-right meme practice, the mixture of which I cannot theorize fully here. Yet, a relational approach that incorporates the concretizing process of performativity allows us to conceptualize how other apolitically intentioned users become tangled up with far-right violence, helping build collective avatars and concretizing their political self in relation to the avatar. As the allegedly former anon quoted at the beginning of this chapter says, participation with objectively racist, political action *does have* material consequences: participants are 'radicalized to do abhorrent things' whether this is ever admitted or intended (figure 12.11).

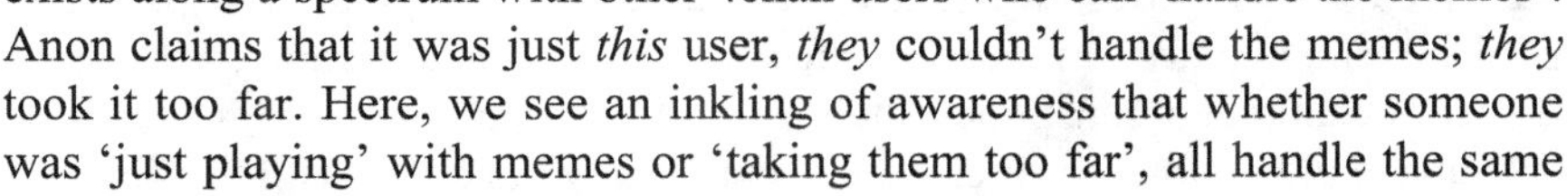

>>206275436
>I'll go on a rampage and get everything I want
Somebody couldn't handle the memes

Figure 12.10. 'Somebody Couldn't Handle the Memes'.
Source: Screenshot of public post from 4/chan. Original creator Anonymous: Author.

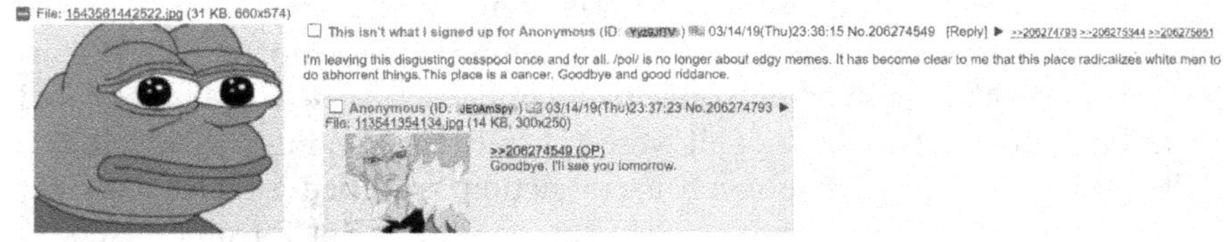

Figure 12.11. Anon Decides to Leave. 'Goodbye and Good Riddance'.
Source: Screenshot of public post from 4/chan. Original creator Anonymous: Author.

Unbinding: 'Goodbye and Good Riddance'

As the first user denounces the board 'once and for all', anon replies, 'Goodbye. I'll see you tomorrow' (figure 12.11). Together, these two goodbyes express the contradiction and ideological heterogeneity within colloquially far-right spaces. The model of the collective avatar is designed to work in spite of this heterogeneity.

It is important to remember that no collective avatar is indestructible. As indicated on the night of New Zealand shooting, global political events can force light upon the mixed internal intentions of those performing the same avatar, rupturing its homogeneity and affording fleeting release from its expectations. These events don't have to be violent ones. On the morning of 20 January 2021, Joe Biden was peacefully inaugurated as president of the United States, ending the presidency of Donald Trump, who infamously encouraged conspiracy theories that the election was rigged. These unfounded allegations of voter fraud were rapidly linked up with the far-right Qanon conspiracy theory by online users across Facebook, 4chan and its sister site 8Kun, which alleges that Trump's destiny in the White House was to overthrow the deep state, a secret cabal of globalist, Satanist paedophiles that rule at the upmost echelons of government. Many Qanon adherents who discussed their theories on 4chan's /pol/ and other online locations expressed that the truth of this conspiracy would be revealed in a violent unveiling, right before President Biden's inauguration.

As the inauguration proceeded as planned, however, there occurred another unravelling of collectively performed far-right political extremeness. Instead, as the successful inauguration indicated that the Q-conspiracy was a lie, many 4chan users were emboldened to mock people that were 'serious' about Q (figure 12.12), and to share progressive (figure 12.13), Pro-Biden and even generally more friendly content (figure 12.14). In other words, this event provided a rupture where users no longer felt the dominance of the far-right, ultra-abrasive, conspiracy-posting anon avatar. For the moment, there was less need to perform a certain type of politics in order to participate with the 4chan collective.

Elsa of Arendelle !Frozen/S0A (ID: QRr0wHIB) 01/20/21(Wed)12:08:37 No.303958742 ▶
File: AADA50B0-8C3A-4913-B9CA-5(...).gif (771 KB, 620x720)

>QAnon-tards actually thought the National Guard was going to mass-arrest every politician in Washington and charge them with election fraud

Wait.

QAnon WASN'T a meme? You fuckers actually believed this???

Figure 12.12. Anon Says They Thought Qanon Was Just a Meme for Everyone Else Too.
Source: Screenshot of public post from 4/chan. Original creator Anonymous: Author.

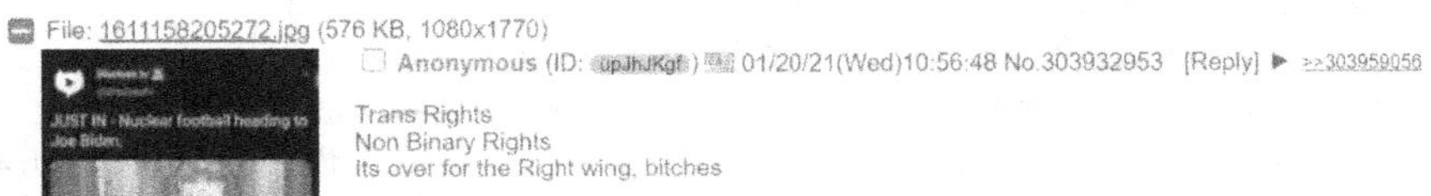
File: 1611158205272.jpg (576 KB, 1080x1770)
Anonymous (ID: upJhJKgf) 01/20/21(Wed)10:56:48 No.303932953 [Reply] ▶ >>303959056

Trans Rights
Non Binary Rights
Its over for the Right wing, bitches

Figure 12.13. 'It's Over for the Right Wing'.
Source: Screenshot of public post from 4/chan. Original creator Anonymous: Author.

File: file.png (904 KB, 1136x646)

Lady Gaga sings the national anthem
Anonymous (ID: PDCZVYR9) 01/20/21(Wed)11:38:50 No.303945798 [Reply] ▶
>>303950235 >>303950355 >>303950402 >>303946504 >>303946582 >>303946609 >>303946813 >>303946892 >>303946986 >>303947045 >>303947234 >>303947467 >>303947656 >>303947723 >>303948162 >>303948188 >>303948476 >>303948575 >>303948790 >>303948855 >>303948857 >>303949816 >>303950011

LADY GAGA C-SPAN LIVE

The next 4 years are gonna be great

Showing all replies.

Anonymous (ID: +Yih7p30) 01/20/21(Wed)11:39:39 No.303946104 ▶ >>303946635 >>303947527 >>303949370

She was pretty good to be honest

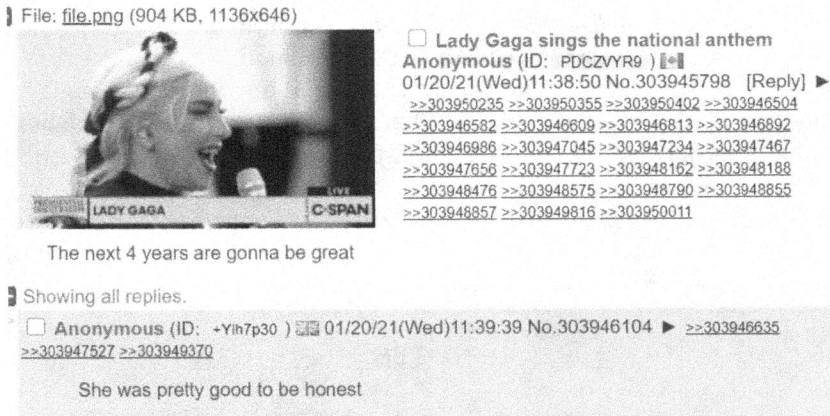

Figure 12.14. Speaking of the Biden presidency: 'The Next 4 Years Are Gonna Be Great'.
Source: Screenshot of public post from 4/chan. Original creator Anonymous: Author.

Within studies of the contemporary far right, our models have mostly described The Alt Right as a homogenous entity, listing its features, ideologies and discursive patterns. In doing so, we conceptualize an entity that is fully formed, and that acts coherently (even with infighting and contradiction) towards its unchanging political, racist and violent aspirations. But this image of the collective Alt-Right on 4chan dissolved on the night of the Christchurch Massacre, as distress and regret spilled out of /pol/ amidst a doubling down or racist, far-right sentiment. Similarly, on the sunny morning of U.S. president Joe Biden's inauguration, /pol/ displayed progressive dissent and resistance, if only for a day. In this sense, the far-right 4chan collective avatar was again disrupted, making room for alternative practices and sentiments. These varying events implicate the complexity and potential for variance underneath commonly mobilized, but not fully recruited, far-right collectives.

In this chapter, I have resisted further describing and categorizing what the online Alt-Right *is*, and instead have attempted to trace the connection between the practices of politically varied or ambivalent users and the manifestation of far-right political consequences. The model of the collective avatar indicates that users can be moved towards recruitment at varying rates through the concretizing and relational processes of performativity. In applying the collective avatar as a conceptual tool to track processes of mobilization and potential recruitment, I attest that deeply qualitative analysis is not limited to providing a culturalist or symbolic level of analysis of memes or posts. Ethnographic methods can trace relational networks of practice (Desmond 2014), and the material interactions between humans, social systems, technologies and racist histories that *together* produce far-right ends. Furthermore, the collective avatar indicates that an important element of halting the process from far-right mobilization to recruitment is *disruption* – events which surface internal misalignment between users underneath the collective avatar's smooth appearance.

I am hopeful that the collective avatar will be one theoretical model of many that use digital ethnographic methods to produce unbounded, relational mappings of how these online cultural-political systems *work*: how they mobilize, and how they insidiously politicize and recruit participants. From this position, we can begin to conceptualize the contemporary far right differently – not as a bounded culture or ideology, but as a set of material practices and outcomes composed of everyday digital actions.

NOTES

1. *Who Killed Captain Alex?* (Nabwana I.G.G., 2015).
2. Safiya Noble advises against the re-printing of this slur in her book *Algorithms of Oppression: How Search Engines Reinforce Racism* (2018).
3. Consider here Kelty's (2005) concept of recursive publics.
4. See ADL's description of Pepe for details as to how the cartoon has evolved to perform far-right function: https://www.adl.org/education/references/hate-symbols/pepe-the-frog.

REFERENCES

Abrahams, Yvette. 1998. 'Images of Sara Bartman: Sexuality, Race, and Gender in Early-Nineteenth-Century Britain', In *Nation, Empire, Colony: Historicizing Gender and Race*, edited by Ruth Roach Pierson and Nupur Chaudhuri, 220–36. Bloomington: Indiana University Press.

Beran, Dale. 2019. *It Came from Something Awful: How a Toxic Troll Army Accidentally Memed Donald Trump into Office*. New York, NY: All Points Books.

Boellstorff, T., B. Nardi, C. Pearce, and T. L. Taylor. 2012. *Ethnography and Virtual Worlds: A Handbook of Method*. Princeton, NJ: Princeton University Press.

Brett, Noel. 2019. Hetero-Comfortable Avatars. *Platypus: The CASTAC Blog*. 27 August. http://blog.castac.org/2019/08/hetero-comfortable-avatars/.

Butler, Judith. 1988. 'Performative Acts and Gender Constitution: An Essay in Phenomenology and Gender Theory'. *Theatre Journal*, 40(4).

Butler, Judith. 1993. *Bodies that Matter: On the Discursive Limits of Sex*. New York, NY: Routledge.

Coleman, E. G. 2014. *Hacker, Hoaxer, Whistleblower, Spy: The Many Faces of Anonymous*. London: Verso.

Desmond, Matthew. 2014. 'Relational Ethnography'. *Theory and Society* 43: 54779.

Desmond, Matthew. 2016. *Evicted: Poverty and Profit in the American City*. New York: Broadway Books.

Devries, M. 2021. 'Archetypes Vs. Homophilic Avatars: Re-defining Far/Right Facebook Practice'. Manuscript submitted for publication.

Ellis, Emma Grey. 2019. 'The Year the Alt-Right Went Underground'. *Wired*. 2 January. https://www.wired.com/story/alt-right-went-underground/.

Evans-Pritchard, E. E. [1940] 1969. *The Nuer: A Description of the Modes of Livelihood and Political Institutions of a Nilotic People*. New York: Oxford University Press.

Gordillo, Gastón. 2014. *Rubble: The Afterlife of Destruction*. Durham, NC: Duke University Press.

Hall, Stuart. [1992] 2019. 'The West and the Rest: Discourse and Power'. *In Essential Essays, Volume 2: Identity and Diaspora*, edited by David Morley, 141–84. Durham, NC: Duke University Press.

Hawley, George. 2017. *Making Sense of the Alt-Right*. Chichester, NY: Columbia University Press.

Hughes, Brian. 2019. 'Thriving from Exile: Toward a Materialist Analysis of the Alt-Right'. *boundary2*, 24 September.

Kelty, Christopher. 2005. 'Geeks, Social Imaginaries, and Recursive Publics'. *Cultural Anthropology* 20 (2): 185–214.

Knuttila, L. 2011. 'User Unknown: 4chan, Anonymity and Contingency'. *First Monday* 16 (10).

Malinowski, Bronislaw. [1922] 2013. *Argonauts of the Western Pacific*. Long Grove: Waveland Press, Inc.

McCoy, Terrance. 2018. '"Imploding": Financial Troubles. Lawsuits. Trailer Park Brawls. Has the Alt-Right Peaked?' *The Washington Post*, 20 April. https://www.washingtonpost.com/local/social-issues/imploding-lawsuits-fundraising-troubles-trailer-park-brawls-has-the-alt-right-peaked/2018/04/20/0a2fb786–39a6–11e8–9c0a-85d477d9a226_story.html.

Milner, Ryan. 2017. *The World Made Meme: Public Conversations and Participatory Media*. Cambridge: MIT Press.

Nagle, Angela. 2017. *Kill All Normies: Online Culture Wars from 4Chan and Tumblr to Trump and the Alt-Right*. Washington, D.C.: Zero Books.

Nakamura, Lisa. 1995. 'Race in/for Cyberspace: Identity Tourism and Racial Passing on the Internet'. *Works and Days* 13 (1–2): 181–93.

Nakamura, Lisa. 2014. ' "Gender and Race Online'. In *Society and the Internet: How Networks of Information and Communication Are Changing Our Lives*, edited by Mark Graham and Willidam H. Dutton. Oxford, UK: Oxford University Press.

Neiwert, D. 2017. *Alt-America: The Rise of the Radical Right in the Age of Trump*. New York: Verso.

Noble, Safyia. 2018. *Algorithms of Oppression: How Search Engines Reinforce Racism*. New York, NY: NYU Press.

Phillips, Whitney. 2015. *This Is Why We Can't Have Nice Things: Mapping the Relationship between Online Trolling and Mainstream Culture*. Cambridge, MA: MIT Press.

Phillips, W., and R. Milner. 2017. *The Ambivalent Internet*. Malden, MA: Polity Press.

Powell, Christopher. 2013. 'Radical Relationism: A Proposal'. In *Conceptualizing Relational Sociology: Ontological and Theoretical Issues*, edited by Christopher Powell and Francois Depelteau. New York, NY: Palgrave Macmillan.

Salter, Michael. 2018. 'From Geek Masculinity to Gamergate: The Technological Rationality of Online Abuse'. *Crime, Media, Culture* 14 (2) (August): 247–64.

Sheller, Mimi. 2003. 'Eating Others: Of Cannibals, Vampires, and Zombies'. In *Consuming the Caribbean*, 143–73. Routledge: New York.

Tuters, Marc, and Sal Hagen. 2019. '(((They))) Rule: Memetic Antagonism and Nebulous Othering on 4chan'. *New Media & Society* 1 (20): 1–20.

Weill, Kelly. 2018. 'Less than a Year after Charlottesville, the Alt-Right Is Self-Destructing'. *The Daily Beast*, 29 March. https://www.thedailybeast.com/less-than-a-year-after-charlottesville-the-alt-right-is-self-destructing.

Wendling, Mike. 2018. *Alt-Right: From 4chan to the White House*.Winnipeg: Fernwood Publishing.

Chapter 13

'Resisting' the Far Right in Racial Capitalism: Sources, Possibilities and Limits

Tanner Mirrlees

Since the so-called digital revolution of the 1990s, innumerable far-right white supremacist organizations, movements and activists have used the Internet to 'connect with the like-minded' and 'recruit new members, some of which have gone on to commit hate crimes and terrorism' (Conway, Scrivens and Macnair 2019, 1). Entangled with digital devices (smartphones and laptop computers) and social media platforms (e.g. 4Chan and 8Chan /pol/ boards, Parler, Gab, Reddit, Discord, Facebook, Twitter and YouTube), the white supremacist right strives to attract white people to its dream of a territorial ethno-state while fomenting hate and violence against racialized minorities and everything its leaders and followers perceive to be instigating so-called white genocide (Hawley 2018; Nagle 2017; Neiwert 2018; Wendling 2018). While this far right is in no way a technologically determined phenomenon, the chapters in this volume have shown that multi-faceted far-right formations exist in different nation-states and have been empowered by digital media technologies. However, what sometimes falls outside of the purview of important research on the contemporary far right's mobilization and recruitment through digital technologies are the growing efforts to counter and oppose the spread of its harmful ideologies and practices. To contribute to studies of contemporary anti-fascism, the goal of this chapter is to provide an overview of the governmental, corporate and activist institutions and tactics that aim to resist the far-right mobilization and recruitment processes examined by this volume.

Focusing on the United States, this chapter highlights efforts by actors within the political sphere (e.g. the American State's repressive and judicial apparatuses), the economic sphere (e.g. the corporate news, entertainment and high-tech industries) and civic sphere (e.g. Left anti-fascist activism) to resist the far right. While efforts by State and corporate actors to take on and take down white supremacist individuals and hate groups are positive and needed, it is important to consider the political possibilities and limits of these challenges to the far right as related to the continuing inequalities and oppressions of the reigning political economy. Racial capitalism and a largely white ruling class persists in the United States, and so the institutional sources and practices of far-right resistance must be critically examined with regard to that social context (Burden-Stelly 2020; Issar 2020; Rahman 2020; Roediger 2017, 2019; Taylor 2016; Virdee 2019). To this end, the first section contextualizes American racial capitalism, the role of the State and political parties in propping up this system and the enduring power of a mostly white and male American ruling class. Following this, the second and third sections identify some U.S. State and corporate sources of opposition to the white supremacist far right, and assess the politics of these within a country whose 'mainstream' political and economic institutions have long been enmeshed with the system of racial capitalism and white supremacy. For a potentially emancipatory source of resistance to the far right and to the system of racial capitalism that emboldens it, the third section looks to broad-based left anti-fascist activism.

RACIAL CAPITALISM AND THE ENDURING RULE OF RICH WHITE FOLKS

The histories of racism and capitalism are coterminous in the United States, and the genesis of the old and new American far right's white supremacist ideology is the U.S. system of 'racial capitalism' (Jenkins and Leroy 2021; Post 2020). Even though the founding of the American liberal democratic State embraced Enlightenment ideals of natural human equality and freedom for all, the country's capitalist development was forged through a white settler colonial project, Black chattel slavery and racially inscribed social class hierarchies, inequities and oppressions (Leroy and Jenkins 2021; Post 2020). The doctrine of white supremacy – the notion that a separate race of white people exists and is superior to non-white people due to intrinsic biological or essential cultural characteristics – was integral to justifying the inequality and unfreedom of Black people, and over time, the new immigrants who entered the ranks of America's racialized waged workers. As white supremacy developed from within capitalism, it was over time interwoven with America's major institutions and national narratives, buttressing a white ruling class's power and dividing working-class white folks from those racialized as 'non-white' others. Despite America's militant history of anti-racism, forms of white supremacy endured the abolition of slavery, the Civil Rights era and the Obama presidency (Alexander 2016; Kendi 2016; Omi and Howard 2015; Post 2020; Robinson 2000; Roediger 2019; Taylor 2016a, 2016b; Virdee 2019). For the past fifty years, Republican *and* Democratic parties and presidents pursued a neoliberal policy and regulatory framework that sustained racial capitalism and helped wealthy white men get richer while working-class people, especially Black, Indigenous and people of colour, got poorer (Fraser 2019; Harvey 2007). The United States is in no way a 'colour blind' country and capitalism's 'colour lines' persist (Bonilla-Silva 2017). In fact, 56% of American voters recently polled believe that the United States is a thoroughly racist society, and 58% saw racism as 'built into' the U.S. economy, government and media (Miller 2020).

The evidence for this is significant. Over the past two decades, the number of white American millionaires and billionaires increased, and at present, America's twenty-five richest people are all white (Dolan, Peterson-Withorn and Wang 2021). All but one of the CEOs of the top twenty-five highest valued American corporations is a white man, and apropos hashtags such as #SiliconValleySoWhite and #HollywoodSoWhite, high-tech and entertainment industries are mostly run by white men too (Guynn 2020; Harrison 2019; Herman 2020; Low and Jackson 2020; Lu et al. 2020; McIlwain 2019; Vary 2020). Even when American gross domestic product rises, most wealth flows to wealthy white people at the top of the social hierarchy, and does not 'trickle down' to everyone else, certainly not to Black working-class people: the white–Black working-class disparities in wages, wealth, employment and health are stark (Hart-Landsberg 2020). The average American CEO-to-worker pay ratio is about 320 to 1, but the lowest paid workers are most often Black workers who earn approximately 14.9% less than white workers even when doing the same jobs (Hart-Landsberg 2020). The median Black household wealth is about $13,024 as compared to the median white household wealth of $149,703. Over 20% of Black Americans live in poverty, twice the rate of white people, and Black people are discriminated against in the housing market and targeted by a predatory loan industry (Taylor 2019).

Also, the U.S. State's repressive apparatus has long secured racial capitalism and white supremacy (Socialist Project 2020). From the colonial era to modern times, American 'policymakers and officials at all levels of government have used criminal law, policing, and imprisonment as proxies for exerting social control in predominantly Black communities', and they have frequently stereotyped Black people as 'internal enemies' and 'volatile threats to state authority' and 'social order' (Hinton and Cook 2021, 2.1). U.S. law enforcement routinely over-police Black folks and deliver them to white-owned carceral corporations (Wang 2018). Most often, the main targets of the prison-industrial complex which metaphorically constitutes the 'New Jim Crow' are poor Black people, who are more likely than whites to be arrested, convicted and imprisoned for longer sentences (Alexander 2020; Barrow 2020; Gramlich 2020). Also, in 2019, Black Americans were almost three times more likely to die from police violence than white Americans: even though just 13% of the U.S. population is Black, that year, 24% of all police killings were of Black Americans (Roper 2020; Statista Research Department 2020). During the Covid-19 pandemic, white police officers killed Jacob Blake, George Floyd and Breonna Taylor. The U.S. State's repressive apparatus and much news and entertainment media that over-represents Black men as criminals (Sun 2019) feed into white people's fears of Black people that too often get translated into anti-Black discrimination in employment, housing, education, voting and social services (Hinton and Cook 2021). Moreover, far-right white supremacist groups prey upon stereotypes of Black criminality, and many have infiltrated the police and military (German 2020; Robinson 2019; Schulkin 2020; Speri 2017). All too often, security forces are whiter than the communities they are paid to 'protect and serve', and they've made the streets 'safe' for white far-right rallies and 'unsafe' for the racial minorities afflicted by their hate and violence (Shepherd 2020). In these material and ideological conditions, it is no surprise that the white supremacist far right is continuously renewed and able to recruit and mobilize so many people.

To be sure, some of racial capitalism's key beneficiaries – rich white men – put their money and their media behind far-right politicians and groups. The billionaire Robert Mercer backed Donald Trump's 'Make America Great Again' election campaign with $15.5 million and funded Steve Bannon's rebranding of Breitbart News into the platform of the alt-right. The millionaire William H. Regnery II, who is a 'race-conscious' supporter of an American 'ethno-state' that would 'exclude, as a rule of thumb, non-whites', also funded some white nationalist organizations such as alt-right spokesperson Richard Spencer's National Policy Institute (Roston and Anderson 2017). But while some white and male bourgeoisie directly support far-right white supremacy, most of the American bourgeoisie do not collectively advocate overt racism, publicly promote racialized class discrimination or openly bankroll the far right's genocidal dreams. Those who currently preside over and profit most from racial capitalism do not as a whole appear to be in cahoots with overt white supremacist far-right figures, movements and groups.

Nowadays, many business elites publicly express a commitment to the civic and social rights of women, racial minorities and LGBTQ+ people; pledge their support for an 'equitable', 'diverse' and 'inclusive' America; and extol a meritocratic politics of recognition typified by initiatives to acknowledge, include and represent members of minoritized groups in society's dominant institutions. The mostly white and male shareholders and CEOs of corporate America seem to embrace folks from under-represented groups who support capitalism and shun democratic socialism (e.g. Kamala Harris, not Alexandria Ocasio-Cortez), and they welcome the gradual diversification of America's upper strata so long as that doesn't disrupt the system's overall class hierarchy (Fraser 2019). That said, a 'rainbow ruling class' that is proportionally representative of America's changing demography is very far from becoming a reality, and even if it came to be, the 'racial permeability of the upper classes' would likely continue to be 'accompanied by an increased and inverse racial permeability of the underclass' (Rossi and Táíwò 2020). Yet, during Donald Trump's presidency, some of the powerful State apparatuses that prop up racial capitalism and corporate strongholds of white class power started combatting the white supremacist far right. These sources of resisting the far right are discussed in the following sections.

THE U.S. STATE AND THE FAR RIGHT

Given its role in maintaining racial capitalism, the State's repressive apparatus is an unlikely source of opposition to white supremacist groups. Even still, by late 2019, the U.S. government had identified the racially motivated violence of far-right groups as a 'persistent, pervasive threat' to national security (Gilsinan 2019; Sherman 2020; Woodward 2020). Christopher Wray, director of the Federal Bureau of Investigation (FBI), described white supremacist groups as America's greatest domestic terrorist threat. Chad Wolf, secretary of The Department of Homeland Security (DHS), reported that 'white supremacist extremists' were 'the most persistent and lethal threat in the Homeland'. In 2020, the FBI arrested two leaders of an insurrectionary accelerationist neo-Nazi hate group called The Base, and charged them with conspiring to kill anti-fascists (Snell and LeBlanc 2020). In that same year, the metropolitan police of DC arrested Proud Boys leader Enrique Tarrio and charged him with vandalism (for burning a BLM banner at an African American church) and weapons possession (carrying high-capacity ammo magazines). Tarrio now faces three years in jail. Post the 6 January 2021 'March for Trump' rally and eventual 'Stop the Steal' riot on Capitol Hill, the FBI has tracked and arrested over 100 far-right activists, including Jake Angeli, a QAnon propagandist, and others from the 3% far-right militias, Boogaloo Boys and Oath Keepers. Some Federal and state-level law enforcement agencies can do some good in countering the far right, but their centrality to the security of racial capitalism, infiltration by white supremacists and alliances with far-Right groups when cracking down on the Left is a problem that has elicited calls for radical institutional reform, democratization, and abolishment (Kopyto 2020).

The State's judicial apparatus may be a more appropriate means through which the civilians terrorized and victimized by the far Right can take on perpetrators of white supremacist hate and violence. That is what some are doing. On 11 October 2017, ten residents of Charlottesville, Virginia (the majority of which are people of colour) teamed up with Integrity for America to launch a lawsuit (*Sines v. Kessler*) against twenty-five of the key organizers of the 'Unite the Right' rally (e.g. Jason Kessler, Richard Spencer, Andrew Anglin, Nathan Damigo, Eli Mosley, Matthew Heimbach and others; Integrity First for America 2020). Represented by Roberta Kaplan, the plaintiffs, all who were peaceful counter-demonstrators who suffered significant physical and psychological injury at the rally, argue that these alt-Right leaders conspired to commit violence in violation of numerous Federal and state laws. They are making the case with help from the digital videos, tweets, posts, texts and chat messages that far-Right leaders produced, transmitted and consumed in the months leading up to the rally (Coaston 2018). Regardless of *Sines v. Kessler*'s outcome, lawsuits like this are a significant judicial tactic for depleting the far Right's financial resources, time and energy. Describing this as 'lawfare' or 'warfare by legal means', Richard Spencer says it has been 'debilitating and consuming, regardless of the facts and regardless of the ultimate judgement' (Smith 2018). In this sense, the courts can be effective in civilian-led cases to slow the recruitment and mobilization efforts of some of the U.S. white supremacist groups. However, even though lawfare can succeed in neutralizing the far Right's individual leaders and possibly even deterring people from joining their cause, it is no magic bullet for racial capitalism as a whole: the government's judicial branch is supposed to be unbiased, fair and impartial, but racism persists throughout the Federal and state court system (Wu 2020).

The U.S. State also permits far-Right hate speech that targets racialized minorities and promotes racial discrimination, separation and segregation, thanks in part to America's libertarian media law, policy and regulatory regime. While the U.S. Constitution does not protect speech that incites imminent lawless action (e.g. a Ku Klux Klan post of a manifesto that directly motivates violence towards Black folk) or true threats (e.g. a neo-Nazi's call to shoot and kill a Muslim American or member of Congress), America does not have an official Federal hate speech Law; the U.S. Supreme Court takes hate speech to be protected free speech, and the Federal Communication Commission (FCC) takes a 'hands-off' or laissez-faire approach to hate speech governance which empowers corporations to define and deal with hate as they choose. Looking to the State to censor the far Right presents risks because the State's repression of far-Right oppressive speech has historically also been used to silence the Left's emancipatory speech (Marcetic 2018), but when a far-Right propagandist calls for the establishment of an authoritarian ethno-state that is genocidally 'cleansed' of non-white people, their speech act does put racialized minorities at risk of harm because this type of speech has motivated people to commit hate crimes, even terrorism. For the protection of all citizens, the far Right's hate speech should be curbed, even in the United States. For now, though, the American State protects the rights of far-Right Americans to impart and receive hate speech through any available communications medium. As a result, the far Right's freedom to spread white supremacist ideology seems more protected in the United States than the millions of people who want to live free from the threat of injury or violence promoted or instigated by it.

In sum, the U.S. State can do some good in combating the far Right, but it is no panacea for the problem of white supremacy. The State's repressive and judicial apparatus can bring far-Right criminals and terrorists to justice after they've broken the law, but their work in doing so is reactive, not proactive, and not very well suited to deterring or pre-empting the far Right's mobilization and recruitment. Racial capitalism's wellspring of white supremacist ideology, the U.S. State's libertarian communications regime, and the Internet and spread of digital devices combine to create an environment in which myriad platforms and sites are used by the far Right to interactively produce, distribute, exhibit and consume a glut of hateful content. All efforts to press the State into action against the white supremacist far Right are important and should be carefully assessed, but given that an end to racial capitalism will not come without radically reforming and transforming the State, it will take a massive democratic movement outside and inside of the State to bring about this bigger social change. For now, some news, Hollywood and Big Tech companies are symbolically countering the far Right with media products and de-platforming campaigns.

THE NEWS, HOLLYWOOD, SILICON VALLEY AND THE FAR RIGHT

Over the past few years, centrist and liberal journalists have been working as effective watchdogs of white supremacist individuals and groups. This is thanks in part to their sources of information: the university researchers and non-profit advocacy organizations that monitor, investigate, research, report on and educate about the far Right in order to counter its spread (e.g. The International Network for Hate Studies, The Southern Poverty Law Centre, the Anti-Defamation League, Political Research Associates, One People Project and the Canadian Anti-Hate Network). News organizations have produced documentary videos about the far Right, and some notable works include *Charlottesville: Race and Terror* (VICE, 2017), *Alt-Right: Age of Rage* (Gravitas Ventures, 2018), *Generation Hate* (Al Jazeera, 2018), *Why People Become Neo-Nazis* (Al Jazeera, 2019), *Beyond the Wall* (Al-Jazeera, 2020), *White Right: Meeting the Enemy* (TVI Docs, 2017), *Documenting Hate: Charlottesville* (Frontline, 2019), *Undercover in the Alt-Right* (Silverfish Films, 2018) and *White Noise: Inside the Racist Right*

(The Atlantic, 2020). In 2018, the Canadian Anti-Hate Network and *VICE* magazine named and shamed the two hosts of 'This Hour Has 88 Minutes', a neo-Nazi podcast (Lamoureux and Patriquin 2018). These liberal media corporations that shed light on the far Right, debunk its conspiracy theories and inform citizens about its threat to democracy are tremendously important as a counterweight to right-wing media corporations such as Fox, Breitbart, the Sinclair Broadcast Group, Rebel Media and One America News (OAN), whose talking points and dog whistles often articulate with white supremacist worldviews. Yet, currently the most liberal media corporations don't go far enough to inform citizens of the ways racial capitalism also supports the rise of the far Right, nor do they help the public to understand how the white billionaires and millionaires that own liberal and conservative news outlets prioritize their bottom-line over a democracy-nourishing media or how the over-presentation of white people in newsrooms leads to racially biased coverage of the world (Cobb 2018; Thrasher 2017).

Hollywood has also spoken out against the far Right, and produced and circulated TV shows and films oriented to popularizing public animosity towards white supremacist hate groups and organizations. In 2017, Hollywood celebrities such as Lady Gaga, Seth Rogen and Mark Hamill condemned the 'Unite the Right' rally, and some TV and film studios have released entertainments that script home-grown and foreign white supremacists and fascists as evil threats to America. For example, HBO's *Watchmen* series draws a line from the Tulsa Massacre of 1921 to present-day racist violence against Black people, and lionizes a Black female hero's beating, shooting and defeating of white supremacist villains. HBO's *The Plot Against America* and Amazon Prime's *The Man in the High Castle* (based upon novels by Philip Roth and Philip K. Dick, respectively) narrate alternative dystopian histories in which the United States loses World War II (WWII) and becomes a full-fledged fascist regime. These positively depict the anti-fascist action of Americans, who heroically join together and rise up in revolt against the Nazi State. *Hunters*, another TV show, uses the fictional plot of post-WWII Nazi hunters to get viewers to contemplate the present-day reality of twenty-first-century fascists trying to take the White House. The super-villain of the second season of *The Boys* is 'Stormfront', a Nazi who uses her smartphone, social media and 'edge' and 'wit' to dissimulate and promote a white supremacist agenda. Similarly, movies such as *Imperium* (2016) and *BlacKkKlansman* (2018) represent white supremacists as a security threat which the State's repressive apparatus diligently neutralizes.

In the Trump era, Hollywood responded to real anxieties about the growth of far-Right groups with TV shows and films that symbolically attack them, and that is somewhat positive. At worst, Hollywood's anti-fascist movies and TV shows may feed into the far Right's notion that Hollywood is ruled by 'cultural Marxists' who dislike and discriminate against the worldview of white conservative Americans. Also, save Boots Riley's *Sorry to Bother You* (2018), Hollywood failed to probe how racism and classism frequently go hand in glove, and it has yet to make a blockbuster movie about its starring role in racial capitalism: the top CEOs of Hollywood's eleven major and mid-major studios are *still* over 90% white and more than 80% male (Vary 2020). While Hollywood studios publicize their support for Black Lives Matter (BLM) and make some headway in diversifying their workforces and representations, it is unlikely that Hollywood's multicultural rebranding will disrupt the power of the white men atop the industry's hierarchy, and subsequently can only get so far in working to resist the ideological spread of racist far-Right beliefs.

The same important but politically limited symbolic politics can be found in video games that enlist their players in a virtual uprising and violent revolution against racist Right-wing terror regimes. For example, *Wolfenstein: The New Colossus* (2017) immerses players in the dystopic world of a 1960s America that has become a satellite State of the Third Reich. William 'B. J.' Blazkowicz (a white male war veteran) and Grace Walker (a Black female leader of the American Resistance) team up to bring down the Nazi regime. Although the game is set in a fictitious past, marketing for the game transformed Donald Trump's 'Make America Great Again' slogan to '#MakeAmericaNaziFreeAgain'. It also repurposed Donald Trump's infamous moral equivalence between the anti-fascists and fascists at the Unite the Right rally into a principled position against the far Right. The game states: 'There is only one side' and 'These are not "fine people"'. In the same year real neo-Nazis were marching in U.S. streets, its trailer 'No More Nazis' depicts historical Nazis doing the same. Instead of passively sitting back and watching it happen, the trailer agitates for violent resistance. 'You still got some Nazi fighting and killing skills in you' shouts Walker to B. J., 'Well, I've got some plans that will send shockwaves throughout the nation!' In the comments section for the game's YouTube trailer, far-Right gamers lambast the game as an 'SJW wet dream' and issue blunt apologias for Hitler (Robertson 2017). From #Gamergate to neo-Nazi mods of *Counter-Strike* to 'whites only' groups on Steam and Discord, many digital games are significant propaganda tools and recruiting platforms for white supremacists (see also Brett, in this volume). In this milieu, *Wolfenstein II* is a positive symbolic attack on the racist Right, old and new. And yet, video games like this are still sold by an industry interlinked with racial capitalism and whose CEOs, high-end workers and playable protagonists are mostly white men. The individual fun of play-leading an insurgency against a virtual Nazi State and blasting fascist avatars from one's bedroom is no substitute for building and participating in brave social movements to push beyond racial capitalism.

Possibilities and pitfalls also surround the efforts by Big Tech corporations to police and prohibit the free flow of far-Right hate speech on the websites and social media platforms they own. All kinds of Big Tech corporations have established hate speech policies and have enforced these in part stirred by calls like the June 2020 '#StopHateForProfit' campaign to boycott Facebook unless it did more to counter digital hate. Facebook's Community Standards section on 'Hate Speech', the Twitter Rules' 'Hateful conduct policy' and YouTube's 'Hate speech policy' rely upon a mix of algorithmic and user agency to flag and report the personalities, pages, channels, posts and content suspected to be in violation of these hate speech policies to the platform's 'content moderators'. These moderators then review, assess and act upon the users and their content (Mirrlees 2021). If a user's conduct subverts the policy, the user may be warned or have their account suspended. If the content violates the policy, the moderators may remove or delete it from the platform.

Big Tech has been deleting and deplatforming the far Right for the past few years. In 2017, Facebook took down fan or group pages for White Nationalists United, Vanguard America and Radical Agenda, as well as pages for Richard Spencer's National Policy Institute and AltRight.com website. In early 2020, Facebook removed nearly 10 million posts and nearly 200 accounts linked to hate groups for violating its rules (Klepper 2020). In 2018, Twitter banned Jared Taylor and his American Renaissance website; in 2020, it permanently banned David Duke (Dowd 2020), and in 2021, it permanently removed @realDonaldTrump. In 2020, YouTube terminated over 25,000 channels for violating its hate speech policies, ridding the site of Richard Spencer, Stefan Molyneux (an anti-Semitic holocaust and Indigenous genocide denier) and others (Hern 2020). Concurrently, Internet infrastructure service companies such as GoDaddy and Google refuse to service The Daily Stormer and AltRight.com. Spotify and Apple have deleted some 'white power' bands, playlists and tracks (Paul 2017), while Reddit removed subreddit pages for r/altright and r/alternativeright and also took down r/The_Donald (Newton 2020).

In this sense, Big Tech's hate speech rules have thrown a monkey wrench into the social media machinery of some far Right's propagandist-entrepreneurs and denied them some platforms to make money, mobilize and recruit in the digital mainstream. But these companies are doing this less for the politics of racial justice, and more to appease shareholders and advertisers and build socially responsible brands. For example, the advertisers that annually buy billions of dollars in Facebook ad services each year do not want their clients' brands inter-mingled with 'swastikas', '14/88' or 'Moon Man' (an alt-Right meme figure), as they recognize these hate symbols will offend the multicultural demographic of prosumers they pay Facebook to aggregate and reach. Furthermore, Big Tech's deplatforming of the far Right has of course not in itself stopped white supremacist activity on the Internet. After being 'de-platformed', far-Right figures tend to create clandestine profiles on the same platforms, or take their business elsewhere to far-Right-friendly or Alt-Tech sites such as Gab, GoyFundMe, BitChute, SubscribeStar and Parler (see Jasser, this volume). When Facebook, Instagram and Twitter banned the Proud Boys, this hate group quickly built a following of over 70,000 followers on Parler. After being pushed off Parler, those running the online group hopped over to Gab, and onto more difficult-to-monitor end-to-end encrypted messaging platforms such as WeMe and Rumble (Daly and Fischer 2021). There seems to be no shortage of Silicon Valley start-ups looking to turn a quick buck by innovating safe spaces for the far Right to commune. Additionally, as 'woke' as Big Tech's major social media platform owners may appear when publicizing their efforts to de-platform and delete the farthest representatives of the far Right and diversify this predominantly white and male-centred industry, they will not disruptively innovate a way out of racial capitalism or creatively destroy their own class privilege.

In sum, while news outlets, Hollywood and interactive game studios and Big Tech firms are doing some good when shedding light on and symbolically challenging far-Right white supremacists, these corporations are also integrated with racial capitalism and are key to the rule of the white men at their helm. Corporations should not be relied upon to solve the substantive social problem of the far Right, as they are not democratic vehicles for human emancipation, nor capable of delivering universal social or economic justice. Leaning on corporations to do something about the far Right may yield positive returns in some instances, but exercising one's consumer or 'user' sovereignty in media markets (e.g. demanding more anti-fascist flicks from Walt Disney or calling on Facebook to censor hate speech) is in the end a neoliberal approach to anti–far Right politics, and no substitute for the civic and community work of participating in grassroots social movements and building democratic political organizations capable of defeating the far Right *and* making a world beyond racial capitalism. For a potentially emancipatory source of resistance to the white supremacist Right and the system of racial capitalism, the next section looks to broad-based Left anti-fascist activism.

CIVIL SOCIETY: LEFT ANTI-FASCIST ACTIVISM

In the early twentieth century, anti-fascist activism emerged across Europe to try to stop the rise of Italian and German fascism, but in the United States, it developed within the subcultural punk scenes of the 1980s and 1990s, and manifested in Skinheads Against Racial Prejudice (SHARP) and the anti-racist action network (ARA) (Bray 2017; Mogelson 2020; Vysotsky 2020). In the twenty-first century, anti-fascist activism grew in response to Donald Trump's presidency and the rise of the white supremacist far Right. Anti-fascism is not housed in one big organization. Rather, it is the ethos of a de-centralized network of many Leftists – anarchists, communists, socialists and sometimes liberals – who are united by the goal of resisting fascism and challenging all forms of oppression and exploitation. Significant nodal points for anti-fascist coordination are the Torch Network (TN) and Rose City Antifa. These, however, are not the only sources of anti-fascism because innumerable people, from those multi-racial BLM activists to the 90,000-person-strong Democratic Socialists of America (DSA) to folks dedicated to the Showing Up for Racial Justice (SURJ) network also organize people's movements against racial capitalism, white supremacy and the far Right (Rein 2021). In the United States, there is a broad-based anti-fascist Left that uses a diversity of tactics – union organizing, solidarity campaigns, community education and direct action – to fight fascism.

Although the anti-fascist Left mostly confronts the far Right in nonviolent ways, some in this milieu have used violence to defend comrades and local minorities from racist threats and attacks (Bray 2017). For example, during the 2017 Unite the Right rally, anti-fascists defended Dr. Cornel West and various clergy from a violent mob of neo-Nazis and white supremacists by beating them back with fists and bats. As West avers, 'The anti-fascists saved our lives, actually. We would have been completely crushed, and I'll never forget that' (Democracy Now! 2017). Anti-fascists also directly confront the far Right with the tactic of 'no platforming', or, preventing its propagandists from spreading their hateful ideas by trying to shut down their events or tours. For example, in 2017, Richard Spencer planned a national speaking tour, but after being 'no platformed' by anti-fascists in Michigan, Spencer had to cancel his tour. Spencer noted that being alt-Right was 'no fun' anymore, and blamed anti-fascists for disrupting his plan and deterring others from joining. In this sense, certain anti-fascist-led and on-the-ground tactics like 'defensive violence' and 'no platforming' have a basic and immediate impact upon those fascists they wish to halt. That said, Antifa's direct action sometimes feeds into media stereotypes of the Left as a violent threat to democracy, even though the far Right is the greatest threat, as recognized by the FBI.

Anti-fascists are also experimenting with forms of digital direct action. It's Going Down (https://itsgoingdown.org/) is an open access hub for 'fist-hand' accounts, reflexive essays and user-generated videos from counter-fascist rallies and demos. Similarly, We Hunted the Mammoth (http://www.wehuntedthemammoth.com) monitors and mocks 'New Misogyny' influencers, exposing the most anti-feminist far-Right figures and practices. As well, the members of Unicorn Riot sometimes infiltrate 'members only' far-Right spaces online to report their mobilizing and recruitment activities: in March 2019, they leaked more than 770,000 Discord messages from Identity Evropa's (IE) 'Nice Respectable People Group', resulting in a massive anti-white nationalist doxxing campaign (Lavin 2020a). Megan Squire's Whack-a-Mole software aggregates data from over 400,000 far-Right user accounts across the Web and feeds it into a centralized database, which is used for organizations pursuing legal action against the far Right (Clark 2018).

Across Facebook and Twitter, a number of anti-fascist community organizations, social movements and activists organize and communicate about public protests and counter-demos against the far Right. Positively, many public rallies organized by the far Right in major cities across North America have been countered (and are often outnumbered) by a plurality of residents who quite literally say 'not in our town'. In that regard, social media platforms are significant to the groups organizing against the far Right. In Toronto, for example, Toronto Against Fascism is a 'non-sectarian leftist organization serving to mobilize communities against fascism'; SAFE (Solidarity Against Fascism Everywhere) is an 'intersectional anti-oppressive committee formed to counter the rise of the islamophobia, white supremacy and fascism'; the GTA Overt Bigotry Response is 'aimed at directly confronting displays of overt bigotry in the Greater Toronto Area'. These are just a few of the many activist groups that use social media platforms such as Facebook to build campaigns, initiate rallies and spark counter-demos against the far Right, wherever it goes.

While YouTube is often used by the far Right to recruit and mobilize (Lewis 2018), Left-Tubers and anti-fascist creators are also taking on the far Right. In doing so, they have delivered sharp arguments against its thinkers, and deterred other users from falling into its red-pilling matrix. In this sense, where comment sections sometimes indicate this effective prevention of further far-right recruitment, YouTube is one of the most exciting digital media entertainment sources of resistance to far-Right ideology. Some of the most significant creators, channels and videos include Natalie Wynn aka Contrapoints (e.g. 'Decrypting the Alt-Right: How to Recognize a F@scist', 'Incels' and 'Jordan Peterson'); Three Arrows (e.g. 'How to Fall Down the Anti-SJW Rabbit Hole' and 'Debunking the Alt-Right: Twisting Words'); 'hbomberguy' (e.g. 'Cultural Marxism: A Measured Response' and 'The Golden One: A Measured Response'); 'Shaun' (e.g. 'The Fate of the Frog Guy' and 'The Great Replacement Isn't Real – ft. Lauren Southern'); Peter Coffin (e.g. 'White Nationalist Terrorism' and 'Taking the Red Pill . . . Back'); Vaush ('Richard Spencer Shows Us – There Are No Civil Nazis' and 'Debating Stefan Molyneux and OBLITERATING him with Facts, Logic, & Arguments'); Philosophy Tube (e.g. 'White Supremacist Propaganda vs Truth' and 'Steve Bannon'); Angie Speaks (e.g. 'Esoteric Fascism – The Occult and the

Far Right' and 'Exit the Vampire Castle'); and Inuendo Studios (e.g. 'The Alt-Right Playbook: How to Radicalize a Normie'). Anti-fascist YouTubers produce captivating videos that signal confidence in the idea that better arguments can be made than those advanced by the far Right. Combined with their shareability, their creative works aim to deter people from succumbing to far-Right ideology. Importantly, what differentiates these anti-fascist YouTube creators from many liberal news journalists, Hollywood studios, gamemakers and Big Tech firms is their ability to launch spirited critiques of the political economy of racial capitalism and white class power. In this sense, these video-creation and streaming initiatives to deter far-Right recruitment and mobilization are important to resisting both far-Right propagandists and the system from which their ideology arises.

In terms of further Internet activism, anti-fascist 'hackers' are waging cyber-war against the far Right by firing a bevy of distributed denial-of-service attacks ('DDoS attacks') at far-Right websites to disrupt or shut them down (Ashok 2017). To remind everyone that the 'alt-right' is a rebranding of white supremacy, 'George Zola', a New York City creative, made a Google Chrome extension called 'Stop Normalizing The Alt Right', which automatically replaces all search references to the 'alt-right' with 'neo-Nazi' (Workney 2016). The far Right is also being attacked, mocked, satirized and degraded with memes, or assemblages of text and images. For example, one anti-fascist meme slogan is 'Good Night Alt-Right', and this phrase has encircled an image of the *DOOM* space soldier wearing a Three Arrows vest crushing Pepe the frog, a giant fist smashing a swastika and Richard Spencer being sucker punched (Sargent 2017). A popular rendition of this meme features 'Gritty', the Philadelphia Flyers' mascot, which was in 2018 appropriated by anarchists, pummelling a 'Keke' flag-wearer (Timsit 2018). Indeed, independent actors mobilized instead by anti-fascist ethics work to circulate criticisms of far-Right talking points in the comments sections of news stories and social media posts, and in discussion forum threads. A Swedish Facebook group called #Jagärhär (#Iamhere), for example, battles far-Right disinformation online and defends those on the receiving end of its racist hate across social media platforms.

CONCLUSION: BEYOND THE FAR RIGHT AND RACIAL CAPITALISM

From the 'top-down' efforts of States and corporations, to the 'bottom-up' activism of a broad-based anti-fascist Left, a wide range of social actors are resisting the white supremacist far Right. While State and corporate efforts to combat the white supremacist far Right are positive and have had some success in thwarting some far-Right leaders and hate groups, this top-down 'resistance' has not slowed or stopped the reproduction of the system of racial capitalism and the power of its mostly white male bourgeoisie, which have long been conducive to the renewal of such far-right movements. In that regard, as significant as State and corporate efforts to combat racist white supremacist individuals and hate groups in America are, they do not disrupt the enduring wealth and power of white men, nor do they redress long-standing forms of racialized class inequality and oppression. Left anti-fascist activists have played a vital role in building grassroots resistance to the rising far Right while simultaneously opposing racial capitalism and white supremacy. However, they have not yet built a multi-racial working-class movement or organization capable of disrupting, let alone building a viable alternative to the reigning political economy.

Far from representing a new 'united front', the main sources of opposition to the far Right are at odds with one another. For example, the FBI, Facebook and anti-fascists all seek to neutralize the threat of white nationalist terrorism, but they are neither 'natural allies' nor 'comrades'. In fact, the FBI reportedly started investigating the potential 'extremist' threat posted by some anti-fascists after the Trump Administration labelled Antifa a 'domestic terrorist organization' (Hosenball and Lunch 2020). Facebook is used by the police to covertly infiltrate and monitor Left and anti-fascist groups (Fariver and Solon 2020), but it does not wish to be regulated by the State. Anti-fascists tend to view the police as a repressive apparatus of the State, and some see Facebook as an algorithmic-ideological enforcer of anti-Black racism. While different and dis-united, each of these entity's specific actions nonetheless contribute to resisting the far Right. Yet, the FBI and Facebook largely sustain racial capitalism while anti-fascist activism intersects with emancipatory movements and organizations that aim to go beyond this system.

As Donald Trump's presidency comes to an end, and Joe Biden's begins, racial capitalism endures. In the future, the Biden presidency will try to unite and heal the country with a centrist approach that emphasizes progressive neoliberal solutions to the problem of white supremacy and the major State apparatuses and corporations will try to crack down on and knock out the farthest Right. But in the absence of massive structural reforms geared to universal social and economic justice, the Biden presidency's efforts to rebuild national unity are likely to fail. Racial capitalism will continue to polarize American society along class and colour lines, and the white supremacist ethos Trump recharged will live on in new far-Right politicians, think-tanks and media outlets, some police and border control agents, organized groups and millions of white conservatives. The far Right's recruitment and mobilization campaigns, hate speech and hate crimes against minorities and harassment and violence against liberals and democratic socialists, will likely continue.

In the years ahead, it will be incumbent upon the Left to continually educate, agitate, and organize against the far Right, in the streets, in communities and across the Internet. For the short term, 'Dismantling the rise of fascism is best not left to lone vigilantes, nor to the punitive mechanisms of the state, but to people working together to stamp out hate wherever it arises' (Lavin 2020, 198). In the long term, the Left's chances of defeating the far Right will greatly increase when it builds multi-racial working-class solidarity into a viable political force that has the capacities and resources to radically reform and one day go beyond racial capitalism (Sunkara 2019; Taylor 2016a, 2016b).

REFERENCES

Alexander, Amy. 2016. 'How Politicians Divide, Conquer and Confuse American Workers Based on Race'. *The Atlantic*, 19 January. https://www.theatlantic.com/politics/archive/2016/01/how-politicians-divide-conquer-and-confuse-american-workers-based-on-race/458835/.

Alexander, Michelle. 2020. *The New Jim Crow: Mass Incarceration in the Age of Colorblindness*. New York: The New Press.

Ashok, India. 2017. '#OpDomesticTerrorism: Anonymous Hackers Take Down over a Dozen Neo-Nazi Sites'. *International Business Times*, 16 November. https://www.ibtimes.co.uk/opdomesticterrorism-anonymous-hackers-take-down-over-dozen-neo-nazi-sites-new-wave-attacks-1647385.

Barrow, Holly. 2020. 'Systemic Racism and the Prison-Industrial Complex in the "Land of the Free"'. *Hampton Institute*, 4 July. https://www.hamptonthink.org/read/systemic-racism-and-the-prison-industrial-complex-in-the-land-of-the-free.

Bonilla-Silva, Eduardo. 2017. *Racism without Racists: Color-Blind Racism and the Persistence of Racial Inequality in America*. New York: Rowman & Littlefield.

Bray, Mark. 2017. *Antifa: The Anti-Fascist Handbook*. New York: Melville House.

Burden-Stelly, Charisse. 2020. 'Modern U.S. Racial Capitalism'. *Monthly Review*, 1 July. https://monthlyreview.org/2020/07/01/modern-u-s-racial-capitalism/.

Clark, Doug Bock. 2018. 'Meet Antifa's Secret Weapon against Far-Right Extremists'. *Wired*, 16 January. https://www.wired.com/story/free-speech-issue-antifa-data-mining/.

Coaston, Jane. 2018. 'The Alt-Right Is Going on Trial in Charlottesville'. *Vox*, 8 March. https://www.vox.com/2018/3/8/17071832/alt-right-racists-charlottesville.

Cobb, Jelani. 2018. 'When Newsrooms Are Dominated by White People, They Miss Crucial Facts'. *The Guardian*, 5 November. https://www.theguardian.com/world/commentisfree/2018/nov/05/newsroom-diversity-media-race-journalism.

Conway, Maura, Ryan Scrivens, and Logan Macnair. 2019. 'Right-Wing Extremists' Persistent Online Presence: History and Contemporary Trends'. *ICCT Policy Brief*, no. 1: 1–24. https://icct.nl/wp-content/uploads/2019/11/Right-Wing-Extremists-Persistent-Online-Presence.pdf.

Congressional Research Service. 2020. 'Are Antifa Members Domestic Terrorists? Background on Antifa and Federal Classification of Their Actions'. https://fas.org/sgp/crs/terror/IF10839.pdf.

Daly, Kyle, and Sara Fischer. 2021. 'The Online Far Right Is Moving Underground'. *Axios*, 21 January. https://www.axios.com/the-online-far-right-is-moving-underground-e429d45d-1b30-46e0-82a3–6e240bf44fef.html.

Democracy Now! 2017. 'Cornel West & Rev. Traci Blackmon'. Democracy Now!, 14 August. https://www.democracynow.org/2017/8/14/cornel_west_rev_toni_blackmon_clergy.

Dolan, Kerry, Chase Peterson-Withorn, and Jennifer Wang. 2020. 'The Forbes 400: The Definitive Ranking of the Wealthiest Americans in 2020'. *Forbes*, 2 January. https://www.forbes.com/forbes-400/#2d1fc8bd7e2.

Dowd, Trone. 2020. 'It Only Took Twitter 11 Years to Ban Former KKK Grand Wizard'. *VICE*, 31 July. https://www.vice.com/en_ca/article/z3ewp8/it-only-took-twitter-11-years-to-ban-former-kkk-grand-wizard-david-duke.

Du Bois, W. E. B. 1965. *Black Reconstruction in America*. New York: The Free Press.

Farivar, Cyrus, and Olivia Solon. 2020. 'FBI Trawled Facebook to Arrest Protesters for Inciting Riots, Court Records Show'. *NBC News*, 19 June. https://www.nbcnews.com/tech/social-media/federal-agents-monitored-facebook-arrest-protesters-inciting-riots-court-records-n1231531.

Fraser, Nancy. 2019. *The Old Is Dying and the New Cannot Be Born*. New York: Verso.

German, Michael. 2020. 'Hidden in Plain Sight: Racism, White Supremacy and Far-Right Militancy in Law Enforcement'. Brennan Center, 20 August. https://www.brennancenter.org/our-work/research-reports/hidden-plain-sight-racism-white-supremacy-and-far-right-militancy-law.

Gilsinan, Kathy. 2019. 'DHS Is Finally Going After White Supremacists'. *The Atlantic*, 20 September. https://www.theatlantic.com/politics/archive/2019/09/new-strategy-fight-white-supremacist-violence/598501/.

Gramlich, John. 2020. 'Black Imprisonment Rate in the U.S. Has Fallen by a Third since 2006'. Pew Research Centre, 6 May. https://www.pewresearch.org/fact-tank/2020/05/06/share-of-black-white-hispanic-americans-in-prison-2018-vs-2006/.

Guynn, Jessica. 2020. '#SiliconValleySoWhite: Black Facebook and Google Employees Speak Out on Big Tech Racism'. *USA Today*, 10 February. https://www.usatoday.com/story/tech/2020/02/10/racial-discrimination-persists-facebook-google-employees-say/4307591002/.

Harrison, Sara. 2019. 'Five Years of Tech Diversity Reports – and Little Progress'. *Wired*, 1 October. https://www.wired.com/story/five-years-tech-diversity-reports-little-progress/.

Hart-Landsberg, Michael. 2020. 'Racism, COVID-19, and the Fight for Economic Justice'. *The Bullet*, 9 July. https://socialistproject.ca/2020/07/racism-covid-19-fight-for-economic-justice/?fbclid=IwAR2VwpU-a2CcFL5kKMv3pMAnfc9yeHUCG2f7oaJhfb2GiFpsG0S9zOb-HOA.

Harvey, David. 2007. *A Brief History of Neoliberalism*. New York: Oxford University Press.

Hawley, George. 2017. *Making Sense of the Alt-Right*. New York: Columbia University Press.

Herman, Alison. 2020. 'Amid the Black Lives Matter Movement, Hollywood Examines Its Own History of Racism'. *The Ringer*, 10 July. https://www.theringer.com/tv/2020/7/10/21319242/hollywood-racism-blackface-tv-episodes-song-of-the-south.

Hern, Alex. 2020. 'YouTube Bans David Duke and Other US Far-Right Users'. *The Guardian*, 30 June. https://www.theguardian.com/technology/2020/jun/30/youtube-bans-david-duke-and-other-us-far-right-users.

Hinton, Elizabeth, and DeAnza Cook. 2021. 'The Mass Criminalization of Black Americans: A Historical Overview'. *Annual Review of Criminology* 4 (2): 261–86.

Hosenball, Mark, and Sarah Lynch. 2020. 'FBI Chief Says U.S. "Antifa" Demonstrators Are Targets of Multiple Probes'. *Reuters*, 24 September. https://www.reuters.com/article/us-usa-security-threats-idUSKCN26F3C2.

Integrity First for America. 2020. 'IFA's Charlottesville Case: *Sines v. Kessler*'. https://www.integrityfirstforamerica.org/our-work/case/charlottesville-case.

Issar, Siddhant. 2020. 'Listening to Black Lives Matter: Racial Capitalism and the Critique of Neoliberalism'. *Contemporary Political Theory* 1 (2): 1–23.

Jenkins, Destin, and Justin Leroy, eds. 2021. *Histories of Racial Capitalism*. New York: Columbia University Press.

Johnson, Walter. 2018. 'To Remake the World: Slavery, Racial Capitalism and Justice'. *Boston Review*, 10 February. http://bostonreview.net/forum/walter-johnson-to-remake-the-world.

Kendi, Ibram X. 2016. *Stamped from the Beginning: The Definitive History of Racist Ideas in America*. New York: Nation Books.

Klepper, David. 2020. 'Facebook Removes Nearly 200 Accounts Tied to Hate Groups'. ABC News, 5 June. https://abcnews.go.com/Business/wireStory/facebook-removes-200-accounts-tied-hate-groups-71101914.

Kopyto, Harry. 2020. 'Can We Ever Truly Transform or Democratize the Police?' *Canadian Dimension*, 28 May. https://canadiandimension.com/articles/view/can-we-truly-transform-or-democratize-the-police.

Lamoureux, Mack, and Martin Patriquin. 2018. 'This Is the Man Who Ran Canada's Biggest Neo-Nazi Podcast'. *VICE*, 14 June. https://www.vice.com/en_ca/article/zm8ky4/this-is-the-man-who-ran-canadas-biggest-neo-nazi-podcast.

Lavin, Talia. 2020a. *Culture Warlords: My Journey into the Dark Web of White Supremacy*. New York: Hatchette Books.

Lavin, Talia. 2020b. 'How to Be an Antifascist from Your Couch'. *The Nation*, June 5. https://www.thenation.com/article/politics/antifa-online/.

Lewis, Rebecca. 2018. 'Alternative Influence: Broadcasting the Reactionary Right on YouTube'. *Data & Society Research Institute*. https://datasociety.net/wpcontent/uploads/2018/09/DS_Alternative_Influence.pdf.

Low, Elaine, and Angelique Jackson. 2020. 'The Reckoning over Representation: Black Hollywood Speaks Out, But Is the Industry Listening?' *Variety*, 30 June. https://variety.com/2020/biz/features/black-representation-hollywood-inclusion-diversity-entertainment-1234693219/.

Lu, Denise, Jon Huang, Ashwin Seshagiri, Haeyoun Park, and Troy Griggs. 2020. 'Faces of Power: 80% Are White, Even as U.S. Becomes More Diverse'. *The New York Times*, 9 September. https://www.nytimes.com/interactive/2020/09/09/us/powerful-people-race-us.html?action=click&module=Editors%20Picks&pgtype=Homepage.

Marcetic, Branko. 2018. 'The Anti-Fascist Boomerang'. *Jacobin*, 14 August. https://jacobinmag.com/2018/08/fascist-free-speech-repression-far-right.

McIlwain, Charlton. 2019. *Black Software: The Internet & Racial Justice, from the AfroNet to Black Lives Matter*. New York: Oxford University Press.

Miller, Joshua Rhett. 2020. 'Majority of US Voters Believe American Society Is Racist: Poll'. *New York Post*, 21 July. https://nypost.com/2020/07/21/majority-of-us-voters-say-american-society-is-racist-poll/.

Mirrlees, Tanner. 2021. 'GAFAM and Hate Content Moderation: Deplatforming and Deleting the Alt-Right'. In *Media and Law: Between Free Speech and Censorship*, edited by Mathieu Deflem and Derek M. D. Silva, 81–96. Bingley, UK: Emerald Publishing.

Mogelson, Luke. 2020. 'In the Streets with ANTIFA'. *The New Yorker*, 2 November. https://www.newyorker.com/magazine/2020/11/02/trump-antifa-movement-portland.

Nagle, Angela. 2017. *Kill All Normies: Online Culture Wars from 4Chan and Tumblr to Trump and the Alt-Right*. Washington, DC: Zero Books.

Newton, Casey. 2020. 'Reddit Bans r/The_Donald and r/ChapoTrapHouse as Part of a Major Expansion of Its Rules'. *The Verge*, 29 June. https://www.theverge.com/2020/6/29/21304947/reddit-ban-subreddits-the-donald-chapo-trap-house-new-content-policy-rules.

Omi, Michael, and Howard Winant. 2015. *Racial Formation in the United States*. New York: Routledge.

Paul, Kari. 2017. 'These Are All the Companies Are Trying to Stop White Supremacists from Raising Money'. MarketWatch, 20 August. https://www.marketwatch.com/story/discover-terminates-merchant-agreements-with-white-supremacist-groups-following-moves-by-paypal-and-godaddy-2017-08-16.

Post, Charles. 2020. 'Beyond Racial Capitalism'. *The Brooklyn Rail*, 1 October. https://brooklynrail.org/2020/10/field-notes/Beyond-Racial-Capitalism-Toward-A-Unified-Theory-of-Capitalism-and-Racial-Oppression.

Rahman, K. Sabeel. 2020. 'Dismantle Racial Capitalism'. *Dissent*, 1 August. https://www.dissentmagazine.org/article/dismantle-racial-capitalism.

Rein, Marcy. 2021. 'Can We Crack the Right's White Bloc? These Organizers Say Yes'. Organizing Upgrade, 12 January. https://organizingupgrade.com/can-we-crack-the-rights-white-bloc-these-organizers-say-yes/.

Robertson, Adi. 2017. 'Watching Internet Nazis Get Mad at Wolfenstein II Is Sadder than the Game's Actual Dystopia'. The Verge, 12 June. https://www.theverge.com/2017/6/12/15780596/wolfenstein-2-the-new-colossus-alt-right-nazi-outrage.

Robinson, Cedric J. 2000. *Black Marxism: The Making of the Black Radical Tradition*. Oakland, CA: University of North Carolina Press.

Robinson, Rashad. 2019. 'We Can't Trust Police to Protect Us from Racist Violence. They Contribute to It'. *The Guardian*, 21 August. https://www.theguardian.com/commentisfree/2019/aug/21/police-white-nationalists-racist-violence.

Roediger, David. 2017. *Class, Race and Marxism*. London: Verso.

Roediger, David. 2019. *How Race Survived US History: From Settlement and Slavery to the Eclipse of Post-racialism*. New York: Verso.

Roper, Willem. 2020. 'Black Americans 2.5× More Likely than Whites to Be Killed by Police'. Statista, 2 June. https://www.statista.com/chart/21872/map-of-police-violence-against-black-americans/.

Rossi, Enzo, and Olúfẹ́mi O. Táíwò. 2020. 'What's New about Woke Racial Capitalism (and What Isn't)'. *Spectre*, 18 December. https://spectrejournal.com/whats-new-about-woke-racial-capitalism-and-what-isnt/.

Roston, Aram, and Joel Anderson. 2017. 'The Moneyman behind the Alt-Right'. BuzzFeedNews, 23 July. https://www.buzzfeednews.com/article/aramroston/hes-spent-almost-20-years-funding-the-racist-right-it#4ldqpgc.

Sargent, Jordan. 2017. 'Our Favorite Memes of Richard Spencer Getting Punched in the Face'. *Spin*, 23 January. https://www.spin.com/2017/01/our-favorite-memes-of-richard-spencer-getting-punched-in-the-face/.

Schulkin, Danielle. 2020. 'White Supremacist Infiltration of US Police Forces: Fact-Checking National Security Advisor O'Brien'. *Just Security*, 1 June 2020. https://www.justsecurity.org/70507/white-supremacist-infiltration-of-us-police-forces-fact-checking-national-security-advisor-obrien/.

Shepherd, Katie. 2020. 'Portland Police Stand by as Proud Boys and Far-Right Militias Flash Guns and Brawl with Antifa Counterprotesters'. *The Washington Post*, 23 August.

Sherman, Amy. 2020. 'FBI Director Warned about White Supremacist Violence'. Politifact.com, 6 October. https://www.politifact.com/factchecks/2020/oct/06/joe-biden/fbi-director-warned-about-white-supremacist-violen/.

Smith, David. 2018. 'After Charlottesville: How a Slew of Lawsuits Pin Down the Far Right'. *The Guardian*, 29 March 2018. https://www.theguardian.com/world/2018/may/29/charlottesville-lawsuits-heather-heyer-richard-spencer-alt-right.

Snell, Robert, and Beth LeBlanc. 2020. 'FBI Arrests White Supremacy Leader in Extremism Crackdown in Michigan'. *The Detroit News*, 29 October 2020. https://www.detroitnews.com/story/news/local/michigan/2020/10/29/fbi-arrests-accused-neo-nazis-michigan-crackdown-extremism/6067038002/.

Socialist Project. 2020. 'All Out: Policing, Racism and Our Collective Response'. *The Bullet*, 10 June 2020. https://socialistproject.ca/2020/06/all-out-policing-racism-collective-response/.

Speri, Alice. 2017. 'The FBI Has Quietly Investigated White Supremacist Infiltration of Law Enforcement'. *The Intercept*, 31 January. https://theintercept.com/2017/01/31/the-fbi-has-quietly-investigated-white-supremacist-infiltration-of-law-enforcement/.

Statista Research Department. 2020. 'People Shot to Death by U.S. Police, by Race 2017 to 2020'. *Statista*, 6 August. https://www.statista.com/statistics/585152/people-shot-to-death-by-us-police-by-race/.

Sun, Elizabeth. 2019. 'The Dangerous Racialization of Crime in U.S. News Media'. Center for American Progress, 29 August. https://www.americanprogress.org/issues/criminal-justice/news/2018/08/29/455313/dangerous-racialization-crime-u-s-news-media/.

Sunkara, Bhaskar. 2019. *The Socialist Manifesto: The Case for Radical Politics in an Era of Extreme Inequality*. New York: Basic Books.

Taylor, Keeanga-Yamahtta. 2016a. *From #BlackLivesMatter to Black Liberation*. Chicago: Haymarket Books.

Taylor, Keeanga-Yamahtta. 2016b. 'What about Racism?" *Jacobin*, 16 March. https://www.jacobinmag.com/2016/03/black-lives-matter-slavery-discrimination-socialism.

Taylor, Keeanga-Yamahtta. 2019. *Race for Profit: How Banks and the Real Estate Industry Undermined Black Homeownership*. Chapel Hill: The University of North Carolina Press.

Thrasher, Steven. 2017. 'The Media Isn't Diverse – And This Leads to Appalling Reporting'. *The Guardian*, 28 November. https://www.theguardian.com/commentisfree/2017/nov/28/media-diversity-neo-nazis-reporting.

Timsit, Annabelle. 2018. 'The Internet Has Chosen a Bizarre Orange Mascot Named Gritty to Lead the Antifa Resistance'. *Quartz*, 16 October. https://qz.com/1425540/how-the-internet-turned-gritty-into-an-antifa-icon/.

Vary, Adam. 2020. Women and People of Color Still Underrepresented behind the Scenes, Study Says'. Variety, 28 February. https://variety.com/2020/film/news/diversity-hollywood-behind-the-scenes-ucla-study-1203494631/.

Virdee, Satnam. 2019. 'Racialized Capitalism: An Account of Its Contested Origins and Consolidation'. *The Sociological Review* 67 (1): 13–28.

Vysotsky, Stanislav. 2020. *American Antifa: The Tactics, Culture and Practice of Militant Antifascism*. New York: Routledge.

Wang, Jackie. 2018. *Carceral Capitalism*. Cambridge: MIT Press.

Wendling, Mike. 2018. *Alt Right: From 4chan to the White House*. Halifax and Winnipeg: Fernwood.

Woodward, Alex. 2020. 'FBI Raises Neo-Nazi Threat Level to Same as Isis." *Independent*, 7 February. https://www.independent.co.uk/news/world/americas/fbi-neo-nazi-isis-us-terror-threat-level-trump-a9323786.html.

Workney, Lilly. 2016. 'Google Chrome Extension Replaces "Alt-Right" with "White Supremacy"'. *The Huffington Post*, 28 November. https://www.huffingtonpost.ca/entry/google-chrome-extension-replaces-alt-right-with-white supremacy_n_583c6106e4b09b60560157b6?ri18n=true.

Wu, Jason. 2020. 'Pervasive Racial Bias in Courts Requires Transformative Social Change'. Truthout, 9 November. https://truthout.org/articles/pervasive-racial-bias-in-courts-requires-transformative-social-change/.

Index

www.ingramcontent.com/pod-product-compliance
Lightning Source LLC
Chambersburg PA
CBHW050630280326
41932CB00015B/2594

* 9 7 8 1 5 3 8 1 5 8 9 0 6 *